INDEX TO MAPS OF THE AMERICAN REVOLUTION

IN

BOOKS AND PERIODICALS

INDEX TO MAPS OF THE AMERICAN REVOLUTION

IN

BOOKS AND PERIODICALS

Illustrating

The Revolutionary War

and

Other Events of the Period 1763-1789

by

David Sanders Clark

This is a T.N. Dupuy Associates Book

Greenwood Press

Westport, Connecticut • London, England

Library of Congress Cataloging in Publication Data

Clark, David Sanders
　　Index to maps of the American Revolution in books
and periodicals.

　　Bibliography; P.
　　1. United States—History—Revolution, 1775-1783—
Maps—Indexes. 2. United States—Historical geography—
Maps—Indexes. I. Title.
Z6027.U5C57 1974　　911'.73'016　　　74-7543
ISBN 0-8371-7582-8

Library of Congress Catalog Card Number: 74-7543
ISBN: 0-8371-7582-8

First published in 1974

Greenwood Press, a division of Williamhouse-Regency Inc.
51 Riverside Avenue, Westport, Connecticut 06880

Manufactured in the United States of America

CONTENTS

PREFACE

The approaching bicentennial of the American Revolution is certain to give great impetus to the production of books, articles, films, and television programs on historical themes, the staging of pageants and re-enactment of battles, and the marking of historic sites. For all these activities, maps depicting events of the Revolutionary Period will be essential source material.

Extensive collections of manuscript and printed maps dating from the time of the Revolution are to be found, however, only in the Library of Congress and a few other leading American libraries. In the historical atlases now generally available, the battles and campaigns from 1775 to 1781 and contemporaneous events receive little space. Therefore, except for the comparatively small number of scholars so fortunate as to have ready access to a major map collection, Americans with an interest in the history of the Revolution must rely chiefly on whatever maps they can find in books and periodicals in their own university, college, high school, or public library. But no comprehensive, up-to-date guide to these scattered maps exists.

The last person to undertake a comprehensive listing was the librarian Justin Winsor. Since the appearance of his *Reader's Handbook of the American Revolution* in 1880 and Volume 6 of his *Narrative and Critical History of America* in 1888, hundreds of additional maps have been published, and many which he cites have become rare.

This *Index to Maps of the American Revolution* is designed to make maps in books and periodicals available to any interested American who lives within reach of a library, whether it be large or small. Consequently the publications chosen for indexing range from monographs and journals issued in limited editions to general histories of the United States, standard reference works, and widely-used textbooks.

Most of the research was done at the Library of Congress, in the evening and on weekends, whenever time could be spared from the compiler's regular occupation and family and civic responsibilities. Books and periodicals were selected with the aid of the Library's card catalog, Winsor's aforementioned two volumes, standard bibliographies such as the *Harvard Guide to American History, The American Historical Association's Guide to Historical Literature, Writings on American History,* and *A Guide to the Study of the United States of America,* and, in the case of the more recent publications, the *American Historical Review.* The task of selection was complicated by the fact that some of the principal bibliographies, and even some Library of Congress cards, fail to list the presence of maps in books, and maps in periodicals have largely been ignored. Accordingly it was necessary to examine not only the publications specifically noted as having maps, but also literally hundreds of other books and articles whose titles suggested that maps might be included.

Preparation of the *Index* would have been impossible without the cooperation of members of the Library staff who tracked down book after book first reported to be "not on shelf" and hauled from the stacks to the reading room several times as many volumes as were finally selected. Their help is warmly appreciated.

The process of editing and arranging the map references was made easier by three compendia which frequently shortened or eliminated the research that would otherwise have been required to identify persons and places or determine dates and sequences of events: the *Encyclopedia of the American Revolution* by Mark Mayo Boatner III (New York, 1966); the revised *Encyclopedia of American History* edited by Richard B. Morris (New York, 1965); and *The Annals of America* by Abiel Holmes (Cambridge, 1829). Also useful were *American Maps and Map Makers of the Revolution* by Peter J. Guthorn (Monmouth Beach, N.J., 1966) and the list of battles and engagements of the Revolutionary War in *The Army Almanac* (Washington, 1950).

Over ninety-five percent of the publications ultimately indexed are held by the Library of Congress. Copies of the rest are in the District of Columbia Public Library or the Army Library at the Pentagon, except for a few in the compiler's own collection.

Although the majority of the maps cited illustrate military or naval engagements and the movements of forces, "American Revolution" has been broadly interpreted to apply also to social, economic, and political developments which took place in America between the signing of the Treaty of Paris in 1763 and the establishment of the government of the United States under the Constitution in 1789. Thus the *Index* includes references to maps showing such things as state and county boundaries, frontier lines, roads and trails, proposed colonies and actual settlements west of the Allegheny Mountains, population distribution and density, and the manner of selecting delegates to the First Continental Congress.

A small mimeographed trial edition of the *Index* was issued late in 1969. The welcome it has received from librarians and scholars has encouraged publication of the present revised and much enlarged edition.

The compiler will welcome hearing from readers about good maps that escaped his attention.

David Sanders Clark

PART I
MAP REFERENCES

The sections and subsections into which the references are divided are shown in the Table of Contents. This arrangement was adopted primarily for the purpose of enabling users of the *Index* to see what maps are available to illustrate the history of a particular region, state, or area during the Revolutionary Period. Persons looking for maps on a specific subject, such as a battle, a fort, or the operations of a certain military commander, will probably find them more quickly by first consulting the alphabetical listing in Part II, which is keyed to entries in Part I.

References to maps of a general nature normally precede those to maps which are more detailed or more limited in scope. For example, in the section devoted to Northern New York, references to maps of the country between Canada and Albany appear ahead of references to maps of Burgoyne's invasion route, which in turn are followed by references to maps of the Battle of Freeman's Farm. Within this framework, entries are arranged chronologically insofar as possible. The majority of the maps are listed only once, but those dealing with a complex subject may be cited under a number of headings. This is the case, for instance, with a map depicting the movements of American, French, and British forces in Virginia in 1781, which has been cited under the names of the principal commanders, Washington, Rochambeau, and Cornwallis, and under Wayne, Steuben, Lafayette, and Tarleton as well.

Because this is an index, not a cartobibliography, no attempt has been made to describe individual maps in minute detail. Entries are brief, intended mainly to tell the reader in a line or two what the map is about, how big it is, and in what book or periodical he can find it. They include:

- Subject of the map.

- Date of the situation depicted; or, in some instances, the year of initial publication, if the map was published during the Revolutionary Period.

- Last name of author or editor of the publication in which the map appears.

- Short title of the publication.

- Volume number of the publication, plus the date of issue in the case of a periodical, followed by a colon.

- Page on which, or next to which, the map will be found; plate number of the map; or map number.

- Height and width of the map, from border to border, to the nearest 1/8 of an inch.

- Name of the maker, engraver, publisher, or original user (if a person of historical interest), in the case of maps made during the Revolutionary Period.

If dimensions are not given, the map was either missing from the volume being indexed or was available only on microfilm.

From the 18th century to the present, it has been a common practice of publishers to reproduce or re-draw maps without identifying who first made them or the works in which they initially appeared. In consequence a user of the *Index* may sometimes discover that several of the maps listed under a particular heading are in fact duplicates or variants differing in size, clarity, and degree of detail. Except for certain older maps which were readily attributable to a specific maker, engraver, or publisher, it was not practical to undertake to identify duplicates and variants in the *Index*. Instead, effort was concentrated on recording as many references as possible, in order to increase the user's chances of finding a map suited to his needs on the shelves of the nearest library.

Key to Abbreviations

col.   in color

engr.   engraved

frontis.   frontispiece

pub.   published

For expansions of the abbreviations used in short titles see Bibliography in Part III.

NORTH AMERICA

```
North America
  1763, after Treaty of Paris                                        01005
    Alvord, Lord Shelburne, end, 1 1/2 x 1 3/4 col.
    Avery, Hist. of U.S., 4:352, 6 3/4 x 5 1/2 col.
    Burpee, Hist. Atlas of Canada, 18, map 47, 4 5/8 x 3 5/8 col.
    Caughey, Hist. of U.S., 79, 3 1/2 x 5 7/8
    Coggins, Ships and Seamen, 18-19, 8 5/8 x 11 1/2
    Craven, U.S., 48, 5 3/8 x 4 1/2
    Current, Am. Hist., 2d ed., 71, 2 7/8 x 2 1/2
    DeConde, Foreign Policy, 22, 6 x 4 5/8
    Entick, Hist. of Late War, 1:167, 7 5/8 x 9
    Faulkner, Am. Political & Social Hist., 87, 1 7/8 x 2 1/2
    Gipson, Br. Empire, 9:46, 5 1/2 x 4 5/8
    Hart, Am. Nation, 7:268, 6 1/2 x 4 1/8 col.
    Hawke, Colonial Experience, 521, 5 3/4 x 5
    Kerr, Hist. Atlas of Canada, 30, 8 x 8 3/4 col.
    Kraus, U.S. to 1865, 157, 3 3/4 x 5
    Newsome, Growth of N.C., 119, 2 1/2 x 2
    Pag. Am., 6:105, 3 7/8 x 3
    Savelle, Foundations, 437, 5 7/8 x 4 1/8
    Todd, America's Hist., 107, 5 1/8 x 5 1/8
  1774, after Quebec Act                                             01010
    Burpee, Hist. Atlas of Canada, 19, map 49, 4 3/4 x 3 5/8
    Gewehr, United States, 69, 4 1/2 x 5 1/4
  1775                                                               01015
    Avery, Hist. of U.S., 5:212, 4 1/2 x 7 1/8 col.
  1778                                                               01020
    Fite, Book of Old Maps, 274, 9 1/4 x 10, by Capt. Johathan
      Carver
  1783, after Treaty of Versailles                                   01025
    Alvord, Lord Shelburne, end, 7 3/4 x 9 3/8 col., 1 1/2 x
      1 3/4 col.
    Avery, Hist. of U.S., 6:362, 6 3/4 x 5 col.
    Baldwin, Adult's History, 112, 4 1/4 x 5 5/8
    Burpee, Hist. Atlas of Canada, 19, map 50, 4 3/4 x 3 5/8
    Hart, Am. Nation, 10:40, 6 3/8 x 4 col.
    Ludlow, War of Am. Independence, 210, 4 1/4 x 3 1/4 col.
  1785                                                               01030
    Wheat, Mapping West, 1:148, 12 5/8 x 4 3/8, by Antonio Zatta
British North America by Royal Proclamation, 1763                    01035
    Burpee, Hist. Atlas of Canada, 18, map 48, 4 3/4 x 7 1/4 col.
    Neatby, Quebec, 5, 4 3/8 x 7 1/4
British posessions in North America, 1763-1775                       01040
    Alden, Hist. of Am. Rev., 40, 8 5/8 x 5 5/8
    Barck, Colonial Am., 2d ed., 475, 5 x 4 1/2
    Bourinot, Canada under Br. Rule, end, 5 1/8 x 4 7/8 col.
    Greene, Foundations, 389, 4 x 6 col.
    Ludlow, War of Am. Independence, 66, 4 1/4 x 3 1/4 col.
    Palmer, Atlas of World Hist., 150, 5 5/8 x 5 col.
    See also 02005 et seq.
Eastern North America
  1763, after Treaty of Paris                                        01045
    Alden, Rise of Am. Republic, 115, 5 x 4 1/4
    Barck, Colonial Am., 473, 7 x 4 5/8
```

THE THIRTEEN COLONIES AND STATES

```
English Colonies in North America                    02005
   Adams, Atlas, pl.66, 9 1/4 x 6 1/4
   Clarke, Am. Revolution, front lining paper, 9 1/8 x 5 7/8
      col.
   Fortescue, British Army, 3:pl.v, 10 1/4 x 17 5/8 col.;
      pl.vi, 8 3/4 x 16 1/4 col.
   Ludlow, War of Am. Independence, 24, 7 1/8 x 5 1/2 col.
   MacMunn, Am. War., 12-13, 8 x 6 1/8
   Naval Docs. of Am. Rev., 2:XLIV, 5 1/8 x 7 5/8
1763                                                 02010
   Current, Am. Hist., 2d ed., 73, 8 x 5 1/4
   Fite, Book of Old Maps, 218, 9 3/8 x 11 1/4, from Gentle-
      man's Mag.
   Gentleman's Mag., 33(Oct.1763):477, 8 x 9 1/4, engr. by
      J. Gibson
   Gipson, Br. Empire, 10:32, 7 7/8 x 9 1/2, by Thomas Kitchin
   Malone, Am. Origins, 107, 6 3/4 x 4 1/4
   Mitchell, Twenty Battles, 201, 2 1/2 x 3 1/8
   Paxon, Am. Frontier, 9, 7 x 4 1/4
   Perkins, U.S. of Am., 128, 7 1/8 x 4 5/8
   Scheer, Rebels and Redcoats, lining papers, 9 1/4 x 12 1/4
   Sosin, Whitehall and Wilderness, 64, 6 x 5 3/8
   Wright, Fabric of Freedom, 14, 6 x 4 1/8
1763-1775                                            02015
   Lord, Atlas, map 36, 4 1/2 x 3 3/8
   Wilson, Am. People, 2:320, 7 x 4 3/8 col.
1763-1783                                            02017
   Wells, Am. War of Independence, 21, 5 3/4 x 4
1765                                                 02020
   Gipson, Coming of Rev., 122-123, 8 1/2 x 6 1/2
1767                                                 02025
   Hart, Am. Nation, 8:4, 8 1/2 x 6 1/2 col.
1774, after Quebec Act                               02030
   Alvord, Lord Shelburne, end, 1 3/8 x 1 3/4 col.
   Bolton, Colonization, 405, 4 3/4 x 4
   Hawke, Colonial Experience, 566, 5 1/4 x 4 1/2
   Hofstadter, Am. Republic, 166, 2 3/8 x 2 5/8
   Lanctot, Canada and Am. Revolution, 210, 7 x 5
   Naval Docs. of Am. Rev., 1:xliv, 7 7/8 x 5, by Samuel Dunn
   Nettels, Roots of Am. Civ., 645, 3 7/8 x 4 1/8
   Paullin, Atlas, pl.46A, 8 1/4 x 9 col.
   Roosevelt, Winning of West, 2:end, 8 x 6 1/2 col.
1775                                                 02035
   Am. Heritage Atlas, 94, 9 3/4 x 4 3/8 col.
   Baldwin, Adult's History, 59, 8 1/2 x 5 5/8
   Gipson, Coming of Rev., 130-131, 8 1/2 x 6 1/2
   Hart, Am. Nation, 8:298, 8 1/2 x 6 1/2 col.
   James, Br. Navy in Adversity, 20, 6 1/2 x 4
   Mackesy, War for America, 3, 6 7/8 x 4 1/4, 2 5/8 x 3 5/8
1776                                                 02040
   Hamilton, Grenadier Guards, 2:209, 6 5/8 x 4 1/2
1777, engr. by William Faden                         02045
   Clinton, Am. Rebellion, end, 9 1/8 x 12
   Fite, Book of Old Maps, 232, 9 3/8 x 11 1/4
```

Naval Docs. of Am. Rev., 3:8, 6 5/8 x 8 1/4
United States in the Revolutionary Period   02047
    Royaumont, La Fayette et Rochambeau, 2, 5 x 6 7/8,
        French map
United States, 1778   02050
    Avery, Hist. of U.S., 6:142, 10 1/8 x 7 1/2, French map
Northeastern United States, 1776   02052
    Palmer, River and Rock, 9 x 7 7/8 col.
Northern colonies and Canada, 1777   02055
    Hughes, Journal, end, 6 1/2 x 4 1/2
    Naval Docs. of Am. Rev., 4:1434, 6 1/4 x 5 1/2, by William
        Faden
Northern New York, Vermont, and New Hampshire, 1777, by   02060
    Bernard Romans
    Crockett, Vermont, 190, 8 x 10
    Pearson, Schenectady Patent, 296, 9 7/8 x 12 3/8
    Vt. Hist. Soc., Proc., 11(June 1943):96-97, 8 x 9
New England and Middle States, 1780-1782   02065
    Chastellux, Travels, 1:front lining paper, 8 x 10 1/4;
        2: end lining paper, 8 x 10 1/4
Maryland, Delaware, and Virginia   02070
    Mag. of Am. Hist., 6(Jan. 1881):25, 7 5/8 x 6 5/8
    1782   02075
    Hilliard d'Auberteuil, Essais, 2:101, 9 x 12 7/8 col.
Virginia and Maryland, with part of Pennsylvania, New Jersey,   02080
    and North Carolina, 1775
    Fite, Book of Old Maps, 242, 8 x 12 7/8, by Joshua Fry
        and Peter Jefferson, pub. by Thomas Jefferys
North Carolina, South Carolina, Georgia, and East and West   02085
    Florida
    Naval Docs. of Am. Rev., 2:773, 5 1/4 x 6 5/8, by Bernard
        Romans, pub. by Robert Sayer and John Bennett

GOVERNMENT

Manner of selection of delegates to Stamp Act Congress, 1765   02100
    Gipson, Coming of Rev., 97, 3 3/4 x 2 1/2
    Hart, Am. Nation, 8:154, 3 5/8 x 2 1/4
Manner of selection of delegates to First Continental Congress,   02105
    1774
    Gipson, Coming of Rev., 229, 3 3/4 x 2 1/2
Manner of selection of delegates to Second Continental   02110
    Congress, 1775
    Gipson, Coming of Rev., 229, 3 3/4 x 2 1/2
Travels of the Continental Congress, 1776-1785   02115
    Gewehr, United States, 91, 4 5/8 x 5 1/4
Seating plan of Continental Congress, Independence Hall, Phila-
    delphia, when receiving credentials of M. Conrad Alexandre
    Gerard, French minister plenipotentiary, Aug. 3, 1778
    Tower, La Fayette, 2:29, 7 1/2 x 4 1/4
Estimated degree of severity of legislation against Loyalists   02125
    Hart, Am. Nation, 9:250, 6 1/2 x 4 1/8

POPULATION

Growth of settlement
  1760-1775   02205
    Channing, Hist. of U.S., 3:528, 15 1/4 x 15 1/4 col.
  1775-1790   02210
    Channing, Hist. of U.S., 3:528, 15 1/4 x 15 1/4 col.
Settled areas
  1770   02215
    Brown, Hist. Geog., 54, 1 7/8 x 1 1/2
  1774   02220
    Becker, Beginnings of Am. People, 272, 5 3/4 x 3 3/8
  1775   02225
    Palmer, Atlas of World Hist., 151, 5 5/8 x 4 3/8 col.
    Paullin, Atlas, pl.60D, 6 x 4 3/8 col.
  1780   02230
    Brown, Hist. Geog., 54, 1 7/8 x 1 1/2
  1783   02235
    Caughey, Hist. of U.S., 119, 3 1/2 x 5 3/4
  1790   02240
    Channing, Hist. of U.S., 3:528, 15 1/4 x 15 1/4 col.
New York, New England, and Eastern Canada, 1775   02245
    Ellis, New York, 138, 4 1/8 x 6
Distribution of population
  1770   02250
    Geog. Rev., 30(July 1940):464, 7 1/4 x 6 1/4 col.
    Nettels, Roots of Am. Civ., 539, 5 1/8 x 4 1/8
  1780   02255
    Geog. Rev., 30(July 1940):464, 7 1/4 x 6 1/4 col.
    Nettels, Roots of Am. Civ., 693, 5 1/4 x 4 1/8
New England and New York, 1771-1776   02260
    Sutherland, Population Distrib., 62, 17 5/8 x 17 3/4
New Jersey, Pennsylvania, Delaware, Maryland, and Virginia,   02265
    1778-1787
    Sutherland, Population Distrib., 158, 17 1/2 x 22
North Carolina, South Carolina, and Georgia, 1775   02270
    Sutherland, Population Distrib., 222, 17 3/8 x 19 5/8
The Southeast, 1770   02275
    De Vorsey, Indian Boundary, 24, 3 x 2 1/2
The Southeast, 1780   02280
    De Vorsey, Indian Boundary, 24, 3 x 2 1/2
Population density in Thirteen Colonies, 1775   02285
    Nickerson, Turning Point, 48, 6 1/4 x 3 1/4
Frontier line (approximate limit of settlement)
  1770   02290
    Kraus, U.S. to 1865, 177, 4 7/8 x 7 7/8
  1774   02295
    Roosevelt, Winning of West, 2:end, 8 x 6 1/2 col.
  1775   02300
    Becker, Beginnings of Am. People, 180, 5 3/4 x 3 3/8
    Faust, German Element, 1:264, 5 1/2 x 3 7/8
    Van Every, Co. of Heroes, viii, 6 1/2 x 4; 221, 4 1/4 x 4
  1784   02305
    Van Every, Ark of Empire, 1, 6 x 4

German settlements, 1775   02310
    Becker, Beginnings of Am. People, 180, 5 3/4 x 3 3/8
    Faust, German Element, 1:264, 5 1/2 x 3 7/8
Towns, 1775   02315
    Paullin, Atlas, pl.61D, 6 x 4 3/8 col.
Principal towns in Southern New England and the Middle Colonies   02317
    1759-1778
    Freemen, Washington, abridgment, 374, 8 5/8 x 11, by Harold
    K. Faye
Towns with newspapers, 1775   02320
    Lord, Atlas, map 45, 6 1/2 x 4 3/4

CHURCHES

Location of churches in the Thirteen Colonies, 1775-1776
Baptist   02405
    Paullin, Atlas, pl.82D, 6 x 2 7/8
Catholic   02410
    Paullin, Atlas, pl.82K, 6 x 2 7/8 col.
Congregationalist   02415
    Paullin, Atlas, pl.82A, 6 x 2 7/8 col.
Dunker   02420
    Paullin, Atlas, pl.82L, 6 x 2 7/8 col.
Dutch Reformed   02420
    Paullin, Atlas, pl.82H, 6 x 2 7/8 col.
French Protestant   02430
    Paullin, Atlas, pl.82L, 6 x 2 7/8 col.
Friends   02435
    Paullin, Atlas, pl.82E, 6 x 2 7/8 col.
German Reformed   02440
    Paullin, Atlas, pl.82F, 6 x 2 7/8 col.
Jewish   02445
    Paullin, Atlas, pl.82M, 6 x 2 7/8 col.
Lutheran   02450
    Paullin, Atlas, pl.82G, 6 x 2 7/8 col.
Mennonite   02455
    Paullin, Atlas, pl.82L, 6 x 2 7/8 col.
Methodist   02460
    Paullin, Atlas, pl.82J, 6 x 2 7/8 col.
Moravian   02465
    Paullin, Atlas, pl.82L, 6 x 2 7/8 col.
Presbyterian   02470
    Paullin, Atlas, pl.82B, 6 x 2 7/8 col.
Protestant Episcopal   02475
    Paullin, Atlas, pl.82C, 6 x 2 7/8 col.
Rogerene   02480
    Paullin, Atlas, pl.82M, 6 x 2 7/8 col.
Sandemanian   02485
    Paullin, Atlas, pl.82M, 6 x 2 7/8 col.
Separatist and Independent   02490
    Paullin, Atlas, pl.82M, 6 x 2 7/8 col.
Friends Meetings in New England, 1782   02495
    Quaker Hist., 52(Spring 1963):frontis., 10 1/2 x 5 7/8
Valley of Virginia churches, 1776   02497
    Hart, Valley of Va., 35, 5 x 7 3/8

COLLEGES

AGRICULTURE AND COMMERCE

ROADS AND TRAILS

GENERAL MAPS OF THE REVOLUTIONARY WAR

Major campaigns and battles, 1775-1781   03040
    Caughey, Hist. of U.S., 105, 7 1/2 x 5 3/4
    Collier's Enc., 2:81, 6 5/8 x 6 3/4
    Craven, U.S., 105, 6 3/4 x 4 1/2
    Enc. Americana, 1:721, 9 3/8 x 6 1/4, 2 3/4 x 2 5/8
    Garner, Hist. of U.S., 2:502, 6 x 4 1/4 col.
    Hawke, Colonial Experience, 614-615, 4 7/8 x 9 5/8
    Lacy, Meaning of Am. Rev., 153, 6 5/8 x 3 3/4;
        155, 6 5/8 x 3 3/4
    Mitchell, Twenty Battles, 201, 8 1/2 x 5 col.
    Palmer, Atlas of World Hist., 150, 5 5/8 x 3 3/4 col.
Northern campaigns (New England, Middle States, and Canada)
  1775-1776   03045
    Faulkner, Am. Political & Social Hist., 121, 4 5/8 x 2 1/2
    Hicks, Federal Union, 4th ed., 178, 2 5/8 x 1 3/8
  1775-1777   03050
    Morison, Growth of Am. Republic, 5th ed., 210 5 1/2 x 4 1/2
    Todd, America's Hist., 139, 6 5/8 x 5 1/8
    World Book, 16:261, 3 1/4 x 4 5/8 col.
  1775-1781   03060
    Barck, Colonial Am., 624, 7 x 4 5/8
    Barck, Colonial Am., 2d ed., 598, 7 x 4 5/8
    Chron. Am., 12:180, 7 x 5 3/4 col.
    Stanley, Canada's Soldiers, 107, 4 5/8 x 7 1/2
  1777   03065
    Faulkner, Am. Political & Social Hist., 133, 4 5/8 x 2 1/2
    Hicks, Feberal Union, 4th ed., 178, 2 5/8 x 1 3/8
    Hofstadter, Am. Republic, 184, 4 1/8 x 3 1/8
Southern campaigns
    See 23050-23085
Western campaigns
    See 38040, et seq.
Campaigns of 1775-1776   03070
    Lord, Atlas, map 46, 6 x 4 col.
    Pag. Am., 6:154-155, 10 7/8 x 8 1/2
    Paullin, Atlas, pl.160A, 8 1/2 x 4 1/4 col.
Campaigns of 1776   03075
    Perkins, U.S. of Am., 156, 7 3/8 x 4 5/8
Campaigns of 1777   03080
    Current, Am. Hist., 2d ed., 109, 5 5/8 x 2 1/2
    Dupuy, Mil. Heritage of Am., 93, 5 1/2 x 4 1/8
    Lord, Atlas, map 47, 6 x 4 col.
    Pag. Am., 6:176-177, 10 7/8 x 8 1/2
    Paullin, Atlas, pl.160B, 8 1/2 x 5 3/8 col.
Campaigns of 1778   03085
    Lord, Atlas, map 48, 6 x 4 col.
    Pag. Am., 6:210-211, 10 7/8 x 8 1/2
    Paullin, Atlas, pl.160C, 4 1/2 x 4 3/8 col.;
        pl.160E, 3 5/8 x 2 5/8 col.
Campaigns of 1779   03090
    James, Br. Navy in Adversity, 157, 6 1/4 x 4
    Lord, Atlas, map 49, 6 x 4 col.
    Pag. Am., 6:220-221, 10 7/8 x 8 1/2
    Paullin, Atlas, pl.160C, 4 1/2 x 4 3/8 col.;
        pl.160E, 3 5/8 x 2 5/8 col.

Campaigns of 1780   03095
   Lord, Atlas, map 50, 6 x 4 col.
   Pag. Am., 6:226-227, 10 7/8 x 8 1/2
   Paullin, Atlas, pl.160F, 3 5/8 x 3 1/8 col.;
     pl.160G, 1 3/8 x 1 3/4 col.
Campaigns of 1781   03100
   Billias, Washington's Opponents, xxxii, 7 1/4 x 4 5/8
   Lord, Atlas, map 51, 6 x 4 col.
   Pag. Am., 6:242, 6 5/8 x 5 5/8; 247, 7 x 5 7/8
     3 5/8 x 3 1/8 col., 1 3/4 x 2 1/2 col.
   Willcox, Portrait, 407, 7 3/8 x 4 5/8
Campaigns in which Hessian troops participated, 1776-1781   03102
   Kipping, Truppen von Hessen-Kassel, 16, 8 7/8 x 6 1/2;
     17, 8 7/8 x 6 1/2
Military operations
 From Lexington to Bunker Hill, Apr.-June 1775   03105
   Mitchell, Battles Am. Rev., 25, 7 1/2 x 5
 From Bunker Hill to evacuation of Boston, June 1775-Mar. 1776   03110
   Mitchell, Battles Am. Rev., 38-39, 7 1/2 x 5, 7 1/2 x 5
 From evacuation of Boston to battles around New York,   03115
   Mar.-Aug. 1776
   Mitchell, Battles Am. Rev., 46-47, 7 1/2 x 5, 7 1/2 x 5
 From loss of New York City to Trenton and Princeton,   03120
   Oct. 1776-Jan. 1777
   Mitchell, Battles Am. Rev., 70, 7 1/2 x 5
 From Trenton and Princeton to Saratoga, Jan.-Oct. 1777   03125
   Mitchell, Battles Am. Rev., 91, 7 1/2 x 5
 From Saratoga to Mommouth, Oct. 1777-June 1778   03130
   Mitchell, Battles Am. Rev., 137, 7 1/2 x 5
 From Monmouth to Camden, June 1778-Aug. 1780   03135
   Mitchell, Battles Am. Rev., 154-155, 7 1/2 x 5, 7 1/2 x 5
 From Camden to Guilford Court House, Aug. 1780-Mar. 1781   03140
   Mitchell, Battles Am. Rev., 172-173, 7 1/2 x 5, 7 1/2 x 5
 From Guilford Court House to Yorktown, Mar.-Oct. 1781   03145
   Mitchell, Battles Am. Rev., 189, 7 1/2 x 5
Parts of U.S. held by British forces, April 1779   03148
   Bemis, Hussey-Cumberland Mission, front lining paper,
     7 5/8 x 10 7/8
Parts of U.S. held by British and Spanish forces, June 1781   03150
   Bemis, Diplomacy of Am. Rev., 182, 7 5/8 x 10 3/4
   Bemis, Hussey-Cumberland Mission, end lining paper,
     7 5/8 x 10 7/8
Areas under British control in North America, late summer 1781   03155
   Fleming, Battle of Yorktown, 16, 7 x 6 3/4

INTERNATIONAL RELATIONS

Attitude of European states toward the American Revolution   03700
   Avery, Hist. of U.S., 6:279, 4 1/2 x 6 3/4 col.
Division of Europe as to war with England, 1778-1782   03705
   Greene, Foundations, 476, 2 5/8 x 2 3/4
   Hart, Am. Nation, 9:228, 4 1/8 x 6 1/2
British world-wide involvement in warfare with French, Spanish,   03710
   and Dutch
   McDowell, Revolutionary War, 188-189, 5 5/8 x 10 1/2 col.

WAR PRISONS

NEW ENGLAND

```
New England                                                    04000
    Holbrook, Ethan Allen, 274, 6 7/8 x 4 1/8
  By Carington Bowles                                          04005
    Fite, Book of Old Maps, 235, 11 3/8 x 9 1/4
    Lee, Hist. of N. America, 5:373, 8 3/8 x 6 1/2 col.
    Naval Docs. of Amer. Rev., 2:986, 6 5/8 x 5 3/8
  c.1775                                                       04007
    Lauvrière, Brève Histoire, 96, 4 3/8 x 6 1/4
  1782                                                         04010
    Hillard d'Auberteuil, Essais, 1:137, 9 x 12 3/4 col.
New Hampshire, Vermont, and Maine                              04015
    Gordon, Hist. of U.S.A., 2:584, pl.V, 14 x 13 3/4,
      engr. by T. Condor
New Hampshire and Vermont, 1781                                04020
    Wilbur, Ira Allen, 1:234, 5 x 4
Southern New England                                           04022
    Allen, Naval Hist. of Am. Rev., 1:332, 4 x 6
    Coggins, Ships and Seamen, 105, 4 7/8 x 7 1/2
Southern New England coast, from Boston Harbor to the          04023
      Connecticut River, 1774
    Naval Docs. of Am. Rev., 3:98, 6 1/2 x 9 5/8
Connecticut and Rhode Island, 1780                             04025
    Naval Docs. of Am. Rev., 2:453, 5 1/8 x 6 3/4, from
      Universal Mag., Oct. 1780
New York to Newport, R.I., 1776-1783                           04030
    Adams, Atlas, pl. 79, 6 1/4 x 9 1/4
```

MILITARY OPERATIONS

```
Washington's routes in New England
  New York to Cambridge, Mass., via Springfield, Mass.,        04035
      June 27 - July 2, 1775
    Sons of Am. Rev., Washington's Journey, 6, 8 1/2 x 9 7/8
    Washington Atlas, pl.26, 11 x 15 1/2 col.
    Washington Bicentennial, 1:406, 7 1/8 x 10 1/8
  Cambridge to New York, via Providence, R.I., and Norwich,    04040
      Conn., Apr. 4-13, 1776
    Washington Atlas, pl.26, 11 x 15 1/2 col.
    Washington Bicentennial, 1:406, 7 1/8 x 10 1/8
  Fredericksburg, N.Y., to Danbury, Conn., and return, Oct. 1778  04045
    Washington Bicentennial, 1:406, 7 1/8 x 10 1/8
  Peekskill, N.Y., to Hartford, Conn., and return, Sept. 18-24, 04050
      1780
    Washington Atlas, pl.26, 11 x 15 1/2 col.
    Washington Bicentennial, 1:406, 7 1/8 x 10 1/8
  New Windsor, N.Y., to Newport, R.I., going via Hartford and  04055
      Lebanon, Conn, returning via Bristol and Providence, R.I.,
      and Hartford, Mar. 2-20, 1781
    Newport Hist. Soc., Bul., No.6(Feb. 1913):frontis., 4 1/4 x
      6 3/8
    Washington Atlas, pl.26, 11 x 15 1/2 col.
    Washington Bicentennial, 1:406, 7 1/8 x 10 1/8
```

New Windsor, N.Y., to Wethersfield, Conn., and return,   04060
    May 18-25, 1781
    Washington Atlas, pl.26, 11 x 15 1/2 col.
    Washington Bicentennial, 1:406, 7 1/8 x 10 1/8
Route of Rochambeau's troops through New England, from   04065
    Providence, R.I., across Connecticut to the Hudson River,
    June 1781
    Avery, Hist. of U.S., 6:306, 4 1/2 x 7 1/2 col.
    Balch, French in Am., 1:end, 4 x 10 1/8
    Chastellux, Travels, 1:64, 5 3/8 x 8 1/4
    Chron. Am., 12:180, 7 x 5 3/4 col.
    Closen, Journal, lining papers, 11 3/4 x 9 col.
    Flexner, Washington in Am. Rev., lining papers, 6 5/8 x
      4 7/8, by Samuel H. Bryant
    Forbes, France and New Eng., 1:132, 4 3/4 x 8
    Freeman, Washington, abridgment, 471, 7 3/4 x 5 1/2
    Greene, Revolutionary War, 150, 4 1/2 x 7 1/2 col.
    Landers, Va. Campaign, map 3, 12 3/8 x 15 3/8
    Mag. of Am. Hist., 4(Apr. 1880):298, 1 1/4 x 3 5/8, 2 1/4 x 8,
      1 1/2 x 3 7/8; 5(Dec. 1880):442, 2 1/2 x 7 1/8, 4 x 13 1/2,
      3 1/2 x 8 1/8; 7(July 1881):8, 4 7/8 x 7
    Pag. Am., 6:252, 2 x 5 7/8, French chart
    See also 09215-09220, 10140
Route of French army across Connecticut, Rhode Island, and   04070
    Massachusetts, on way from Yorktown, Va., to Boston,
    autumn 1782
    Balch, French in Am., 1:end, 4 x 10 1/8
    Closen, Journal, lining papers, 11 3/4 x 9 col.
    Crofut, Guide, 1:78, 8 5/8 x 9 5/8
    Forbes, France and New Eng., 1:132, 4 3/4 x 8
    Mag. of Am. Hist., 7(July 1881):8, 4 7/8 x 7
    See also 08275-08280, 09225-09235, 10155-10190

MAINE

Maine, 1771   05005
    Gipson, Br. Empire, 3:30, 5 5/8 x 5 5/8, by Carington Bowles
Eastern Maine and Nova Scotia, 1775-1776   05010
    Ahlin, Maine Rubicon, 29, 3 7/8 x 6
Twelve townships east of the Penobscot granted by Massachusetts   05015
    General Court in 1762, conditional upon the King's approval
    Ahlin, Maine Rubicon, 3, 3 7/8 x 6

DEFENSES

Fort George, Castine, Me., built in June 1779   05020
    Wheeler, Castine, Penobscot, and Brooksville, 188,
      3 1/2 x 3 1/2
Fort Machias, Me., 1775-1777   05025
    Dunnack, Maine Forts, 26, 3 7/8 x 4
Fort McClary (formerly Fort William), Kittery, Me.   05030
    Dunnack, Maine Forts, 160, 4 1/4 x 4 3/8
Fort Pownall, Stockton, Me.   05035
    Dunnack, Maine Forts, 4 x 5 7/8, 1759 plan

MILITARY OPERATIONS

Capture of *Margaretta,* June 12, 1775, and *Diligent,*   05040
    July 15, 1775, near Machias, Me.
  Ahlin, Maine Rubicon, 13, 6 x 3 7/8
Burning of Falmouth Neck (now Portland), Me., by British,   05045
    Oct. 18, 1775
  Kaler, Old Falmouth, 118, 5 1/2 x 7 3/4
  Naval Docs. of Am. Rev., 2:591, 5 3/8 x 8
  Willis, Portland, 520
Col. Benedict Arnold's march through Maine to Quebec, fall 1775
  See 46125
Capt. Jonathan Eddy's expedition to Fort Cumberland, Aug.-Nov.
    1776
  See 47030
John Allen's expedition to the St. John River, May 30-Aug. 2,
    1777
  See 47040
British attack on Machias, Me., Aug. 13-15, 1777   05050
  Ahlin, Maine Rubicon, 89, 6 x 3 7/8
Penobscot expedition, July-Aug. 1779
  See 50120, 50125

NEW HAMPSHIRE

New Hampshire, 1771   06005
  Gipson, Br. Empire, 3:46, 5 5/8 x 5 1/2 by Carington Bowles
New Hampshire counties at time of the Revolution   06010
  Brown, King's Friends, 3, 5 5/8 x 3 1/4
Meredith, N.H., 1770   06015
  Paullin, Atlas, pl.44D, 7 1/2 x 11 col.
Portsmouth, N.H., 1782   06020
  Morison, Jones, 328, 3 5/8 x 4 1/8
Portsmouth and Piscataqua Harbor, N.H.   06021
  Naval Docs. of Am. Rev., 3:744, 5 3/8 x 7 3/4
Approaches to Piscataqua River and Isles of Shoals, N.H.   06025
  Naval Docs. of Am. Rev., 2:1243, 6 7/8 x 5 1/2

VERMONT

Vermont
 1774, by Thomas Jefferys   07005
   Newton, Vermont Story, 55, 8 3/8 x 7 7/8
   Williamson, Vt. in Quandary, 38-39, 8 1/4 x 7 3/4
 1776   07010
   Gipson, Br. Empire, 3:47, 7 1/2 x 5 3/8
 1777, by Capt. Bernard Romans   07015
   Crockett, Vermont, 2:190, 8 x 10
   Pearson, Schenectady Patent, 296, 9 7/8 x 12 3/8
   Vt. Hist. Soc., Proc., n.s., 11(June 1943):96-97, 8 x 9
 1778-1782   07020
   Thompson, Independent Vt., lining papers, 8 3/4 x 11
 1779, by Claude Joseph Sauthier   07025
   Newton, Vermont Story, 54, 10 5/8 x 7 3/8

```
1781                                                              07030
   Newton, Vermont Story, 86, 4 1/4 x 3 3/4
   Williamson, Vt. in Quandary, 95, 4 1/4 x 3 3/4
1783                                                              07035
   Collins, Hist. of Vermont, 122, 5 3/4 x 3 1/2
Undated map in Duane Papers                                      07040
   Wilbur, Ira Allen, 1:116, 6 3/4 x 3 1/2
New Hampshire grants                                             07045
   Jellison, Ethan Allen, front, 11 x 8 1/8
   Mag. of Am. Hist., 8(Jan. 1882):1, 12 x 6 1/8
   N.H. State Papers, 25:frontis., 11 x 11 1/2
1770                                                             07050
   Pell, Ethan Allen, 30, 5 7/8 x 3 5/8
1771                                                             07055
   Newton, Vermont Story, 52, 9 1/4 x 6 1/2
   Williamson, Vt. in Quandary, 38, 6 x 4 1/8
1777-1778                                                        07060
   Newton, Vermont Story, 81, 4 1/2 x 3 3/4
   Williamson, Vt. in Quandary, 83, 4 1/2 x 3 3/4
New York grants, 1779                                            07065
   Williamson, Vt. in Quandary, 39, 7 1/2 x 5 1/4, by
      Claude Joseph Sauthier
Vermont as divided into counties by New York                    07070
   Collins, Hist. of Vermont, 74, 4 x 3 1/2
   Kimball, Vermont, 89, 5 x 3 1/2
Lake Champlain-Vermont frontier                                 07072
   Sosin, Revolutionary Frontier, 48, 7 1/2 x 5 1/8
Vermont roads at the time of the Revolution
   Roads and forts in the Whitehall-Rutland-Crown Point area    07075
      Vermont Hist., 27(Apr. 1959):94-95, 8 1/2 x 7
   Bayley-Hazen military road, Wells River to Hazen's Notch,    07080
      1776-1779
      Crockett, Vermont, 2:180, 4 3/4 x 3 3/4
      Vermont Hist., 27(Jan. 1959):68, 7 1/8 x 2 3/4
      Vermont Life, 9(Spring 1955):32, 6 1/2 x 4 3/8;
         34, 10 1/4 x 2 3/4 col.
   Mount Independence-Hubbardton military road, 1776            07085
      Vermont Hist., 27(July 1959):199, 6 3/4 x 3 7/8; 202,
         5 3/4 x 4; 208-209, 6 3/8 x 8; 217, 5 3/4 x 4;
         27(Oct. 1959): 336-339, 6 1/4 x 8
   Hydeville branch military road, 1780-1781                    07090
      Vermont Hist., 27(Oct. 1959):344, 6 1/2 x 2 1/4
Vermont-Canada frontier and Hazen Road                          07100
   Smith, Struggle for 14th Colony, 2:518, 3 3/4 x 2
```

MILITARY OPERATIONS

1777

```
Route of Brig. Gen Simon Fraser and Gen. Riedesel to and        07103
      from Hubbardton, Vt., July 1777
   Lancaster, Guns in the Forest, lining papers, 7 7/8 x 10 3/4,
      by Samuel H. Bryant
   Lancaster, Guns of Burgoyne, frontis., 6 7/8 x 4 3/8
```

Hubbardton, Vt., Battle of, July 7, 1777   07105
   Avery, Hist. of U.S., 6:94, 2 1/2 x 1 3/4 col.
   Boatner, Enc. of Am. Rev., 71, 4 x 7; 527, 4 1/8 x 4 1/8
   Burgoyne, State of Expedition, plan 2, 10 3/4 x 13 3/4 col.,
     by P. Gerlach, engr. and pub. by William Faden, 1780
   Carrington, Battles, 322, 7 3/4 x 4 3/4
   Coffin, Boys of '76, 164, 4 x 2 1/2
   Greene, Revolutionary War, 102, 2 1/2 x 1 3/4 col.
   Lossing, Field-Book of Rev., 1:146, 2 1/8 x 4 1/8
   Nickerson, Turning Point, 148, 5 1/4 x 3 1/4; 152,
     5 3/4 x 3 1/4
Route of British to and from Bennington, Aug. 1777   07109
   Lancaster, Guns in the Forest, lining papers, 7 7/8 x
     10 3/4, by Samuel H. Bryant
   Lancaster, Guns of Burgoyne, frontis., 6 7/8 x 4 3/8
Col. John Stark's march to Bennington, Aug. 1777   07110
   Gewehr, United States, 75, 2 1/4 x 2 1/2
   Rayback, Richards Atlas, 30, 16 x 10 1/8
Bennington, Vt., Battle of, Aug. 16, 1777   07115
   Avery, Hist. of U.S., 6:100, 2 3/4 x 4 1/4 col.
   Bird, March to Saratoga, 98, 1 7/8 x 3 1/2, 4 3/8 x 3 1/2
   Carrington, Battles, 334, 7 3/4 x 4 5/8
   Channing, Hist. of U.S., 3:277, 4 x 6 1/2
   Coburn, Bennington, 33, 2 3/4 x 2 3/4; end, 5 7/8 x 8 7/8
   Coffin, Boys of '76, 190, 3 x 3 1/8
   Crockett, Vermont, 2:120, 3 1/4 x 3 3/8, from Lossing
   Drake, Burgoyne's Invasion, 71, 2 5/8 x 3; 79, 3 x 4 1/4
   Dupuy, Compact Hist., 217, 4 1/2 x 7 1/4
   Ellis, Saratoga Campaign, 53, 3 x 4
   Forbes, Second Battle, 81, 2 7/8 x 2 7/8
   Fuller, Battles, 52, 2 1/4 x 4
   Fuller, Decisive Battles of W. World, 2:295, 2 1/4 x 4 1/8
   Garner, Hist. of U.S., 2:449, 2 x 2 1/4
   Gilmore, N.H. Soldiers, 44, 3 7/8 x 5 7/8
   Granite State Mag., 6(July-Sept. 1909):25, 3 x 4 1/8
   Greene, Revolutionary War, 102, 2 3/4 x 4 1/4 col.
   Hall, School Hist., 224, 6 x 3 3/8
   Harper's Mag., 21(Aug. 1860):325, 3 1/8 x 3 1/8; 55(Sept.
     1877):515, 3 x 4 1/4
   Lossing, Field-Book of Rev., 1:395, 3 x 3
   Mitchell, Battles Am. Rev., 106, 7 1/2 x 5 col.
   Montross, Rag, Tag and Bobtail, 207, 2 1/2 x 4 1/4
   Moore, Gen. John Stark, 292, 4 1/4 x 7 1/2
   New York, Am. Rev. in N.Y., 165, 3 5/8 x 4
   N.Y., Bennington Program, 23, 3 5/8 x 4
   Nickerson, Turning Point, 234, 5 3/4 x 3 1/4; 250, 5 1/2 x 3
   Niles, Hoosac Valley, xxiv, 3 3/8 x 6
   Pag. Am., 6:164, 1 7/8 x 4
   Stiles, Diary, 3:242, 3 1/8 x 3 7/8, by Ezra Stiles
   Ward, Revolution, 1:427, 7 1/8 x 4 3/8
 By Lt. Durnford, engr. by William Faden, 1780   07120
   Burgoyne, State of Expedition, plan 3, 10 3/4 x 13 5/8 col.
   Hall, Bennington, front, 4 x 5 1/8
   Jennings, Memorials, frontis., 4 x 5 1/8
   Newton, Vermont Story, 73, 5 1/2 x 7
   Ridpath, New Complete Hist., 6:2602, 4 1/2 x 4
   Sylvester, Rennselaer Co., 49, 7 1/4 x 9 col.

MASSACHUSETTS

Massachusetts, 1771   08005
   Gipson, Br. Empire, 3:31, 5 x 8, by Carington Bowles
Eastern Massachusetts, 1775   08007
   Hart, Am. Nation, 8:310, 4 1/8 x 6 1/2
Massachusetts counties at time of the Revolution   08010
   Brown, King's Friends, 19, 7 1/8 x 4 1/2
Density of Massachusetts population, 1765   08015
   Hart, Commonwealth Hist. of Mass., 2:410, 3 3/8 x 4 7/8
Craft industries in Massachusetts, 1767   08020
   Hart, Commonwealth Hist. of Mass., 2:410, 3 x 4 7/8
Massachusetts ports   08021
   Coggins, Ships and Seamen, 25, 3 1/2 x 3 1/2

TOWNS AND LOCALITIES

Boston
1765-1775   08025
   Avery, Hist. of U.S., 5:165, 7 1/8 x 4 3/4 col.
1769   08027
   Forbes, Paul Revere, front lining paper, 8 3/4 x 11 3/4 col.
   Gipson, Br. Empire, 10:129, 4 7/8 x 7
   Zobel, Boston Massacre, 197, 7 3/4 x 10, pub. by
     William Price
1771   08029
   Hall-Quest, Guardians of Liberty, 8, 6 7/8 x 4 5/8,
     after A. Hamilton, Jr.
1774   08030
   Am. Heritage Atlas, 84, 5 5/8 x 3 3/4
     by Lt. Thomas Hyde Page. See also 08170
1775   08035
   Falkner, Forge of Liberty, front lining paper, 5 1/4 x
     7 1/2 by C.H. Williams, 1959
   Pulsifer, Bunker Hill, frontis., 11 5/8 x 5 3/8
   Willard, Letters on Am. Rev., 146, 5 7/8 x 4 1/4, from
     Gentleman's Magazine
Boston and environs
1775   08040
   Falkner, Forge of Liberty, front lining paper, 5 1/4 x
     7 1/2, by C.H. Williams, 1959
   Martyn, Artemas Ward, 92, 5 3/4 x 4 3/4
   See also 08155-08175
1776   08041
   Hall-Quest, Guardians of Liberty, 128-129, 4 1/4 x 8 3/4,
     after A. Hamilton, Jr.
Nov. 1782   08045
   Chastellux, Travels, 2:494, 6 x 5 1/2
100 miles around Boston, 1-75   08050
   Gipson, Br. Empire, 12:43, 5 1/8 x 5 1/2
Boston Harbor
1775   08053
   Winsor, Boston, 3:ii, 4 x 5, from Gentleman's Magazine
1781   08055
   Roscoe, Picture Hist., no.452.6, 4 x 5 5/8, from Atlantic
     Neptune

Cambridge, Mass.
  1775   08060
    Lillie, Cambridge in 1775, frontis., 8 1/4 x 13 3/4
  1776   08061
    Gilman, Cambridge of 1776, 2, 4 x 6 1/2, by Mary Isabella
    James
Cambridge and vicinity in Revolutionary times   08065
  Batchelder, Burgoyne, 80, 16 3/4 x 21 1/4
Cambridge and Boston localities associated with Geo. Washington
  Washington Atlas, pl.42, 15 1/2 x 11
Charlestown, Mass., 1775   08075
  Hunnewell, Century of Town Life, 114, 7 x 5 1/4; 129, 8 x 5;
    142, 7 x 5 1/4; 148, 7 x 5 1/4
Dorchester Neck, Mass., 1775   08080
  Simonds, South Boston, 31, 5 1/2 x 3 3/8
  Stark, Antique Views, 273, 5 3/8 x 3 3/8
Lynn, Mass., 1775   08085
  Sanderson, Lynn in Rev., 1:30, 5 1/2 x 9 1/4
Massachusetts Bay   08087
  Allen, Naval Hist. of Am. Rev., 1:6, 6 x 3 3/4
New Bedford and Fair Haven, Mass., and vicinity, 1778   08090
  André, Journal, 2:28, 10 3/8 x 8 3/8, by Maj. John André
Plymouth Bay, Mass., 1781   08092
  Naval Docs. of Am. Rev., 3:1032, 7 3/4 x 5 1/2, from J.F.W.
  Des Barres, Atlantic Neptune
Salem and Marblehead, Mass.   08093
  Billias, Gen. John Glover, frontis., 4 5/8 x 5

PRE-REVOLUTIONARY EVENTS

Boston Massacre, Mar.5, 1771, by Paul Revere   08095
  Russell, Lexington, 56, 5 5/8 x 3 5/8
  Warden, Boston, 230, 7 1/4 x 4 3/4
  Winsor, America, 6:48, 7 7/8 x 5 1/8
  Zobel, Boston Massacre, 197, 4 x 2 1/2
Boston Tea Party, Dec. 16, 1773
 Route taken by Americans from the Old South Church to the wharf   08100
  Drake, Tea Leaves, LXXV, 3 3/4 x 6 3/8
Griffin's wharf, where tea ships lay   08105
  Drake, Tea Leaves, CLXXIII, 3 1/2 x 4 1/2
Places in Boston connected with Boston Tea Party   08107
  Miers, Yankee Doodle Dandy, 13, 5 3/8 x 4 3/4

MILITARY OPERATIONS

1775-1776

Road maps by General Gage's agents, 1775
Between Boston and Marlborough, Mass.   08110
  Winsor, America, 6:121, 5 1/2 x 2 5/8
Roxbury, Mass., and beyond   08115
  Winsor, America, 6:120, 4 x 2 5/8
British expeditions to Marshfield, Jan. 23, 1775, and Salem,   08120
  Mass., Feb. 26, 1775
  Hart, Am. Nation, 8:310, 4 1/8 x 6 1/2

Col. Alexander Leslie's repulse at Salem, Feb. 26, 1775   08125
    Stiles, Diary, 1:523, 3 1/2 x 4 5/8, by Ezra Stiles
Routes of Paul Revere, William Dawes, Jr., and Dr. Samuel   08130
    Prescott, Apr. 18-19, 1775
    Adams, Atlas, pl.64, 6 1/4 x 9 1/4
    Am. Heritage Atlas, 94-95, 4 1/8 x 6 col.
    Azoy, Paul Revere's Horse, 39, 3 3/8 x 5
    Caughey, Hist. of U.S., 100, 3 1/2 x 5 3/4
    Chidsey, Siege of Boston, lining papers, 8 1/4 x 11
    Clarke, Am. Rev., 10, 2 7/8 x 4
    Coburn, Battle of Apr. 19, 1775, 114, 9 1/4 x 9 col.
    Cook, Golden Bk. of Am. Rev., 19, 5 7/8 x 8
    Forbes, Paul Revere, back lining paper, 8 5/8 x 11 3/4 col.
    French, Day of Con. and Lex., front lining paper,
      8 3/4 x 11 1/2
    Hawke, Colonial Experience, 575, 5 x 4 1/2
    Lexington-Concord Battle Rd., 116, 4 1/8 x 6 1/2
    McDowell, Revolutionary War, 38-39, 2 7/8 x 8 1/2 col.
    Mil. Affairs, 1(Spring 1937):2, 5 1/4 x 7
    Morison, Growth of Am. Republic, 5th ed., 183, 3 3/4 x 4 1/4
    Nettels, Washington, 51, 3 3/4 x 5 1/2
    Russell, Lexington, 16-17, 8 1/4 x 12 1/4, by Cal Sachs
    Soc. for Army Hist. Res., Jl., 15(Spring 1936):18,
      5 1/4 x 7 1/8
    Tourtellot, Wm. Diamond's Drum, front lining paper, 8 3/8 x
      11 1/2 col.
    World Book, 16:259, 3 1/4 x 4 3/4
Lexington and Concord, Mass., Battles of, Apr. 19, 1775,   08135
    including British march to and from
    Adams, Address, 24, 13 7/8 x 18 7/8
    Adams, Atlas, pl.64, 6 1/4 x 9 1/4
    Adams, Letter, front, 9 x 10 3/4
    Alden, Rise of Am. Republic, 138, 2 3/8 x 4 3/8
    Am. Heritage, 8(Feb. 1957):75, 2 1/4 x 7 1/2
    Am. Heritage Atlas, 94-95, 4 1/8 x 6 col.
    Army, Am. Military Hist., 32, 4 1/8 x 7 1/2
    Avery, Hist. of U.S., 5:240-241, 1 5/8 x 2 7/8, 7/8 x 1 1/2
      3 x 2 col.
    Baldwin, Adult's History, 96, 3 3/8 x 5 5/8
    Boatner, Enc. of Am. Rev., 624, 4 x 4; 628, 2 1/2 x 4
    Caughey, Hist. of U.S., 100, 3 1/2 x 5 3/4
    Chidsey, Siege of Boston, lining papers, 8 1/4 x 11
    Coburn, Battle of Apr. 19, 1775, 1, 4 1/8 x 3; 58, 8 x 8 1/2
      61, 3 x 5 1/4; 73, 5 1/2 x 7 1/2; 101, 3 x 5 3/8; 114,
      9 1/4 x 9 col.; 131, 3 x 5 3/8
    Collier's Enc., 14:535, 4 x 5
    Coffin, Boys of '76, 38, 2 3/8 x 4 3/8
    Commager, Spirit of '76, 1:72-73, 5 3/4 x 9 1/4
    Drake, Middlesex Co., 2:10, 7 x 3 3/4
    Dupuy, Compact Hist., 32, 1 1/4 x 2 1/4
    Fleming, Now We Are Enemies, lining papers, 3 1/2 x 4 5/8
    French, Day of Con. and Lex., lining papers, 8 3/4 x 11 1/2,
      8 3/4 x 11 1/2
    French, Historic Concord, 67, 3 3/4 x 5 3/8
    Frothingham, Siege, 70, 3 1/2 x 3 5/8

Gewehr, United States, 72, 1 5/8 x 2 1/2
Greene, Revolutionary War, 4, 1 5/8 x 2 7/8, 7/8 x 1 1/2
  3 x 2 col.
Gurney, Pict. Hist. U.S. Army, 21, 4 1/8 x 7 1/2
Harper's Mag., 50(May 1875):784, 3 3/8 x 2 1/8; 796, 2 3/8
  x 4 3/8
Hart, Am. Nation, 8:310, 4 1/8 x 6 1/2
Hart, Commonwealth Hist. of Mass., 2:574, 4 5/8 x 4 7/8
Hawke, Colonial Experience, 575, 5 x 4 1/2
Hersey, Heroes of Battle Rd., 16-17, 4 3/4 x 11
Hicks, Federal Union, 4th ed., 177, 2 5/8 x 2 3/4
Hofstadter, Am. Republic, 167, 2 3/8 x 2 5/8
Lancaster, Trumpet to Arms, front lining paper, 7 5/8 x 10 3/8
  col., 2 1/2 x 5 col.
Leckie, Wars of America, 98, 4 1/8 x 6 3/4
Lexington-Concord Battle Rd., 116, 4 1/8 x 6 1/2; 118,
  4 1/8 x 6 1/2; 119, 4 1/8 x 6 1/2; 120, 4 1/8 x 6 1/2;
  121, 4 1/8 x 6 1/2; 122, 4 1/8 x 6 1/2; 123, 4 1/8 x 6 1/2
Lossing, Field-Book of Rev., 1:527, 1 7/8 x 1 3/4
Matloff, Am. Military History, 45, 4 1/8 x 7 5/8
Mil. Affairs, 1(Spring 1937):2, 5 1/4 x 7; 5, 4 1/8 x 3 3/4;
  9, 5 3/4 x 5 3/4; 13, 2 5/8 x 3 3/4, 1 1/4 x 1 1/8; 14,
  5 1/4 x 7
Miller, Triumph of Freedom, 39, 4 1/4 x 7
Montross, Rag, Tag and Bobtail, 9, 3 x 4 1/4
Morison, Growth of Am. Republic, 5th ed., 183, 3 3/4 x 4 1/4
Morison, Hist. of Am. People, 213, 1 5/8 x 2 1/8
Nettels, Washington, 51, 3 3/4 x 5 1/2
Payne, Concord Bridge, lining papers, 7 3/4 x 10 1/2
Perkins, U.S. of Am., 146, 2 3/8 x 2 3/8
Rankin, Am. Rev., 35, 2 1/2 x 4
Reeder, Story of Rev. War, 4, 2 3/8 x 4 1/8
Ridpath, New Complete Hist., 5:2424, 2 1/2 x 1 5/8, 2 1/4 x
  2 1/8
Scheer, Rebels and Redcoats, 22-23, 7 3/8 x 10
Soc. for Army Hist. Res., Jl., 15(Spring 1936):18, 5 1/4 x
  7 1/8; 21, 4 1/8 x 3 3/4; 27, 3 5/8 x 3 3/4; 28, 5 3/8 x
  7 1/8; 30-31, 5 3/4 x 5 3/4
Tourtellot, Wm. Diamond's Drum, 48, 5 3/8 x 8 3/8 col; 96,
  8 3/8 x 5 3/8 col.; 216, 5 3/8 x 8 3/8 col.; 264, 8 3/8
  x 5 3/8 col.; end lining paper, 8 3/8 x 11 1/2 col.
Varney, Patriot's Day, 27, 5 3/8 x 3 1/8; 39, 3 1/2 x 3 1/4;
  61, 5 1/2 x 3 1/4
Wallace, Appeal to Arms, 19, 4 x 6 1/4
Winsor, America, 6:179, 4 3/4 x 2 5/8; 180, 2 1/2 x 2 1/4
Winsor, Boston, 3:102, 3 1/2 x 2 1/8
World Book, 16:259, 3 1/4 x 4 3/4
By J. De Costa   08140
  Am. Heritage, Revolution, 113, 5 x 6 7/8 col.
  Cook, Golden Bk. of Am. Rev., front lining paper, 10 1/8 x
    13 1/4
  Fite, Book of Old Maps, 254, 9 3/8 x 12 5/8
  Murdock, 19th Apr. 1775, end, 9 x 12 1/8
  Naval Docs. of Am. Rev., 1:197, 5 1/8 x 7 1/8
  Niles, Chronicles, VIII, 5 x 6 1/2
  Russell, Lexington, 20-21, 9 1/4 x 9 5/8

By Lt. Frederick Mackenzie   08145
   French, Gage's Informers, 78, 7 x 7 1/4
   Mackenzie, Br. Fusilier, 78, 7 1/4 x 7; 81, 7 1/4 x 7
   Mil. Affairs, 1(Spring 1937):8, 6 1/8 x 5 3/4
   Soc. for Army Hist. Res., Jl., 15(Spring 1936):30-31,
      6 x 5 3/4
Lord Percy's maps of British retreat from Concord   08146
   Am. Heritage, 20(Aug. 1969):28, 6 3/8 x 10; 29,
   4 3/4 x 7 1/4 col.
Towns in Massachusetts from which minutemen came in response   08147
   to Lexington Alarm
   Miers, Yankee Doodle Dandy, 44, 3 3/8 x 4 5/8
Routes travelled by "Expresses" carrying news of Battle of   08149
   Lexington southward to other colonies as far south as
   Virginia, April 1775
   Md. Hist. Mag., 41(June 1946):95, 4 7/8 x 4 3/8
Chelsea, Mass., Battle of, May 27, 1775   08150
   Sons of Am. Rev., Old Suffolk Reg., 27, 4 1/2 x 7
Boston, Mass., siege, May 1775 - Mar. 1776   08155
   Adams, Atlas, pl.65, 9 1/4 x 6 1/4
   Alden, Hist. of Am. Rev., 172, 4 1/8 x 5 5/8
   Anderson, Howe Bros., 72, 3 1/2 x 3 3/4
   Avery, Hist. of U.S., 5:295, 4 7/8 x 7 col.
   Boatner, Enc. of Am. Rev., 95, 4 1/8 x 4 1/8
   Bolton, Colonization, 460, 4 1/4 x 4
   Boston, Evacuation, 138, 6 7/8 x 4 5/8
   Boston, Memorial of Am. Patriots, 139, 7 3/4 x 4 3/4
   Bryant, Popular Hist. of U.S., 3:427, 7 1/8 x 4 3/4
   Callahan, Henry Knox, 45, 5 x 4 7/8
   Carrington, Battles, 154, 7 3/4 x 4 3/4
   Carrington, Washington, 69, 5 3/4 x 3 1/2
   Channing, Hist. of U.S., 3:166, 3 7/8 x 4
   Chitwood, Colonial America, 554, 4 1/4 x 4 1/8
   Coffin, Boy's of 76, 64, 5 x 4 5/8
   Cunliffe, Washington, 66, 3 1/2 x 2 1/2
   Cutter, Israel Putnam, 185, 5 7/8 x 3 1/4
   Duncan, Medical Men, 51, 4 1/8 x 5
   Dupuy, Compact Hist., 32, 4 1/2 x 6 1/2
   Egleston, John Paterson, 50, 4 1/4 x 5 1/4
   Esposito, Am. Wars Atlas, 1:map 4b, 5 3/8 x 3 7/8 col.
   Esposito, Civil War Atlas, map 4b, 5 3/8 x 3 7/8 col.
   Fisher, Struggle for Am. Ind., 1:316, 4 7/8 x 3 1/2
   Fiske, Am. Rev., 1:181, 6 x 3 3/4
   Fleming, Now We Are Enemies, lining papers, 7 7/8 x 10 1/2
   Flexner, Washington in Am. Rev., 31, 7 3/8 x 4 3/4, by
      Samuel H. Bryant
   Force, Am. Archives, 4th series, 3:32, 7 1/8 x 10 1/4
   Fortescue, British Army, 3:pl.II, 4 x 4 1/8 col.
   Freeman, Washington, 3:479, 6 1/4 x 5
   Freeman, Washington, abridgment, 229, 7 3/4 x 5 1/2
   French, First Year, front, 8 3/8 x 11 3/4; 10, 3 1/2 x 4 1/2
   Frothingham, Siege, 91, 6 3/8 x 9 1/4
   Frothingham, Washington, 40, 4 5/8 x 6 7/8, 2 1/4 x 1 3/4
   Garner, Hist. of U.S., 1:397, 4 1/4 x 7
   Gilman, Story of Boston, 209, 7 3/4 x 12 1/8
   Gipson, Br. Empire, 12:42, 7 1/4 x 5 1/4

Gordon, Hist. of U.S.A., 2:frontis, pl.II, 9 x 12 3/4
Greene, Revolutionary War, 12, 4 7/8 x 7 col.
Guizot, Atlas, pl.10, 7 1/8 x 4 3/8
Guthorn, Am. Maps, 37, 3 1/8 x 5 7/8, 2 1/2 x 2 5/8, from
  Bickerstaff's New-England Almanack for 1776
Hall, School History, 184, 6 1/4 x 7 1/2
Harper's Mag., 47 (June 1873):20, 3 1/8 x 4 1/2
Hart, Am. Nation, 8:310, 2 x 2 3/4
Hart, Commonwealth Hist. of Mass., 3:8, 4 1/8 x 5 7/8
Hawke, Colonial Experience, 575, 5 x 4 1/2
Hicks, Federal Union, 4th ed., 177, 2 5/8 x 2 3/4
Hofstadter, Am. Republic, 167, 2 3/8 x 2 5/8
Infantry Jl., 44(July-Aug. 1937):292, 5 1/4 x 3 1/8
Ketchum, Bunker Hill, end, 8 1/2 x 10 1/2 col.
Lossing, Field-Book of Rev., 1:566, 5 x 4 5/8
Lossing, Life of Washington, 1:619, 5 1/2 x 9
Lossing, Washington, A Biography, 1:675, 4 3/8 x 7
Lossing, Washington and Am. Republic, 1:619, 5 1/2 x 9
Mackesy, War for America, 81, 2 7/8 x 2 3/8
MacMunn, Am. War, 103, 2 7/8 x 3
Marshall, Atlas, map 1, 6 1/4 x 9 1/2
Mass. Hist. Soc., Battle of Bunker Hill, 7, 7 1/4 x 9 1/8
Mass. Hist. Soc., Proc., 17(1879-1880);frontis, 16 3/4 x 17,
  July 25, 1775
Mather, Refugees of 1776, 26, 2 1/4 x 2 1/4
Mil. Engineer, 31(Nov.-Dec. 1939):410, 4 1/2 x 3 1/4; 40(Sept.-
  Oct. 1948):415, 4 3/4 x 4 1/4; 55(May-June 1963):160, 4 3/4 x
  3 3/8
Montross, Rag, Tag and Bobtail, 82, 5 x 4 1/4
Morison, Growth of Am. Republic, 5th ed., 183, 3 3/4 x 4 1/4
Morison, Hist. of Am. People, 213, 1 5/8 x 2 1/8
Naval Docs. of Am. Rev., 1:985, 7 1/2 x 5 1/2
Pag. Am., 6:136, 3 3/4 x 5
Ridpath, New Complete Hist., 5:2424, 4 7/8 x 5
Scheer, Rebels and Redcoats, 77, 5 1/8 x 4 3/8
Seelye, Story of Washington, 130, 3 1/4 x 3 1/4
Sparks, Washington's Writings, 3:26, 7 x 4 1/2
Steele, Am. Campaigns, 2:10, 5 5/8 x 4 1/8 col.
Tharp, Baroness and General, 241, 4 x 5 5/8
Trevelyan, Am. Revolution, 1:394, 8 7/8 x 13 1/4 col.
Vestal, Washington, 12, 4 1/8 x 4
Ward, Revolution, 1:57, 4 1/2 x 6 1/2
Washington Bicentennial, 1:110, 4 1/8 x 4
Wheildon, Siege, 33, 64
Whitton, Am. War of Ind., 318, 4 1/4 x 5 7/8
Wilson, Am. People, 2:234, 6 1/8 x 3 1/4
Winsor, America, 6:206, 6 1/4 x 5 1/8; 208, 4 7/8 x 6 5/8;
  210, 5 1/2 x 5 1/2
By Robert Aitken   08160
  Guthorn, Am. Maps, 7, 5 1/2 x 4, from Pennsylvania Mag.,
    July 1775
By J. De Costa   08165
  Am. Heritage, Revolution, 113, 5 x 6 7/8 col.
  Cook, Golden Bk. of Am. Rev., front lining paper, 10 1/8 x
    13 1/4

Fite, Book of Old Maps, 254, 9 3/8 x 12 5/8
Labaree, Boston Tea Party, frontis, 6 x 5 3/8
Murdock, 19th Apr. 1775, end, 9 x 12 1/8
Naval Docs. of Am. Rev., 1:197, 5 1/8 x 7 1/8
Niles, Chronicles, VIII, 5 x 6 1/2
Russell, Lexington, 20-21, 9 1/4 x 9 5/8
By Lt. Thomas Hyde Page, pub. by William Faden   08170
  Fite, Book of Old Maps, 246, 13 x 9
  Frothingham, Siege, frontis, 17 1/8 x 11 7/8
  Frothingham, Washington, 56, 4 5/8 x 7
  Honyman, Colonial Panorama, end, 13 1/2 x 9 1/2
  Lee, Hist. of N. America, 6:240, 5 1/2 x 3 3/4
  Paullin, Atlas, pl.156, 12 3/8 x 9 col.
  Winsor, Boston, 3:iv, 7 7/8 x 5 1/2
By Henry Pelham   08175
  Boston, Evacuation, front, 38 1/4 x 27
  Drake, Historic Fields, 1, 10 1/4 x 6 3/4
  May, Brookline in Rev., 18, 6 x 5 1/4, part of Pelham's map
  Moore, Diary of Am. Rev., 1:212, 10 x 7
  Russell, Lexington, 128, 8 3/4 x 6 1/4
  Stark, Antique Views, 263, 20 1/2 x 14 1/4
  Stark, Loyalists of Mass., end, 20 1/2 x 14 1/2
  Warden, Boston, 326-327, 8 1/4 x 12
  Winsor, Boston, 3:vi, 10 3/8 x 7 1/2
By Ezra Stiles   08180
  Stiles, Diary, 1:612, 4 x 3 1/8
By John Trumbull, Sept. 1775   08185
  Meredith, Am. Wars, 55, 3 1/8 x 4 5/8
  Trumbull, Autobiography, 23, 7 1/8 x 10 7/8
  Washington Atlas, pl.40, 7 3/4 x 10 1/2
  Washington Bicentennial, 1:420, 5 x 4 1/8
  Winsor, Boston, 3:80, 3 7/8 x 5 1/2
By George Washington   08190
  Washington Bicentennial, 1:391, 3 3/4 x 5
American defenses in vicinity of Boston   08195
  Mil. Engineer, 55(Sept.-Oct. 1963):346, 3 x 3
Roxbury Fort   08200
  Lossing, Field-Book of Rev., 1:592, 1 1/4 x 1 1/4
Breed's Hill redoubt   08205
  Avery, Hist. of U.S., 5:267, 1 5/8 x 3 1/8 col.
  Bunker Hill Mon. Assn., Proc., 1876, frontis, 8 1/2 x 1 3/8
  Coolidge, Brochure, 13, 1 x 1
  Frothingham, Bunker Hill, 117, 3 1/4 x 3 1/2
  Frothingham, Charlestown, 365, 3 3/8 x 3 5/8
  Frothingham, Siege, 198, 3 1/4 x 3 1/2
  Greene, Revolutionary War, 6, 1 5/8 x 3 1/8 col.
  Irving, Life of Washington, 1:467, 1 7/8 x 1 1/2
  Lossing, Field-Book of Rev., 1:540, 2 1/8 x 2 1/8
  Mass. Hist. Soc., Battle of Bunker Hill, 13, 6 3/8 x 7 1/4
  Mil. Engineer, 40(Sept.-Oct. 1948):414, 1 1/2 x 3 1/8
  Winsor, Boston, 3:82, 3 x 4 3/4
Bunker Hill, Mass., Battle of, June 17, 1775   08210
  Adams, Album of Am. Hist., 1:371, 6 5/8 x 3 1/8
  Alden, Am. Revolution, 37, 4 1/4 x 4 1/4
  Anderson, Howe Bros., 79, 3 x 3 3/4

Am. Heritage, 8(Feb. 1957):86, 4 3/4 x 4 3/4; 13(Aug. 1962):
   80, 9 3/4 x 7 1/2 col.
Am. Heritage, Revolution, 106, 4 3/4 x 2 1/4
Army, Am. Military Hist., 32, 1 7/8 x 2 1/8
Avery, Hist. of U.S., 5:267, 6 7/8 x 4 1/2 col.; 271, 6 3/4 x
   3 3/8
Boatner, Enc. of Am. Rev., 121, 5 3/4 x 4 1/8; 126, 3 1/4 x
   4 1/8; 127, 3 1/2 x 4 1/8; 128, 2 1/4 x 4 1/8
Botta, War of Ind., 1:189, 4 1/4 x 6 5/8
Bryant, Popular Hist. of U.S., 3:399, 3 1/4 x 4 1/4
Carrington, Battles, 112, 7 7/8 x 4 7/8
Coffin, Boys of '76, 48, 3 3/8 x 4 3/4
Coggins, Boys in Revolution, 21, 5 1/8 x 5 1/2
Commager, Spirit of '76, 1:121, 4 5/8 x 4 5/8
Drake, Tea Leaves, 264-265, 11 1/4 x 5 1/2
Duncan, Medical Men, 47, 5 x 4 1/8
Dupuy, Brave Men and Great Captains, 10, 4 1/2 x 4
Dupuy, Compact Hist., 48, 4 7/8 x 4 1/2
Ellis, Bunker's Hill, frontis, 4 7/8 x 6 7/8
Esposito, Am. Wars Atlas, 1:map 4c, 4 x 3 7/8 col.
Esposito, Civil War Atlas, map 4c, 4 x 3 7/8 col.
Falls, Great Mil. Battles, 84, 5 1/2 x 8 1/2 col.
Fisher, Struggle for Am. Ind., 1:336, 3 1/2 x 6
Fiske, Am. Rev., 1:150, 6 x 3 3/4 col.
Fleming, Now We Are Enemies, frontis, 7 7/8 x 10 1/2
Fortescue, British Army, 3:pl.II, 3 3/8 x 3 3/4 col.
Frothingham, Bunker Hill, 43, 4 3/4 x 3 1/2
Frothingham, Charlestown, 313, 18 1/8 x 16 5/8
Frothingham, Siege, 139, 4 3/4 x 3 1/2
Grant, British Battles, 2:144, 8 1/2 x 5 5/8
Greene, Revolutionary War, 6, 5 7/8 x 4 1/2 col.
Gurney, Pict. Hist. U.S. Army, 21, 1 7/8 x 2 1/8
Hall, School History, 188, 6 1/8 x 3 1/2
Hart, Commonwealth Hist. of Mass., 3:12, 4 1/8 x 6 1/4,
   overlay on modern street plan
Infantry Jl., 44(July-Aug. 1937):293, 5 x 6 5/8
Ketchum, Bunker Hill, front, 8 1/8 x 10 1/2 col.
Lossing, Field-Book of Rev., 1:543, 3 3/8 x 4 7/8
McDowell, Revolutionary War, 62-63, 10 x 13 1/2 col.
MacMunn, Am. War, 104, 2 1/2 x 2 3/4
Mass. Hist. Soc., Battle of Bunker Hill, 8, 6 3/4 x 6 3/4,
   by an officer on the spot, pub. by R. Sayer and J. Bennett;
   9, 8 1/4 x 7 1/2, engr. by Jefferys and Faden
Mil. Engineer, 40(Sept.-Oct. 1948):414, 5 3/4 x 4 3/8;
   55(July-Aug. 1963):267, 2 3/4 x 3
Miller, Triumph of Freedom, 49, 4 1/4 x 7
Mitchell, Battles Am. Rev., 33, 7 1/2 x 5 col.
Montross, Rag, Tag and Bobtail, 31, 4 1/4 x 4 1/4
Moore, Gen. John Stark, 144, 5 x 5 5/8
Murdock, Earl Percy Dines Abroad, 38, 8 x 7 1/4, engr.
   and pub. by Jefferys and Faden, Aug. 1775
Pag. Am., 6:124, 3 1/4 x 4 1/2
Pulsifer, Bunker Hill, frontis, 11 5/8 x 5 3/8
Reeder, Story of Rev. War, 38, 4 3/8 x 4
Roscoe, Picture Hist., no.28, 1 7/8 x 2 1/4
Russell, Lexington, 104-105, 8 7/8 x 13 7/8, by Cal Sachs

Scheer, Rebels and Redcoats, 58, 4 5/8 x 4 1/2
Tarbox, Israel Putnam, 184, 5 3/8 x 6 7/8
Wallace, Appeal to Arms, 31, 4 3/8 x 4
Ward, Revolution, 1:83, 5 1/2 x 4 1/2
Wheildon, Bunker Hill, 56, 13 1/2 x 6 1/8
Willcox, Portrait, 47, 7 3/8 x 4 5/8
Wilson, Am. People, 2:234, 6 1/8 x 3 1/4
By Henry De Berniere   08215
Dearborn, Bunker Hill, 16, 12 1/4 x 19 5/8 col.
French, First Year, 226-227, 8 x 11 1/2
Ketchum, Bunker Hill, 112, 6 3/4 x 9 3/4
Winsor, America, 6:199, 5 x 7 3/8, after De Berniere
By John Norman   08220
Am. Heritage Atlas, 95, 9 3/4 x 4 1/2
Winsor, America, 6:201, 8 x 4 1/8
By Lt. Thomas Hyde Page   08225
Am. Hist., 2(Nov. 1967):9, 6 1/8 x 6 7/8 col., after Lt. Page
Boston, Memorial of Am. Patriots, 73, 10 1/2 x 9 1/8
Coolidge, Brochure, 13, 3 3/8 x 4 7/8, after Lt. Page
Frothingham, Bunker Hill, frontis, 6 x 9 1/4, 19 x 16 3/4
Frothingham, Siege, 133, 6 1/8 x 9 1/4, 18 7/8 x 16 1/2
Hunnewell, Bibliography, 16, 9 x 8, by D. Martin after Lt.
   Page, pub. by C. Smith, 1797
Irving, Life of Washington, 1:467, 7 1/4 x 8 1/2
Kinnaird, Geo. Washington, 74, 5 3/8 x 6 3/8
Lodge, Story of Rev., 72, 4 5/8 x 4 1/8
Murdock, Bunker Hill, end, 8 x 9 3/8
Scribner's Mag., 23(1898):191, 5 3/8 x 4 3/4, after Lt. Page
Stark, Antique Views, 245, 10 1/2 x 9 1/8
Stedman, Am. War, 1:126, 19 1/8 x 16 7/8, 6 1/8 x 9
By Ezra Stiles   08230
Historical Mag., 2d series, 3(June 1868):393, 1 3/4 x 2 3/8
Stiles, Diary, 1:579, 2 3/4 x 4
Stiles, Letters and Papers, 41, 2 3/8 x 4
British fortifications erected on and near Bunker Hill after   08235
   the battle
Avery, Hist. of U.S., 5:267, 1 5/8 x 3 1/8 col.
Carter, Genuine Detail, 1, 5 1/2 x 8 1/4
Frothingham, Siege, 330, 3 1/8 x 6 3/8
Greene, Revolutionary War, 6, 1 5/8 x 3 1/8 col.
Kinnaird, Geo. Washington, 74, 1 3/8 x 1 1/8
Lossing, Field-Book of Rev., 1:574, 3 1/4 x 1 1/2
Mil. Engineer, 40(Sept.-Oct. 1948):414, 1 1/2 x 3
By Capt. Edward Barron   08238
Am. Heritage, 20(Aug. 1969):30, 6 3/8 x 8 3/4 col.
By John Montrésor, Dec. 1775   08240
Adams, Hq. Papers, 11, 5 3/4 x 8 7/8
Brun, Guide, 62, 5 3/8 x 8 1/4
Ketchum, Bunker Hill, 113, 3 1/2 x 5 1/8
Winsor, America, 6:198, 3 1/8 x 4 3/4
British fortifications on Boston Neck   08245
Force, Am. Archives, 4th series, 3:32, 7 3/8 x 7 1/8
Guthorn, Am. Maps, 35, 10 1/8 x 8 1/2, by John Trumbull, with
   table prob. by Thomas Mifflin
Naval Docs. of Am. Rev., 2:325, 7 1/4 x 5 1/2, from Hibernian
   Mag., Sept. 1775

Wheildon, Siege, 34
Winsor, America, 6:211, 5 1/8 x 3 7/8, after Lt. Page
Winsor, Boston, 3:80, 4 5/8 x 5 7/8, by Col. Thomas Mifflin
Col. Henry Knox's route transporting cannon from Fort   08250
    Ticonderoga to Cambridge, Mass., Dec. 1775 - Jan. 1776
  Am. Heritage, 6(Apr. 1955):14, 8 5/8 x 7 7/8 col.
  Callahan, Henry Knox, 44-45, 8 3/8 x 10 7/8

1777

Hull, Mass., fortifications, Feb. 27, 1777   08255
  Smith, French at Boston, 20, 4 1/8 x 5 3/4, by Joseph Palmer
March of Burgoyne's surrender army, Saratoga, N.Y., to   08260
    Cambridge, Mass., Oct.-Nov. 1777
  Lancaster, Guns in the Forest, lining papers, 3 5/8 x 4 5/8,
    by Samuel H. Bryant
  Tharp, Baroness and General, lining papers, 7 3/4 x 5 1/8
Parole limits of Burgoyne's officers, Cambridge, Mass., 1777   08265
  Batchelder, Bits, 64, 16 3/4 x 21 1/4
  Batchelder, Burgoyne, 80, 16 3/4 x 21 1/4

1778

Route of the Convention Army, Massachusetts to Virginia,   08270
    Nov. 1778 - Feb. 1779
  Anburey, Travels, 1:frontis, 8 1/4 x 7 1/2
  Tharp, Baroness and General, lining papers, 7 3/4 x 5 1/8
  Wall, Convention Army, 18, 7 7/8 x 7 1/4

1782

French army camp sites in Massachusetts on march from Yorktown,
    Va., to Boston
Fifty-third camp, Wrentham, Dec. 1, 1782   08275
  Forbes, France and New Eng., 1:176, 4 x 2 7/8
Fifty-fourth camp, Dedham, Dec. 2-5, 1782   08280
  Dedham Hist. Reg., 12(Jan. 1901):8, 4 3/4 x 6 7/8
  Forbes, France and New Eng., 1:176, 4 x 2 7/8

RHODE ISLAND

Rhode Island   09000
  Mackesy, War for America, 81, 6 1/2 x 4 1/4
1777   09005
  Brown, Hist. Geog., 32, 6 7/8 x 4 3/4, aft. Chas. Blaskowitz
Rhode Island counties at time of the Revolution   09010
  Brown, King's Friends, 45, 1 7/8 x 2 3/4
Narragansett Bay and vicinity   09015
  Mahan, Navies, 70, 7 1/2 x 5
  Serle, Am. Journal, 275, 5 7/8 x 4
1777, by Charles Blaskowitz, pub. by William Faden   09020
  Mag. of Am. Hist., 3(July 1879):424, 6 1/2 x 5
  Naval Docs. of Am. Rev., 3:668, 7 3/4 x 5 3/8
  R.I. History, 7(Jan. 1948):16-17, 11 1/4 x 7 7/8

1778   09025
   Cullum, Fortification Defenses, end, 7 x 11 3/8
   See also 09175
Newport, R.I., and vicinity   09027
   Coffins, Ships and Seamen, 143, 3 3/8 x 3 7/8
 1776   09028
   Mason, Stars on the Sea, end lining paper, 7 3/4 x 10 1/2
Newport, R.I., 1777, by Charles Blaskowitz, engr. and pub.   09030
   by William Faden
   Gipson, Br. Empire, 10:64, 5 1/4 x 5 5/8
   Lee, Hist. of N. America, 6:288, 3 3/4 x 4 1/8
   Mag. of Am. Hist., 3(July 1879):417, 6 3/8 x 9
   Morgan, Gentle Puritan, 120, 5 3/8 x 4 3/8
   Naval Docs. of Am. Rev., 1:957, 3 3/8 x 5 1/2
   Pag. Am., 6:209, 2 3/8 x 3 3/8
   Winsor, America, 6:597, 5 x 6
Newport Harbor, R.I., 1781 or 1782   09035
   Ristow, Services, pl.VIII, 5 x 5 1/8
Block Island and vicinity   09037
   Coggins, Ships and Seamen, 29, 4 3/4 x 3 3/4

MILITARY OPERATIONS

George Washington's journeys through Rhode Island, 1776, 1781   09040
   Haley, Washington and R.I., 8, 5 x 4 1/8
Revolutionary fortifications in Rhode Island   09045
   Field, Defences in R.I., 147, 9 5/8 x 8
 Defenses of Narragansett Bay
 American Battery, North Point, 1776   09050
   Cullum, Fortification Defenses, pl.I, 3 x 2 1/8
 Battery on the Bonnet, 1777-1778   09055
   Cullum, Fortification Defenses, pl.I, 1 7/8 x 2 1/8
 Battery or Fort on Conanicut Is., 1777-1778   09060
   Cullum, Fortification Defenses, pl.I, 2 7/8 x 2 1/4
   Field, State of R.I., 1:454, 2 3/4 x 2
 Fort Chastellux, Hallidon Hill, 1780   09065
   Cullum, Fortification Defenses, pl.I, 1 1/2 x 2 1/4
 Hog Pen Point Fort   09070
   Field, State of R.I., 1:451, 3 x 1 3/4
 Robin Hill Fort   09075
   Field, State of R.I., 1:448, 3 1/8 x 2 7/8
 Tonomy Hill (or Beacon Hill) Fort   09080
   Field, State of R.I., 1:453, 1 3/4 x 2 1/4
 Defenses of Newport, R.I.   09085
   Newport Hist. Soc., Bul., No.51(Oct. 1924):15, 5 1/4 x
    4 3/8
 1781   09090
   Mag. of Am. Hist., 4(Mar. 1880):213, 8 1/8 x 15 1/4,
    French chart
 Defenses of Providence, R.I.   09095
   Stone, Our French Allies, 20, 5 1/2 x 4, after Charles
    Blaskowitz
Prospect Hill Fort, Providence, 1777   09100
   Stone, Our French Allies, 18, 1 3/4 x 2 3/8

1776

British attack on Prudence Is., R.I., Jan. 12, 1776, by   09105
    Ezra Stiles
    Stiles, Diary, 1:655, 6 3/4 x 4
    Stiles, Itineraries, 375, 4 x 2 3/8

1777

Howland's Ferry, R.I., skirmish, Feb. 22, 1777   09110
    Stiles, Diary, 2:140, 4 1/4 x 4, by Ezra Stiles
Howland's Ferry, R.I., skirmish, Mar. 18, 1777   09115
    Stiles, Diary, 2:149, 3 x 3 3/4, by Ezra Stiles
Area of operations, north end of Island of Rhode Island,   09120
    June 1777?
    Mackenzie, Diary, 1:132, 8 3/4 x 9, prob. by Lt. Frederick
    Mackenzie
Commonfence Neck, R.I., skirmish, June 10, 1777   09125
    Mackenzie, Diary, 1:138, 6 1/2 x 5 1/2, prob. by Lt.
    Frederick Mackenzie
Capture of Brig. Gen. Richard Prescott, Redwood's, R.I.,   09130
    July 10, 1777
    Mackenzie, Diary, 1:148, 7 5/8 x 12, prob. by Lt.
    Frederick Mackenzie
Disposition of British night sentries from the Town Pond to   09135
    Howland's Bridge, R.I., Sept. 2, 1777
    Mackenzie, Diary, 1:172, 8 x 12, prob. by Lt. Frederick
    Mackenzie
British post, Conanicut Is., R.I., Dec. 9, 1777   09140
    Mackenzie, Diary, 1:222, 12 1/8 x 8 1/4, prob. by Lt.
    Frederick Mackenzie
Military operations on Island of Rhode Island, 1777-1778   09145
    Cullum, Fortification Defenses, pl.II, 7 3/8 x 23 7/8

1778

Sir Henry Clinton's plans of attack against Rhode Island,   09150
    1778, 1780
    Willcox, Portrait, 327, 7 3/8 x 4 5/8
Clinton's map of Rhode Island   09155
    Journal of Mod. Hist., 17(Dec. 1945):309, 11 7/8 x 14 3/8
Disposition of British advanced posts, sentries, and patrols, 09160
    north end of Island of Rhode Island, July 11, 1778
    Mackenzie, Diary, 1:308, 8 3/4 x 11, prob. by Lt. Frederick
    Mackenzie
Newport, R.I. siege, July 29 - Aug. 29, 1778   09165
    Am. Heritage, 20(Aug. 1969):33, 7 x 9 1/8, by Lt. Thomas
    Fage
    Am. Heritage, Revolution, 265, 2 x 2 1/8
    Angell, Diary, 6, 17 7/8 x 8 1/2
    Avery, Hist. of U.S., 6:182, 4 7/8 x 2 7/8 col.
    Billias, Gen. John Glover, 167, 7 3/8 x 4 1/4
    Boatner, Enc. of Am. Rev., 791, 6 5/8 x 4 1/8
    Carrington, Battles, 456, 8 x 4 3/4
    Coffin, Boys of'76, 285, 4 3/4 x 2 1/2
    Commager, Spirit of '76, 2:716, 7 1/2 x 4 5/8

Dinman, Capture of Gen. Prescott, 10, 11 1/2 x 6 3/4
Dupuy, Compact Hist., 289, 4 1/2 x 4 1/2
Dupuy, Rev. War Naval Battles, 66, 5 3/4 x 6
Field, Defences in R.I., 142, 8 1/2 x 17 3/4
Fiske, Am. Rev., 2:76, 6 x 3 3/4 col.
Fite, Book of Old Maps, 272, 12 3/4 x 7 3/4
Freeman, Washington, 5:63, 5 1/2 x 4 3/8
Frothingham, Washington, 266, 7 x 3 1/4
Gottschalk, Lafayette Joins Am. Army, 248, 3 5/8 x 9 1/2
Greene, Gen. Greene, 116, 6 1/8 x 4
Greene, Revolutionary War, 152, 4 7/8 x 2 7/8 col.
Guthorn, Am. Maps, 13, 6 5/8 x 8 1/2, by J. Denison
James, Br. Navy in Adversity, 103, 6 1/8 x 4
Lossing, Field-Book of Rev., 1:648, 4 7/8 x 2 1/4
Marshall, Atlas, map 7, 9 3/8 x 6
Mass. Hist. Soc., Proc., 20(Oct. 1883):350, 18 1/8 x 22
Montross, Rag, Tag and Bobtail, 292, 6 1/2 x 4 1/4
Preston, Battle of R.I., end, 7 x 14 5/8, French map
R.I. Hist. Mag., 5(Oct. 1884):119, 7 7/8 x 4 3/4
Rider, Battle of R.I., front, 11 3/8 x 6 3/4
Ridpath, New Complete Hist., 6:2754, 4 1/2 x 3 1/8
Royaumont, La Fayette et Rochambeau, 115, 2 1/8 x 5 1/2,
    French map
Stone, Our French Allies, 68, 4 x 3 5/8, by S. Lewis
Ward, Revolution, 2:589, 7 1/8 x 4 1/8
Whittemore, John Sullivan, 87, 6 3/4 x 4
Winsor, America, 6:596, 7 5/8 x 4 7/8; 602, 3 x 4 5/8
Sullivan's campaign map, Aug. 9-30, 1778, by J. Denison   09170
    Stone, Our French Allies, 108, 3 7/8 x 7
Lafayette's map of Narragansett Bay, 1778   09175
    Tower, La Fayette, 1:456, 3 3/4 x 9 5/8
    Winsor, America, 6:600, 8 x 4 1/2
American trenches, Aug. 17-25, 1778   09180
    Preston, Battle of R.I., 48, 6 x 4, by Lt. Edw. Fage,
        British Artillery
Rhode Island, Battle of, Aug. 29, 1778   09185
    Dinman, Capture of Gen. Prescott, 10, 11 x 6 3/4
    Preston, R.I.'s Hist. Background, 30, 6 x 5 1/4
    Rider, Battle of R.I., front, 11 3/8 x 6 3/4
    See also 09165
Positions occupied by American troops after their retreat from
        island of Rhode Island, Aug. 30, 1778
    Royaumont, La Fayette et Rochambeau, 89, 3 3/4 x 6 1/8
    Tower, La Fayette, 2:8, 6 1/4 x 10, French map

1779

Position of American forces in Rhode Island, Oct. 8, 1779   09195
    Stiles, Diary, 2:377, 3 7/8 x 4, by Ezra Stiles

1780

French positions at Newport, R.I., 1780   09200
    Brun, Guide, 68, 5 3/8 x 6 5/8, by Edouard Colbert
    Forbes, France and New Eng., 1:107, 4 7/8 x 8
    Pag. Am., 6:248, 4 3/4 x 2 7/8
    Washington-Rochambeau Celeb., 20-21, 10 3/8 x 14 7/8

French encampment, North Providence, R.I., 1780-1782   09205
    Forbes, France and New England, 1:170, 3 5/8 x 2 1/2
    Pag. Am., 6:250, 3 3/4 x 3
    Stone, Our French Allies, 310, 17 7/8 x 13 3/4; 317,
      6 1/8 x 3 7/8

1781

First French camp, Providence, R.I., June 10-18, 1781, at start 09210
    of Rochambeau's march to Hudson River, by Louis-Alexandre
    Berthier
    Maggs Bros., Berthier, 12, 7 1/2 x 5
    R.I. Hist., 24(July 1965):86, 6 x 4 1/8
Route of Rochambeau's troops
From Providence to Waterman's Tavern, R.I., June 18, 1781   09215
    Maggs Bros., Berthier, 6, 5 7/8 x 7 1/2, by Louis-Alexandre
    Berthier
    Preston, Rochambeau, 14, 4 3/4 x 3 7/8
From Providence to Canterbury, Conn.   09220
    Pell, Rochambeau and R.I., 2, 6 3/4 x 4

1782

French army camp sites in Rhode Island on march from Yorktown,
    Va., to Boston, by Louis-Alexandre Berthier
Fiftieth camp, Waterman's Tavern, R.I., Nov. 9, 1782   09225
    Maggs Bros., Berthier, 30, 7 1/8 x 4 7/8
Fifty-first camp, Providence, R.I., Nov. 10, 1782   09230
    Maggs Bros., Berthier, 30, 7 1/8 x 4 7/8
Fifty-second camp, North Providence, R.I., Nov. 13-Dec.1, 1782
    Forbes, France and New Eng., 1:169, 4 3/8 x 2 7/8
    Maggs Bros., Berthier, 30, 7 1/8 x 4 7/8

CONNECTICUT

Connecticut
1766   10005
    Van Dusen, Connecticut, 125, 5 1/4 x 7 1/4, by Moses Park
1774, by Thomas Jefferys   10010
    Howard, Seth Harding, 26, 5 x 6 5/8
    Mather, Refugees of 1776, 160, 7 1/2 x 9 7/8
    Middlebrook, Maritime Conn., 2:frontis, 5 7/8 x 6
1775, including Connecticut claims to Pennsylvania   10015
    Fite, Book of Old Maps, 250, 5 3/8 x 12 7/8, by John Trumbull
Connecticut counties at time of the Revolution   10020
    Brown, King's Friends, 59, 4 1/4 x 6 1/8
Connecticut, Long Island, and New York   10025
    Ingles, Queen's Rangers, 34, 5 1/4 x 7
Shoreline from Port Chester, N.Y., to Compo Hill, Conn.   10030
    Mather, Refugees of 1776, 231, 3 1/4 x 7
Fairfield, Conn., about 1780   10033
    Garvan, Arch. and Town Planning, 41, 4 x 5 1/8, from Clinton
      Papers, Wm. L. Clements Library
Greenwich and Stamford, Conn.   10035
    Mather, Refugees of 1776, 195, 3 1/8 x 4
Lebanon, Conn., 1772   10038
    Garvan, Arch. and Town Planning, 57, 4 3/8 x 5 1/2,
      by Nathaniel Webb

Lyme, Conn., 1768   10040
   Stiles, Itineraries, 266, 5 x 3 3/4, by Ezra Stiles
Middletown, Conn., Main Street, 1770-1775
   Van Dusen, Middletown, front, 5 1/8 x 4
Mouth of Connecticut River   10050
   Mather, Refugees of 1776, 199, 2 1/2 x 2
New Haven, Conn., dwelling houses, Sept. 16, 1772   10055
   Stiles, Itineraries, 355, 4 1/2 x 4, by Ezra Stiles
New Haven, Conn., 1775, by Ezra Stiles   10060
   Middlebrook, Maritime Conn., 1:17, 3 1/2 x 4 1/2
   Morgan, Gentle Puritan, 310, 5 1/4 x 4 1/2
   Naval Docs. of Am. Rev., 2:552, 6 3/4 x 5 3/8
   Stiles, Diary, 2:275, 6 x 4
New Haven Harbor, 1780   10065
   Stiles, Diary, 2:413, 5 x 4, by Ezra Stiles
New London, Conn., and its defenses, Apr. 1776   10070
   Middlebrook, Maritime Conn., 1:13, 5 1/8 x 3 1/2, from
     Gov. Jonathan Trumbull papers
New London Harbor   10075
   Mather, Refugees of 1776, 235, 2 5/8 x 2
 April 1776   10076
   Naval Docs. of Am. Rev., 4:848, 5 x 6 5/8, by Richard Gridley
Saybrook Bar, Conn., 1771, by Capt. Abner Parker, engr. by
   Abel Buell
   Comstock, Enc. of Am. Antiques, 2, pl.282A, 3 1/2 x 5 1/8
   Hoadly, Pub. Rec. Col. Conn., 13:503, 7 3/8 x 10 7/8
   Wroth, Abner Buell, 57, 5 3/4 x 8 1/2
Tashua Hill observation point, Trumbull, Conn.   10085
   Middlebrook, Maritime Conn., 1:243, 6 x 3 3/8
Old North Road, Litchfield Co., Conn.
   Crofut, Guide, 1:451, 5 x 4 1/2
Homes of loyalists in vicinity of Chippeny Hill, Bristol, Conn.   10092
   Pond, Tories of Chippeny Hill, 10, 5 3/8 x 3 3/4

MILITARY OPERATIONS

George Washington's journeys in Connecticut, 1775, 1776, 1780, 1781 10095
   Burpee, Story of Conn., 1:438, 5 x 6 5/8
   Crofut, Guide, 1:68, 7 1/4 x 10 col.
   Dutcher, Washington, end, 8 1/2 x 11 1/2 col.
Site of Revolutionary War cannon foundry, Salisbury, Conn.   10100
   Middlebrook, Salisbury Cannon, 6, 3 1/2 x 3 1/4

1777

Gov. Wm. Tryon's first raid into Connecticut, Apr. 25-28, 1777   10105
   Avery, Hist. of U.S., 6:66, 3 3/4 x 2 3/4 col.
   Case, Tryon's Raid, front, 6 7/8 x 4
   Dupuy, Compact Hist., 190, 6 x 4 1/2
   Greene, Revolutionary War, 80, 3 3/4 x 2 3/4 col.
   Leake, John Lamb, 160, 8 1/2 x 5
   Mather, Refugees of 1776, 225, 2 5/8 x 1 3/4
   Pag. Am., 6:160, 2 3/4 x 2 3/4
   Ward, Revolution, 2:493, 7 x 4 1/2

1779

Connecticut shore, Fairfield to New London, May 1779   10110
   Brown, Loyalist Operations, 6 x 8, by Capt. Patrick Ferguson
    of 71st Highlanders

Tryon's second raid into Connecticut, July 5-13, 1779   10115
    Avery, Hist. of U.S., 6:235, 3 3/4 x 4 1/4 col.
    Greene, Revolutionary War, 158, 3 3/4 x 4 1/4 col.
British invasion of New Haven, July 5, 1779, by Ezra Stiles   10120
    Sons of Am. Rev., Rev. Characters, 33, 4 x 3 3/8
    Stiles, Diary, 2:352, 4 3/4 x 4
    Townshend, British Invasion, 20, 5 1/8 x 4 3/8
Fairfield, Conn., July 7, 1779   10125
    Lathrop, Black Rock, 30, 4 3/8 x 3 1/2
    Middlebrook, Maritime Conn., 1:57, 4 3/8 x 3 1/2

1781

Whaleboat raid by Long Island Loyalists on New Haven Harbor,   10130
    Feb. 2, 1781
    Stiles, Diary, 2:507, 4 1/2 x 4, by Ezra Stiles
Capt. Nathan Hubbel's raid on Black Rock Fort guarding entrance   10135
    to New Haven Harbor, Apr. 19, 1781
    Brown, Loyalist Operations, 8 5/8 x 12 col.
Route of Lauzun's French cavalry from Lebanon, Conn., to Bedford,   10140
    N.Y., and Hudson River, June 1781
    Forbes, France and New England, 1:132, 4 3/4 x 8
British attack on New London, Sept. 6, 1781   10145
    Avery, Hist. of U.S., 6:311, 2 3/4 x 2 col.; 312, 6 5/8 x
      4 3/4 col.
    Carrington, Battles, 630, 7 3/4 x 4 5/8
    Greene, Revolutionary War, 152, 2 3/4 x 2 col.
    Harris, Groton Heights, frontis, 6 3/8 x 5 3/8
    Krafft, Journal, pl.5, 8 1/8 x 6 5/8, by Lt. John Charles
      Philip von Krafft
    Lossing, Field-Book of Rev., 1:609, 1 3/8 x 1 3/8
    Rogers, Conn. Naval Office, 4, 6 3/8 x 3 3/4; end lining
      papers, 9 3/8 x 9 1/8 col., by William Faden
    Rogers, Groton Heights, 23, 4 5/8 x 3 1/2
Fort Griswold, Groton Heights, Conn.   10150
    Avery, Hist. of U.S., 6:312, 6 7/8 x 5 5/8
    Harris, Groton Heights, 172, 3 7/8 x 5
    Rogers, Groton Heights, 83, 4 3/8 x 7; 86, 3 7/8 x 5

1782

Route of French army, Crompond, N.Y., to Hartford, Conn.,   10155
    Oct. 22-29, 1782
    Chastellux, Travels, 2:478, 5 1/2 x 8
French army camp sites in Connecticut on March from Yorktown,
    Va., to Boston
   Forty-fourth camp, Farmington, Oct. 28, 1782   10165
    Forbes, France and New Eng., 1:158, 4 x 2 3/4
   Forty-fifth camp, East Hartford, Oct. 29 - Nov. 4, 1782   10170
    Forbes, France and New Eng., 1:159, 3 7/8 x 2 7/8
   Forty-sixth camp, Bolton, Nov. 4, 1782   10175
    Forbes, France and New Eng., 1:159, 3 7/8 x 2 7/8
   Forty-seventh camp, Windham, Nov. 5-6, 1782   10180
    Forbes, France and New Eng., 1:163, 4 1/2 x 2 3/4
   Forty-eighth camp, Canterbury, Nov. 7, 1782   10185
    Forbes, France and New Eng., 1:163, 4 1/2 x 3
   Forty-ninth camp, Voluntown (now Sterling), Nov. 8, 1782   10190
    Forbes, France and New Eng., 1:169, 4 3/8 x 2 7/8

THE MIDDLE STATES

New York and New Jersey, 1777   11005
    Jones, Hist. of N.Y., 1:748, 23 1/4 x 16 7/8 col.,
      by Claude Joseph Sauthier, engr. and pub. by Matthew
      Albert Lotter
Mohawk-Susquehanna frontier   11007
    Sosin, Revolutionary Frontier, 54, 5 1/8 x 7 1/2
Fort Stanwix, N.Y., to Chesapeake Bay, Aug. 1777   11010
    Nickerson, Turning Point, 214, 6 1/8 x 3 1/4
Lower Hudson Valley and New Jersey   11015
    Mackesy, War for America, 92, 6 7/8 x 4 1/4
West of the Hudson, King's Ferry, N.Y., to Bound Brook, N.J.   11020
    Mag. of Am. Hist., 5(July 1880):8, 7 x 5 5/8, after Robert
      Erskine
Northern New Jersey and environs of New York City   11025
    Trevelyan, Am. Revolution, 2:end, 12 3/8 x 12;
      3:end, 12 3/8 x 12
    Wickwire, Cornwallis, 91, 4 1/2 x 4 1/8
Northern New Jersey and New York Harbor   11030
    Serle, Am. Journal, 29, 5 7/8 x 4
New York City area, New Jersey, and Eastern Pennsylvania,   11032
    1777
    Willard, Letters on Am. Rev., 326, 5 3/8 x 4 1/4
New York City to Philadelphia   11035
    Coffin, Boys of '76, 271, 2 3/8 x 4 7/8
New York City to Delaware Bay   11040
    Fortescue, British Army, 3:pl.III, 7 3/8 x 4 3/8 col.
    Hart, Am. Nation, 6:26, 6 1/2 x 3 3/8 col.
    Soc. for Army Hist. Res., Jl., 8(Oct. 1929):238,
      7 3/8 x 4 3/8 col.
New York City to Chesapeake Bay, Sept. 1776   11045
    Stoudt, Ordeal at Valley Forge, 24, 3 1/2 x 4 1/4,
      from Gentleman's Mag.
Morristown, N.J., to Head of Elk, Md.   11050
    Bolton, Colonization, 501, 4 3/8 x 4
    Trevelyan, Am. Revolution, 4:end, 12 x 13 1/4 col.
Raritan River, N.J., to Head of Elk, Md.   11055
    Channing, Hist. of U.S., 3:254-255, 6 x 9
    Lossing, Field-Book of Rev., 2:182, 2 1/2 x 4 3/4
New Jersey and Eastern Pennsylvania   11060
    Alden, Hist. of Am. Rev., 293, 8 5/8 x 5 5/8
    Baurmeister, Revolution, 147, 7 1/4 x 5
    Clarke, Am. Revolution, end lining paper, 4 1/4 x 3 1/8
      col.
    Frothingham, Washington, 254, 3 5/8 x 4 1/2
    Lodge, Story of Am. Rev., 317, 1 7/8 x 6 1/2
    MacMunn, Am. War, 217, 5 7/8 x 3 1/2
 1777   11065
    Rogers, New Doane Book, 26, 9 1/4 x 8 1/4, by William
      Faden
 1782   11070
    Hilliard d'Auberteuil, Essais, 2:153, 9 x 12 3/4 col.

Southern New Jersey and Eastern Pennsylvania   11075
  Freeman, Washington, 4:277, 6 3/8 x 5
The Nose (or Elbow) of the Delaware River   11080
  Freeman, Washington, 4:305, 5 1/4 x 4 7/8
  Smith, Princeton, 7, 6 x 4
Philadelphia to Cape Henry, Sir Henry Clinton's map   11085
  Cooch, Cooch's Bridge, 27, 5 3/8 x 3
Eastern Maryland and Delaware, 1777   11090
  Honyman, Colonial Panorama, end, 9 1/8 x 9 3/8
Chesapeake and Delaware Bay area   11095
  Serle, Am. Journal, 243, 5 7/8 x 4
 1777   11100
  Popp, Hessian Soldier, 20, 4 1/2 x 6 5/8
Delmarva Peninsula, c.1786   11105
  Comstock, Enc. of Am. Antiques, 2:pl.279B, 3 1/2 x
   2 3/4

MILITARY OPERATIONS

Area of operations
 Middle States   11110
  Steele, Am. Campaigns, 2:13, 6 x 3 7/8
 1775-1780   11115
  Nettels, Roots of Am. Civ., 701, 6 1/2 x 3 1/4
 1776-1778   11120
  Mahan, Navies, 40, 7 1/2 x 5
 1776-1780   11125
  Ward, Del. Continentals, front, 11 3/4 x 8 7/8 col.
 1778-1780   11130
  Palmer, Steuben, 178, 9 7/8 x 8 1/8
 New York and New Jersey
 1776-1777   11135
  Fiske, Am. Rev., 1:236-237, 6 x 7 1/2
  Passano, Hist. of Md., 101, 4 7/8 x 3 1/8
 1779   11137
  Miers, Yankee Doodle Dandy, 167, 2 1/2 x 5
 New York, New Jersey, and Pennsylvania, 1776-1777   11138
  Hall-Quest, From Colony to Nation, 133, 6 1/8 x 3 3/4
 New Jersey, Pennsylvania, and Delaware   11140
  Hall, School History, 238, 3 1/4 x 6 1/8
 1776-1777   11145
  Baurmeister, Letters, frontis., 4 1/2 x 6 3/8
  Botta, War of Ind., 1:393, 4 1/8 x 6 1/2
  Marshall, Atlas, map 5, 6 3/8 x 9 1/2
  Miers, Yankee Doodle Dandy, 97, 6 1/4 x 3 1/4
 Pennsylvania and New Jersey, 1777-1778   11150
  Army, Am. Military Hist., 67, 5 1/2 x 4 1/2
  Gurney, Pict. Hist. U.S. Army, 46, 5 1/2 x 3 1/2
  Matloff, Am. Military History, 73, 5 1/2 x 4 3/8
  Miers, Yankee Doodle Dandy, 138, 3 1/2 x 4
  Reeder, Story of Rev. War, 125, 3 3/4 x 4 1/8
 Maryland, Delaware, and Pennsylvania, 1777   11155
  Pleasants, John André, 18, 4 1/8 x 5 1/8, by S. Lewis

New York and Pennsylvania back country   11157
    Sosin, Revolutionary War, 113, 5 1/8 x 7 1/2
Strategic points in New Jersey, Delaware, and Maryland   11160
    from which British could keep the Middle Colonies
    "in subjection with a few troops and Frigates prop-
    erly placed so as to communicate with each other"
    André, Journal, 2:50, 13 5/8 x 8 1/8, by Maj. John
    André
Region between Hudson and Delaware Rivers, in New York   11163
    and New Jersey, showing relation of geology and
    physiography and movements of Washington's armies,
    and advantage of the rugged topography as screens
    for American line of march, and sources of supplies
    Scenic and Historic Am., 2(Mar. 1930):24-25, 11 x 7 1/4
Campaigns in the Middle States   11165
    Hicks, Federal Union, 4th ed., 188, 2 5/8 x 2 3/4
1776   11170
    Kraus, U.S. to 1865, 227, 5 1/8 x 4 1/4
1776-1777   11175
    World Book, 16:261, 3 1/4 x 4 5/8 col.
1776-1778   11180
    Hofstadter, Am. Republic, 83, 4 x 2 1/2, 4 x 2 1/2
    Malone, Am. Origins, 175, 7 1/8 x 4 1/2
1776-1781   11185
    Chron. Am., 12:180, 7 x 5 3/4 col.
1777   11190
    Kraus, U.S. to 1865, 229, 5 x 4; 231, 4 1/2 x 7
1778   11195
    Kraus, U.S. to 1865, 232, 4 1/4 x 4 3/8
Washington's Movements in the Middle States
1776-1777   11200
    Am. Heritage Atlas, 97, 9 3/4 x 7 1/2 col.
    Avery, Hist. of U.S., 6:38, 5 1/4 x 4 5/8 col.
    Esposito, Am. Wars Atlas, 1:map 5a, 9 3/8 x 7 3/8 col.
    Esposito, Civil War Atlas, map 5a, 9 3/8 x 7 3/8 col.
    Faulkner, Am. Political & Social Hist., 135, 5 x 3 5/8
    Flexner, Washington in Am. Rev., 155, 7 3/8 x 4 3/4,
      by Samuel H. Bryant
    Greene, Revolutionary War, 60, 5 1/4 x 4 5/8 col.
    Harlow, United States, 110, 5 1/2 x 3 1/2
    Hawke, Colonial Experience, 604, 6 1/4 x 4 1/2
    McDowell, Revolutionary War, 103, 3 x 3 1/4 col.
    Morison, Hist. of Am. People, 242, 7 1/4 x 4 1/2
    Paullin, Atlas, pl.160A, 8 1/2 x 4 1/4 col.
    Washington Atlas, pl.36, 15 1/2 x 11 col.
    Washington Bicentennial, 1:416, 10 1/8 x 7 1/8
1776-1783   11205
    Baldwin, Adult's History, 106, 5 3/4 x 5 5/8
1777   11210
    Paullin, Atlas, pl.160B, 8 1/2 x 5 3/8 col.,
      2 3/4 x 2 3/4 col.
    Reed, Campaign to Valley Forge, 24, 6 1/4 x 5;
      87, 6 1/4 x 5
    Washington Atlas, pl.37, 15 1/2 x 11 col.
    Washington Bicentennial, 1:417, 10 1/8 x 7 1/8

1777 and 1778   11215
    Am. Heritage Atlas, 99, 7 x 7 1/2 col.
    Avery, Hist. of U.S., 6:76-77, 3 3/4 x 5 7/8 col.
    Esposito, Am. Wars Atlas, 1:map 7a, 9 3/8 x 8 1/4 col.
    Esposito, Civil War Atlas, map 7a, 9 3/8 x 8 1/4 col.
    Flexner, Washington in Am. Rev., 218, 3 7/8 x 4 5/8,
        by Samuel H. Bryant
    Greene, Revolutionary War, 76, 3 3/4 x 5 7/8 col.
    Hawke, Colonial Experience, 604, 6 1/4 x 4 1/2
    Ingles, Queen's Rangers, 41, 5 1/4 x 8
1778   11220
    Washington Atlas, pl.38, 15 1/2 x 11 col.
    Washington Bicentennial, 1:418, 10 1/8 x 7 1/8
1778-1779   11225
    Paullin, Atlas, pl.160C, 4 1/2 x 4 3/8 col.
Movements of Sir William Howe and Lord Cornwallis in New   11230
        York and New Jersey, Aug. 1776 - Jan. 1777
    Am. Heritage Atlas, 97, 9 3/4 x 7 1/2 col.
    Avery, Hist. of U.S., 6:38, 5 1/4 x 4 5/8 col.
    Esposito, Am. Wars atlas, 1:map 5a, 9 3/8 x 7 3/8 col.
    Esposito, Civil War Atlas, map 5a, 9 3/8 x 7 3/8 col.
    Greene, Revolutionary War, 60, 5 1/4 x 4 5/8 col.
    Harlow, United States, 110, 5 1/2 x 3 1/2
    James, Br. Navy in Adversity, 36, 6 5/8 x 4
Movements of Sir William Howe and Sir Henry Clinton in the   11235
        Middle States, 1777-1778
    Adams, Hq. Papers, 20, 4 1/4 x 9 1/8, by John Hills
    Am. Heritage Atlas, 99, 7 x 7 1/2 col.
    Avery, Hist. of U.S., 6:76-77, 3 3/4 x 5 7/8 col.
    Bruce, Brandywine, 13, 4 3/4 x 7 1/4, by William Faden
    Esposito, Am. Wars Atlas, 1:map 7a, 9 3/8 x 8 1/4 col.
    Esposito, Civil War Atlas, map 7a, 9 3/8 x 8 1/4 col.
    Flexner, Washington in Am. Rev., 218, 3 7/8 x 4 5/8,
        by Samuel H. Bryant
    Greene, Revolutionary War, 76, 3 3/4 x 5 7/8 col.
    Ingles, Queen's Rangers, 41, 5 1/4 x 8
    James, Br. Navy in Adversity, 62, 6 1/8 x 4
    Paullin, Atlas, pl.160B, 8 1/2 x 3 5/8 col.,
        2 3/4 x 2 3/4 col.
Disposition of American and British forces in Pennsylvania   11240
        and New Jersey, late Dec. 1776
    Military Review, 43(Jan. 1963):91, 3 3/8 x 2 3/8
Winter Quarters of Washington's army, New Jersey, New York   11245
        and Connecticut, 1778-1779
    Washington Atlas, pl.38 inset, 5 5/8 x 4 3/4 col.
    Washington Bicentennial, 1:418, 3 5/8 x 3
Movements of American and British forces in New York and   11250
        New Jersey, 1780
    Paullin, Atlas, pl.160G, 1 3/8 x 1 3/4 col.
Routes of Washington's and Rochambeau's forces through
        Middle States on way to Yorktown, Va., 1781
    See 24265
Route of French army through Middle States on way from
        Yorktown to Boston, autumn 1782
    See 24350

NEW YORK

New York State
 During the Revolutionary War   12005
  Clinton, Public Papers, 7:frontis., 18 3/4 x 13 7/8,
   after Sauthier
  Cochran, N.Y. in Confed., 3, 7 5/8 x 5 1/8
  Munger, Hist. Atlas, 17, 16 1/8 x 20 1/8 col.
  N.Y., New York in Rev., 2d ed., 1:frontis., 12 1/8 x 9
  Prentice, Hist. of N.Y. State, 225, 3 5/8 x 5 1/4 col.
  Thomas, Marinus Willett, lining papers, 7 x 9 1/2
 1779   12010
  O'Callaghan, Doc. Hist. of N.Y., 1:526, 37 1/8 x 27 1/2,
   by Claude Joseph Sauthier, engr. and pub. by William
   Faden
 1782   12015
  Hilliard d'Auberteuil, Essais, 2:1, 9 x 12 3/4 col.
 1783   12020
  Munger, Hist. Atlas, 15, 16 x 20 col.
 1788   12025
  Mohr, Fed. Indian Relations, frontis., 4 x 5 3/8
Southern New York, 1774   12027
  Ford, Gen. Orders of Israel Putnam, frontis., 17 x
   18 3/4, by Claude Joseph Sauthier, pub. by William
   Faden
From Fort Chambly to New York City, 1776   12028
  Lucas, Appendiculae, 104, 13 5/8 x 9 1/8, in three
   sections, by Claude Joseph Sauthier, engr. and pub.
   by William Faden
New York counties
 1770   12030
  Munger, Hist. Atlas, 9, 7 7/8 x 10 col.
 At time of the Revolution   12035
  Brown, King's Friends, 77, 5 1/2 x 4 5/8
  Cochran, N.Y. in Confed., 3, 7 5/8 x 5 1/8
  N.Y., New York in Rev., 2d ed., 1:frontis, 12 1/8 x 9
 1788   12040
  Mohr, Fed. Indian Relations, frontis., 4 x 5 3/8
Tryon County, N.Y., and surrounding territory, 1777 12045
  Campbell, Annals of Tryon Co., 1, 10 1/8 x 6 1/2, by
   Claude Joseph Sauthier
New York senatorial districts   12050
  Cochran, N.Y. in Confed., 3, 7 5/8 x 5 1/8
New York boundary adjustments, 1770-1786   12055
  Rayback, Richards Atlas, 24, 7 5/8 x 9 7/8 col.
Hudson River area
 From Saratoga to New York City   12060
  Gerlach, Schuyler, 43, 6 1/8 x 4
 From Albany to Tappan Zee, 1779   12065
  Gipson, Br. Empire, Caxton ed., 3:308, 10 1/8 x 5, by
   Claude Joseph Sauthier

From Albany to New York City   12070
    Fortescue, British Army, 3:pl.III, 7 1/2 x 3 3/8 col.
    Hart, Am. Nation, 9:26, 6 1/2 x 2 1/2 col.
    Nickerson, Turning Point, 334, 4 7/8 x 2 3/4
    1779   12075
    Gipson, Br. Empire, 3:118, 7 5/8 x 4 3/4, by Claude
       Joseph Sauthier
East side of Hudson River, from Fishkill to Dobbs Ferry, N.Y.   12080
    Stimson, My Story, 562, 6 x 3 3/4
Albany-Schenectady region, 1779   12085
    Pearson, Schenectady Patent, 290, 11 1/4 x 10 3/8
Albany
  1763, from Rocque, Set of Plans and Forts in America   12090
    Avery, Hist. of U.S., 4:122, 2 x 2 1/2
    Munsell, Annals of Albany, 4:344, 5 x 6 1/2
  c.1770, by Robert Yates   12095
    Munsell, Annals of Albany, 4:frontis., 8 1/4 x 12 1/8
    O'Callaghan, Doc. Hist. of N.Y., 3:697, 8 1/8 x 11 3/4
    Smith, Tour of Four Great Rivers, 16, 2 5/8 x 4
  1786, by Ezra Stiles   12097
    Stiles, Itineraries, 394, 3 7/8 x 4 3/4
Rensselaerswyck Manor, 1767, by John R. Bleecker (or Bleaker)   12100
    O'Callaghan, Doc. Hist. of N.Y., 3:552, 14 7/8 x 8 3/4
    Pag. Am., 3:45, 6 3/8 x 5 7/8
    Sylvester, Rensselaer Co., 27, 10 x 7 1/8
Schenectady, 1768   12105
    Pearson, Schenectady Patent, 328, 5 1/4 x 5 3/8, by Vrooman
Tappan, N.Y., 1779   12110
    Mag. of Am. Hist., 3(Dec. 1879):746, 2 1/2 x 2 1/2
Long Island and Connecticut   12115
    Ingles, Queen's Rangers, 34, 5 1/4 x 7
Long Island Sound   12120
    Boatner, Enc. of Am. Rev., 658, 4 1/8 x 6 3/4
  East part, 1777   12121
    Naval Docs. of Am. Rev., 3:923, 6 1/2 x 9 1/8, by Lt.
       Knatchbull
  1779   12122
    Naval Docs. of Am. Rev., 3:604, 5 1/2 x 6 5/8, by Claude
       Joseph Sauthier, pub. by William Faden

                            MILITARY OPERATIONS

Washington's headquarters in New York State   12125
    Washington Atlas, pl.27, 15 1/2 x 11, 4 1/4 x 3 1/2 col.
    Washington Bicentennial, 1:407, 10 1/8 x 7 1/4
See 13375 et seq., 14040 et seq., and 15140 et seq.

                      NEW YORK CITY AND VICINITY

New York City
  1764   13005
    Hall-Quest, From Colony to Nation, 13, 6 1/8 x 3 3/4
    N.Y. Common Council Manual for 1861, 596, 6 3/8 x 6 3/8

1766   13010
    Kouwenhoven, Columbia Hist. Port., 68, 4 3/8 x 5, by
      Capt. John Montrésor. Upper part of city only
1767   13015
    Wilson, Mem. Hist. of N.Y., 2:455, 4 3/4 x 8 1/8
  By Lt. Bernard Ratzer   13020
    Avery, Hist. of U.S., 5:83, 6 3/8 x 4 1/2
    Bliven, Battle for Manhattan, 32, 4 x 6
    Decker, Brink of Rev., 38, 10 3/4 x 8 1/4
    Fitch, N.Y. Diary, frontis., 9 x 5 1/2
    Gipson, Br. Empire, 10:209, 4 1/2 x 7 1/8
    Greene, Rev. Generation, 58, 2 5/8 x 4
    Jones, Hist. of N.Y., 1:389, 17 1/4 x 26
    Kouwenhoven, Columbia Hist. Port, 68, 4 3/8 x 5. Upper
      part of city only
    Lamb, Hist. of N.Y., 1:757, 10 3/4 x 8 3/8
    Naval Docs. of Am. Rev., 1:617, 6 1/4 x 5 1/2, pub. by
      William Faden
    N.Y. City during Rev., frontis., 10 x 15
    N.Y. Common Council, Manual for 1854, frontis., 12 x 16 7/8
    Smith, Tour of Four Great Rivers, 16, 4 1/8 x 4
    Wertenbaker, Knickerbocker, 14, 5 5/8 x 7 3/4, engr. by
      Thomas Kitchin
    Wilson, Am. People, 2:103, 5 1/4 x 3 3/4
    Wilson, Mem. Hist. of N.Y., 2:344, 4 3/4 x 6 1/4
    Winsor, America, 6:332, 4 3/4 x 7 7/8
1775   13025
    Ford, Peculiar Service, front lining papers, 7 3/4 x 10 1/2
    Hamilton, Papers, 1:510, 7 x 5 3/4
    Naval Docs. of Am. Rev., 2:380, 6 3/4 x 5 3/8, by John
      Montrésor, engr. by P. Andrews, pub. by Andrew Drury
1776   13030
    Gerson, Nathan Hale, 16-17, 7 1/8 x 10 col.
    Paullin, Atlas, pl.159a, 7 3/8 x 9 col., by Maj. Holland
    Rankin, Am. Rev., 81, 6 1/4 x 4
1782, by John Hills   13035
    Harper's Mag., 67(Nov. 1883):911, 4 3/4 x 7 7/8
    Kenyon, Something Gleamed, lining papers, 8 x 10 3/4
    N.Y. Common Council, Manual for 1857, frontis., 19 x 21 5/8
    Wilson, Mem. Hist. of N.Y., 2:494, 4 3/4 x 7 3/4
During the Revolution   13040
    Barck, N.Y. City, 5, 6 3/8 x 4
    Duncan, Medical Men, 111, 6 1/8 x 3 7/8
    Mather, Refugees of 1776, 50, 2 3/4 x 4
1789   13045
    N.Y. Common Council, Manual for 1857, 372, 8 3/4 x 14 1/8
Ground to be railed around the statue of George III erected in   13050
    Bowling Green, 1770
    N.Y. Hist. Soc., Quar. Bul, 3(Apr. 1920):39, 4 x 6 1/8, by
      Gerard Bancker
Great Fires in New York City
Sept. 21, 1776   13055
    Lamb, Hist. of N.Y., 2:136, 4 1/2 x 4 3/8
    N.Y. Common Council, Manual for 1866, 766, 14 1/2 x 13 1/2
    col.

Aug. 3, 1778   13060
   N.Y. Common Council, Manual for 1866, 766, 14 1/2 x
     13 1/2 col.
The Battery, New York City, 1783 and 1883   13065
   Harper's Mag., 67(Nov. 1883):916, 3 7/8 x 3 3/8
De Lancey Bowery farm, New York City, at time of the Revolution 13070
   Jones, Hist. of N.Y., 2:558, 14 5/8 x 20 1/8 col., by
     James De Lancey
New York City area   13075
   Adams, Pilgrims, Indians, and Patriots, 181, 6 5/8 x 4 1/4
     from Gordon, Hist. of U.S.A.
   Allen, Naval Hist. of Am. Rev., 1:86, 6 x 3 5/8
   Boatner, Enc. of Am. Rev., front lining paper, 7 5/8 x 4 3/4
   Gordon, Hist. of U.S.A., 2:310, pl.III, 10 3/8 x 6 5/8, engr.
     by T. Conder
   Haycox, Winds of Rebellion, 17, 2 1/2 x 3 1/4
   Meredith, Am. Wars, 61, 4 5/8 x 4, Washington's map
   Serle, Am. Journal, 73, 5 7/8 x 4
  1766   13080
   Abbott, N.Y. in Am. Rev., end, 11 1/2 x 8 3/4, by Capt.
     John Montrésor
  1766-1767   13085
   Kouwenhoven, Columbia Hist. Port., 69, 7 5/8 x 7, by Lt.
     Bernard Ratzer
  1774, by Claude Joseph Sauthier, pub. by William Faden in 1779 13090
   Baurmeister, Revolution, 290, 7 1/2 x 4 3/4
   Clinton, Am. Rebellion, 40, 9 1/8 x 6
   Winsor, America, 6:340, 8 x 4 3/4
  1775   13095
   Avery, Hist. of U.S., 5:344, 8 1/4 x 6 5/8 col., by Capt.
     John Montrésor
   Ford, Peculiar Service, back lining papers, 5 x 2 1/8,
     7 3/4 x 10 1/2
  1776   13100
   Adams, Atlas, pl. 70, 9 1/4 x 6 1/4
   Alden, Hist. of Am. Rev., 264, 8 5/8 x 5 5/8
   Clarke, Am. Revolution, end lining paper, 4 1/4 x 3 5/8 col.
   Freeman, Washington, abridgment, 269, 7 3/4 x 5 1/2
   Hall-Quest, From Colony to Nation, 83, 6 1/8 x 3 3/4
   Ingles, Queen's Rangers, 18, 7 3/4 x 5 1/4
   Johnston, Campaigns of 1776, frontis., 6 3/4 x 4 1/8
   Lucas, Appendiculae, 102, 7 1/2 x 5 3/8 col., by Maj. Holland
   Mather, Refugees of 1776, 31, 6 1/2 x 4
   Wilson, Mem. Hist. of N.Y., 2:523, 7 5/8 x 5 3/4, by Thomas
     Kitchin
   Winsor, America, 6:343, 7 7/8 x 4 1/4
   See also 13375
  1778   13105
   N.Y. Common Council, Manual for 1869, xvi, 9 5/8 x 7 3/8,
     by Thomas Kitchin
  c.1781   13110
   Leiby, Hackensack Valley, 150, 10 1/2 x 8
New York Bay and Port
  1764, by S. Bellin   13115
   N.Y. Common Council, Manual for 1861, 597, 8 5/8 x 6 5/8
   Wilson, Mem. Hist. of N.Y., 2:332, 7 1/8 x 5 1/2

1777   13117
    Naval Docs. of Am. Rev., 4:339, 7 1/2 x 5 1/2, pub. by
      R. Sayer and J. Bennett
New York Harbor and vicinity   13120
    Clowes, Royal Navy, 3:381, 4 1/4 x 7 3/8
    Frothingham, Washington, 124, 6 7/8 x 3 1/8
  c.1774-1784   13125
    Ristow, Services, pl.VII, 7 x 5 1/8
  1781   13127
    Fleming, Battle of Yorktown, 38, 8 7/8 x 5 1/8 col.
Manhattan Island
  1776   13130
    Fiske, Am. Rev., 1:226-227, 2 3/4 x 7 1/2
  1776 and 1956   13135
    Bliven, Battle for Manhattan, front, 8 x 10 1/2 col.
  During the Revolution   13140
    Lamb, Hist. of N.Y., 2:68, 8 3/8 x 4 3/8
  Northern part, July 1778   13145
    André, Journal, 2:51, 14 1/8 x 29 1/2 col., by Ens.
      Jno. Wilson
  Localities associated with George Washington   13150
    Washington Atlas, pl.43, 15 1/2 x 11, 9 7/8 x 2 1/4
Staten Island, N.Y., 1781   13155
    Staten Is. Inst. Arts Sci., Proc., 7(Oct. 1932-May 1933):5,
      6 x 9 5/8, by George Taylor and A. Skinner, British Army
      surveyors
Long Island, N.Y.
 North Shore
  From Oyster Bay to Fort Slongo   13160
    Mather, Refugees of 1776, 221, 3 3/8 x 7
  From Setauket to Miller's Place   13165
    Mather, Refugees of 1776, 223, 1 3/4 x 4
 Towns and localities
  Bedford Corners, 1766-1767 and 1867   13170
    Stiles, Brooklyn, 1:267, 7 x 4 col.
  Brookland Ferry, 1766-1767 and 1867   13175
    Stiles, Brooklyn, 1:311, 6 x 4 1/8
  Brooklyn and vicinity, 1766-1767   13180
    Stiles, Brooklyn, 1:62, 10 3/4 x 15 7/8
  Brooklyn at time of the Revolutionary War   13185
    N.Y. Common Council, Manual for 1858, 112, 9 5/8 x 20 1/4
  Setauket   13190
    Ford, Peculiar Service, back lining paper, 3 1/4 x 4 1/8
  Southampton, Bridge Hampton, Sag Harbor, and East Hampton   13195
    Mather, Refugees of 1776, 217, 3 1/8 x 4
  Southold, Shelter Island, and Sag Harbor   13200
    Mather, Refugees of 1776, 3 3/4 x 4
Westchester County, N.Y. during the Revolution
 1775-1783   13203
    Hough, Neutral Ground, lining papers, 10 3/4 x 7 3/4 col.
 1778-1780   13205
    Irving, Life of Washington, 2:226, 8 3/8 x 6 1/2, after
      surveys by Robert Erskine
 Northern section   13210
    Hough, If Not Victory, lining papers, 7 7/8 x 11 col.
    Hufeland, Westchester Co., end, 18 x 13 3/4 col.

Southern section (now the Bronx)   13215
  Hufeland, Westchester Co., 102, 7 3/4 x 9 col.
  Westchester Co. Hist. Soc., Soc., Quar. Bul., 8(Apr. 1932):51,
    4 x 4 5/8
Towns and localities
 Frog's Point, 1781   13220
  Mag. of Am. Hist., 4(Apr. 1880):294, 3 7/8 x 5 3/8,
    French map
  Kingsbridge, 1645-1783   13225
   Scharf, Westchester Co., 1:746, 8 3/4 x 9 3/4
  Kingsbridge, Aug. 31, 1778   13230
   Ingles, Queen's Rangers, 98, 5 x 6 1/4
  Morrisania, 1781   13235
   Mag. of Am. Hist., 4(Apr. 1880):294, 3 5/8 x 5 3/8,
     French map
  Port Chester   13240
   Mather, Refugees of 1776, 195, 3 1/8 x 4
  Tarrytown and White Plains section   13245
   Pleasants, John André, 36, 4 3/4 x 4 1/4
  White Plains, 1776   13250
   Scharf, Westchester Co., 1:727, 5 1/2 x 3 1/8
 Roads about White Plains, 1779   13255
   Scharf, Westchester Co., 1:732, 8 5/8 x 5 3/4, by
     Robert Erskine
 Road from New York to New Rochelle, 1789   13260
   N.Y. Common Council, Manual for 1871, 778, 6 3/4 x 4 1/2,
     6 3/4 x 4 1/2, by Christopher Colles

DEFENSES AROUND NEW YORK CITY

American defenses, 1776
 Manhattan Island   13265
   Bryant, Popular Hist. of U.S., 3:491, 7 x 2 3/4
   Decker, Brink of Rev., end, 13 3/8 x 33
   Johnston, Campaign of 1776, end, 14 1/4 x 35
 Fort George   13270
   Abbott, N.Y. in Am. Rev., 170, 3 1/4 x 6 1/2, by Claude
     Joseph Sauthier, 1773
   Lossing, Field-Book of Rev., 2:593, 1 1/4 x 1 1/4
   Wilson, Mem. Hist. of N.Y., 2:470, 1 1/2 x 1 5/8
 Fort Washington and outworks   13275
   Am. Scenic Hist. Pres. Soc., Annual Rept. 1902, 96,
     7 x 14 7/8
   Cook, Golden Bk. of Am. Rev., 90, 3 5/8 x 3 1/8
   Ft. Washington Account, 40, 5 x 10 1/2
   Ft. Washington Memorial, 14-15, 5 x 10 1/2
   See also 13505, 13 510
 Fort Washington in relation to modern streets
   1898: Ft. Washington Memorial, 8, 5 1/8 x 5   13280
   1902: Ft. Washington Account, 80, 7 x 15 1/4   13285
   1923: Calver, Hist. with Pick and Shovel, 47, 3 5/8 x 4 1/2   13290
 Hellgate Fort, Oct. 10, 1776   13295
   Mackenzie, Diary, 1:81, 7 1/8 x 5 1/2
 Independent Battery   13300
   Lossing, Field-Book of Rev., 2:593, 1 1/8 x 1 1/4

Brooklyn, by Ezra Stiles   13305
  Johnston, Campaign of 1776, 70, 7 x 4 3/4
  Stiles, Diary, 2:152, 5 1/2 x 4
British defenses and camps, 1776-1783
  New York City defenses, 1781, pub. by J. Bew   13310
  Avery, Hist. of U.S., 6:181, 6 3/4 x 3 7/8
  N.Y. Common Council, Manual for 1871, 844, 16 5/8 x 9 5/8
Manhattan Island
  Camp of 17th Foot Regiment, Dyckman Farm, 1776-1783   13315
    Calver, Hist. with Pick and Shovel, 14-15, 5 1/8 x 8 5/8
    N.Y. Hist. Soc., Quar. Bul., 2(Oct. 1918):90-91, 6 1/4 x
     11 1/2
  Defenses in vicinity of Fort Knyphausen (formerly Fort   13320
    Washington), 1779
    Krafft, Journal, pl.6, 3 3/8 x 7 1/2, by Lt. John Charles
     Philip von Krafft
    Wilson, Mem. Hist. of N.Y., 2:525, 2 7/8 x 6
  Defenses at northern end of Manhattan
    1781   13325
     Mag. of Am. Hist., 4(Apr. 1880):306, 7 1/2 x 6 1/2
     N.Y. Common Council, Manual for 1854, 548, 3 1/2 x 7 1/2
    1782, British headquarters map   13327
     Bolton, Washington Hts., 279, 7 1/2 x 4 1/4
    1783   13330
     Scenic and Hist. Am., 4(May 1936):27, 3 3/8 x 4 1/2
Staten Island
  Fort and camp site, Richmond   13335
    Calver, Hist. with Pick and Shovel, 32-33, 7 x 8 7/8
    N.Y. Hist. Soc., Quar. Bul., 3(Oct. 1919):86-87, 6 7/8 x
     9 3/8
  Redoubts, Richmond, Oct. 30, 1779   13340
    Staten Is. Historian, 4(Jan.-Mar. 1941):1, 4 1/2 x 3 7/8
  British-Hessian camp, 1780-1783   13345
    Staten Is. Historian, 7(July-Sept. 1944):21, 10 7/8 x
     7 7/8, French map
Long Island
  Brooklyn defenses, 1776-1783   13350
    Stiles, Brooklyn, 1:251, 2 x 2 5/8
  Brooklyn Fort, 1780   13355
    Stiles, Brooklyn, 1:315, 2 1/8 x 2 1/8
  Encampment of Queen's Rangers, Oyster Bay, 1778-1779,   13360
    by Lt. Col. John Graves Simcoe
    Ingles, Queen's Rangers, 104, 4 7/8 x 5 5/8
    Simcoe, Military Jl., 94, 7 1/2 x 8 5/8
  Hessian encampment near Bedford, Aug. 1783   13365
    Baurmeister, Revolution, 581, 3 x 4 1/2
American and British defenses along Harlem River, in northern   13370
    part of Manhattan Is. and Westchester County, 1775-1783
  Schwab, Fort No. Eight, frontis, 8 1/8 x 10 3/8

MILITARY OPERATIONS

Area of operations, Aug.-Nov. 1776   13375
  Adams, Atlas, pl.70, 9 1/4 x 6 1/4
  Anderson, Howe Bros., 128, 5 x 3 3/4
  Channing, Hist. of U.S., 3:231, 6 1/4 x 4

Fortescue, British Army, 3:pl.II, 7 1/2 x 2 5/8 col.
Guthorn, Am. Maps, 37, 2 1/2 x 1 7/8, from Isaac Warren's
    North American Almanack for 1777, 2 1/2 x 1 7/8 from
    Nathaniel Low's Astronomical Diary for 1777
Freeman, Washington, 4:185, 4 7/8 x 5; 213, 7 1/8 x 5
MacMunn, Am. War, 140, 6 x 3 3/4; 177, 6 5/8 x 3 1/8
Miers, Yankee Doodle Dandy, 81, 8 x 3 3/8
Rankin, Am. Rev., 81, 6 1/4 x 4
Scheer, Rebels and Redcoats, 144, 7 1/2 x 4 1/2
Vestal, Washington, 16, 3 7/8 x 2, 3 7/8 x 1 7/8
Wallace, Appeal to Arms, 109, 6 1/2 x 4 1/8
Washington Bicentennial, 1:111, 3 7/8 x 2, 3 7/8 x 1 7/8
Winsor, America, 6:342, 4 1/2 x 3 3/8
See also 13380
Movements of forces of Washington and Howe during New York   13380
    campaign, Aug.-Nov. 1776
Alden, Gen. Chas. Lee, 143, 5 3/8 x 4 1/8
Alden, Rise of Am. Republic, 142, 6 5/8 x 4
Am. Heritage, Revolution, 194, 8 5/8 x 7 7/8 col.
Anderson, Howe Bros., 171, 4 7/8 x 3 3/4
Avery, Hist. of U.S., 6:11, 7 1/4 x 4 7/8 col.
Billias, Gen. John Glover, 113, 7 1/4 x 4 7/8
Billias, Washington's Opponents, xxviii, 7 1/2 x 4 5/8,
    3 1/2 x 2 3/8
Carrington, Battles, 228, 7 5/8 x 4 5/8
Carrington, Washington, 125, 5 7/8 x 3 1/2
Coffin, Boys of '76, 117, 7 3/8 x 4 3/4
Cook, Golden Bk. of Am. Rev., 84, 8 5/8 x 7 7/8 col.
Cunliffe, Washington, 73, 4 1/2 x 2 1/2 col.
Dupuy, Compact Hist., 120, 6 1/8 x 4 1/2
Dupuy, Mil. Heritage of Am., 87, 5 1/4 x 4 1/2
Ellis, New York, 143, 8 1/8 x 6
Ellis, Short Hist., 107, 5 1/4 x 4 3/8
Fast, The Unvanquished, lining papers, 7 x 4 3/4 col.
Fisher, Struggle for Am. Ind., 1:526, 6 x 3 1/2
Flexner, Washington in Am. Rev., 88, 7 3/4 x 5 5/8, by
    Samuel H. Bryant
Fortescue, British Army, 3:pl.II, 7 1/2 x 2 5/8
Freeman, Washington, 4:172, 4 x 5; 220, 5 x 3 1/2
Frothingham, Washington, 152, 6 5/8 x 4 1/2
Greene, Revolutionary War, 28, 7 1/4 x 4 7/8 col.
Hamilton, Grenadier Guards, 2:219, 7 1/2 x 4 1/2
Johnston, Campaigns of 1776, end, 14 1/4 x 35
Leckie, Wars of America, 142, 6 3/4 x 4 1/8
Lossing, Field-Book of Rev., 2:618, 7 1/2 x 4 7/8
McDowell, Revolutionary War, 89, 4 x 3 1/2 col.
Mackesy, War for America, 84, 7 3/8 x 4 1/4
Marshall, Atlas, map 2, 9 1/2 x 6 1/2
Mather, Refugees of 1776, 57, 6 1/2 x 4 1/4, from Lossing
Mitchell, Battles Am. Rev., 57, 7 1/2 x 5 col.
Montross, Rag, Tag and Bobtail, 119, 4 3/4 x 4 1/4; 129,
    6 x 4 1/4; 148, 6 1/8 x 4 1/4
Morison, Growth of Am. Republic, 5th ed., 207, 6 1/4 x 4 1/2
N.Y. Common Council, Manual for 1864, 668, 31 1/2 x 22 5/8
    pub. by J.F.W. Des Barres, 1777

Niles, Chronicles, XXIII, 7 1/4 x 6 1/2
Pag. Am., 6:146, 5 5/8 x 2 7/8; 149, 5 3/8 x 3 1/8; 151,
   4 3/4 x 4 5/8
Paullin, Atlas, pl.160A, inset, 2 1/8 x 1 7/8 col.
Rayback, Richards Atlas, 28, 15 7/8 x 10 1/2 col.
Seelye, Story of Washington, 162, 5 x 3
Sparks, Washington's Writings, 4:68, 7 3/8 x 4 3/8; 160,
   7 5/8 x 4 3/8
Ward, Revolution, 1:249, 5 3/4 x 4 1/2
Wertenbaker, Knickerbocker, 94, 7 x 4 3/8
Whitton, Am. War of Ind., 318, 6 x 3 1/2
Willcox, Portrait, 103, 3 3/8 x 2 1/4
Wilson, Mem. Hist. of N.Y., 2:488, 10 x 9, eng. and pub.
   by William Faden, 1776
Winsor, America, 6:335, 3 1/8 x 7 7/8; 343, 7 7/8 x 4 1/4;
   344, 4 3/8 x 4 7/8; 345, 4 5/8 x 3 3/4, Hessian map;
   404, 5 3/8 x 4 3/4
   See also 13450, 13455
Actions of Col. John Glover's marine regiment during New York   13385
   campaign
   Lancaster, Trumpet to Arms, end lining paper, 7 5/8 x 5 1/8 col.
   Marine Corps Gaz., 34(Jan. 1950):35, 7 1/4 x 5 col.
Positions of American and British armies before, at, and after
   Battle of Long Island, Aug.-Sept. 1776, engr. by W. Kemble
   Kinnaird, Geo. Washington, 95, 9 3/8 x 5 7/8
   Lossing, Life of Washington, 2:262, 8 7/8 x 5 1/2
   Lossing, Washington, A Biography, 2:123, 7 x 4 3/8
   Lossing, Washington and Am. Republic, 2:262, 8 7/8 x 5 1/2
Long Island, N.Y., Battle of (also known as Battle of Brooklyn),   13390
   Aug. 27, 1776
   Alden, Am. Revolution, 98, 4 3/4 x 4 3/8
   Anderson, Howe Bros., 131, 3 3/4 x 3 3/4
   Army, Am. Military Hist., 53, 3 1/8 x 2 1/8
   Avery, Hist. of U.S., 6:16, 4 3/4 x 4 1/2 col.
   Bailey, Brooklyn, 55, 8 x 5 3/8
   Baurmeister, Revolution, 38, 4 7/8 x 4 1/2
   Belcher, First Am. Civil War, 2:155, 4 x 3 7/8 col.
   Billias, Gen. John Glover, 98, 5 5/8 x 4 7/8
   Bliven, Battle for Manhattan, 32, 5 x 4 1/2
   Boatner, Enc. of Am. Rev., 648, 3 1/4 x 4 1/8; 650, 2 1/8 x
     4 1/8; 652, 2 1/8 x 4 1/8; 653, 2 x 4 1/8
   Botta, War of Ind., 1:369, 6 1/2 x 4 1/4
   Carrington, Battles, 214, 7 3/4 x 4 5/8
   Carrington, Washington, 105, 5 7/8 x 3 1/2
   Clinton, Public Papers, 1:328, 9 1/2 x 8 3/8, by Maj. Holland
   Coffin, Boys of '76, 99, 3 1/4 x 4 5/8
   Commager, Spirit of '76, 1:429, 5 1/8 x 4 5/8
   Decker, Brink of Rev., end, 23 1/8 x 18 3/8
   Drake, Campaign of Trenton, 28, 3 5/8 x 3 1/4
   Duer, Sterling, 162, 7 1/4 x 4 1/4
   Duncan, Medical Men, 131, 5 1/8 x 4 1/8
   Dupuy, Compact Hist., 129, 4 1/2 x 6 1/4
   Dupuy, Mil. Heritage of Am., 87, 5 1/4 x 4 1/2
   Esposito, Am. Wars Atlas, 1:5b, 5 5/8 x 4 3/4 col.
   Esposito, Civil War Atlas, 5b, 5 5/8 x 4 3/4 col.
   Field, Battle of L.I., 310, plan I, 8 1/4 x 10 1/4 col.; plan II

Fisher, Struggle for Am. Ind., 1:494, 3 1/2 x 3 1/2
Fiske, Am. Rev., 1:218, 6 x 3 3/4 col.
Fitch, N.Y. Diary, 32, 6 x 4 7/8
Fite, Book of Old Maps, 258, 12 7/8 x 8 1/8
Flexner, Washington in Am. Rev., 89, 3 3/4 x 5 1/8, by
   Samuel H. Bryant
Fortescue, British Army, 3:pl.II, 1 3/8 x 2 3/8 col.
Freeman, Washington, 4:160-161, 6 3/8 x 8
Freeman, Washington, abridgment, 287, 6 5/8 x 4 5/8
Garner, Hist. of U.S., 2:429, 6 7/8 x 4 1/4
Greene, Revolutionary War, 36, 4 3/4 x 4 1/2 col.
Guizot, Atlas, pl.11, 7 1/8 x 4 1/2
Gurney, Pict. Hist. U.S. Army, 37, 2 3/4 x 1 7/8
Hall, School History, 204, 6 x 3 1/2
Hamilton, Grenadier Guards, 2:217, 7 3/8 x 4 1/2
Harper's Mag., 53(Aug. 1876):337, 3 1/4 x 4 5/8
Hughes, Washington, 2:441, 5 1/4 x 4
Irving, Life of Washington, 2:308, 5 3/8 x 4 5/8
Johnston, Campaign of 1776, 50, 2 7/8 x 6 1/2; 300,
   25 3/4 x 20 3/8
Knickerbocker Mag., 13(Apr. 1839):288, 7 5/8 x 5
Lamb, Hist. of N.Y., 2:106, 3 1/4 x 4 3/8
Lodge, Story of Rev., 186, 4 1/2 x 4 1/8
Long Is. Hist. Soc. Quar., 1(Apr. 1939):48-49, 7 x 8
Lossing, Field-Book of Rev., 2:600, 2 1/4 x 2 5/8; 603,
   3 3/8 x 3 1/4
Lowell, Hessians, 63, 3 1/4 x 4 5/8
MacMunn, Am. War, 140, 6 x 3 3/4
Marshall, Atlas, map 2, 9 1/2 x 6 1/2
Mather, Refugees of 1776, 35, 6 1/4 x 4
Matloff, Am. Military History, 64, 3 1/8 x 2
Miller, Triumph of Freedom, 123, 4 1/4 x 7
Mitchell, Battles Am. Rev., 57, 7 1/2 x 5 col.
Niles, Chronicles, XXIII, 7 1/4 x 6 1/2
Onderdonk, Rev. Incidents, frontis., 6 5/8 x 7 3/8
Pag. Am., 6:144, 5 7/8 x 4 5/8
Reeder, Story of Rev. War. 77, 4 1/2 x 4 1/8
Ridpath, New Complete Hist., 6:2514, 7 3/4 x 4 7/8
Roscoe, Picture Hist., no.92, 2 5/8 x 2 1/8
Scharf, Hist. of Md., 2:244, 8 3/8 x 6 5/8, by T.W. Field, 1869
Scheer, Rebels and Redcoats, 164-165, 4 3/8 x 10
Scribner's Mag., 23(1898):403, 5 1/8 x 4 3/4
Seelye, Story of Washington, 149, 4 1/4 x 3 7/8
Sons of Rev., N.Y., Year Book 1896, 42, 8 3/4 x 14
Sparks, Washington's Writings, 4:68, 7 3/8 x 4 3/8
Stedman, Am. War, 1:195, 13 7/8 x 10 1/2
Steele, Am. Campaigns, 2:14, 6 3/8 x 3 3/4 col.
Stephenson, Washington, 1:360, 4 5/8 x 4
Stiles, Brooklyn, 1:250, 12 7/8 x 9 3/4, 3 5/8 x 2 3/8
Stone, Hist. of N.Y. City, 246, 8 3/4 x 5 1/2
Vestal, Washington, 18, 3 7/8 x 4
Ward, Battle of L.I., 14, 8 1/8 x 5
Ward, Del. Continnentals, 36, 4 x 6
Ward, Revolution, 1:217, 4 1/2 x 6 1/2
Washington Bicentennial, 1:111, 3 7/8 x 4
Wertenbaker, Knickerbocker, 94, 7 x 4 3/8

Whittemore, Heroes of Am. Rev., xix, 6 1/2 x 4 3/8
Whittemore, Sullivan, 34, 4 3/4 x 4
Whitton, Am. War of Ind., 318, 3 1/2 x 3 1/2
Wickwire, Cornwallis, 87, 3 1/2 x 4 1/8
Willard, Letters on Am Rev., 354, 4 1/4 x 6 3/4, from
  Gentleman's Magazine
Winsor, America, 6:327, 3 5/8 x 4 3/4, Hessian map; 328,
  6 1/4 x 5 1/8
 Engraved and published by William Faden   13395
  Belcher, First Am. Civil War, 2:154, 4 3/4 x 4
  Fraser, Stone House, 74, 9 5/8 x 7 3/4
  Frothingham, Washington, 132, 5 x 4 1/2
  Kouwenhoven, Columbia Hist. Port., 71, 7 x 5 7/8
  Wilson, Mem. Hist. of N.Y., 2:488, 10 x 9
Movements of Nathan Hale, Sept. 10-22, 1776   13400
  Avery, Hist. of U.S., 6:28, 3 5/8 x 3 7/8 col.
  Greene, Revolutionary War, 52, 3 5/8 x 3 7/8 col.
Site of Hale's execution, New York, Sept. 22, 1776   13405
  Avery, Hist. of U.S., 6:28, 3 5/8 x 2 col.
  Greene, Revolutionary War, 52, 3 5/8 x 2 col.
  Johnston, Nathan Hale, 162, 4 x 4 1/2
  N.Y. Hist. Soc., Quar. Bul., 2(Apr. 1918):13, 2 1/2 x 2 1/8
British landing at Kip's Bay, Manhattan Is., Sept. 15, 1776   13410
  Coggins, Boys in Revolution, 72, 4 7/8 x 5 1/2
  N.Y. Hist. Soc. Quar., 32(Oct. 1948):253, 9 x 5 3/4
Kip's Bay, N.Y., Battle of, Sept. 15, 1776   13415
  Bliven, Battle for Manhattan, end, 8 x 5 col.
  Mitchell, Battles Am. Rev., 57, 7 1/2 x 5 col.
Position of British army on Manhattan Is., evening of Sept. 15,
  1776
  Johnston, Harlem Heights, 46, 6 1/2 x 4 col.
Harlem Heights, N.Y., Battle of, Sept. 16, 1776   13425
  Am. Heritage, Revolution, 185, 2 1/2 x 2 1/8
  Avery, Hist. of U.S., 6:23, 4 1/4 x 1 7/8 col.
  Bliven, Battle for Manhattan, end, 5 1/8 x 8 col.
  Boatner, Enc. of Am. Rev., 489, 6 1/2 x 4
  Coggins, Boys in Revolution, 72, 4 7/8 x 5 1/2
  Cook, Golden Bk. of Am. Rev., 90, 3 5/8 x 3 1/8
  Dupuy, Compact Hist., 145, 6 1/8 x 4 1/2
  Freeman, Washington, 4:199, 3 3/4 x 7 1/4
  Greene, Gen. Greene, 48, 3 1/2 x 5 1/4
  Greene, Revolutionary War, 48, 6 1/8 x 10 col.
  Johnston, Campaign of 1776, 259, 4 3/4 x 7
  Johnston, Harlem Heights, 70, 5 3/4 x 10 1/2 col.; 122,
    5 1/4 x 3 7/8, 1 3/4 x 1 3/4
  Lamb, Hist. of N.Y., 2:129, 5 1/2 x 2 3/4
  Mag. of Am. Hist., 4(May 1880):362, 6 1/2 x 6 1/8; 368,
    4 x 2 3/4
  Mather, Refugees of 1776, 55, 4 x 6 1/8
  Mil. Affairs, 15(Spring 1951):18, 5 x 7 3/4, by Maj. John
   André
  Mitchell, Battles Am. Rev., 57, 7 1/2 x 5 col.
  N.Y. Common Council, Manual for 1868, 812, 14 5/8 x 28 1/8 col.
  Seelye, Story of Washington, 166, 4 5/8 x 3 1/2
  Shepherd, Harlem Heights, front, 3 1/2 x 6 1/2 col.

By Ezra Stiles   13430
    Johnston, Harlem Heights, 116, 4 1/2 x 3 5/8
    Stiles, Diary, 2:65, 4 3/8 x 4
American position, Harlem Heights, night of Sept. 16, 1776   13435
    Mag. of Am. Hist., 6(Jan. 1881):97, 5 7/8 x 4 5/8
Position of American and British armies near Harlem, Sept. 16-   13440
    Oct. 12, 1776
    Johnston, Harlem Heights, 50, 4 3/4 x 10 1/2 col.
Positions of American and British armies, Oct. 12-28, 1776   13445
    Hall, School History, 209, 6 1/8 x 3 3/8
    Marshall, Atlas, map 3, 9 3/4 x 6 1/8
By S. Lewis   13450
    Dawson, Westchester Co. in Rev., 238, 12 1/4 x 6 3/4
    N.Y. Hist. Soc. Quar., 42(Jan. 1958):24, 6 7/8 x 5 1/4
    Scharf, Westchester Co., 1:414, 12 1/4 x 6 3/4
Positions of American and British armies, Oct. 12 - Nov. 28, 1776, 13455
    by Claude Joseph Sauthier, engr. by William Faden, 1777
    Clinton, Public Papers, 1:622, 12 1/2 x 8 1/2
    Dawson, Westchester Co. in Rev., end, 28 x 19 5/8
    O'Dea, Washington, 18, 9 1/2 x 6 1/2
    Scharf, Westchester Co., 1:402, 28 1/2 x 19 1/4
    Scull, Evelyns in Am., 319
    Stedman, Am. War, 1:215, 28 1/4 x 19 1/4
    Winsor, America, 6:336, 4 1/8 x 8
American and British advance posts, Manhattan Is., Oct. 12, 1776   13460
    Mackenzie, Diary, 1:76, 12 1/8 x 7 1/2, prob. by Lt. Frederick
       Mackenzie
American and British positions, Manhattan Is., Oct. 24, 1776   13465
    Mackenzie, Diary, 1:85, 5 1/2 x 7 1/2, prob. by Lt. Frederick
       Mackenzie
British misconception of Washington's "detached camps" west of   13470
    Bronx River, N.Y., Oct. 1776
    Freeman, Washington, 4:223, 6 x 5
Survey of Frog's Neck and route of British army to Oct.24, 1776,   13475
    by Charles Blaskowitz
    Hufeland, Westchester Co., frontis., 19 1/2 x 11 1/4, 6 1/8 x
       4 3/8
    Lamb, Hist. of N.Y., 2:140, 8 1/4 x 4 3/8
Pelham Bay, N.Y., Battle of, Oct. 18, 1776   13480
    Abbatt, Pell's Point, end, 8 x 10 3/8
By S. Lewis   13485
    Dawson, Westchester Co. in Rev., 238, 12 1/4 x 6 3/4
    N.Y. Hist. Soc. Quar., 42(Jan. 1958):24, 6 7/8 x 5 1/4
White Plains, N.Y., Battle of, Oct. 28, 1776   13490
    Anderson, Howe Bros., 189, 4 1/8 x 3 3/4
    Avery, Hist. of U.S., 6:33, 3 x 2 1/4 col.
    Dupuy, Compact Hist., 151, 5 x 4 1/2
    Flexner, Washington in Am. Rev., 89, 3 3/8 x 4 3/4, by
       Samuel H. Bryant
    Freeman, Washington, 4:228, 3 7/8 x 5
    Frothingham, Washington, 152, 6 5/8 x 4 1/2
    Grant, British Battles, 2:147, 5 3/4 x 7 5/8
    Greene, Revolutionary War, 52, 3 x 2 1/4 col.
    Hamilton, Hist. of Republic, 1:133, 7 1/8 x 10 1/2
    Hufeland, Westchester Co., 131, 7 3/4 x 13 7/8 col.
    Pag. Am., 6:148, 2 3/8 x 5 1/4

Robertson, Diaries, pl.44, 6 7/8 x 5 3/8
Seelye, Story of Washington, 173, 5 7/8 x 3 7/8
Vestal, Washington, 20, 2 1/4 x 2, 2 1/4 x 2
Ward, Revolution, 1:263, 5 x 4 3/8
Washington Bicentennial, 1:112, 2 1/4 x 2, 2 1/4 x 2
Westchester Co. Hist. Soc., Quar. Bul., 8(Jan. 1932):24-25,
  6 1/2 x 10
By Claude Joseph Sauthier, engr. by William Faden, 1777   13495
  Clinton, Public Papers, 1:622, 12 1/2 x 8 1/2
  Coles, Washington Hq., 26, 5 1/8 x 3 1/2
  Dawson, Westchester Co. in Rev., end, 28 x 19 5/8
  O'Dea, Washington, 18, 9 1/2 x 6 1/2
  Scharf, Westchester Co., 1:402, 28 1/2 x 19 1/4
  Winsor, America, 6:336, 4 1/8 x 8
American earthworks, Miller Hill   13500
  Westchester Co. Hist. Soc., Quar. Bul., 8(Jan. 1932):33,
    3 3/4 x 6 3/8
Fort Washington, N.Y., British capture of, Nov. 16, 1776   13505
  Am. Heritage, Revolution, 186, 1 1/2 x 1 7/8 col.
  Avery, Hist. of U.S., 6:34, 5 x 2 col.
  Belcher, First Am. Civil War, 2:174, 6 3/8 x 4 1/2 col.
  Britt, Hungry War, pl.iv, 3 7/8 x 5 3/8
  Carrington, Battles, 254, 7 5/8 x 4 3/4
  Carrington, Washington, 132, 5 3/4 x 3 5/8
  Drake, Campaign of Trenton, 37, 5 5/8 x 3 1/4
  DeLancey, Capture of Mt. Washington, frontis., 5 1/2 x 7 5/8
  Freeman, Washington, 4:244, 6 1/2 x 5
  Greene, Gen. Greene, 58, 3 1/2 x 5 3/4
  Greene, Revolutionary War, 80, 5 x 2 col.
  Guizot, Atlas, pl.12, 7 1/8 x 4 1/8
  Hall, School History, 211, 6 x 3 3/8
  Johnston, Campaign of 1776, end, 14 1/4 x 35
  Lossing, Field-Book of Rev., 2:610, 7/8 x 1 1/8
  Mag. of Am. Hist., 1(Feb. 1877):65, 5 1/2 x 7 5/8, German plan
  N.Y. Common Council, Mannual for 1861, 428, 16 1/2 x 21 3/4 col.
  N.Y. Pub. Lib., Bul., 37(July 1933):587, 6 1/2 x 4, by
      Lt. Gen. Archibald Robertson
  Scharf, Westchester Co., 1:790, 5 7/8 x 9
  Sparks, Washington's Writings, 4:96, 7 1/4 x 4 1/8
By Claude Joseph Sauthier, pub. by William Faden, 1777   13510
  Am. Heritage, 20(Aug. 1969):31, 9 3/4 x 5 1/2
  Am. Scenic Hist. Pres. Soc., Annual Rept. 1902, 91,
    15 5/8 x 8 1/2
  Avery, Hist of U.S., 6:34, 9 x 5 col.
  Bliven, Battle for Manhatten, 96, 6 1/2 x 3 5/8
  Bolton, Washington Hts., 221, 7 1/2 x 4 1/8, after Sauthier
  Clinton, Public Papers, 1:432, 15 5/8 x 8 1/2
  DeLancey, Capture of Mt. Washington, 30, 6 7/8 x 4 3/8,
    after Sauthier
  Ft. Washington Account, 64, 15 5/8 x 8 1/2
  Frothingham, Washington, 140, 6 1/2 x 3 3/8
  Kouwenhoven, Columbia Hist. Port., 72, 8 7/8 x 5 1/4
  Lee, Hist. of N. America, 6:256, 6 x 3 3/8 col.
  Mag. of Am. Hist., 4(May 1880):351, 7 5/8 x 4 7/8
  N. Y. Calendar of Hist. MSS., 1:532, 14 1/8 x 7 1/2

N.Y. Common Council, Manual for 1859, 120, 17 1/8 x 10 col.
Scenic and Hist. Am., 4(May 1936):14, 7 x 4 1/8
Stedman, Am. War, 1:210, 6 1/8 x 10
Winsor, America, 6:339, 8 x 4
Diagram of opposing forces, Nov. 16, 1776   13515
Fort Washington Account, 96, 8 1/8 x 14 1/8

1777

House in which American prisoners were billeted, New Lots,   13520
   Long Island, 1777
Fitch, N.Y. Diary, 105, 6 1/4 x 6

1778-1779

Situation of American and British armies in vicinity of New   13525
   York City, Aug. 1778 - May 1779
Pag. Am., 6:208, 4 1/4 x 3 1/4
Washington's headquarters, Wright's Mills, Westchester Co., N.Y., 13530
   July 1778
Westchester Co. Hist. Soc., Quar. Bul., 8(Jan. 1932):13,4 x 6
Headquarters of Washington and Gates, White Plains, N.Y.,   13535
   July - Sept. 1778
Westchester Co. Hist. Soc., Quar. Bul., 9(July 1933):56, 4 x
   6 1/2, by Robert Erskine
Washington's headquarters, White Plains, N.Y., and vicinity, 1778 13540
   Westchester Co. Hist. Soc., Quar. Bul., 8(Jan. 1932):17,
   6 1/2 x 4, by Robert Erskine
Indian ambuscade, Kingsbridge, N.Y., Aug. 31, 1778   13550
   Ingles, Queen's Rangers, 98, 5 x 6 1/4, after Simcoe
Simcoe, Military Jl., 86, 6 1/4 x 8, by Lt. Col. John Graves
   Simcoe
Babcock's, N.Y., skirmish, Sept. 16, 1778   13555
   Ingles, Queen's Rangers, 101, 4 5/8 x 6
Old Tappan, N.Y., Massacre, Sept. 28, 1778   13560
   Leiby, Hackensack Valley, 168, 4 3/4 x 5 1/4, by Maj.
   John André

1780

Young's House (or Four Corners), Westchester County, N.Y.,   13565
   skirmish, Feb. 3, 1780
   Abbatt, Young's House, 22, 7 7/8 x 7 7/8
Position of British, Phillips, Westchester County, N.Y., July 1780 13570
   Putnam, Memoirs, 166, 5 1/8 x 4
Maj. Benjamin Tallmadge's map of his operations against Long   13575
   Island
   Mather, Refugees of '76, 237, 2 1/2 x 4
Fort St. George, Long Island, captured by Americans, Nov. 23,   13580
   1780
   Lossing, Field-Book of Rev., 2:628, 3/4 x 7/8
By Maj. Benjamin Tallmadge   13585
   Am. Heritage, Revolution, 265, 2 3/8 x 2
   Guthorn, Am. Maps, 6, 10 1/8 x 8 3/8
   Mather, Refugees of 1776, 232, 3 1/8 x 4

1781

Scene of Americans operations near New York City, 1781, by   13590
    Robert Erskine
    Clinton, Public Papers, 6:646, 7 1/8 x 6 1/4
    Mag. of Am. Hist., 4(Jan. 1880):23, 7 1/8 x 6 1/4,
    after Erskine
Expedition of Lt. Col. William Hull against Morrisania, Jan.   13595
    22-23, 1781
    Campbell, Gen. William Hull, 188, 7 3/8 x 5 1/8
American military works, Crow Hill, Westchester County, N.Y.,   13600
    prob. constructed Spring 1781
    N.Y. Hist. Soc., Quar. Bul., 8(July 1924):37, 4 1/8 x 7
    Westchester Co. Hist. Soc., Quar. Bul., 12(July 1936):76,
    4 x 6
American attempt on British posts at Kingsbridge, N.Y., July 3,   13605
    1781
    Mag. of Am. Hist., 4(Jan. 1880):2, 6 7/8 x 5 5/8
Position of American and French armies, Phillipsburg, N.Y.,   13610
    July 1781
    Avery, Hist. of U.S., 6:306, 6 5/8 x 7 3/4 col.
    Clinton, Public Papers, 7:108, 6 3/4 x 8
    Mag. of Am. Hist., 4(Jan. 1880):10, 6 1/2 x 8, French map;
    4(Apr. 1880):296, 5 1/2 x 6 3/4
Washington's and Rochambeau's headquarters, Greensburgh, N.Y.,   13615
    July 1781
    Westchester Co. Hist. Soc., Quar. Bul., 8(July 1932):103,
    4 x 6 1/2, French map
Rochambeau's headquarters, Odell House, Westchester County, N.Y.   13620
    July-Aug. 1781
    Mag. of Am. Hist., 4(Jan. 1880):48, 3 7/8 x 4 1/8
Location of French ovens near Rochambeau's headquarters, Odell   13625
    House
    Scharf, Westchester Co., 2:180, 1 1/2 x 2 1/2
French camps, by Louis-Alexandre Berthier
 Phillipsburg, N.Y., July 5, 1781   13630
    Maggs Bros., Berthier, 14, 7 x 4 7/8
 Suffern, N.Y., Aug. 25, 1781   13635
    Leiby, Hackensack Valley, 300, 4 1/2 x 3
March of the Queen's Rangers against Col. Gist's camp near   13640
    Babcock's, N.Y., Sept. 1781
    Simcoe, Military Jl., 88, 6 1/4 x 8, by Lt. Col. John Graves
    Simcoe

1783

Washington's line of march through New York City on Evacuation   13645
    Day, Nov. 25, 1783
    Riker, Evacuation Day, 11, 4 3/8 x 3 5/8

NORTHERN NEW YORK

Territory claimed or occupied by the Six Nations   14005
   Godcharles, Chronicles, 1:25, 3 7/8 x 4 3/4
   Williams, N.Y.'s Part in Hist., 6, 2 7/8 x 3 3/4
Limits of the Iroquois according to contemporary maps, 1755-1769   14010
   Channing, Hist. of U.S., 2:553, 6 1/2 x 4
Country of the Six Nations, 1771, by Guy Johnson   14015
   Am. Heritage, 20(Oct. 1969):32, 4 3/4 x 6 7/8 col.
   Am. Heritage, Revolution, 318, 4 3/4 x 6 7/8 col.
   Avery, Hist. of U.S., 5:292, 6 x 9
   Beauchamp, N.Y. Iroquois, 408, 7 x 7
   Cook, Golden Bk. of Am. Rev., 160, 4 1/2 x 6 5/8 col.
   Fite, Book of Old Maps, 228, 8 1/2 x 12 7/8
   Flexner, Mohawk Baronet, 20-21, 6 x 9, after Guy Johnson
   Howard, Thundergate, end lining paper, 6 1/4 x 11 1/4
   Hulbert, Indian Thoroughfares, 69, 5 1/8 x 7 7/8
   Johnson, Papers, 8:264, 8 x 11 7/8
   O'Callaghan, Doc. Hist. of N.Y., 4:660, 7 7/8 x 12
   Pearson, Schenectady Patent, 432, 12 1/8 x 8
   Pouchot, Memoir, 2:148, 7 7/8 x 11 5/8
   Rochester Hist. Soc. Pub., 3:78, 5 3/8 x 8
   Smith, Struggle for 14th Colony, 1:297, 3 1/2 x 6 3/8
   Winsor, America, 6:609, 5 x 7 7/8
   Winsor, Westward Movement, 18-19, 5 1/4 x 7 5/8
Six Nations in New York at beginning of the Revolution   14020
   Pag. Am., 2:60, 4 5/8 x 6 5/8
Mohawk Indian towns on or near Mohawk River, 1580-1779   14020
   Greene, Mohawk Valley, 1:140, 4 1/4 x 7
Settlements, forts, and Indian trails in region between Hudson 14030
  River and Lake Erie and Lake Ontario
   Matthews, Mark of Honour, 52, 9 x 24 1/2
Northern New York State, illustrating New York-New Hampshire   14035
    controversy over Vermont
   O'Callaghan, Doc. Hist. of N.Y., 4:330, 10 x 12 3/8
   See also 07065 and 07070

MILITARY OPERATIONS

New York frontiers during the Revolutionary War
 Northern frontier   14040
   Billington, W. Expansion, 2d ed., 178, 3 x 4 1/8
   Clarke, Am. Revolution, 44, 3 3/8 x 4
   Halsey, Old N.Y. Frontier, 1, 4 5/8 x 6 3/8
   Matthews, Mark of Honour, 27, 8 5/8 x 6, after C.J. Sauthier
   Reeder, Story of Rev. War, 172, 3 7/8 x 4 1/8
   Van Every, Co. of Heroes, 93, 4 x 4
 Northwestern frontier   14045
   Johnson, Orderly Book, clxii, after Claude Joseph Sauthier
   Ontario History, 52(Mar. 1960):5, 3 3/8 x 5
Area of operations   14050
   Alden, Hist. of Am. Rev., 318, 8 5/8 x 5 5/8; 435, 4 1/8
    x 5 5/8
   Bolton, Colonization, 494, 4 x 4 1/2
   Hilliard d'Auberteuil, Essais, 2:203, 7 7/8 x 14 7/8 col.

Jacobs, Tarnished Warrior, 8, 11 1/2 x 7 3/8
McDowell, Revolutionary War, 57, 5 1/8 x 2 5/8 col.
Reeder, Story of Rev. War, 28, 4 7/8 x 4 1/8
Reynolds, Albany Chronicles, 294, 7 1/8 x 4
Williams, N.Y.'s Part in Hist., 249, 4 1/2 x 3 3/4
Lake Champlain, Hudson River, and Mohawk River area   14055
  Dupuy, Compact Hist., 203, 5 7/8 x 4 1/2
  Nickerson, Turning Point, 54, 5 3/4 x 3 1/4
  Scott, Ft. Stanwix, 10, 3 5/8 x 6 1/4
  Sherwin, Arnold, 140, 5 7/8 x 4
Water route between Canada and Albany, N.Y.   14060
  Am. Heritage, Revolution, 122, 10 7/8 x 1 5/8
  Channing, Hist. of U.S., 3:259, 12 3/4 x 2
  Fortescue, British Army, 3:pl.III, 7 1/2 x 3 3/8 col.
  Hart, Am. Nation, 9:26, 6 1/2 x 2 5/8 col.
  Mather, Refugees of 1776, 69, 7 x 2 1/8, 7 x 2 1/8
  See also 46035
Lake Champlain   14065
  Allen, Naval Hist. of Am. Rev., 1:162, 6 x 3 5/8
  Beebe, Journal, frontis., 2 x 7 1/2, French map
  Coggins, Ships and Seamen, 55, 10 x 3 7/8
  Drake, Burgoyne's Invasion, 7, 4 5/8 x 2 1/2
1762, by William Brassier   14070
  Fite, Book of Old Maps, 212, 12 7/8 x 9 3/8
  Naval Docs. of Am. Rev., 1:365, 7 3/8 x 5 1/2
1776   14075
  Decker, Arnold, 62, 6 x 1 3/4, by William Faden
  See also 46050, 46055
Lake George, 1756, by Capt. Jackson   14080
  Fite, Book of Old Maps, 212, 6 1/2 x 3 1/4
  Naval Docs. of Am. Rev., 1:365, 3 3/4 x 1 7/8
St. Johns to Ticonderoga   14085
  Nickerson, Turning Point, 180, 6 1/8 x 3 1/4
Corlear Bay to Albany, 1774   14087
  Lucas Appendiculae, 114, 15 x 7 1/2, by Thomas Jefferys
Crown Point to Albany   14090
  Decker, Arnold, 246, 5 5/8 x 3 3/8
  See also 46045
Region of Ticonderoga and Crown Point   14095
  French, First Year, 143, 4 1/4 x 4
Ticonderoga to the Hudson   14100
  Moore, Diary of Am. Rev., 1:79, 7 1/8 x 4 1/4
  Nickerson, Turning Point, 164, 5 1/4 x 3
Fort Ticonderoga to Albany   14105
  Mitchell, Discipline and Bayonets, 42, 3 1/8 x 4 1/4
Fort Edward to Stillwater   14110
  Nickerson, Turning Point, 186, 5 3/8 x 3
Fort Miller to Albany   14115
  Nickerson, Turning Point, 292, 5 3/4 x 3 1/4
Freeman's Farm to New York   14120
  Nickerson, Turning Point, 334, 4 7/8 x 2 3/4
Albany to Oswego   14125
  Irving, Life of Washington, 3:183, 2 1/8 x 7 3/4
1775   14127
  Lucas, Appendiculae, 120, 9 1/2 x 14 3/4, by Capt. Holland,
    pub. by Thomas Jefferys

Mohawk River, Wood Creek, and Lake Oneida route to Oswego   14130
    Lake Ontario, 1778
    Winsor, Westward Movement, 501, 2 7/8 x 6 7/8, after Sauthier   14135
    and Ratzer, pub. by Le Rouge
Mohawk Valley   14140
    Boatner, Enc. of Am. Rev., 250, 4 1/8 x 6 3/4
    Johnson, Orderly Book, clxii
Road between Albany and Kinderhook, N.Y., 1779   14145
    Guthorn, Am. Maps, 16, 7 1/8 x 3 7/8, by Robert Erskine
War in Canada and Northern New York   14150
    Baldwin, Adult's History, 108, 4 7/8 x 5 5/8
    Roberts, Rabble in Arms, lining papers, 10 x 7 col.
Forts in the Mohawk Valley region, 1775-1783   14151
    Clarke, Bloody Mohawk, 201, 2 3/4 x 4 1/4
Fort Ontario, Oswego, N.Y., built 1763   14153
    Stotz, Defense in Wilderness, 186, 3 3/8 x 9
Fort Plain, N.Y.   14155
    Lossing, Field-Book of Rev., 1:261, 1 1/8 x 1 1/8

1775

Routes of Ethan Allen and Benedict Arnold to Fort Ticonderoga   14160
    and Fort St. John, May 1775
    Faulkner, Am. Political & Social Hist., 121, 4 5/8 x 2 1/2
    Miers, Yankee Doodle Dandy, 63, 4 1/4 x 3 5/8
    Rayback, Richards Atlas, 28, 15 7/8 x 9 3/8 col.
Fort Ticonderoga, N.Y., American capture of, May 10, 1775   14165
    Scribner's Mag., 23(1898):196, 1 1/4 x 1 1/4
    Vt. Hist., 24(July 1956):22, 4 x 4
Col. Henry Knox's route transporting cannon from Fort Ticonderoga
    to Cambridge, Mass., Dec. 1775 - Jan. 1776
    See 08250
Route of Col. Guy Johnson from Mohawk Valley via Oswego to   14166
    Montreal, 1775
    Clarke, Bloody Mohawk, 189, 4 7/8 x 4 3/8
    Vrooman, Clarissa Putman, front lining paper, 8 1/4 x 11

1776

Flight of Sir John Johnson from Mohawk Valley thru Adirondacks   14170
    to Montreal, May 1776
    Clarke, Bloody Mohawk, 189, 4 7/8 x 4 3/8
Crown Point and vicinity, 1776   14175
    Hadden, Journal, 33, 1 5/8 x 1 1/2
Fort Ticonderoga and outlying defenses, 1776
  By Capt. Ichabod Norton   14180
    Norton, Orderly Book, end, 10 x 7 1/2
  By Col. John Trumbull, Aug. 1776   14185
    Am. Heritage, Revolution, 237, 2 3/8 x 2
    Fiske, Am. Rev., 1:280, 3 3/4 x 6
    Gilchrist, Ft. Ticonderoga, 51, 4 1/4 x 5 1/4
    Meredith, Am. Wars, 55, 3 1/2 x 4 5/8
    Pag. Am., 6:134, 3 3/8 x 4 1/4
    Palmer, L. Champlain, 119, 3 1/2 x 3 3/8
    Pell, Ft. Ticonderoga, 83, 4 1/4 x 5 1/4

Ridpath, New Complete Hist., 6:2572, 5 x 6 3/4
Trumbull, Autobiography, 33, 8 3/8 x 11 3/8
Vt. Hist., 27(Apr. 1959):98, 4 1/2 x 6 7/8
Watson, Essex Co., 89, 3 3/8 x 3 1/2
Winsor, America, 6:352, 6 3/4 x 5
On powder horn, Dec. 17, 1776   14190
   Ft. Ticonderoga Museum, Bul., 9, no.4(Winter 1954):cover,
    4 1/8 x 3 7/8
Valcour Island, Battle of, Oct. 11, 1776.   See 50070
Lake Cahmplain, Second Battle of, Oct.13, 1776.   See 50080

1777

Military operations in Northern New York, 1777   14193
   Greene, Mohawk Valley, 1:787, 6 3/4 x 5
Maj. Gen. John Burgoyne's invasion of Northern New York,   14195
   June 17-Oct. 17, 1777
   Adams, Atlas, pl.72, 9 1/4 x 6 1/4
   Alden, Am. Republic, 147, 3 1/4 x 4 3/8
   Alden, Am. Revolution, 137, 4 1/2 x 7
   Am. Heritage Atlas, 98, 6 3/4 x 4 1/8 col.
   Am. Heritage, Revolution, 239, 3 x 1 7/8; 251, 5 1/2 x 3 1/4
    col.
   Anburey, With Burgoyne from Quebec, 20, 6 5/8 x 3 7/8
   Army, Am. Military Hist., 71, 5 1/4 x 4 1/2
   Avery, Hist. of U.S., 6:90, 6 1/2 x 4 3/4 col.
   Barck, Colonial Am., 2d ed., 598, 7 x 4 5/8
   Belcher, First Am. Civil War, 2:227, 6 1/4 x 4 1/8 col.
   Billias, Washington's Opponents, xxx, 4 5/8 x 7 1/8
   Bird, March to Saratoga, front, 8 1/4 x 10 1/2 col.; 30,
    6 3/8 x 3 1/2
   Boatner, Enc. of Am. Rev., 175, 5 1/2 x 4 1/8
   Botta, War of Ind., 1:432, 6 1/2 x 4 1/4
   Burgoyne, Orderly Book, frontis., 22 3/8 x 11 col.
   Carrington, Battles, 312, 7 3/4 x 4 3/4
   Caughey, Hist. of U.S., 107, 3 1/2 x 5 3/4
   Chitwood, Colonial Am., 557, 6 3/4 x 3 1/4
   Chron. Am., 12:180, 7 x 5 3/4 col.
   Clarke, Am. Revolution, end lining paper, 4 1/4 x 3 3/4 col.
   Commager, Spirit of '76, 1:540, 4 5/8 x 7 1/8
   De Puy, Ethan Allen, 360, 6 1/4 x 3 3/8
   Duncan, Medical Men, 245, 6 x 4 1/8; 249, 4 7/8 x 4 1/4
   Ellis, New York, 147, 7 1/2 x 6
   Ellis, Short Hist., 110, 5 1/4 x 4 3/8
   Ellis, Saratoga Campaign, 6, 6 3/4 x 3 7/8, 2 1/4 x 2 1/8
   Esposito, Am. Wars Atlas, 1:map 6a, 9 3/8 x 7 5/8 col.
   Esposito, Civil War Atlas, map 6a, 9 3/8 x 7 5/8 col.
   Falls, Great Mil. Battles, 95, 10 1/2 x 4 col.
   Faulkner, Am. Political & Social Hist., 133, 4 5/8 x 2 1/2
   Fisher, Struggle for Am. Ind., 2:63, 6 x 3 1/2
   Fiske, Am. Rev., 1:273, 6 x 3 3/4
   Ft. Ticonderoga Museum, Bul., 9, no.2(Winter 1953):114,
    6 1/2 x 4 1/2
   Fuller, Battles, 43, 5 1/8 x 4
   Fuller, Decisive Battles of W. World, 2:287, 6 1/8 x 4 3/4

Gewehr, United States, 75, 2 1/4 x 2 1/2
Greene, Revolutionary War, 96, 6 1/4 x 5 1/4 col.
Gurney, Pict. Hist. U.S. Army, 48, 5 1/4 x 4 3/8
Hadden, Journal, 90, 14 3/4 x 4 5/8
Harlow, United States, 111, 5 x 1 5/8
Hart, Am. Nation, 9:26, 6 1/2 x 2 5/8 col.
Higginbotham, Morgan, 31, 5 3/8 x 4 1/8
Hofstadter, Am. Republic, 184, 4 1/8 x 3 1/8
Hudleston, Burgoyne, 162, 6 1/4 x 4 1/2
Irving, Life of Washington, 3:93, 8 1/2 x 3 7/8
James, Br. Navy in Adversity, 59, 6 1/4 x 4
Kerr, Hist. Atlas of Canada, 33, 6 1/2 x 8 5/8 col.
Kraus, U.S. to 1865, 231, 4 1/2 x 7
Lancaster, Guns in the Forest, lining papers, 7 7/8 x 10 3/4,
   3 5/8 x 4 5/8, by Samuel Bryant
Lancaster, Guns of Burgoyne, frontis., 6 7/8 x 4 3/8
Lancaster, Ticonderoga, 166, 4 x 3 3/4 col.
Lodge, Story of Rev., 231, 5 1/2 x 2 3/8
McDowell, Revolutionary War, 117, 3 1/8 x 4 col.
MacMunn, Am. War, 177, 6 5/8 x 3 1/8
Mag. of Am. Hist., 1(May 1877):273, 8 1/2 x 5
Malone, Am. Origins, 166, 5 3/8 x 4 1/2
Md. Hist. Mag., 57(Dec. 1962):288, 7 1/2 x 2 3/8
Matloff, Am. Military History, 76, 5 1/4 x 4 3/8
Miers, Yankee Doodle Dandy, 116, 2 3/8 x 4
Mitchell, Battles Am. Rev., 99, 7 1/2 x 5 col.
Mitchell, Discipline and Bayonets, 42, 3 1/4 x 4 1/4
Mitchell, Twenty Battles, 205, 4 7/8 x 5 col.
Montross, Rag, Tag and Bobtail, 201, 6 1/4 x 4 1/4
Morison, Growth of Am. Republic, 5th ed., 210, 5 1/2 x 4 1/2
New York, Am. Rev. in N.Y., 163, 4 3/4 x 4
N.Y. State Hist. Assn., Quar. Jl., 8(Jan. 1927):32, 4 3/4 x 4
Pag. Am., 6:160, 6 3/8 x 3
Paullin, Atlas, pl.160B inset, 2 7/8 x 1 7/8 col.
Perkins, U.S. of Am., 159, 3 1/2 x 2 3/4
Rankin, Am. Rev., 123, 3 1/4 x 4
Rayback, Richards Atlas, 30, 16 x 10 1/8 col.
Scheer, Rebels and Redcoats, 252, 7 1/2 x 4 1/2
Scribner's Mag., 23(1898):552, 5 1/2 x 2 3/8
Snell, Saratoga, 2, 5 7/8 x 4 3/8
Steele, Am. Campaigns, 2:11, 6 x 3 1/2
Sullivan, Hist. of N.Y. State, 3:994, 4 3/4 x 4
Tharp, Baroness and General, lining papers, 7 3/4 x 5 1/8
Wallace, Appeal to Arms, 149, 4 1/8 x 6 3/8
Walworth, Saratoga, frontis., 8 1/2 x 5
By Thomas Kitchin   14200
   Fite, Book of Old Maps, 268, 12 x 9 3/8
   Gilchrist, Ft. Ticonderoga, 10, 5 x 3 3/4
By Medcalfe, engr. and pub. by William Faden, 1780   14205
   Burgoyne, State of Expedition, frontis., 10 5/8 x 10 7/8 col.
   Newton, Vermont Story, 58, 8 1/2 x 4 1/8
   Stanley, For Want of a Horse, frontis., 18 x 8 1/2
Fort Ticonderoga, N.Y., British siege of, June 30-July 6, 1777   14207
   Avery, Hist. of U.S., 6:93, 4 1/8 x 3 col.
   Bird, March to Saratoga, 30, 1 3/4 x 1 1/2

Boatner, Enc. of Am. Rev., 1105, 5 3/4 x 4 1/8
Drake, Burgoyne's Invasion, 41, 4 1/4 x 3
Dupuy, Compact Hist., 199, 5 3/4 x 4 1/2
Ellis, Saratoga Campaign, 6, 1 3/8 x 2 1/8
Ft. Ticonderoga Museum, Bul., 9, no.2(Winter 1953):143, 5 1/4 x
    6 1/2, no.4(Winter 1954):246, 5 1/4 x 6 1/2
Fuller, Decisive Battles of W. World, 2:287, 2 7/8 x 2
Greene, Revolutionary War, 102, 4 1/8 x 3 col.
Hadden, Journal, 83, 3 7/8 x 4 1/2
Hamilton, Ft. Ticonderoga, 185, 5 7/8 x 4 7/8
Holden, Hist. of Queensbury, 435, 3 1/4 x 3 1/2
Lancaster, Ticonderoga, 143, 4 3/8 x 5 3/8 col.
Lonergan, Ticonderoga, lining papers, 7 3/4 x 10 3/8, map
    prepared for Gen. Burgoyne
Nickerson, Turning Point, 130, 7 1/2 x 10 1/4, by Lt. Chas.
    Wintersmith; 142, 6 1/4 x 3 1/2
N.Y. Hist. Soc., Collections, 13:172, 9 3/8 x 7 3/4
Smith, St. Clair Papers, 1:76, 8 3/8 x 11 3/8
Smith, Struggle for 14th Colony, 2:468, 2 1/4 x 1 1/2
Van de Water, Lake Champlain and Lake George, 185, 4 1/4 x 5 1/4
Vt. Hist., 27(Apr. 1959):106, 6 3/8 x 4
Whitton, Am. War of Ind., 318, 6 x 3 1/2
Winsor, America, 6:353, 6 3/4 x 4 1/4
Maj. Gen. Arthur St. Clair's retreat from Fort Ticonderoga,   14210
    July 1777
    Drake, Burgoyne's Invasion, 49, 4 x 3
    Gewehr, United States, 75, 2 1/4 x 2 1/2
Burgoyne's advance from Fort Ticonderoga to Fort Edward, July   14215
    6-29, 1777
    Drake, Burgoyne's Invasion, 49, 4 x 3
Hubbardton, Vt., Battle of, July 7, 1777
    See 07105
Fort Anne, N.Y., skirmish near, July 8, 1777   14220
    Nickerson, Turning Point, 156, 3 1/4 x 3 1/4
Fort Edward, N.Y.   14225
    Drake, Burgoyne's Invasion, 63, 2 x 2 7/8
 Blockhouse   14230
    Am. Heritage, Revolution, 238, 3 x 2 1/8
Bennington, Vt., Battle of, Aug. 16, 1777
    See 07115
Col. John Brown's expedition against Fort Ticonderoga and Diamond 14235
    Island, N.Y., Sept. 1777
    Infantry Jl., 36(May 1930):476, 4 1/2 x 2 3/8
    N.Y. State Hist. Assn., Quar. Jl., 3(Jan. 1922):49, 7 x 4 3/4
    Sullivan, Hist. of N.Y. State, 3:936, 7 x 4 3/4
Saratoga campaign   14240
    Ellis, Saratoga Campaign, 6, 2 1/4 x 2 1/8
    Flick, Hist. of State of N.Y., 4:102, 6 1/8 x 4
    Hall, School History, 226, 7 3/4 x 6 1/4
    N.Y., Saratoga and Burgoyne, 43, 7 5/8 x 5
Burgoyne's camp, Sept. 17-19, 1777, by Lt. W.C. Wilkinson,   14245
    engr. and pub. by William Faden, 1780
    Burgoyne, State of Expedition, plan 4, 12 5/8 x 13 1/2 col.
    Clinton, Public Papers, 2:334, 8 1/2 x 9 1/8
    Sylvester, Saratoga Co., 60, 7 1/4 x 7 3/4 col.

Burgoyne's order of battle, Sept. 19, 1777   14250
   Drake, Burgoyne's Invasion, 103, 4 3/8 x 3
Freeman's Farm, N.Y., Battle of (also known as First Battle   14255
   of Saratoga), Sept. 19, 1777
   Alden, Am. Revolution, 146, 3 7/8 x 3 3/4
   Armstrong, 15 Battles, 57, 2 3/4 x 2 1/2
   Army, Am. Military Hist., 71, 2 1/4 x 2 1/4
   Avery, Hist. of U.S., 6:113, 5 3/8 x 3 3/4 col.
   Belcher, First Am. Civil War, 2:327, 5 1/2 x 4 col.
   Billias, Gen. John Glover, 145, 5 1/4 x 4 7/8
   Bird, March to Saratoga, 174, 3 1/2 x 6 1/4
   Boatner, Enc. of Am. Rev., 970, 4 x 4 7/8; 972, 3 7/8 x 4
   Brandow, Old Saratoga, end, 13 5/8 x 4
   Callahan, Daniel Morgan, 134, 5 1/8 x 3 7/8
   Campbell, Gen. Wm. Hull, 92, 7 3/8 x 5 1/8
   Carrington, Battles, 344, 7 5/8 x 4 5/8
   Commager, Spirit of '76, 1:578, 4 3/4 x 4 5/8
   Drake, Burgoyne's Invasion, 109, 4 x 3
   Duncan, Medical Men, 252, 5 3/4 x 4 1/8
   Dupuy, Brave Men and Great Captains, 44, 5 1/2 x 4 1/8
   Dupuy, Compact Hist., 247, 4 5/8 x 4 1/2
   Dupuy, Enc. of Mil. History, 715, 3 1/4 x 2 3/8
   Egleston, John Paterson, 88, 6 1/4 x 4
   Ellis, Saratoga Campaign, 77, 6 1/4 x 3 7/8
   Esposito, Am. Wars Atlas, 1:map 6b, 4 5/8 x 4 1/2 col.
   Esposito, Civil War Atlas, map 6b, 4 5/8 x 4 1/2 col.
   Fiske, Am. Rev., 1:334, 6 x 3 3/4 col.
   Ft. Ticonderoga Museum, Bul., 9, no.2(Winter 1953):99,
     6 x 3 3/8
   Fortescue, British Army, 3:pl.II, 3 3/4 x 4 col.
   Greene, Revolutionary War, 116, 5 3/8 x 3 3/4 col.
   Gurney, Pict. Hist. U.S. Army, 48, 2 1/4 x 2 1/4
   Higginbotham, Morgan, 66, 4 5/8 x 4 1/8
   Jacobs, Tarnished Warrior, 36, 4 1/4 x 3
   Matloff, Am. Military History, 76, 2 1/4 x 2 1/4
   Mitchell, Battles Am. Rev., 127, 7 1/2 x 5 col.
   Mitchell, Discipline and Bayonets, 88, 4 1/4 x 3 1/8
   Mitchell, Twenty Battles, 205, 3 3/4 x 2 1/2 col.
   Montross, Rag, Tag and Bobtail, 216, 5 5/8 x 4 1/4
   Neilsen, Burgoyne's Campaign, 283, 8 3/4 x 7
   N.Y. State Hist. Assn., Quar. Jl., 8(Jan. 1927):57,
     5 1/8 x 4 1/4
   Nickerson, Turning Point, 310, 5 7/8 x 3 3/8
   Pag. Am., 6:165, 3 7/8 x 3 1/2
   Pausch, Journal, 163, 5 1/8 x 4 1/8
   Reeder, Story of Rev. War, 119, 3 3/4 x 4 1/8
   Ridpath, New Complete Hist., 6:2638, 3 3/4 x 3 1/4
   Royal United Service Instn., Journal, 57(Dec. 1913):1642
     7 1/2 x 7 5/8
   Sherwin, Arnold, 196, 5 1/2 x 3 3/4
   Snell, Saratoga, 13, 6 1/2 x 4 3/8
   Steele, Am. Campaigns, 2:16, 6 x 3 7/8 col.
   Stone, Burgoyne, 9, 16 x 13 1/2; 45, 1 1/2 x 3 1/4
   Sullivan, Hist. of N.Y. State, 3:998, 5 1/8 x 4 1/8
   Tharp, Baroness and General, 241, 2 1/2 x 1

Wallace, Appeal to Arms, 160, 4 x 4
Walworth, Saratoga, end, 7 1/8 x 3 col.
Ward, Revolution, 2:509, 6 3/4 x 4 3/8
By Lt. W.C. Wilkinson, engr. and pub. by William Faden, 1780   14260
   Burgoyne, State of Expedition, plan 4, 12 5/8 x 13 1/2 col.,
    4 1/4 x 5 1/2 col.
   Clinton, Public Papers, 2:334, 8 1/2 x 9 1/8
   Sylvester, Saratoga Co., 60, 7 1/4 x 7 3/4 col., 2 1/4 x
    3 1/4 col.
Saratoga National Military Park   14265
   Snell, Saratoga, 16-17, 7 5/8 x 10
American and British camps and fortifications, Saratoga, Sept.   14267
   19 and Oct. 7, 1777
   Ellis, Saratoga Campaigns, 94, 3 7/8 x 4 7/8
Burgoyne's camp, Sept. 20-Oct. 7, 1777, by Lt. W.C. Wilkinson,   14270
   engr. and pub. by William Faden, 1780
   Burgoyne, State of Expedition, plan 5, 13 5/8 x 14 col.
   Clinton, Public Papers, 2:430, 8 1/4 x 8 1/2
   De Fonblanque, Burgoyne, 292, 10 3/4 x 11 1/4 col.
   Sylvester, Saratoga Co., 62, 7 x 7 3/8 col.
Bemis Heights, N.Y., Battle of (also known as Second Battle of   14275
   Freeman's Farm, Second Battle of Saratoga, Battle of
   Stillwater), Oct. 7, 1777
   Alden, Am. Revolution, 147, 3 7/8 x 3 3/4
   Am. Heritage Atlas, 108-109, 9 5/8 x 16 3/4 col.
   Armstrong, 15 Battles, 57, 2 3/4 x 2 1/2
   Army, Am. Military Hist., 71, 2 1/4 x 2 1/4
   Avery, Hist. of U.S., 6:122, 5 3/8 x 3 3/4 col.
   Belcher, First Am. Civil War, 2:327, 5 1/2 x 4 col.
   Billias, Gen. John Glover, 148, 5 1/4 x 5
   Bird, March to Saratoga, 224, 3 1/8 x 3 1/2, 3 1/8 x 3 1/2
   Boatner, Enc. of Am. Rev., 970, 4 x 4 7/8; 976, 4 1/8 x 4 1/8
   Brandow, Old Saratoga, end, 13 5/8 x 14
   Campbell, Gen. Wm. Hull, 101, 5 x 7 1/2
   Carrington, Battles, 350, 7 3/4 x 4 5/8
   Caughey, Hist. of U.S., 107, 1 7/8 x 2 3/8
   Coffin, Boys of '76, 234, 2 7/8 x 2 3/4
   Commager, Spirit of '76, 1:591, 4 3/4 x 4 5/8
   Decker, Arnold, 254, 5 7/8 x 4
   Duncan, Medical Men, 252, 5 3/4 x 4 1/8
   Dupuy, Brave Men and Great Captains, 44, 5 1/2 x 4 1/8
   Dupuy, Compact History, 257, 4 1/2 x 4 1/2
   Dupuy, Enc. of Mil. History, 715, 3 1/4 x 2 3/8
   Dupuy, Mil. Heritage of Am., 96, 5 x 4 1/2
   Egleston, John Paterson, 86, 6 1/4 x 4 1/4
   Ellis, Saratoga Campaign, 98, 6 1/4 x 4
   Esposito, Am. Wars Atlas, 1:map 6c, 4 3/4 x 4 1/2 col.
   Esposito, Civil War Atlas, map 6c, 4 3/4 x 4 1/2 col.
   Fiske, Am. Rev., 1:338, 6 x 3 3/4 col.
   Fortescue, British Army, 3:pl.II, 3 3/4 x 4 col.
   Fuller, Battles, 60, 5 1/8 x 4
   Fuller, Decisive Battles of W. World, 2:305, 5 1/4 x 4 1/4
   Gurney, Pict. Hist. U.S. ARmy, 48, 2 1/4 x 2 1/4;
    51, 6 3/8 x 4 1/2
   Greene, Revolutionary War, 122, 5 3/8 x 3 3/4 col.

Haiman, Kosciusko, 27, 5 x 4, by Thaddeus Kosciusko
Higginbotham, Morgan, 74, 4 5/8 x 4 1/8
Hudleston, Burgoyne, 198, 5 3/8 x 3 3/4
Jacobs, Tarnished Warrior, 36, 4 1/4 x 2 7/8
Lossing, Field-Book of Rev., 1:46, 3 3/8 x 2 7/8
McDowell, Revolutionary War, 118-119, 10 x 13 1/2 col.
Mitchell, Battles Am. Rev., 130, 7 1/2 x 5 col.
Mitchell, Discipline and Bayonets, 88, 4 1/4 x 3 1/8
Mitchell, Twenty Battles, 205, 3 3/4 x 2 1/2 col.
Montross, Rag, Tag and Bobtail, 222, 5 5/8 x 4 1/4
Morison, Hist. of Am. People, 213, 4 1/2 x 4 1/2
Neilsen, Burgoyne's Campaign, 283, 8 3/4 x 7
N.Y., Saratoga and Burgoyne, 42, 7 x 5
N.Y. State Hist. Assn., Quar. Jl., 8(Jan. 1927):57,
   5 1/8 x 4 1/4
Nickerson, Turning Point, 360, 6 x 3 3/8
Ostrander, Old Saratoga, end, 3 x 4 7/8
Pag. Am., 6:167, 3 7/8 x 3 1/2
Reeder, Story of Rev. War, 121, 3 3/8 x 4 1/8
Ridpath, New Complete Hist., 6:2638, 3 3/4 x 3 1/4
Royal United Service Instn., Journal, 57(Dec. 1913):1642,
   7 1/2 x 7 5/8
Sherwin, Arnold, 193, 5 1/2 x 3 3/4
Snell, Saratoga, 19, 4 5/8 x 4 3/8
Steele, Am. Campaigns, 2:17, 6 x 3 7/8 col.
Stone, Burgoyne, 9, 16 x 13 1/2
Sullivan, Hist. of N.Y. State, 3:998, 5 1/8 x 4 1/8
Tharp, Baroness and General, 241, 5 5/8 x 4 1/2
Wallace, Appeal to Arms, 161, 4 x 4
Walworth, Saratoga, end, 17 1/4 x 14 1/8 col.
Ward, Revolution, 2:527, 6 1/2 x 4 1/2
By Lt. W.C. Wilkinson, engr. and pub. by William Faden, 1780   14280
   Burgoyne, State of Expedition, plan 5, 13 5/8 x 14 col.
   Clinton, Public Papers, 2:430, 8 1/4 x 8 1/2
   De Fonblanque, Burgoyne, 292, 10 3/4 x 11 1/4 col.
   Sylvester, Saratoga Co., 62, 7 x 7 3/8 col.
Breymann Redoubt   14285
   Mil. Affairs, 1(Summer 1937):88, 4 1/4 x 4 3/8
Position of Burgoyne's army, Oct. 8, 1777   14290
   Walworth, Saratoga, end, 3 7/8 x 2 1/8 col.
By Lt. W.C. Wilkinson, engr. and pub. by William Faden, 1780   14295
   Burgoyne, State of Expedition, plan 6, 5 7/8 x 3 1/2 col.
   Sylvester, Saratoga Co., 62, 1 7/8 x 3 col.
British and American positions at Saratoga till Burgoyne's   14300
   surrender
   Belcher, First Am. Civil War, 2:321, 4 1/4 x 6 1/4 col.
   Brandow, Old Saratoga, end, 7 3/8 x 10 5/8
   Drake, Burgoyne's Invasion, 125, 5 x 3
   Nickerson, Turning Point, 378, 5 1/8 x 3
   Ridpath, New Complete Hist., 6:2638, 2 7/8 x 4 7/8
   Tharp, Baroness and General, 241, 5 5/8 x 4 1/2
   Walworth, Saratoga, end, 17 1/4 x 14 1/8 col.
By William Faden, 1780   14305
   Avery, Hist. of U.S., 6:124, 4 3/4 x 9 col.
   Burgoyne, State of Expedition, plan 7, 8 3/4 x 18 5/8 col.

Clinton, Public Papers, 2:446, 7 1/8 x 15 5/8
De Fonblanque, Burgoyne, 302, 7 5/8 x 16 1/2 col.
Stedman, Am. War, 1:352, 8 1/2 x 18 5/8
Sylvester, Saratoga Co., 66, 7 1/8 x 10 1/8 col.
Burgoyne's surrender, Saratoga, N.Y., Oct. 17, 1777   14310
  Avery, Hist. of U.S., 6:126, 2 1/4 x 2 col.
  Carrington, Battles, 354, 7 3/4 x 4 5/8
  Coffin, Boys of '76, 242, 4 1/2 x 2 3/8
  Drake, Burgoyne's Invasion, 135, 4 1/2 x 3
  Egleston, John Paterson, 89, 6 1/4 x 4 1/4
  Fiske, Am. Rev., 1:344, 6 x 3 3/4 col.
  Garner, Hist. of U.S., 2:454, 3 3/8 x 1 3/4
  Grant, British Battles, 2:150, 4 1/4 x 5 7/8
  Greene, Revolutionary War, 126, 2 1/4 x 2 col.
  Hudleston, Burgoyne, 212, 4 1/8 x 3 5/8
  Lossing, Field-Book of Rev., 1:77, 4 5/8 x 2 3/8
  Lowell, Hessians, 163, 4 1/2 x 2 3/8
  N.Y., Saratoga and Burgoyne, 37, 4 5/8 x 8
  Pag. Am., 6:167, 2 1/2 x 3 5/8
  Winsor, America, 6:362, 4 3/4 x 7 7/8, by Isaac A. Chapman
  See 08260 and 08270 for subsequent movements of Burgoyne's
    surrendered army
Lt. Col. Barry St. Leger's expedition to Mohawk Valley, July 26-   14315
  Aug. 22, 1777
  Adams, Atlas, pl.72, 9 1/4 x 6 1/4
  Alden, Am. Revolution, 137, 4 1/2 x 7
  Alden, Rise of Am. Republic, 147, 3 1/4 x 4 3/8
  Am. Heritage Atlas, 98, 6 3/4 x 4 1/8 col.
  Am. Heritage, Revolution, 241, 1 3/4 x 1 7/8; 251, 5 1/2 x
    3 1/4 col.
  Avery, Hist. of U.S., 6:102, 3 7/8 x 4 1/2 col.; 187, 4 1/2
    x 6 3/4 col.
  Barck, Colonial Am., 2d ed., 598, 7 x 4 5/8
  Billias, Washington's Opponents, xxx, 4 5/8 x 7 1/8
  Chitwood, Colonial Am., 557, 6 3/4 x 3 1/4
  Chron. Am., 12:180, 7 x 5 3/4 col.
  Clarke, Am. Revolution, end lining paper, 4 1/4 x 3 3/4 col.
  Commager, Spirit of '76, 1:540, 4 5/8 x 7 1/8
  Drake, Burgoyne's Invasion, 90, 1 3/8 x 3
  Ellis, New York, 147, 7 1/2 x 6
  Ellis, Short Hist., 110, 5 1/4 x 4 3/8
  Esposito, Am. Wars Atlas, 1:map 6a, 9 3/8 x 7 5/8 col.
  Esposito, Civil War Atlas, map 6a, 9 3/8 x 7 5/8 col.
  Faulkner, Am. Political & Social Hist., 133, 4 5/8 x 2 1/2
  Gewehr, United States, 75, 2 1/4 x 2 1/2
  Greene, Revolutionary War, 96, 6 1/4 x 5 1/4 col.
  Hofstadter, Am. Republic, 184, 4 1/8 x 3 1/8
  Hudleston, Burgoyne, 162, 6 1/4 x 6 1/2
  James, Br. Navy in Adversity, 59, 6 1/4 x 4
  Kraus, U.S. to 1865, 231, 4 1/2 x 7
  McDowell, Revolutionary War, 117, 3 1/8 x 4 col.
  Malone, Am. Origins, 166, 5 3/8 x 4 1/2
  Mitchell, Battles Am. Rev., 99, 7 1/2 x 5 col.
  Mitchell, Twenty Battles, 205, 4 7/8 x 5 col.
  Montross, Rag, Tag and Bobtail, 201, 6 1/4 x 4 1/4

Morison, Growth of Am. Republic, 5th ed., 210, 5 1/2 x 4 1/2
Morison, Hist. of Am. People, 213, 4 1/2 x 4 1/2
Nickerson, Turning Point, 194, 5 1/4 x 3
Pag. Am., 6:161, 2 1/8 x 3 1/2
Perkins, U.S. of Am., 159, 3 1/2 x 2 3/4
Rayback, Richards Atlas, 30, 16 x 10 1/8 col.
Scheer, Rebels and Redcoats, 252, 7 1/2 x 4 1/2
Snell, Saratoga, 2, 5 7/8 x 4 3/8
Wallace, Appeal to Arms, 149, 4 1/8 x 6 3/8
Ward, Revolution, 2:479, 7 1/8 x 4 1/8

St. Leger's line of march   14317
Durant, Hist. of Oneida Co., 93, 6 1/4 x 3
Stone, Joseph Brant, 1:219, 6 1/2 x 3 1/2

Fort Stanwix, N.Y. (also known as Fort Schuyler), siege,   14320
    Aug. 3-22, 1777
Avery, Hist. of U.S., 6:105, 4 3/8 x 6 3/4 col.; 107,
    2 7/8 x 3 1/8 col.
Clark, Bloody Mohawk, 223, 2 5/8 x 4 3/8
Coffin, Boys of '76, 172, 2 3/4 x 3 1/2
Greene, Revolutionary War, 126, 2 7/8 x 3 1/8 col.
Gurney, Pict. Hist. U.S. Army, 50, 7 1/8 x 4 1/2
Lossing, Field-Book of Rev., 1:249, 2 3/4 x 3 1/2
N.Y. State Hist. Assn., Proc., 14(1915):114, 4 1/4 x 7
Nickerson, Turning Point, 200, 3 7/8 x 3 1/4
Ridpath, New Complete Hist., 6:2586, 2 1/2 x 3 1/8

By Francois Louis Teissedre de Fleury, presented to   14325
    Col. Peter Gansevoort
Cookinham, Hist. of Oneida Co., 505, 4 1/4 x 7
Durant, Hist. of Oneida Co., 102, 4 1/4 x 6 1/2
Scott, Ft. Stanwix, 237, 2 3/4 x 3 1/2
Stone, Joseph Brant, 1:230, 9 1/2 x 15 1/8
Winsor, America, 6:355, 4 3/4 x 4 3/4

Fort Stanwix, 1763   14330
N.Y. Hist., 19(Oct. 1938):400, 4 x 5 3/8, pub. by
    Mary Ann Rocque

Fort Stanwix, Oct. 1777   14335
Willett, Narrative, 43, 4 1/8 x 4

Fort Stanwix superimposed on street plan of Rome, N.Y.   14340
Cookinham, Hist. of Oneida Co., 22, 4 x 5 1/4
Pouchot, Memoir, 206, 10 1/8 x 15 1/4
Scott, Ft. Stanwix, 160, 8 1/2 x 15 3/4

Brig. Gen. Nicholas Herkimer's march for relief of Fort   14345
    Stanwix, Aug. 3-6, 1777
Billias, Washington's Opponents, xxx, 4 5/8 x 7 1/8
Clarke, Bloody Mohawk, 215, 2 1/8 x 4 3/8
New York, Am. Rev. in N.Y., 150, 3 1/8 x 6 1/2
N.Y. State Hist. Assn., Proc., 14(1915):416, 3 1/8 x 6 1/2
Rayback, Richards Atlas, 30, 16 x 10 1/8 col.
Scott, Ft. Stanwix, 194, 3 1/8 x 6 1/2
Sullivan, Hist. of N.Y. State, 3:1008, 3 1/8 x 6 1/2

Oriskany, N.Y., Battle of, Aug. 6, 1777   14350
Clarke, Bloody Mohawk, 217, 2 7/8 x 4 3/8
Durant, Hist. of Oneida Co., 105, 4 3/8 x 6 3/8
Ellis, Saratoga Campaign, 60, 3 1/8 x 4
Johnson, Orderly Book, clxii

Nickerson, Turning Point, 204, 5 3/4 x 3 1/4
Ward, Revolution, 2:487, 7 1/8 x 4 1/4
Brig. Gen Benedict Arnold's march to Fort Stanwix, Aug.9-23, 1777   14353
  Am. Heritage Atlas, 98, 6 3/4 x 4 1/8 col.
  Billias, Washington's Opponents, xxx, 4 5/8 x 7 1/8
  Esposito, Am. Wars Atlas, 1:map 6a, 9 3/8 x 7 5/8 col.
  Esposito, Civil War Atlas, map 6a, 9 3/8 x 7 5/8 col.
  Gewehr, United States, 75, 2 1/4 x 2 1/2
  Kraus, U.S. to 1865, 231, 4 1/2 x 7
  McDowell, Revolutionary War, 117, 3 1/8 x 4 col.
  Munger, Hist. Atlas, 17, 16 1/8 x 20 1/8 col.
  Perkins, U.S. of Am., 159, 3 1/2 x 2 3/4
  Rayback, Richards Atlas, 30, 16 x 10 1/8 col.

FRONTIER WARFARE, *1778-1780*

Raids by Loyalists and Indians on New York frontier
  1778   14355
    Clarke, Bloody Mohawk, 234, 3 1/2 x 4 3/8; 249, 3 x 4 3/8;
     253, 3 x 4 3/8
    Pag. Am., 6:214, 4 1/8 x 8 1/2
    Swiggett, War out of Niagara, 144, 4 1/8 x 7 1/2
  1778-1779   14360
    Am. Heritage Atlas, 101, 4 3/4 x 7 1/2 col.
    Rayback, Richards Atlas, 30, 16 x 9 1/2 col.
  1778-1780   14365
    Avery, Hist. of U.S., 6:187, 4 1/2 x 6 3/4 col.
    Commager, Spirit of '76, 2:1004, 4 5/8 x 6 1/2
    Greene, Revolutionary War, 156, 4 1/2 x 6 3/4 col.
  1780-1781   14370
    Clarke, Bloody Mohawk, 274, 4 x 4 3/8
    Rayback, Richards Atlas, 32, 6 1/2 x 6 1/4 col.
Col. Sir John Johnson's raid on Johnstown, May 1780   14373
  Clarke, Bloody Mohawk, 274, 3 x 4 3/8
  Vrooman, Clarissa Putman, front lining paper, 8 1/4 x 11
Col. Sir John Johnson's raid, Oct. 1780   14375
  Clarke, Bloody Mohawk, 278, 3 x 4 3/8
  Greene, Mohawk Valley, 2:1011, 4 1/2 x 9
  MacWethy, Book of Names, 192, 3 3/4 x 6 1/8
  New York, Am. Rev. in N.Y., 175, 4 3/4 x 4
  Sigsby, Timothy Murphy, 24, 3 1/2 x 6 7/8
  Vrooman, Forts and Firesides, end lining paper, 9 1/2 x 15
Raid of Maj. John Ross and Capt. Walter Butler, Oct. 1781   14377
  Clarke, Bloody Mohawk, 292, 3 1/2 x 4 3/8
American Expeditions
Lt. McClellan's expedition from Fort Stanwix against British   14379
    forts at Oswego
  Clarke, Bloody Mohawk, 247, 3 x 4 3/8
Col. William Butler's march, Oct.-Nov. 1778   14380
  Avery, Hist. of U.S., 6:187, 4 1/2 x 6 3/4 col.
  Clarke, Bloody Mohawk, 247, 3 x 4 3/8
  Greene, Revolutionary War, 156, 4 1/2 x 6 3/4 col.
  Kraus, U.S. to 1865, 231, 4 1/2 x 7
  Pag. Am., 6:214, 4 1/8 x 8 1/2
  Rayback, Richards Atlas, 30, 16 x 9 1/2 col.

By Capt. William Gray   14385
  Egle, Journals, 289, 14 x 18 1/2
  N.Y., Sullivan Journals, 288, 15 3/4 x 19
Expedition of Maj. Gen. John Sullivan and Brig. Gen. James
    Clinton into country of the Six Nations, May-Nov. 1779
Map of country to be traversed by Sullivan's army, by   14390
    George Washington
  N.Y. State Hist. Assn., Quar. Jl., 10(July 1929):205,
    3 1/2 x 4
Routes of Sullivan and Clinton   14395
  Alden, Am. Revolution, 137, 4 1/2 x 7
  Am. Heritage, 20(Oct. 1969):32, 4 3/4 x 6 7/8 col.
  Am. Heritage Atlas, 101, 4 3/4 x 7 1/2 col.
  Am. Heritage, Revolution, 318, 4 3/4 x 6 7/8 col.
  Avery, Hist. of U.S., 6:187, 4 1/2 x 6 3/4 col.
  Billington, W. Expansion, 2d ed., 178, 3 x 4 1/8
  Chalmers, West to Setting Sun, lining papers, 10 5/8 x 7 3/4,
    10 5/8 x 7 3/4
  Clarke, Bloody Mohawk, 260, 2 7/8 x 4 3/8; 268, 2 3/4 x 4 3/8
  Commager, Spirit of '76, 1:540, 4 5/8 x 7 1/8; 2:1004,
    4 5/8 x 6 1/2
  Cook, Golden Bk. of Am. Rev., 160, 4 1/2 x 6 5/8 col.
  Ellis, New York, 147, 7 1/2 x 6
  Ellis, Short Hist., 110, 5 1/4 x 4 3/8
  Eyres, Sullivan Trail, 9, 5 x 5 1/8; 20-21, 7 x 10 1/2 col.
  Flick, Hist. of State of N.Y., 4:192, 4 1/4 x 7
  Geo. Rev., 30(July 1940):442, 5 1/2 x 3 3/4
  Gore, Journal, 11, 4 1/2 x 6 col.
  Greene, Revolutionary War, 156, 4 1/2 x 6 3/4 col.
  Guthorn, Am. Maps, 39, 10 1/8 x 8 3/8
  Mag. of Am. Hist., 3(Nov. 1879):655, 5 7/8 x 7 1/2
  Munger, Hist. Atlas, 17, 16 1/8 x 20 1/8 col.
  N.Y. Hist. Soc. Quar., 41(Jan. 1957):40-41, 8 7/8 x 11 1/2
  N.Y. State Hist. Assn., Quar. Jl., 9(Apr. 1928):217, 5 1/8
    x 4; 10(Oct. 1929):280, 4 1/4 x 7 col.
  N.Y., Sullivan-Clinton Campaign, 18, 4 1/4 x 7 col.
  N.Y., Sullivan Journals, end, 19 1/8 x 13 3/4, 16 1/2 x 8
    5/8, 16 x 13 3/8, 21 x 10 3/8, 12 7/8 x 4 3/4, by Lt.
    Benjamin Lodge
  Norton, Sullivan's Campaign, end, 7 1/4 x 6 3/8
  Pag. Am., 6:217, 4 3/8 x 6 7/8
  Rayback, Richards Atlas, 32, 15 1/2 x 20 col.
  Rogers, Journal, 23, 5 3/4 x 7 7/8
  Simms, Frontiersmen of N.Y., 2:272, 7 x 3 7/8
  Stevens, Exploring Penna., 181, 3 5/8 x 5 3/4
  Stone, Joseph Brant, 1:230, 9 1/2 x 15
  Utica Pub. Lib., Bibliography, end, 7 1/4 x 7
  Wallace, Appeal to Arms, 149, 4 1/8 x 6 3/8
  Weyburn, Following Conn. Trail, 22, 4 1/2 x 3 1/2
  Whittemore, Sullivan, 134, 4 x 4
Encampments, by Lt. Col. Adam Hubley, Jr.   14400
  Pa. Mag. Hist. and Biog., 33(Apr. 1909):133, 4 x 5; 135,
    4 x 5 1/2; 136, 4 3/4 x 4, 4 x 5; 137, 4 x 4 3/4; 138,
    5 1/4 x 4; 140, 4 7/8 x 4; 141, 4 x 5 5/8; 33(July 1909):
    282, 4 1/2 x 4; 284, 5 1/4 x 4; 285, 5 1/8 x 4; 288, 5 x
    4; 290, 4 x 5; 292, 4 7/8 x 4; 293, 4 x 4 7/8; 294, 4 x
    5 7/8, 5 3/8 x 4; 295, 4 3/4 x 4; 296, 4 x 4 1/2;

297, 4 x 4 1/4; 298, 5 3/8 x 3 7/8; 299, 4 x 4 7/8; 300,
4 x 4; 302, 4 1/4 x 4; 33(Oct. 1909):411, 4 x 4 1/2;
412, 3 1/2 x 5 5/8, 4 5/8 x 4, 4 1/8 x 4; 414, 3 1/2 x
5 3/8, 3 7/8 x 5 3/8, 4 x 5 1/2; 415, 4 3/8 x 4; 416,
4 x 4 3/4

Fort Sullivan and Sullivan's camp at Tioga (now Athens, Pa.)   14405
   Aug.-Oct. 1779
   Godcharles, Chronicles, 2:336, 3 x 1 3/4
   N.Y., Sullivan Journals, 580, 4 3/8 x 2 5/8
By Lt. Col. dam Hubley, Jr.   14410
   Guthorn, Am. Maps, 25, 5 1/2 x 4
   Murray, Old Tioga Pt., 151, 3 x 2 1/2, 3 1/8 x 3 3/8
   Pa. Mag. Hist. and Biog., 33(Apr. 1909):143, 4 x 5 1/8
By Lt. Nukerck   14411
   Murray, Order Book of Ft. Sullivan, front, 2 3/8 x 3 1/4
   Pa. Mag. Hist. and Biog., 33(Apr. 1909):143, 4 x 5 1/8
Encounter with Indians at Chemung, Aug. 13, 1779, by   14415
   Lt. Col. Adam Hubley, Jr.
   Pa. Mag. Hist. and Biog., 33(Apr. 1909):145, 6 x 4; 146,
    4 1/2 x 5 7/8
Newtown, N.Y., Battle of, Aug. 29, 1779
   Eyres, Sullivan Trail, 19, 3 x 3 1/8
   Hardenbergh, Journal, 44, 6 1/2 x 9
   Murray, Notes on Sullivan Exped., 23, 2 x 3 5/8; 24,
    14 1/2 x 18 1/4 col., 3 1/2 x 5
   N.Y. Hist. Soc. Quar., 41(Jan. 1957):57, 4 1/2 x 6 1/8
   N.Y., Sullivan-Clinton Campaign, 134, 4 1/2 x 4 1/2
   N.Y., Sullivan Journals, 127, 6 1/2 x 9 1/8
   Pag. Am., 6:217, 1 1/4 x 1 3/4
Groveland, N.Y., ambuscade, Sept. 13, 1779   14425
   Elwood, Episode, 5, 4 3/4 x 6 1/2
   Hardenbergh, Journal, 50, 6 1/2 x 9
   N.Y. State Hist. Assn., Quar. Jl., 11(Jan. 1930):136, 4 1/2
    x 6 1/4
   N.Y., Sullivan-Clinton Campaign, 150, 4 1/2 x 6 1/4
   N.Y., Sullivan Journals, 131, 6 1/2 x 9
   Rochester Hist. Soc. Pub., 3:92, 4 5/8 x 6 1/2
Col. Daniel Brodhead's expedition, Aug. 11-Sept. 14, 1779
   See 20060
Minisink, N.Y., Battle of, July 22, 1779   14427
   Johnston, Minisink Battle, 16, 4 1/2 x 7
Klock's Field, N.Y., Battle of, Oct. 19, 1780   14430
   Johnson, Orderly Book, clxii

1781

American order of battle, Saratoga, N.Y., Nov. 1, 1781   14435
   Duer, Stirling, 226, 7 x 4 5/8

1782-1783

Washington's journeys in Northern New York, 1782, 1783   14440
   Washington Atlas, pl.27, 15 1/2 x 11 col.
   Washington Bicentennial, 1:406, 2 3/4 x 1 1/4; 407,
    10 1/8 x 7 1/4

HUDSON RIVER HIGHLANDS

The Highlands, 1776-1783   15000
  Adams, Atlas, pl.73, 9 1/4 x 6 1/4
  Boatner, Enc. of Am. Rev., 531, 6 3/4 x 4 1/8
  Carrington, Battles, 512, 7 3/4 x 4 5/8
  Carrington, Washington, 255, 5 7/8 x 3 1/2
  Clinton, Public Papers, 2:392, 10 5/8 x 6 1/2
  Crane, West Point, 22, 4 3/4 x 3
  Cutter, Israel Putnam, 81, 5 3/4 x 3 1/2
  Duncan, Medical Men, 189, 6 x 4 1/4
  Dupuy, Brave Captains and Brave Men, 59, 3 1/2 x 4 1/8
  Egleston, John Paterson, 108, 6 3/8 x 4 1/4
  Freeman, Washington, abridgment, 361, 7 3/4 x 5 1/2
  Guthorn, Am. Maps, 27, 4 1/2 x 8 3/8, 4 1/2 x 8 3/8,
    by Thomas Machin
  Harte, River Obstructions, 7, 5 1/4 x 3
  Heusser, Forgotten Gen., 2, 6 x 4, by Robert Erskine
  Irving, Life of Washington, 4:108, 7 1/4 x 5
  Mather, Refugees of 1776, 62, 6 1/2 x 4
  Mil. Affairs, 19 (Summer 1955):84, 9 x 5 1/4
  Mitchell, Discipline and Bayonets, 124, 3 1/4 x 4 1/4
  Nickerson, Turning Point, 334, 2 5/8 x 2 3/4; 420,
    2 5/8 x 2 3/4
  Palmer, River and Rock, lining papers, 11 3/8 x 5 1/8 col.
  Ruttenber, Obstructions of Hudson, frontis., 10 1/2 x 6 1/2
  Spaulding, Geo. Clinton, 66, 7 1/2 x 4 5/8
  Steele, Am. Campaigns, 2:12, 6 x 3 3/4 col.
  Winsor, America, 6:455, 7 7/8 x 2 1/2; 456, 6 7/8 x 2 1/2
    after Maj. Jean de Villefranche; 465, 8 x 4 7/8; 556,
    5 3/4 x 5 5/8
Region west of the Hudson, Newburgh to Haverstraw Bay
  1778-1779, by Robert Erskine   15005
  Cox, Sterling Furnace, frontis., 15 1/4 x 13 1/8
  1779, drawn for Lord Stirling   15007
  Garner, Hist. of U.S., 2:433, 6 7/8 x 4 1/4
  Kinnaird, Geo. Washington, 164, 9 3/8 x 5 3/4
  Lossing, Life of Washington, 2:543, 9 x 5 5/8
  Lossing, Washington and Am. Republic, 2:543, 9 x 5 5/8
West side of the Hudson River, from West Point to Stony   15010
    Point, 1780
  Boynton, West Point, 45, 7 1/4 x 4 7/8, after Maj. Jean
    de Villefranche
The Hudson from West Point to Stony Point, Aug. 1781, by   15015
    Louis-Alexandre Berthier
  Chastellux, Travels, 1:72, 6 x 5 1/4
  Maggs Bros., Berthier, 9, 7 5/8 x 6
Haverstraw, N.Y., at time of the Revolution   15020
  Abbott, Crisis of Rev., 10, 7 5/8 x 4 3/4
New Winsor, N.Y., 1783   15025
  Mag. of Am. Hist., 10(Oct. 1883):363, 6 x 2 3/4
Vicinity of Peekskill, N.Y.   15030
  Patterson, Peekskill, 20, 5 x 4 1/2

AMERICAN DEFENSES IN THE HIGHLANDS

Obstacles to navigation
  Chain across Hudson River, near Fort Montgomery   15035
    Bucks Co. Hist. Soc., Papers, 7(1937):599, 2 x 4
    Harte, River Obstructions, 10, 1 3/4 x 4 1/2
    Kinnaird, Geo. Washington, 161, 1 5/8 x 4
    Palmer, River and Rock, 87, 5 3/4 x 6 7/8, prob. by
      Thomas Machin
    Ruttenber, Obstructions of Hudson, 64, 2 x 5
    Westchester Co. Hist. Soc., Quar. Bul., 12(Jan. 1936):8,
      4 x 6 1/4
    Winsor, America, 6:324, 1 7/8 x 4 3/4
  Chevaux-de-frise, battery, and chains to obstruct the Hudson   15040
    between Breakneck Mt. and Butter Hill
    N.Y. Calendar of Hist. MSS., 2:616, 4 7/8 x 7 3/4
  Great boom and chain at West Point, 1778   15045
    Boynton, West Point, 70, 2 1/2 x 4 5/8
    Crane, West Point, 22, 1 3/4 x 4 1/8
    Reeder, Story of Rev. War, 164, 2 x 4 1/8
Fortifications
  Plans for fortifications at West Point and Martelaer's Rock   15050
    Sept. 14, 1775, by Bernard Romans
    Force, Am. Archives, 4th series, 3:735, 10 x 4 1/8, 9 1/2 x
      6 5/8, 3 3/4 x 4 1/8, 5 3/4 x 4 1/8, 5 1/4 x 4 7/8
    Palmer, River and Rock, 29, 8 7/8 x 6 1/2; 35, 8 1/4 x 6 3/8
  Constitution Island
    Fort Constitution   15055
      Boynton, West Point, 27, 7 1/4 x 4 7/8
      Lossing, Field-Book of Rev., 1:703, 1 x 1 1/8; 1:704,
        1 1/8 x 1
      Martelaer's Rock Assn., 3rd Annual Rept., 20, 4 3/8 x 4 3/8
      N.Y. Hist. Soc., Quar. Bul., 7(Jan. 1924):109, 4 1/2 x 6 3/8
      Winsor, America, 6:325, 3 1/8 x 4 1/2
    Outlying fortifications   15060
      Martelaer's Rock Assn., 3rd Annual Rept., 22, 4 3/4 x 4 1/4;
        25, 4 1/4 x 4 1/8; 30, 4 1/4 x 2 3/4; 32, 1 5/8 x 3 3/4
  Fort Clinton
    See 15145, 15150
  Fort Montgomery, 1776   15065
    Guthorn, Am. Maps, 33, 9 1/4 x 7, by William Smith
    N.Y. Calendar of Hist. MSS., 1:474, 10 x 7 5/8 col., by
      Col. Thomas Palmer
    See also 15145, 15150
  Stony Point, 1779
    By British engineers, pub. by William Faden   15070
    Johnston, Storming of Stony Pt., 173, 3 5/8 x 4 7/8
    By Col. Rufus Putnam   15075
    Johnston, Storming of Stony Pt., 222, 3 1/2 x 3
    Sklarsky, Boldest Venture, 77, 3 1/2 x 3
    See also 15165, 15170
  Stony Point and Verplanck's Point   15080
    Ridpath, New Complete Hist., 6:2836, 2 3/4 x 5
  July 3, 1779, annotated by George Washington   15085
    Washington Atlas, pl.17, 8 5/8 x 10 1/2
    Washington Bicentennial, 1:396, 5 5/8 x 6 3/4

Verplanck's Point, 1779   15090
    Johnston, Storming of Stony Pt., 223, 2 5/8 x 3 1/2, by
      Col. Rufus Putnam, July 1779
    Westchester Co. Hist. Soc., Quar. Bul., 8(Oct. 1932):147,
      5 1/4 x 4
    Winsor, America, 6:557, 2 5/8 x 2 1/2
West Point   15095
    Am. Heritage, 10(Dec. 1958):15, 3 x 3
    Martelaer's Rock Assn., 3rd Annual Rept., end, 12 3/8 x 15
    Palmer, River and Rock, lining papers, 11 3/8 x 10 1/4 col.
Fort Arnold, at West Point, Feb. or Mar. 1778   15097
    Palmer, River and Rock, 141, 8 3/4 x 6 5/8
1779, from Moses Greenleaf Papers, Mass. Historical Soc.   15100
    Winsor, America, 6:451, 5 5/8 x 4 3/4
1779, by Thaddeus Kosciusko   15105
    Boynton, Guide to W. Point, 10, 4 3/4 x 6 7/8
    Fish, Washington in Highlands, 6, 4 x 6
    Haiman, Kosciusko, 45, 5 7/8 x 5; 75, 4 1/8 x 5 1/8, 2 1/4
      x 5 1/8
    Palmer, River and Rock, 173, 2 1/2 x 6 5/8, 4 5/8 x 6 5/8,
      2 1/2 x 6 5/8
1779 and 1850   15110
    Lossing, Field-Book of Rev., 1:705, 3 3/4 x 3 3/8
1780, French map   15115
    Am. Heritage, Revolution, 268, 3 1/8 x 2 1/4
    Barbe-Marbois, Complot d'Arnold, 1:frontis.
    Centennial of West Point, 1:204, 5 1/2 x 4
    Chidsey, Yorktown, 18, 6 3/4 x 4 3/4
    Cook, Golden Bk. of Am. Rev., 128, 4 3/8 x 3 1/8
    Crane, West Point, 29, 4 5/8 x 3 1/4
    Cunliffe, Washington, 95, 3 1/2 x 2 1/2 col.
    Dupuy, Where They Have Trod, 65, 6 1/8 x 4 1/4
    Essex Inst., Hist. Collections, 90(Jan. 1954):96, 5 1/2 x 4
    Mil. Engineer, 41(Sept.-Oct. 1949):362, 4 3/4 x 3 1/4
    Pag. Am., 6:284, 4 1/4 x 3
    Winsor, America, 6:459, 6 x 4 1/4
1780, by Maj. Jean de Villefranche   15120
    Avery, Hist. of U.S., 6:247, 4 1/2 x 6 1/8
    Boynton, West Point, 79, 7 1/4 x 4 7/8; 87, 11 5/8 x 15
    Crane, West Point, 21, 5 3/8 x 7 1/8
    Harte, River Obstructions, 14, 2 7/8 x 4 1/2
    Winsor, America, 6:462, 5 x 7 1/2
1781   15125
    Mag. of Am. Hist., 4(Apr. 1880):304, 5 1/2 x 6 1/2, French
      map
    Palmer, River and Rock, 305, 5 5/8 x 8 1/8, by Louis-Alexandre
      Berthier
1782   15128
    Palmer, River and Rock, 306, 6 x 7 1/2; 307, 6 x 7 1/2,
      by Capt. Ephraim Sergent
Encampments
    Continental Village, Putnam Co., N.Y., established in 1777,   15130
      burned by British Oct. 9, 1777
    Calver, Hist. with Pick and Shovel, 38, 6 1/4 x 4 1/4

Camp Robinson's Farm, Putnam Co., N.Y., occupied by   15135
    Connecticut troops, 1778, 1779-1780
    Calver, Hist. with Pick and Shovel, 38, 6 1/4 x 4 1/4

MILITARY OPERATIONS

1777

Sir Henry Clinton's expedition to the Highlands, Oct. 3-23, 1777   15140
    Am. Heritage Atlas, 98, 6 3/4 x 4 1/8 col.
    Billias, Washington's Opponents, xxviii, 7 1/2 x 4 5/8
    Ellis, New York, 147, 7 1/2 x 6
    Ellis, Short Hist., 110, 5 1/4 x 4 3/8
    Hudleston, Burgoyne, 162, 6 1/4 x 4 1/2
    James, Br. Navy in Adversity, 62, 6 1/4 x 4
    Mitchell, Twenty Battles, 205, 4 7/8 x 5 col.
    Rayback, Richards Atlas, 30, 16 x 10 1/8 col.
    Willcox, Portrait, 103, 7 3/4 x 4 3/4
Fort Clinton and Fort Montgomery, N.Y., capture of by British,   15145
    Oct. 6, 1777
    André, Journal, 1:108, 9 x 17 1/4 col., by Maj. John André
    Avery, Hist. of U.S., 6:117, 4 1/8 x 2 1/2 col.
    Carrington, Battles, 362, 7 5/8 x 4 3/4
    Carrington, Washington, 179, 5 5/8 x 3 1/2
    Dupuy, Compact. Hist., 252, 5 3/8 x 4 1/2
    Greene, Revolutionary War, 96, 6 1/4 x 5 1/4 col.; 126,
        4 1/8 x 2 1/2 col.
    Harper's Mag., 52(Apr. 1876): 648, 5 1/8 x 3 3/8
    Leake, John Lamb, 176, 8 1/2 x 5
    Lossing, Field-Book of Rev., 1:734, 3 1/2 x 3 3/4
    Nickerson, Turning Point, 344, 4 7/8 x 3 1/2
    Pag. Am., 6:166, 2 x 2 3/4
    Palmer, River and Rock, 108, 9 x 7 1/2 col.; 114, 7 5/8
        x 6 5/8 col.
    Popp, Hessian Soldier, 6, 4 7/8 x 6 1/2
    Ridpath, New Complete Hist., 6:2654, 3 5/8 x 2 1/8
    Scenic and Historic Am., 2(Mar. 1930):15, 2 1/8 x 2
    Sparks, Washington's Writings, 5:92, 7 x 4 1/4
    Ward, Revolution, 2:517, 5 1/2 x 4 1/2
    Winsor, America, 6:324, 4 1/4 x 4 3/4; 365, 5 1/8 x 3
  By Lt. John Hills, pub. by William Faden   15150
    Am. Heritage Atlas, 98, 4 1/8 x 3
    Avery, Hist. of U.S., 6:116, 9 5/8 x 7 1/2 col.
    Clinton, Public Papers, 2:380, 16 x 12 3/8
    Irving, Life of Washington, 3:244, 8 3/8 x 6 3/4
    N.Y. Calendar of Hist. MSS., 2:298, 13 x 10 1/8 col.
    Stedman, Am. War, 1:363, 26 1/4 x 20 1/4
    Winsor, America, 6:363, 7 1/8 x 4 7/8
Maj. Gen. John Vaughan's advance to Kingston, N.Y. (burned by   15155
    British Oct. 16, 1777)
    Am. Heritage Atlas, 98, 6 3/4 x 4 1/8 col.
    Billias, Washington's Opponents, xxviii, 7 1/2 x 4 5/8

1779

Movements of Brig. Gen. Anthony Wayne and Sir Henry Clinton   15160
      prior to taking of Stony Point, July 1779
   Preston, Gentleman Rebel, 175, 6 1/2 x 4 3/8
   Rayback, Richards Atlas, 32, 15 1/2 x 20 col.
Stony Point, N.Y., capture by Wayne, July 16, 1779   15165
   Am. Scenic Hist. Pres. Soc., Annual Rpt, 1900, 74, 11 5/8 x
      13 1/2; 84, 4 3/8 x 4, 4 x 4 1/2
   Avery, Hist. of U.S., 6:236, 3 5/8 x 3 3/4 col.
   Boatner, Enc. of Am. Rev., 1064, 4 1/4 x 4 1/4
   Campbell, Gen. Wm. Hull, 159, 7 1/2 x 5
   Coffin, Boys of '76, 267, 2 5/8 x 4 3/4
   Dupuy, Brave Men and Great Captains, 59, 2 5/8 x 2 7/8
   Dupuy, Compact Hist., 334, 3 3/4 x 4 1/2
   Freeman, Washington, 5:117, 5 x 4 1/2
   Gérard, Despatches, 803, 13 5/8 x 9 3/8, 5 7/8 x 4 3/8
   Greene, Revolutionary War, 158, 3 5/8 x 3 3/4 col.
   Guizot, Atlas, pl.17, 7 x 4 1/8
   Hall, Stony Point, 32, 6 x 6 1/4
   Johnston, Storming of Stony Pt., 58, 10 x 6 1/2 col.; 97,
      3 3/4 x 5 1/2, from Ezra Stiles' diary
   Lossing, Field-Book of Rev., 1:743, 2 5/8 x 4 3/4
   Mitchell, Discipline and Bayonets, 124, 3 x 4 1/4
   Montross, Rag, Tag and Bobtail, 322, 5 1/2 x 4 1/4
   Pag. Am., 6:212, 2 3/8 x 4 1/8
   Palmer, River and Rock, 198, 8 3/8 x 6 5/8 col., after
      Capt. Ephraim Sergent
   Pratt, 11 Generals, 46, 3 3/4 x 4
   Revue Historique de l'Armée, 26, 3 1/4 x 5 1/8
   Scenic and Historic Am., 1(Mar. 1929):4, 7 1/2 x 4 7/8;
      10, 2 7/8 x 4 3/4; 2(Dec. 1930):35, 2 7/8 x 4 3/4;
      3(July 1934):9, 7 1/2 x 4 7/8; 13, 2 7/8 x 4 3/4
   Seelye, Story of Washington, 257, 2 5/8 x 2 1/4
   Sparks, Washington's Writings, 6:304, 7 x 4 1/8
   Spears, Anthony Wayne, 160, 6 x 6 1/4
   Stiles, Diary, 2:363, 2 1/2 x 3 7/8, by Ezra Stiles
   Vestal, Washington, 41, 1 3/4 x 1 3/4
   Ward, Del. Continentals, 294, 3 3/8 x 4 1/8
   Ward, Revolution, 2:601, 3 3/4 x 4 1/2
   Washington Bicentennial, 1:118, 1 3/4 x 2
   Winsor, America, 6:557, 2 1/2 x 2
By Lt. John Hills, pub. by William Faden   15170
   Clinton, Public Papers, 5:152, 8 1/2 x 12
   Dawson, Stony Point, 39, 9 5/8 x 13 5/8 col.
   N.Y. Calendar of Hist. MSS., 2:347, 9 3/4 x 14 col.
   Winsor, America, 6:558, 4 3/4 x 3 3/8

1780

Locale of Maj. Gen. Benedict Arnold's treason and the capture   15175
      of Maj. John André, Sept. 1780
   Abbatt, Crisis of Rev., 6, 5 1/4 x 10 3/4; 10, 7 5/8 x 4 3/4
      13, 6 7/8 x 6
   Avery, Hist. of U.S., 6:251, 5 7/8 x 5
   Boynton, West Point, 104, 3 1/8 x 2 1/4

Carrington, Battles, 512, 7 3/4 x 4 5/8
Coffin, Boys of '76, 317, 3 1/8 x 2 1/4
Commager, Spirit of '76, 2:747, 7 1/2 x 4 5/8
Fiske, Am. Rev., 2:225, 3 3/4 x 6
Greene, Revolutionary War, 166, 5 7/8 x 5
Lengyel, I, Arnold, lining papers, 10 7/8 x 8 1/4
Lossing, Field-Book of Rev., 1:715, 3 1/4 x 2 3/8
Mag. of Am. Hist., 3(Dec. 1879):756, 8 1/8 x 5 1/4,
   by Robert Erskine
Pleasants, John André, 42, 2 3/8 x 1 5/8
Sargent, Life of André, end, 14 1/8 x 14
Scenic and Historic Am., 1(Dec. 1929):7, 4 3/4 x 4 3/4
Seelye, Story of Washington, 275, 4 7/8 x 4
Van Doren, Secretary History, 282, 8 x 5 1/4, after Robert
   Erskine
Wallace, Traitorous Hero, 250, 6 7/8 x 4 1/8
Site of André's execution, Tappan, N.Y., Oct. 2, 1780   15180
   Abbatt, Crisis of Rev., 72, 10 1/2 x 6 7/8

1781-1783

Positions occupied by American and French armies along the Hudson, 15185
   1781-1783
   Duncan, Medical Men, 189, 6 x 4 1/4
   Guizot, Atlas, pl.18, 7 x 4 1/4
   Irving, Life of Washington, 4:108, 7 1/4 x 5
   Sparks, Washington's Writings, 7:216, 7 x 4 1/2
   Wilson, Mem. Hist. of N.Y., 2:543, 4 3/4 x 3 1/4
Location of quarters of St. Clair, Gates, and Lafayette,   15190
   Washington Square, N.Y., 1782
   Lossing, Field-Book of Am. Rev., 1:683, 3 3/4 x 1 7/8
Winter cantonment of American army, near New Windsor, N.Y., 1783   15195
   by Simeon DeWitt
   Guthorn, Am. Maps, 15, 6 1/4 x 8 1/2
   Mag. of Am. Hist., 10(Oct. 1883):365, 4 3/4 x 6 5/8
   N.Y. State Hist. Assn., Quar. Jl., 12(Apr. 1931):136,
      4 1/4 x 6
   Ruttenber, New Windsor, 83, 4 3/8 x 6 1/8
Localities associated with George Washington, Newburgh and   15200
   New Windsor, N.Y.
   Fish, Washington in Highlands, 10, 4 1/2 x 4 7/8
   Washington Atlas, pl.44, 4 1/2 x 4 7/8

NEW JERSEY

New Jersey at time of the Revolution   16005
   Boatner, Enc. of Am. Rev., front lining paper, 7 3/4 x 4 3/4
   Bryant, Popular Hist. of U.S., 3:602, 3 7/8 x 4 1/8
   Gordon, Hist. of U.S.A., 2:524, pl.IV, 12 1/8 x 9,
      engr. by T. Conder
   Irving, Life of Washington, 2:430, 6 x 4, after Robert Erskine
   Kinnaird, George Washington, 110, 6 3/4 x 5 1/4
   Lundin, Cockpit, 6, 8 1/2 x 4 3/4
   Steele, Am. Campaigns, 6 x 3 7/8

1777
  By Robert Erskine, annotated by George Washington   16010
    Washington Atlas, pl.14, 15 1/4 x 9 7/8
    Washington Bicentennial, 1:393, 10 1/8 x 7 1/4
  By Bernard Ratzer, engr. and pub. by William Faden   16015
    Naval Docs. of Am. Rev., 2:403, 7 3/8 x 5 1/2
1778
  By William Faden
    Lunny, Early Maps of N. Am., 38, 7 5/8 x 5 1/2
New Jersey today, with selected historic sites   16025
  Bill, N.J. and Rev. War, end, 10 3/8 x 6 7/8 col.
New Jersey coast, Sand Hook to Cape May, 1780   16030
  N.Y. Hist. Soc. Quar., 41(July 1957):280, 5 3/4 x 4 1/4,
    from Atlantic Neptune chart
Northern New Jersey
  1776   16035
    Ward, Revolution, 1:279, 7 1/8 x 4 1/8
  1780   16040
    Richardson, Washington and Powles Hook, 14, 7 x 5
New Jersey counties at time of the Revolution   16045
  Bill, N.J. and Rev. War, front, 10 3/8 x 6 7/8 col.
  Brown, King's Friends, 111, 5 7/8 x 4

TOWNS AND LOCALITIES

New Jersey west of the Hudson, from Closter to Paulus Hook   16050
  Mag. of Am. Hist., 5(Sept. 1880):171, 7 x 5 1/2
  Winfield, Block-House, end, 6 5/8 x 8 1/4
Maneuver area between Tappan, N.Y., and Elizabeth, N.J.,   16055
    1777-1781
  Freeman, Washington, 5:front, 8 5/8 x 11 3/4 col.
Closter, N.J., and Vicinity, 1779   16060
  Leiby, Hackensack Valley, 208, 5 x 4 1/4, by I. Hills
Hackensack Valley, N.J., 1776   16065
  Leiby, Hackensack Valley, front, 11 3/4 x 8 3/4
Passaic Valley in Revolutionary times   16070
  Myers, Story of N.J., 1:120-121, 9 x 7 1/2
Jersey City, N.J., at time of the Revolution   16075
  Richardson, Washington, front, 8 3/4 x 5 1/2
Elizabeth Town, N.J., 1775-1783   16080
  Elizabeth, Rev. Hist., 20-21, 7 7/8 x 6 1/2
  Kelley, Historic Elizabeth, pl.I, 5 3/4 x 4
Chatham, Morris County, N.J., at time of the Revolution   16085
  Hist. of Morris Co., 1:289, 5 3/8 x 4 3/4
Morristown, N.J.   16090
  Heusser, Washington's Map Maker, 109, 5 x 7 1/8, by
    Robert Erskine
  1777   16095
    Hist. of Morris Co., 1:260, 3 5/8 x 5 7/8
  Vicinity of Morristown, N.J., 1778-1780   16100
    Harper's Mag., 18(Feb. 1959):291, 4 1/2 x 4 1/2, after
      Robert Erskine
Monmouth County, N.J., 1775-1781   16105
  Smith, Monmouth, front, 9 5/8 x 12 1/2
  Smith, Sandy Hook, front, 9 5/8 x 12 1/2

Trenton-Princeton, N.J., area   16110
   Vestal, Washington, 24, 3 x 4
   Washington, Bicentennial, 1:113, 3 x 4
Trenton, N.J., 1776   16115
   Butcher, Trenton, 16, 3 5/8 x 3
   Stryker, Trenton, 93, 6 3/8 x 3 3/4
   Trenton Hist. Soc., Hist. of Trenton, 1:105, 4 x 6 1/4

ROADS

Major roads in New Jersey at time of the Revolution   16120
   Bill, N.J. and Rev. War, front, 10 3/8 x 6 7/8
New Jersey roads, by Robert Erskine
 From Brunswick to Bound Brook   16125
   Heusser, Washington's Map Maker, 108, 7 3/4 x 1C 1/8
 "From Duyckinks Mill to the South Branch Garison's, Somerset   16130
   Bound Brook, from South Branch to Reddington Brockaws &
   from near headquarters to So. Branch"
   Heusser, Washington's Map Maker, 108, 6 3/8 x 10 1/4
 From Ringwood, N.J., to Slott's on the New Windsor Road   16135
   Heusser, Washington's Map Maker, 108, 10 1/4 x 7 3/8
 From the Wheat Sheaf through Woodbridge to Amboy, from   16140
   Amboy towards Brunswick
   Heusser, Washington's Map Maker, 108, 7 3/4 x 9 1/8
 In Chatham and vicinity   16142
   Vanderpoel, Hist. of Chatham, N.J., 277, 6 x 4 1/4;
   297, 6 x 4 1/2
 In vicinity of Morristown, Springfield, and Elizabeth   16145
   Freeman, Washington, 5:169, 5 3/8 x 7 5/8

MILITARY OPERATIONS

Area of American and British operations in New Jersey, 1776-1781   16150
   Adams, Atlas, pl.71, 9 1/4 x 6 1/4
   Alden, Gen. Chas. Lee, 206, 3 1/8 x 4 1/8
   Bill, N.J. and Rev. War, 10, 3 3/4 x 6 1/2
   Carrington, Battles, 302, 7 3/4 x 4 3/4
   Dupuy, Compact Hist., 160, 5 1/8 x 4 1/2
   Freeman, Washington, 4:259, 6 x 4 1/4; 277, 6 3/8 x 5
   Freeman, Washington, abridgment, 321, 7 3/4 x 5 1/2
   Frothingham, Washington, 158, 4 5/8 x 4 5/8
   Lancaster, Trumpet to Arms, end lining paper, 7 5/8 x 5 1/8 col.
   Frothingham, Washington, 158, 4 5/8 x 4 5/8
   Leiby, Hackensack Valley, 150, 10 1/2 x 8
   Lowell, Hessians, 85, 2 5/8 x 3 3/8
   Miller, Triumph of Freedom, 142, 7 x 4 1/4
   Mitchell, Discipline and Bayonets, 61, 3 1/2 x 4 1/4
   Ridpath, New Complete Hist., 6:2528, 4 7/8 x 6 3/8
   Scheer, Rebels and Redcoats, 205, 7 1/2 x 4 1/2
   Soc. for Army Hist. Res., Journal, 6(Oct. 1927):196, 8 x 7 1/4
   Ward, Revolution, 1:279, 7 1/8 x 4 1/8
   Wildes, Anthony Wayne, 161, 6 5/8 x 4
   Willcox, Portrait, 103, 7 3/4 x 4 3/4
Washington's headquarters in New Jersey   16155
   Washington Atlas, pl.28, 15 1/2 x 11 col.
   Washington Bicentennial, 1:408, 10 1/8 x 7 1/8

Battlegrounds of the Revolution in Essex, Middlesex, and   16160
   Somerset Counties, N.J., showing only highways then
   existing
   Hoffman, Rev. Scene, 194-195, 7 7/8 x 11
Military movements in New Jersey, 1776-1778   16165
   Lovell, Israel Angell, 126, 7 x 4 3/8
   Pleasants, John André, 15, 6 1/4 x 4 1/4
   Sparks, Washington's Writings, 4:266, 7 x 4 1/4

1776

American positions behind the Hackensack River, Nov. 1776   16170
   Drake, Campaign of Trenton, 47, 4 3/4 x 3 3/4
Fort Lee, N.J., captured by British, Nov. 20, 1776   16175
   Leiby, Hackensack Valley, 67, 4 1/4 x 5 3/8
Movements of American and British forces during Washington's   16180
   retreat across New Jersey, Nov.-Dec. 1776
   Anderson, Howe Bros., 200, 4 1/4 x 3 3/4
   Army, Am. Mil. Hist., 53, 6 1/4 x 4 3/8
   Avery, Hist. of U.S., 6:38, 5 1/4 x 4 5/8
   Current, Am. Hist., 2d ed., 107, 3 x 2 1/2
   Drake, Campaign of Trenton, 76, 2 7/8 x 3 1/2
   Duncan, Medical Men, 167, 5 1/2 x 4
   Fast, The Unvanquished, lining papers, 7 x 5 1/4 col.
   Fisher, Struggle for Am. Ind., 1:536, 6 x 3 1/2
   Fite, Book of Old Maps, 262, 12 3/4 x 7 1/4, by S. Lewis
   Flexner, Washington in Am. Rev., 155, 7 3/8 x 4 3/4, by
     Samuel H. Bryant
   Fisher, Struggle for Am. Ind., 1:536, 6 x 3 1/2
   Fite, Book of Old Maps, 262, 12 3/4 x 7 1/4, by S. Lewis
   Greene, Revolutionary War, 60, 5 1/4 x 4 5/8 col.
   Gurney, Pict. Hist. U.S. Army, 37, 4 7/8 x 3 7/8
   Hall, School History, 213, 6 1/8 x 3 1/2
   Hart, Am. Nation, 6:26, 6 1/2 x 2 1/2 col., 6 1/2 x 3 3/8 col.
   Ingles, Queen's Rangers, 26, 6 x 5 1/4
   Marshall, Atlas, map 4, 9 1/2 x 6 1/2
   Matloff, Am. Military History, 64, 6 1/4 x 4 3/8
   Montross, Rag, Tag and Bobtail, 156, 4 3/8 x 4 1/4
   Morison, Growth of Am. Republic, 5th ed., 207, 6 1/4 x 4 1/4
   Pag. Am., 6:151, 4 3/4 x 4 5/8
   Pratt, 11 Generals, 8, 6 3/4 x 4
   Rayback, Richards Atlas, 28, 15 7/8 x 10 1/2 col.
   Reeder, Story of Rev. War, 85, 6 1/4 x 4 1/8
   Seelye, Story of Washington, 179, 4 1/8 x 3 3/4
   Vestal, Washington, 22, 4 x 4
   Washington Atlas, pl.36, 15 1/2 x 11 col.
   Washington Bicentennial, 1:113, 4 x 4
   Whitton, Am. War of Ind., 318, 6 x 3 1/2
British invasion of Bergen County, N.J., Nov. 20, 1776   16185
   O'Dea, Washington, 27, 6 5/8 x 4 1/4
Washington's route through Bergen County, Nov. 20-21, 1776   16190
   O'Dea, Washington, 20-21, 9 1/4 x 11
Route of American troops under Maj. Gen. Charles Lee (until his   16195
   capture Dec. 12) and Maj. Gen. John Sullivan, from King's
   Ferry, N.Y., through New Jersey, to Pennsylvania, Dec. 2-20,
   1776

Avery, Hist. of U.S., 6:38, 5 1/4 x 4 5/8 col.
Greene, Revolutionary War, 60, 5 1/4 x 4 5/8 col.
Vestal, Washington, 22, 4 x 4
British posts in New Jersey, Dec. 1776   16200
  Am. Heritage, Revolution, 189, 1 1/2 x 2 1/8
  Fisher, Struggle for Am. Ind., 1:554, 5 5/8 x 3 1/2
  Lundin, Cockpit, 169, 3 7/8 x 6 1/4
Position of American and British troops in New Jersey and nearby   16205
  Pennsylvania, Dec. 15-25, 1776
  Smith, Trenton, 10, 5 x 4
Trenton, N.J., Battle of, Dec. 26, 1776   16210
  Alden, Am. Revolution, 108, 3 1/8 x 3 3/4
  Alden, Rise of Am. Republic, 143, 3 1/4 x 4 1/2
  Army, Am. Military Hist., 60, 3 1/8 x 4 1/2
  Avery, Hist. of U.S., 6:46, 3 1/8 x 3 col.; 47, 3 1/4 x 3 7/8
    col.; 52, 4 3/4 x 3 3/4 col.
  Bill, N.J. and Rev. War, 30, 4 x 6 1/2
  Bill, Princeton, 55, 5 x 8 1/8; 91, 5 x 8
  Billias, Gen. John Glover, 13, 4 1/4 x 4 7/8
  Boatner, Enc. of Am. Rev., 1113, 4 1/8 x 6 3/4
  Butcher, Trenton, 28-29, 5 3/8 x 7
  Callahan, Henry Knox, 86, 3 7/8 x 4 1/4
  Carrington, Battles, 270, 4 1/2 x 7 1/2; 278, 3 3/4 x 4 1/2
  Carrington, Washington, 144, 3 1/2 x 5 3/4; 151, 2 7/8 x 3 1/2
  Coast Artillery Jl., 81(Nov.-Dec. 1938):420, 3 3/4 x 7 col.;
    421, 8 1/4 x 7 col.; 425, 8 1/8 x 7 col.
  Coggins, Boys in Revolution, 38, 4 3/4 x 5 1/2
  Commager, Spirit of '76, 1:509, 3 7/8 x 4 5/8
  Cunliffe, Washington, 80-81, 9 3/8 x 14 col.
  Drake, Campaign of Trenton, 73, 4 5/8 x 3 3/4
  Duncan, Medical Men, 174, 5 1/4 x 4 1/8
  Dupuy, Compact Hist., 173, 4 3/8 x 5 5/8
  Egleston, John Paterson, 68, 4 1/4 x 5 5/8
  Freeman, Washington, 4:315, 3 3/4 x 5
  Fuller, Battles, 25, 3 x 4
  Greene, Revolutionary War, 66, 3 1/8 x 3 3/4 col.
  Gurney, Pict. Hist. U.S. Army, 40, 3 1/8 x 4 3/8
  Haven, 30 Days in N.J., front, 7 1/8 x 9 5/8
  Hutton, Washington Crossed Here, frontis., 3 1/2 x 5 1/2
  Jacobs, Tarnished Warrior, 22, 3 3/8 x 4 1/8
  Kinnaird, Geo. Washington, 110, 3 1/8 x 3 3/4
  Lossing, Field-Book of Rev., 2:21, 4 1/4 x 3 1/8
  Lovell, Israel Angell, 104, 7 x 3 7/8
  McDowell, Revolutionary War, 104-105, 10 x 13 1/2 col.
  Mag. of Am. Hist., 4(May 1880):378, 5 1/4 x 6 1/4, French map
  Matloff, Am. Military History, 68, 3 x 4 1/2
  Mil. Affairs, 20(Spring 1956):3, 7 1/2 x 5 7/8, 3 x 2 3/8
  Mitchell, Battles Am. Rev., 78, 7 1/2 x 5 col.
  Montross, Rag, Tag and Bobtail, 161, 5 3/8 x 4 1/4
  Pag. Am., 6:151, 1 3/8 x 1 5/8
  Raum, Trenton, frontis., 7 1/8 x 9 1/2
  Reeder, Story of Rev. War, 94, 3 x 4 1/8
  Richards, Pa.-German in Rev. War, 193, 2 3/4 x 3 3/8
  Ristow, Services, pl.IX, 5 1/8 x 6 3/4
  Seelye, Story of Washington, 185, 2 1/8 x 3 5/8

Smith, Trenton, 13, 4 1/2 x 4 1/8; 18, 4 1/2 x 8 1/2; 21,
    9 x 8 1/2; 23, 9 1/2 x 4; 24, 9 1/8 x 4; 25, 3 7/8 x 4
Steele, Am. Campaigns, 2:15, 3 7/8 x 6 1/2 col.
Wallace, Appeal to Arms, 128, 3 1/4 x 4
Ward, Del. Continentals, 128, 4 1/8 x 5 1/4
Ward, Revolution, 1:299, 4 1/2 x 5 3/4; 313, 4 3/4 x 4 3/8
Whittemore, Sullivan, 46, 3 3/8 x 4
Wilkinson, Diagrams, No. 2, 4 3/8 x 8 1/8
Wilson, Am. People, 2:261, 5 x 3 3/4
Winsor, America, 6:408, 4 5/8 x 7 1/4; 409, 4 3/4 x 3 1/2;
    412, 2 1/2 x 4 7/8
By William Faden   16215
  Am. Heritage, Revolution, 202, 5 7/8 x 7 7/8 col.
  Avery, Hist. of U.S., 6:52, 6 x 8 col.
  Hughes, Washington, 2:590-591, 5 1/4 x 7 3/4
  Winsor, America, 6:410, 4 3/4 x 3 3/4
By Lt. Friederich Fischer   16220
  Avery, Hist. of U.S., 6:48, 3 3/8 x 4 1/2
  Cottrell, Trenton Battle Mon., 8-9, 6 5/8 x 8 7/8
  Freeman, Washington, 4:319, 5 x 6 3/4
  Stryker, Trenton, 128, 6 5/8 x 8 7/8
By Lt. Charles Philip von Krafft   16225
  Krafft, Journal, pl.1, 6 1/4 x 6 5/8
By Lt. Jacob Piel   16230
  Smith, Trenton, 12, 7 1/2 x 8 1/2
  Stryker, Trenton, 124, 7 x 7 7/8
By Lt. Andreas Wiederhold   16235
  Lowell, Hessians, 92, 3 3/8 x 4 1/4
  Stryker, Trenton, 126, 7 x 8 3/4
  Winsor, America, 6:411, 3 7/8 x 4 3/4
See also next entry

1777

Movements of American and British forces during Trenton-Princeton 16240
    campaign and Washington's advance to Morristown, N.J., Dec.
    26, 1776-Jan. 6, 1777
  Am. Heritage Atlas, 106-107, 11 x 17 col.
  Avery, Hist. of U.S., 6:52, 4 3/4 x 3 3/4 col.
  Bill, N.J. and Rev. War, 10, 3 3/4 x 6 1/2
  Bill, Princeton, 8, 4 3/4 x 8 1/8; 91, 5 x 8
  Bill, Valley Forge, 4, 3 1/2 x 4
  Coast Artillery Jl., 81(May-June 1938):176, 6 3/8 x 4 5/8
  Coffin, Boys of '76, 135, 4 x 3 5/8
  Dupuy, Brave Men and Great Captains, 24, 5 1/4 x 4 1/8
  Dupuy, Mil. Heritage of Am., 91, 3 1/2 x 4 1/2
  Egleston, John Paterson, 70, 6 1/4 x 4 1/4
  Esposito, Am. Wars Atlas, 1:map 5c, 3 5/8 x 4 3/4 col.
  Esposito, Civil War Atlas, map 5c, 3 5/8 x 4 3/4 col.
  Flexner, Washington in Am. Rev., 155, 7 3/8 x 4 3/4 by
    Samuel H. Bryant
  Freeman, Washington, 4:347, 6 5/8 x 3 5/8
  Fuller, Battles, 18, 5 1/8 x 4
  Godfrey, Washington's March, front, 6 1/2 x 4
  Greene, Revolutionary War, 66, 4 3/4 x 3 3/4 col.

Guizot, Atlas, pl.13, 7 x 3 3/4
Hall, School Hist., 217, 6 x 3 3/8
Hart, Am. Nation, 6:26, 6 1/2 x 3 3/8 col.
Hughes, Washington, 3:15, 5 7/8 x 3 7/8
Lovell, Israel Angell, 104, 7 x 3 7/8
Military Review, 43(Jan. 1963):90, 7 1/8 x 4 7/8
Montross, Rag, Tag and Bobtail, 169, 6 3/8 x 4 1/4
Montross, War through the Ages, 425, 2 3/8 x 4
Morison, Growth of Am. Republic, 5th ed., 207, 6 1/4 x 4 1/4
Pag. Am., 6:151, 4 3/4 x 4 5/8; 152, 3 1/2 x 3 3/4
Ridpath, New Complete Hist., 6:2528, 4 7/8 x 2
Smith, Princeton, 14, 9 5/8 x 8 3/8; 31, 10 3/8 x 3 7/8
Soc. for Army Hist. Res., Jl., 13(Winter 1934):228, 4 3/8
    x 3 1/4
Sparks, Washington's Writings, 4:258, 7 1/4 x 4
Stryker, Trenton, 279, 3 3/4 x 6 1/2
Wallace, Appeal to Arms, 129, 3 3/4 x 4
Wilkinson, Diagrams, Nos. 3,4,5, 13 1/4 x 13 1/2
  By William Faden   16243
    Avery, Hist. of U.S., 6:52, 6 x 8 col.
    Cook, Golden Bk. of Am. Rev., 92, 5 7/8 x 8 col.
    Godfrey, Washington's March, 8, 4 x 7
    Lee, Hist. of N. America, 6:273, 3 7/8 x 5 1/4
    Stryker, Trenton, 84, 7 x 9
Trenton, N.J., Second Battle of (also known as Battle of the   16245
    Assumpink), Jan. 2, 1777
  Cunliffe, Washington, 80-81, 9 3/8 x 14 col.
  Garner, Hist. of U.S., 2:441, 3 1/8 x 2 5/8
  Haven, 30 Days in N.J., front, 7 1/8 x 9 5/8
  Military Review, 43(Jan. 1963):93, 3 1/2 x 4 7/8
  Smith, Princeton, 16, 9 5/8 x 4
Princeton, N.J., Battle of, Jan. 3, 1777   16250
  Avery, Hist. of U.S., 6:52, 4 3/4 x 3 3/4 col.
  Bill, N.J. and Rev. War, 40, 4 x 6 1/2
  Bill, Princeton, 91, 5 x 8; 102, 4 7/8 x 8 1/8
  Boatner, Enc. of Am. Rev., 892, 4 3/8 x 7 3/4
  Carrington, Battles, 278, 3 3/4 x 4 1/2
  Carrington, Washington, 151, 2 7/8 x 3 1/2
  Coast Artillery Jl., 81(May-June 1938):176, 9 1/8 x 6 5/8,
    5 x 3
  Coffin, Boys of '76, 146, 5 x 3
  Cunliffe, Washington, 80-81, 9 3/8 x 14 col.
  Dupuy, Compact Hist., 181, 4 5/8 x 4 1/2
  Freeman, Washington, 4:351, 3 1/2 x 4 1/4
  Fuller, Battles, 31, 5 1/4 x 4
  Greene, Revolutionary War, 66, 4 3/4 x 3 3/4 col
  Haven, 30 Days in N.J., front, 7 1/8 x 9 5/8
  Kinnaird, Geo. Washington, 113, 6 1/2 x 4 7/8
  Lossing, Field-Book of Rev., 2:28, 5 x 3
  Lovell, Israel Angell, 104, 7 x 3 7/8
  Mil. Affairs, 20(Spring 1956):3, 7 1/2 x 5 7/8
  Mitchell, Battles Am. Rev., 83, 7 1/2 x 5 col.
  Pag. Am., 6:152, 3 1/4 x 5
  Princeton Battle Mon., 75, 3 3/4 x 3; 85, 4 x 3; 92,
    4 x 2 7/8; 98, 4 x 2 7/8; 104, 3 3/4 x 2 7/8

Princeton Univ. Lib. Chron., 13(Summer 1952):177, 5 1/4 x
8 7/8
Raum, Trenton, frontis., 7 1/8 x 9 1/2
Richards, Pa.-German in Rev. War, 233, 3 1/4 x 3 3/4
Ristow, Services, pl.IX, 5 1/8 x 6 3/4
Seelye, Story of Washington, 190, 3 3/8 x 3 7/8
Smith, Princeton, 20, 4 3/8 x 4; 21, 5 1/4 x 8 3/8;
22, 10 1/4 x 8 1/2; 25, 4 1/2 x 4, 4 1/2 x 4
Soc. for Army Hist. Res. Jl., 13(Winter 1934):218, 5 3/4 x
4 1/2; 228, three maps each 4 1/4 x 3 1/4
Steele, Am. Campaigns, 2:15, 3 7/8 x 6 1/2 col.
Stryker, Trenton, 288, 2 x 3 1/2
Ward, Revolution, 1:313, 4 3/4 x 4 3/8
Whittemore, Sullivan, 49, 3 1/4 x 7 1/8
Wilkinson, Diagrams, No.6, 8 3/8 x 6 1/4
Wilson, Am. People, 2:261, 5 x 3 3/4
Winsor, America, 6:408, 4 5/8 x 7 1/4; 409, 4 3/4 x 3 1/2;
413, 6 1/2 x 4 7/8
Woodhull, Princeton, end, 15 5/8 x 12
By William Faden   16255
Am. Heritage, Revolution, 202, 5 7/8 x 7 7/8 col.
Avery, Hist. of U.S., 6:52, 6 x 8 col.
Winsor, America, 6:410, 4 3/4 x 4 3/4
British positions at Princeton, Dec. 31, 1776   16260
Bill, Princeton, 100, 7 3/8 x 4 3/4
Freeman, Washington, 4:340, 6 1/2 x 3 1/2
Lost ground in New Jersey reclaimed by American forces,
Dec. 25, 1776 - Jan. 10, 1777
Montross, Rag, Tag and Bobtail, 169, 1 1/4 x 1 3/8
Morristown, N.J., and related American outposts, 1777   16270
Weig, Morristown, 5, 6 x 4 3/8
Washington's headquarters, Morristown, N.J., Jan. 6-May 28,   16275
1777
Washington Atlas, pl.44, 4 1/2 x 4 7/8
Howe's maneuvers in Northern New Jersey and Washington's   16280
reactions, June 12-30, 1777
Esposito, Am. Wars Atlas, 1:map 7a, 9 5/8 x 8 3/8 col.
Esposito, Civil War Atlas, map 7a, 9 5/8 x 8 3/8 col.
British positions, Middlebush, N.J., June 14, 15, 1777, by   16285
Maj. John André
André, Journal, 1:38, 5 1/4 x 6 7/8; 39, 5 1/4 x 6 7/8
British redoubts, Middlebush, N.J., June 16, 1777, by Capt.   16290
John Montrésor
Meredith, Am. Wars, 21, 2 1/2 x 3 3/4
N.Y. Hist. Soc., Collections, 14:422, 3 1/4 x 4 7/8
Somerset Co. Hist. Quar., 5(Jan. 1916):22, 3 1/8 x 4 3/4
Disposition of British army near New Brunswick, N.J., June 21,   16295
1777, by Maj. John André
André, Journal, 1:40, 5 1/2 x 14
Routes taken by divisions of Washington's army under Major   16300
Generals John Sullivan, Nathanael Greene, Adam Stephen,
and William Alexander, Lord Stirling, through New Jersey
to Pennsylvania, July-Aug. 1777
Reed, Campaign to Valley Forge, 24, 6 1/4 x 5
British invasion of Northern New Jersey, Sept. 12-21, 1777   16305
Leiby, Hackensack Valley, 136, 6 7/8 x 5 3/8

Route of Hessians from Camden to Red Bank, Gloucester Co., N.J.   16310
    Kull, New Jersey, 2:476, 5 1/2 x 4 1/4
    Stewart, Battle of Red Bank, 28, 5 1/2 x 4 1/4
Fort Mercer, Red Bank, Gloucester Co., N.J., siege, Oct. 22-   16315
    Nov. 21, 1777
    Coffin, Spirit of '76, 246, 1 1/2 x 1 3/4
    David, R.I. Chaplain, 43, 10 7/8 x 16 1/2, by William Faden
    Kain, Operations on Del., 195, 4 x 4
    Krafft, Journal, pl.3, 4 5/8 x 7 3/4, by Lt. Charles Philip
      von Krafft
    Lossing, Field-Book of Rev., 2:84, 1 3/8 x 1 3/4
    Reed, Campaign to Valley Forge, 291, 4 5/8 x 2 1/2
    Richards, Pa.-German in Rev. War, 484, 3 5/8 x 1 7/8
    Stewart, Battle of Red Bank, 14, 4 3/8 x 4 1/4
Movements of Maj. Gen. Nathanael Greene in New Jersey, Nov. 1777   16320
    Avery, Hist. of U.S., 6:76-77, 3 3/4 x 7 5/8 col.
    Greene, Revolutionary War, 76, 3 3/4 x 7 5/8 col.
Disposition of American troops, Mount Holly, N.J., Nov. 25, 1777   16325
    Weedon, Orderly Book, 142, 3 1/2 x 6
Gloucester, N.J., skirmish, Nov. 25, 1777   16330
    Gottschalk, Lafayette Joins Am. Army, 80, 7 1/8 x 9
    Royaumont, La Fayette et Rochambeau, 73, 4 3/8 x 5 3/8,
      French map
    Tower, La Fayette, 1:248, 7 1/4 x 9 1/4, Lafayette's map
    Winsor, America, 6:430, 5 1/8 x 4 3/4, French map

1778

Quintan's Bridge, N.J., skirmish, Mar. 18, 1778   16335
    Lossing, Field-Book of Rev., 2:138, 1 1/8 x 1 1/8
    Stewart, Foraging, 20, 4 1/8 x 5 1/8
 By Lt. Col. John Graves Simcoe   16336
    Ingles, Queen's Rangers, 70, 4 7/8 x 6, after Simcoe
    Reed, Valley Forge, 44, 3 1/4 x 3 7/8
    Simcoe, Military Jl., 50, 6 1/4 x 7 1/2
Hancock's Bridge, N.J., skirmish, Mar. 21, 1778   16340
    Ingles, Queen's Rangers, 72, 5 1/8 x 5 5/8, after Lt. Col.
      Simcoe
    Lossing, Field-Book of Rev., 2:139, 1 3/8 x 1 1/4
    Simcoe, Military Jl., 52, 6 3/8 x 7, by Lt. Col. John Graves
      Simcoe
    Stewart, Foraging, 24, 3 7/8 x 4 3/8
Movements of forces of Washington and Clinton during British   16345
    retreat across New Jersey from Philadelphia to New York,
    June-July 1778
    Avery, Hist. of U.S., 6:76-77, 3 3/4 x 5 7/8 col.
    Azoy, Paul Revere's Horse, 111, 3 3/8 x 5 7/8
    Bill, Valley Forge, 4, 3 1/2 x 4
    Billias, Washington's Opponents, xxviii, 7 1/2 x 4 5/8
    Carrington, Battles, 302, 7 3/4 x 4 3/4; 398, 4 5/8 x 7 5/8
    Carrington, Washington, 161, 5 3/4 x 3 1/2
    Doyle, Von Steuben, 112, 4 1/2 x 7
    Duncan, Medical Men, 265, 4 1/8 x 5 3/4
    Faulkner, Am. Political & Social Hist., 135, 5 x 3 5/8
    Fisher, Struggle for Am. Ind., 2:178, 6 x 3 1/2

Flexner, Washington in Am. Rev., 218, 3 7/8 x 4 5/8, by
　　Samuel H. Bryant
Gilman, Monmouth, end papers, 8 1/2 x 10 7/8
Greene, Revolutionary War, 76, 3 3/4 x 5 7/8 col.
Hart, Am. Nation, 6:26, 6 1/2 x 3 3/8 col.
Infantry Jl., 46(Nov.-Dec. 1939):569, 4 x 7
Ingles, Queen's Rangers, 26, 6 x 5 1/4
MacMunn, Am. War, 217, 5 7/8 x 3 1/2
Montross, Rag, Tag and Bobtail, 284, 4 1/4 x 4 1/4
Morison, Growth of Am. Republic, 5th ed., 207, 6 1/4 x 4 1/2
Pag. Am., 6:206, 2 x 5 7/8
Tower, La Fayette, 1:346, 7 3/8 x 9 1/8 col.
Whitton, Am. War of Ind., 318, 6 x 3 1/2
Willcox, Portrait, 103, 7 3/4 x 4 3/4
Winsor, America, 6:442, 3 1/4 x 3 5/8, Hessian map
By Maj. John André   16350
André, Journal, 2:1, 9 1/8 x 13 5/8 col.
By Lt. John Hills   16355
Clinton, Am. Rebellion, 86, 6 x 9 1/4
Smith, Monmouth, 4, 8 1/2 x 10 1/2; 25, 7 1/2 x 10 3/8,
　　prob. by Hills
Alternative British lines of withdrawal, June 1778   16360
Freeman, Washington, 5:13, 4 1/8 x 4 1/2
Positions of British forces during retreat, by Major John André
Evesham, N.J., June 19, 1778   16365
André, Journal, 2:4, 5 x 6 5/8
Mt. Holly, N.J., June 20-21, 1778   16370
André, Journal, 2:5, 5 x 6 7/8
Black Horse, N.J., June 22, 1778   16375
André, Journal, 2:6, 5 1/4 x 6 1/4
Crosswicks, N.J., June 23, 1778   16380
André, Journal, 2:7, 5 3/8 x 6 1/4
Allentown, N.J., June 24, 1778   16385
André, Journal, 2:8, 5 3/8 x 6 1/2
Upper Freehold, N.J., June 25, 1778   16390
André, Journal, 2:9, 5 3/8 x 6 1/2
Freehold, N.J. (Monmouth Court House), June 26-28, 1778   16395
André, Journal, 2:10, 5 3/8 x 6 5/8
June 29, 1778   16400
André, Journal, 2:14, 4 3/4 x 7
Middletown, N.J., June 30, 1778   16405
André, Journal, 2:15, 4 3/4 x 6 3/4
Monmouth, N.J., Battle of, June 28, 1778   16410
Alden, Am. Revolution, 204, 4 1/8 x 6 3/8
Alden, Gen. Chas Lee, 220, 7 1/4 x 10 3/4
Alden, Rise of Am. Republic, 151, 3 1/4 x 4 1/2
Avery, Hist. of U.S., 6:178, 2 3/8 x 4 1/4 col.
Bill, N.J. and Rev. War, 80, 4 1/4 x 6 1/2
Bill, Valley Forge, 213, 4 1/8 x 6 1/2
Boatner, Enc. of Am. Rev., 720, 4 1/8 x 6 1/2
Boyd, Wayne, 122, 4 x 6 1/2
Carrington, Battles, 446, 7 5/8 x 4 3/4
Carrington, Washington, 224, 3 1/2 x 5 5/8
Coffin, Boys of '76, 276, 1 3/4 x 4 3/4
Commager, Spirit of '76, 2:709, 4 5/8 x 7 1/8
Cunningham, N.J. Sampler, 64, 2 x 5 1/2

Dearborn, Journals, 126, 7 x 10 1/2
Duer, Stirling, 196, 2 3/8 x 7 1/8
Dupuy, Brave Men and Great Captains, 37, 3 1/8 x 4 1/8
Dupuy, Compact Hist., 282, 4 1/2 x 3 1/4
Egleston, John Paterson, 103, 4 1/4 x 6 1/4
Esposito, Am. Wars Atlas, 1:map 7d, 2 3/4 x 4 1/4 col.
Esposito, Civil War Atlas, map 7d, 2 3/4 x 4 1/4 col.
Field Artillery Jl., 39(Sept.-Oct. 1949):222, 2 1/2 x 7 1/4
Fiske, Am. Rev., 2:62, 2 3/4 x 6 1/8 col.
Freeman, Washington, 5:21, 4 1/8 x 5
Garner, Hist. of U.S., 2:469, 1 3/8 x 4
Gilman, Monmouth, 5, 3 5/8 x 3 3/4; 28, 6 3/4 x 4
Gottschalk, Lafayette Joins Am. Army, 222, 4 7/8 x 9 3/4
Greene, Revolutionary War, 146, 2 3/8 x 4 1/4 col.
Guizot, Atlas, pl.16, 4 x 7
Hilliard d'Auberteuil, Essais, 2:271, 4 1/4 x 15 3/4 col.
Infantry Jl., 46(Nov.-Dec. 1939):571, 4 1/2 x 7; 575,
    4 1/2 x 7; 577, 4 1/2 x 7; 580, 4 1/2 x 7
Ingles, Queen's Rangers, 88, 4 3/8 x 6 3/4
Irving, Life of Washington, 3:429, 2 1/2 x 6 1/2
Kinnaird, Geo. Washington, 158, 2 1/2 x 6 1/2
Lossing, Field-Book of Rev., 2:150, 1 3/4 x 4 3/4
Mitchell, Battles Am. Rev., 144, 5 x 7 1/2 col.
Mitchell, Discipline and Bayonets, 110, 4 1/4 x 6 3/8
Pag. Am., 6:207, 1 5/8 x 5 7/8
Patterson, Knight Errant, 208, 3 3/4 x 9 1/4; 209, 4 1/8 x
    6 1/4
Pratt, 11 Generals, 43, 2 3/4 x 4
Ridpath, New Complete Hist., 6:2734, 2 x 7 1/2, 2 1/8 x 7
Royaumont, La Fayette et Rochambeau, 84, 3 1/4 x 6 3/8,
    French map
Seelye, Story of Washington, 243, 2 7/8 x 4
Smith, Monmouth, 12, 5 1/2 x 8 1/2; 15, 5 1/2 x 8 1/2; 17,
    5 3/8 x 8 1/2; 20, 5 1/2 x 8 5/8
Sparks, Washington's Writings, 5:430, 4 1/8 x 7 1/8
Steele, Am. Campaigns, 2:21, 2 1/4 x 6 1/4 col.
Stephenson, Washington, 88, 3 3/8 x 4
Stryker, Monmouth, 116, 3 1/2 x 6 1/4
Vestal, Washington, 38, 2 3/8 x 4
Wallace, Appeal to Arms, 183, 4 1/4 x 6 1/2
Ward, Del. Continentals, 276, 4 1/8 x 6 1/2
Ward, Revolution, 2:583, 4 1/2 x 7
Washington Bicentennial, 1:117, 2 3/8 x 4; 420, 1 3/4 x
    6 3/4, French map
Winsor, America, 6:444, 2 1/8 x 7 7/8, French map; 445,
    4 3/4 x 2 3/4, Hessian map
By Maj. John André   16415
    André, Journal, 2:12, 9 1/2 x 17 col.
Sir Henry Clinton's manuscript map   16420
    Gilman, Monmouth, 20, 2 3/8 x 5 5/8; 21, 3 1/4 x 4 3/4
    Hughes, Washington, 3:366, 3 x 6 3/8
    Willcox, Portrait, 228, 5 3/8 x 7 1/2
Lafayette's (?) map   16425
    Freeman, Washington, 5:29, 8 3/8 x 5
    Tower, La Fayette, 1:368, 5 x 10

By Lt. Charles Philip von Krafft   16430
   Krafft, Journal, pl.2, 4 3/4 x 8
Maj. Gen. Charles Grey's expedition into Northern New Jersey,   16435
   Sept. 1778
   André, Journal, 1:46, 16 3/8 x 9 1/2 col., by Maj. John Andre
   See also Old Tappan, N.Y. Massacre, 13560
British positions in Schraalenburgh, Teaneck, and English   16440
   Neighborhood, N.J. Sept. 23-27, 1778
   Leiby, Hackensack Valley, 161, 4 3/4 x 5 1/4, by Maj. John
   Andre
Count Pulaski's headquarters and camp of Pulaski's Legion, Middle 16445
   of the Shore (now Tuckerton), N.J., Oct. 8-15, 1778
   Stryker, Egg Harbor, 14, 5 1/8 x 3 3/4
Egg Harbor, N.J., skirmish, Oct. 15, 1778   16450
   Stryker, Egg Harbor, 18, 6 1/2 x 3 1/2
American encampment, Middlebrook, N.J., 1778-1779   16455
   N.J. Hist. Soc., Proc., 70(Apr. 1952):102-103, 8 x 9 3/4
British raid on Hackensack Valley, N.J., May 18-21, 1779   16460
   Leiby, Hackensack alley, 211, 6 1/2 x 4 1/4, by Capt.
   Patrick Ferguson
Paulus Hook, N.J., American capture of, Aug. 19, 1779   16465
   Boatner, Enc. of Am. Rev., 837, 6 x 4 1/8
   Farrier, Paulus Hook, 34
   Leiby, Hackensack Valley, 222, 3 x 4 1/8
   Lossing, Field-Book of Rev., 2:622, 1 3/8 x 1 3/8
   Lowell, Hessians, 228, 3 3/8 x 3 3/8
   Richardson, Washington and Powles Hook, 4, 7 1/4 x 12 5/8;
     30, 6 1/2 x 4 5/8
   Ward, Del. Continentals, 304, 5 1/2 x 4 1/8
   Ward, Revolution, 2:607, 5 7/8 x 4 1/2
   Winsor, America, 6:559, 2 3/4 x 2 1/8
Positions of the 10 brigades of Washington's army, Morris County, 16470
   N.J., winter 1779-1780
   Journal of Am. Hist., 10(1916):324, 3 3/4 x 3 1/2
   McClintock, Washington's Camp, 3, 5 1/4 x 4
American encampment, Morristown, N.J., winter 1779-1780   16475
   Mil. Engineer, 45(Mar.-Apr. 1953): 119, 6 1/2 x 6 3/4
By Robert Erskine   16480
   McClintock, Washington's Camp, 33, 4 x 5 5/8, Washington's
   plan, Dec. 17, 1779
   Weig, Morristown, 13, 4 7/8 x 7 5/8
By Capt. Bichet de Rochefontaine   16485
   Weig, Morristown, 14, 4 1/8 x 4 3/8
Winter camp of Gen. Stark's brigade, Morristown, N.J.   16487
   Cook, Golden Bk. of Am. Rev., 66, 3 1/8 x 6 5/8
Morristown, N.J., and related American outposts, 1779-1780   16490
   Weig, Morristown, 5, 6 x 4 3/8
Washington's headquarters, Morristown, N.J., Dec. 1, 1779 -   16495
   June 6, 1780
   Washington Atlas, pl.44, 4 1/2 x 4 7/8
Morristown National Historical Park   16500
   Weig, Morristown, 20-21, 7 1/2 x 10; 35, 6 x 4 1/2

1780

Washington's position at Morristown, N.J., 1780   16505
   Lundin, Cockpit, 418, 5 x 4

Operations of British troops under Col. Duncan MacPherson   16510
    and Lt. Col. John Howard against Hackensack and
    Paramus, N.J., Mar. 23, 1780
    Leiby, Hackensack Valley, 242, 6 7/8 x 5 3/8
Hopperstown, N.J., skirmish, Apr. 16, 1780   16515
    Leiby, Hackensack Valley, 248, 3 1/2 x 4 1/4, by
    Cornet George Spencer
General Knyphausen's advance into New Jersey, June 1780   16520
    Avery, Hist. of U.S., 6:240-241, 6 3/4 x 9 3/4 col.
    Carrington, Battles, 302, 7 3/4 x 4 3/4; 502, 7 5/8 x 4 1/2
    Carrington, Washington, 283, 5 7/8 x 3 1/2
    Ingles, Queen's Rangers, 149, 5 1/4 x 7 1/2
    Pag. Am., 6:218, 1 3/4 x 5 7/8
British forces at Elizabethtown Point, N.J., June 8-23, 1780   16525
    Elizabeth, Souvenir Programme, 9, 4 3/8 x 6 5/8
Springfield, N.J., Battle of, June 23, 1780   16530
    Avery, Hist. of U.S., 6:240, 4 x 4 7/8 col.
    Carrington, Battles, 502, 2 x 3 3/8
    Carrington, Washington, 283, 1 1/2 x 2 5/8
    Greene, Revolutionary War, 152, 4 x 4 7/8 col.
    Ingles, Queen's Rangers, 149, 5 1/4 x 7 1/2
    Lossing, Field-Book of Rev., 1:322, 2 3/4 x 1 3/4
    Lovell, Israel Angell, 166, 2 3/8 x 4 3/8
Movements of Continental Army in Northern New Jersey and nearby   16535
    New York, July 1-Sept. 4, 1780
    Leiby, Hackensack Valley, 271, 6 7/8 x 5 3/8
Brig. Gen. Anthony Wayne's expedition against Block House near   16540
    Bull's Ferry, N.J., July 21, 1780
    Mag. of Am. Hist., 5(Sept. 1880):172, 2 1/2 x 3 3/4
    Winfield, Block-House, end, 6 5/8 x 8 1/4
Washington's camp on North River, Bergen County, N.J., Aug. 10,   16545
    1780
    Rogers, New Doane Book, 72, 7 1/2 x 4 3/8
Route of Sergeant Major John Champe through New Jersey on secret   16550
    mission from Washington to kidnap Benedict Arnold, Oct. 20,
    1780
    Am. Heritage, 8(Oct. 1957):26, 7 x 4 1/8 col.
Disposition of American army, Totowa and Preakness, N.J., Oct.   16555
    and Nov., 1780
    Mag. of Am. Hist., 3(Aug. 1879):491, 5 3/8 x 7 1/8
Lafayette's encampment at Wagaraw (now Hawthorne), N.J.,   16560
    Oct.-Nov. 1780
    N.J. Hist. Soc., Proc., 69(Jan. 1951):17, 4 3/8 x 4 5/8,
    4 3/8 x 6 1/4
Camp of Pennsylvania troops, Mt. Kemble, N.J., Dec. 10, 1780   16565
    Van Doren, Mutiny in Jan., 28, 5 1/4 x 4 1/4, by Brig. Gen.
    Anthony Wayne; and explanatory plan, 5 1/4 x 4 1/4, by
    staff of Morristown National Park

1781

Mutiny of the Pennsylvania Line, N.J., Jan. 1781   16570
    Van Doren, Mutiny in Jan., 240, 16 x 10 1/2
Places in New Jersey through which Washington's army marched   16573
    en route to Yorktown, Va., Aug. 1781
    Miers, Yankee Doodle Dandy, 201, 6 1/8 x 3 3/8

Route of Rochambeau's army, Whippany to Bullions Tavern   16575
    (now Liberty Corner), N.J., Aug. 1781
      Whitridge, Rochambeau, 84, 2 7/8 x 5 3/8
Encampments of Rochambeau's troops en route to Yorktown, Va.,
    by Louis-Alexandre Berthier
      Twenty-fourth camp, Princeton, N.J., Aug. 31, 1781   16580
      Magg Bros., Berthier, 15, 7 3/8 x 4 3/4
      Van Doren, Mutiny in Jan., 60, 5 7/8 x 4 1/4
  Camp, Trenton, N.J., Sept. 1781   16585
      Van Doren, Mutiny in Jan., 152, 4 1/4 x 4 1/4
Delaware River ford at Trenton, N.J., crossed by the French   16590
    army en route to Yorktown, 1781
      Lunny, Early Maps of N. Am., 39, 4 1/2 x 4 3/4, by Louis-
      Alexandre Berthier

PENNSYLVANIA

Pennsylvania
  By Thomas Kitchin   17005
      Winsor, Westward Movement, 54-55, 4 3/4 x 6
  1770, by William Scull   17010
      Fite, Book of Old Maps, 224, 8 1/2 x 12 7/8
      Heathcote, Chester Co., VIII, 4 x 5 7/8
Eastern Pennsylvania, 1767   17012
      West. Pa. Hist. Mag., 5(Oct. 1922):257, 9 1/8 x 7 3/8
Pennsylvania counties
  At time of the Revolution   17015
      Brown, King's Friends, 129, 3 5/8 x 6 1/4
  1780   17020
      Godcharles, Chronicles, 1:236, 2 1/8 x 3
      Stevens, Exploring Penna., 93, 3 5/8 x 5 3/4
Pennsylvania frontier, 1775   17025
      Stevens, Exploring Penna., 144, 3 5/8 x 5 3/4; 220,
      3 5/8 x 5 3/4
Thirteen Pennsylvania communities where resolutions and   17030
    declarations of independence were passed, 1774-1776
      Fed. Writers' Proj., Bid for Liberty, 14, 2 5/8 x 4 3/4

MILITARY OPERATIONS

The Revolutionary War in Pennsylvania   17035
      Stevens, Exploring Penna., 181, 3 5/8 x 5 3/4
Washington's headquarters in Pennsylvania   17040
      Washington Atlas, pl.36, 15 3/8 x 11 col.; pl.37,
      15 3/8 x 11 col.
      Washington Bicentennial, 1:408, 6 1/4 x 10 1/8,
      2 3/8 x 3 3/8

PHILADELPHIA AND VICINITY

Philadelphia, 1776   18005
      Naval Docs. of Am. Rev., 2:560, 5 1/4 x 7
      Paullin, Atlas, pl. 157B, 6 1/2 x 18 1/4 col., by
      Benjamin Easburn

Philadelphia and adjacent areas   18007
    Reed, Valley Forge, 39, 6 1/4 x 8 3/8, by Capt. John Montrésor
Philadelphia and environs, 1777   18010
    Adams, Album of Am. Hist., 1:393, 8 3/4 x 6 1/2, by Nicholas
      Scull and George Heap, engr. by William Faden
    Hawke, Colonial Experience, 642, 4 x 3 1/2
Delaware Bay and River, 1776, by Joshua Fisher   18015
    Naval Docs. of Am. Rev., 4:1269, 5 3/8 x 7 3/4
    Pa. Archives, 2d series, 3:frontis., 6 7/8 x 8 7/8
    Stoudt, Ordeal at Valley Forge, 48, 3 3/8 x 4 1/4
Delaware River, from Reedy Is. to Philadelphia, 1776   18020
    Serle, Am. Journal, 255, 5 7/8 x 4, after Joshua Fisher
Schuylkill Valley from Valley Forge to Philadelphia at time   18025
    of Revolutionary War
    Hist. Soc. Montgomery Co., Historical Sketches, 4:end,
      15 5/8 x 30 3/8
Fords and Ferries on the Schuylkill River   18030
    Picket Post, Apr. 1954, 62, 4 1/2 x 6 1/8

MILITARY OPERATIONS

American chevaux-de-frise in Delaware River, 1775   18035
    Pa. Archives, 2d series, 1:769, 14 1/4 x 6 3/4; 770,
      10 1/4 x 14 1/8
Area of operations, 1777-1778   18040
    Adams, Atlas, pl.71, 9 1/4 x 6 1/4
    Bean, Washington, end, 10 7/8 x 16 1/8
    Carrington, Battles, 398, 4 5/8 x 7 5/8
    Carrington, Washington, 204, 3 1/2 x 5 5/8
    Duncan, Medical Men, 210, 5 1/2 x 4 1/8
    Ewing, Geo. Ewing, 23, 4 1/2 x 6 5/8; 25, 5 1/4 x 4 5/8
    Freeman, Washington, 4:461, 5 x 3 3/4
    Freeman, Washington, abridgment, 321, 7 3/4 x 5 1/2
    Mackesy, War for America, 127, 4 5/8 x 4 1/4
    MacMunn, Am. War, 217, 5 7/8 x 3 1/2
    Miller, Triumph of Freedom, 201, 7 x 4 1/4
    Mitchell, Discipline and Bayonets, 61, 2 7/8 x 4 1/4
    Moore, Diary of Am. Rev., 1:494, 7 x 8 1/2
    Paoli Massacre Proc., end, 10 7/8 x 16 1/8
    Popp, Hessian Soldier, 10, 4 1/2 x 6 1/2; 20, 4 1/2 x 6 5/8
    Rankin, Am. Rev., 151, 4 1/2 x 4
    Scheer, Rebels and Redcoats, 231, 5 5/8 x 4 1/2
    Seelye, Story of Washington, 218, 2 7/8 x 3 1/2
    Stryker, Forts on Del., frontis., 4 x 4 7/8
    Wildes, Anthony Wayne, 117, 6 5/8 x 4
By Thomas Kitchin, 1777   18045
    Fite, Book of Old Maps, 264, 9 3/8 x 12 1/4
    Pa. Archives, 2d series, 3:frontis., 7 1/4 x 8 5/8
By Bernard Romans   18050
    Guthorn, Am. Maps, 31, 8 1/2 x 9 3/8

1777

Movements of forces of Washington and Howe during Philadelphia   18055
    campaign, Sept.-Dec. 1777
      Alden, Am. Revolution, 123, 4 1/4 x 3 3/4

Alden, Rise of Am. Republic, 146, 4 7/8 x 4 1/2
Anderson, Howe Bros., 275, 3 3/4 x 3 3/4
André, Journal, 1:32, 10 x 9 1/4, by Maj. John André
Avery, Hist. of U.S., 6:76-77, 3 3/4 x 7 5/8 col.
Bill, Valley Forge, 51, 4 1/2 x 4
Commager, Spirit of '76, 1:607, 5 1/4 x 4 5/8
Cunliffe, Washington, 82, 3 1/2 x 2 1/2 col.
Dupuy, Compact Hist., 224, 3 3/4 x 4 1/2
Faulkner, Am. Political & Social Hist., 135, 5 x 3 5/8
Flexner, Washington in Am. Rev., 218, 3 7/8 x 4 5/8, by
   Samuel H. Bryant
Frothingham, Washington, 214, 7 x 4 7/8
Greene, Revolutionary War, 76, 3 3/4 x 7 5/8 col.
Krafft, Journal, pl.4, 6 7/8 x 9 1/8, by Lt. John Charles
   Philip von Krafft
Morison, Growth of Am. Republic, 5th ed., 221, 4 1/4 x 4 1/2
Pag. Am., 6:169, 3 1/8 x 4 1/2
Paullin, Atlas, pl.160B inset, 2 5/8 x 2 5/8 col.
Pa. Mag. Hist. and Biog., 26(Apr. 1902):24, 7 5/8 x 10 1/2;
   32, 6 1/2 x 10 1/4
Reed, Campaign to Valley Forge, 160, 4 1/4 x 6 1/2
Ridpath, New Complete Hist., 6:2612, 7 1/8 x 5
Scull, Evelyns in America, 253
Sparks, Washington's Writings, 5:66, 7 x 4 1/8
Wallace, Appeal to Arms, 137, 4 1/2 x 4
Ward, Revolution, 1:337, 4 3/4 x 4 3/8
Winsor, America, 6:414, 5 1/4 x 4 7/8, 415, 5 3/8 x 4 3/4
   442, 3 1/4 x 3 5/8
Position of British army at New Garden, Pa., Sept. 8, 1777   18060
   Pleasants, John André, 51, 4 1/4 x 5 1/4, by Maj. John André
Washington's map of Brandywine campaign, by Jacob Broom   18065
   Washington Atlas, pl.15, 15 1/2 x 11
   Washington Bicentennial, 1:394, 10 1/8 x 7 1/8
   Winsor, America, 6:420, 8 x 4 7/8
Brandywine, Pa., Battle of, Sept. 11, 1777   18070
   Anderson, Howe Bros., 283, 3 1/2 x 3 3/4
   Army, Am. Mil. Hist., 67, 2 1/2 x 2 1/8
   Avery, Hist. of U.S., 6:78, 3 3/8 x 3 3/4 col.
   Bean, Washington, 8, 5 x 3 3/4
   Belcher, First Am. Civil War, 2:241, 4 3/8 x 5 3/4 col.
   Boatner, Enc. of Am. Rev., 106, 4 1/8 x 6 1/2
   Boyd, Wayne, 60, 6 5/8 x 4
   Brandywine, 150th Anniversary, 7 x 4 3/8, 2 x 4 3/8
   Bruce, Brandywine, 23, 5 3/4 x 4 3/8; 24-25, 6 3/4 x 9 7/8;
      28, 4 1/4 x 3 1/8, 4 1/4 x 3 7/8
   Canby, Brandywine, 190, 3 7/8 x 5 3/8
   Carrington, Battles, 382, 7 5/8 x 4 5/8
   Carrington, Washington, 186, 5 7/8 x 3 1/2
   Chester Co. Hist. Soc., Lafayette, end, 8 3/8 x 9 1/4
   Coffin, Boys of '76, 200, 4 1/2 x 3 3/4
   Commager, Spirit of '76, 1:612, 4 1/8 x 4 5/8
   Duer, Stirling, 174, 4 1/8 x 4 3/8, 3 3/8 x 4 3/8
   Duncan, Medical Men, 224, 4 1/4 x 4 1/4
   Dupuy, Compact Hist., 227, 4 1/4 x 4 1/2
   Esposito, Am. Wars Atlas, 1:map 7b, 4 5/8 x 3 7/8 col.

Esposito, Civil War Atlas, map 7b, 4 5/8 x 3 7/8 col.
Ewing, Geo. Ewing, 21, 4 1/2 x 6 5/8
Fisher, Struggle for Am. Ind., 2:23, 3 1/4 x 3 1/2
Fiske, Am. Rev., 1:322, 6 x 3 3/4 col.
Fortescue, British Army, 3:pl.II, 3 1/2 x 4 1/8
Freeman, Washington, 4:473, 4 3/4 x 5
Futhey, Hist. of Chester Co., 70, 6 3/4 x 7 1/4 col.
Garner, Hist. of U.S., 2:457, 3 1/8 x 2 3/4
Greene, Revolutionary War, 84, 3 3/8 x 3 3/4
Gurney, Pict. Hist. U.S. Army, 46, 2 1/2 x 2 1/4
Hamilton, Grenadier Guards, 2:227, 7 3/8 x 4 1/2
Hist. Soc. Pa., Bul., 1, no.7(1846):front, col.
Hughes, Washington, 3:157, 3 1/4 x 3 3/4, 2 3/8 x 3 3/4
Ingles, Queen's Rangers, 44, 5 1/4 x 5 7/8
Irving, Life of Washington, 3:205, 3 x 3 1/2, 2 5/8 x 3 1/2
Lossing, Field-Book of Rev., 2:171, 4 1/2 x 3 1/2
Lowell, Hessians, 198, 4 1/4 x 3 3/8
MacElree, Along W. Brandywine, 138, 14 7/8 x 13 1/2 col.,
   by Lt. S.W. Werner, engr. and pub. by William Faden,
   1778; 142, 7 x 4 3/8; 150, 2 x 4 3/8
MacMunn, Am. War, 161, 3 1/4 x 3 1/2
Matloff, Am. Military History, 73, 2 1/2 x 2 1/2
Mitchell, Battles Am. Rev., 114, 7 1/2 x 5 col.
Mitchell, Discipline and Bayonets, 67, 6 3/8 x 4 1/4
Pag. Am., 6:170, 3 3/8 x 3 7/8
Pa. Mag. Hist. and Biog., 26(Apr. 1902):24, 7 5/8 x 10 1/2,
   2 3/4 x 4 3/8
Popp, Hessian Soldier, 20, 1 5/8 x 6 5/8
Reed, Campaign to Valley Forge, 119, 5 5/8 x 5
Ridpath, New Complete Hist., 6:2616, 4 5/8 x 4 1/4, 4 3/8 x 3
Scheer, Rebels and Redcoats, 237, 4 3/4 x 4 1/2
Sedgwick, La Fayette, 38, 4 x 4
Seelye, Story of Washington, 207, 3 7/8 x 3 3/4
Serle, Am. Journal, 248, 4 3/8 x 4 3/8, by Ambrose Serle
Soc. for Army Hist. Res., Jl.,8(Oct. 1929):238, 3 1/4 x
   4 1/8 col.
Sparks, Washington's Writings, 5:58, 4 1/4 x 4 7/8, 3 3/8 x
   4 3/4
Steele, Am. Campaigns, 2:18, 3 7/8 x 4 1/4 col.; 19, 6 1/8 x
   3 3/4 col.
Stephenson, Washington, 28, 4 1/2 x 4
Stone, Brandywine, front, 7 7/8 x 8 1/8
Tower, La Fayette, 1:222, 7 1/2 x 9 1/4
Vestal, Washington, 30, 3 5/8 x 4
Ward, Del. Continentals, 206, 4 1/8 x 4 3/4
Washington Bicentennial, 1:115, 3 5/8 x 4
Whittemore, Sullivan, 57, 3 3/4 x 4
Whitton, Am. War of Ind., 318, 3 1/4 x 3 1/2
Wickwire, Cornwallis, 103, 4 5/8 x 4 1/8
Winsor, America, 6:422, 5 3/4 x 4 1/2, Hessian map
By Major John André   18075
   André, Journal, 1:84, 11 3/8 x 7 col.
   Heathcote, Chester Co., 40, 6 x 3 5/8
   Heathcote, Washington, 4, 6 x 3 5/8
   Nolan, S.E. Penna., 1:206, 8 x 5
   Pleasants, John André, 50, 4 1/4 x 5 1/8

Chad's Ford, Pa.   18080
   Pag. Am., 6:170, 2 5/8 x 3 1/8, annotated by George Washington
Position of British army near the Brandywine, Sept. 12, 1777   18083
   André, Journal, 1:88, 5 5/8 x 7, by Maj. John André
American and British movements between Battle of Brandywine and   18085
   entry of British into Philadelphia, Sept. 26, 1777
   Hist. Soc. Montgomery Co., Bul., 4(Oct. 1943):10, 5 1/8 x 6 1/2
Clouds, Battle of the, Hershey's Mill, Pa., Sept. 16, 1777   18090
   Bean, Washington, 16, 8 1/8 x 4 3/4
   Reed, Campaign to Valley Forge, 170, 4 3/4 x 6 3/8
British camp at Trudruffrin (Tredyffrin), Pa., Sept. 18-21, 1777
   By an officer on the spot, engr. and pub. by William Faden, 1778   18095
   Futhey, Hist. of Chester Co., 84, 6 1/4 x 10 1/8
   Winsor, America, 6:424, 4 7/8 x 8 1/8
   By Maj. John André, Sept. 19, 1777   18100
   André, Journal, 1:90, 5 5/8 x 7
Paoli, Pa., Battle of, Sept. 21, 1777   18105
   Bean, Washington, 16, 8 1/8 x 4 3/4
   Pag. Am., 6:171, 2 5/8 x 4 7/8
   Reed, Campaign to Valley Forge, 170, 4 3/4 x 6 3/8
   Winsor, America, 6:423, 3 1/4 x 3 1/2, Hessian map
   By Maj. John André   18110
   André, Journal, 1:94, 5 5/8 x 7
   Pleasants, John André, 47, 4 1/4 x 5 1/8; 48, 4 1/4 x 5 1/4;
     49, 4 1/4 x 5 7/8
   By an officer on the spot, engr. and pub. by William Faden, 1778   18115
   Futhey, Hist. of Chester Co., 84, 6 1/4 x 10 1/8
   Winsor, America, 6:424, 4 7/8 x 8 1/8
Camp Pottsgrove, Washington's encampment near Fagleysville, Pa.,   18120
   Sept. 21-26, 1777
   Hist. Soc. Montgomery Co., Historical Sketches, 3:28, 6 1/2 x 9
Position of British army, Charlestown, Pa., Sept. 21, 1777, by   18125
   Maj. John André
   André, Journal, 1:95, 5 5/8 x 7
   Pa. Mag. Hist. and Biog., 31(1907):400, 4 x 5 3/4
Position of British army, Norrington, Pa., Sept. 25, 1777, by   18130
   Maj. John André
   André, Journal, 1:98, 5 7/8 x 7
Approaches to Germantown, Pa., from Washington's encampment, Oct.   18135
   1777
   Pa. Archives, 2d series, 11:191, 5 7/8 x 4
   Winsor, America, 6:425, 5 7/8 x 4
Germantown, Pa., Battle of, Oct. 4, 1777   18140
   Am. Heritage, Revolution, 215, 3 3/8 x 1 5/8
   Army, Am. Military Hist., 68, 4 3/8 x 4 3/8
   Avery, Hist. of U.S., 6:84, 4 3/4 x 3 3/4 col.
   Bean, Montgomery Co., 165, 5 7/8 x 4; 166, 6 1/4 x 8 1/8
   Bean, Washington, 20, 8 1/8 x 4 3/4
   Belcher, First Am. Civil War, 2:263, 4 3/4 x 4 3/8 col.
   Boatner, Enc. of Am. Rev., 427, 6 3/8 x 4 1/8
   Boyd, Wayne, 82, 4 1/4 x 6 3/4
   Carrington, Battles, 392, 4 1/2 x 7 5/8
   Carrington, Washington, 196, 3 1/2 x 5 7/8
   Coffin, Boys of '76, 220, 3 1/4 x 2 5/8
   Duer, Sterling, 177, 3 1/2 x 4 3/8, 3 1/2 x 4 3/8
   Dupuy, Compact Hist., 234, 5 5/8 x 4 1/2

Esposito, Am. Wars Atlas, 1:map 7c, 4 3/4 x 3 7/8 col.
Esposito, Civil War Atlas, map 7c, 4 3/4 x 3 7/8 col.
Fisher, Struggle for Am. Ind., 2:37, 6 x 3 1/2
Fiske, Am. Rev., 1:328, 6 x 3 3/4 col.
Fortescue, British Army, 3:pl.II, 4 1/8 x 4 1/8 col.
Freeman, Washington, 4:503, 4 x 5
Germantown Hist. Soc., 150th Anniversary, 7 x 5 1/2
Germantowne Crier, 4(Sept. 1952):19, 5 1/2 x 6 7/8
Greene, Revolutionary War, 92, 4 3/4 x 3 3/4 col.
Guizot, Atlas, pl. 14, 3 1/2 x 4 1/4, 3 1/2 x 4 1/4
Gurney, Pict. Hist. U.S. Army, 46, 4 3/8 x 4 3/8
Hamilton, Grenadier Guards, 2:229, 7 3/8 x 4 1/2
Haycox, Winds of Rebellion, 147, 2 3/4 x 3 1/2
Hughes, Washington, 3:191, 4 x 5 1/4
Ingles, Queen's Rangers, 52, 6 x 5 1/8
Irving, Life of Washington, 3:286, 3 x 3 1/2, 3 x 3 1/2
Lossing, Field-Book of Rev., 2:110, 3 1/4 x 2 5/8
Matloff, Am. Military History, 74, 4 3/8 x 4 3/8
Mitchell, Battles Am. Rev., 119, 7 1/2 x 5 col.
Mitchell, Discipline and Bayonets, 75, 6 3/8 x 4 1/4
Montross, Rag, Tag and Bobtail, 230, 5 1/8 x 4 1/4
Old York Rd. Hist. Soc., Bul., 3(Oct. 1939):42-43, 7 5/8 x 9 7/8
Pag. Am., 6:172, 3 7/8 x 3 1/2
Pa. Archives, 2d series, 11:188, 6 3/8 x 8 1/2
Pa. Mag. Hist. and Biog., 1(1877):368, 8 1/4 x 10 3/4
Reed, Campaign to Valley Forge, 219, 4 7/8 x 6 3/4
Reeder, Story of Rev. War., 129, 3 3/8 x 4 1/8
Scharf, Hist. of Phila., 1:353, 5 7/8 x 4; 354, 6 1/4 x 8 1/8
Scheer, Rebels and Redcoats, 245, 5 5/8 x 4 3/8
Seelye, Story of Washington, 212, 4 5/8 x 3 1/8
Soc. for Army Hist. Res., Jl., 8(Oct. 1929):238, 4 1/8 x 4 1/8
    col.
Sparks, Washington's Writings, 5:86, 3 1/2 x 4 3/8, 3 1/2 x
    4 1/8
Steele, Am. Campaigns, 2:20, 6 1/4 x 3 5/8 col.
Stephenson, Washington, 36, 5 1/4 x 4
Vestal, Washington, 32, 5 1/2 x 4
Ward, Del. Continentals, 226, 5 x 4
Ward, Revolution, 1:367, 5 1/2 x 4 1/2
Washington Bicentennial, 1:115, 5 1/2 x 4
Weedon, Orderly Book, frontis., 3 1/2 x 6
Whittemore, Sullivan, 70, 4 1/4 x 4
Whitton, Am. War of Ind., 318, 6 x 3 1/2
Winsor, America, 6:428, 4 5/8 x 3 1/2, Hessian map
By Capt. John Montrésor   18145
Winsor, America, 426-427, 7 3/4 x 6 1/8
By Maj. John André   18150
André, Journal, 1:102, 15 5/8 x 13 3/4 col.
Pleasants, John André, 46, 4 1/4 x 5
Position of British army after Battle of Germantown, Oct. 6, 1777, 18155
    by Maj. John André
André, Journal, 1:106, 5 3/8 x 7 col.
Operations on the Delaware River, Oct. - Nov. 1777   18160
Avery, Hist. of U.S., 6:86, 3 x 4 1/2 col.
Carrington, Battles, 396, 4 3/4 x 7 5/8
Carrington, Washington, 202, 3 1/2 x 5 5/8

Coffin, Boys of '76, 246, 2 3/8 x 4 3/4
Coggins, Boys in Revolution, 76, 4 1/8 x 5 5/8
Coggins, Ships and Seamen, 94, 5 1/4 x 7 5/8
Fisher, Struggle for Am. Ind., 2:42
Freeman, Washington, 4:527, 3 3/8 x 5
Greene, Revolutionary War, 84, 3 x 4 1/2 col.
Irving, Life of Washington, 3:278, 7 3/8 x 4 1/4
Kain, Operations on Del., 189, 4 x 6 1/2
Kinnaird, Geo. Washington, 122, 7 3/4 x 3 5/8
Knox, Naval Genius of Washington, 36, 6 1/2 x 4
Knox, Navy, 25, 6 5/8 x 4 3/8
Lee, Hist. of N. America, 6:285, 5 3/4 x 8 7/8 col.
Lossing, Field-Book of Rev., 2:92, 2 3/8 x 4 7/8
Pag. Am., 6:174, 3 1/4 x 3 1/4
Reed, Campaign to Valley Forge, 275, 5 x 6 1/2
Ridpath, New Complete Hist., 6:2670, 7 x 4 1/8
Roscoe, Picture Hist., no.138, 4 3/4 x 2 7/8
Scharf, Hist. of Phila., 1:306, 2 3/8 x 4 7/8
Sparks, Washington's Writings, 5:156, 7 1/4 x 4 3/8
Stryker, Forts on Del., frontis., 1 3/4 x 2 3/8
U.S.N. Inst., Proc., 88(Jan. 1962):85, 5 x 5 1/2, after
    J.L. Villefranche
Ward, Revolution, 1:375, 7 1/8 x 4 1/8
By William Faden   18165
    Allen, Naval Hist. of Am. Rev., 242, 1 3/4 x 6, 1 3/4 x 6,
        after Faden
    David, R.I. Chaplain, 43, 10 7/8 x 16 1/2
    Lundin, Cockpit, 336, 6 1/8 x 9 1/2
    Strittmatter, Campaign on Del., end, 6 3/8 x 12 7/8, 3 x 2
    Wallace, Col. Wm. Bradford, 228, 6 3/8 x 13, 3 1/8 x 2 1/8
    Winsor, America, 6:429, 1 5/8 x 4 7/8
See also 17170 and 16315
Fort Mifflin, Pa., siege, Oct. 10 - Nov. 15, 1777   18170
    Bean, Montgomery Co., 164, 2 1/4 x 1 7/8
    Coffin, Boys of '76, 250, 2 1/4 x 1 7/8
    Kain, Operations on Del., 193, 5 1/2 x 4
    Lee, Hist. of N. America, 6:285, 3 1/4 x 3 1/4 col.
    Lossing, Field-Book of Rev., 2:90, 2 1/4 x 1 7/8
    Montross, Rag, Tag and Bobtail, 235, 5 1/4 x 4 1/4
    Pag. Am., 6:175, 3 3/4 x 3 1/2
    Pa. Archives, 1st series, 5:721, 11 7/8 x 17 7/8
    Reed, Campaign to Valley Forge, 291, 4 7/8 x 3 1/4
    Scharf, Hist. of Phila, 1:363, 2 1/4 x 1 7/8
    Scull, Evelyns in Am., 253
    Smith, Delaware Co., 321, 4 3/8 x 6 5/8
    Strittmatter, Campaign on Del., 9, 6 1/4 x 4 3/8
    Stryker, Forts on Del., 6, 4 3/8 x 3 1/4; 32, 3 7/8 x 5 3/4
    Wallace, Col. Wm. Bradford, 240, 6 1/2 x 4 5/8
    Washington Bicentennial, 1:395, 5 1/8 x 6 1/4, annotated
        by Washington
    Winsor, America, 6:431, 4 1/2 x 3; 437, 3 1/2 x 4 1/4;
        438, 5 3/4 x 4 3/4
By Maj. John André   18175
    André, Journal, 1:116, 13 1/2 x 8 1/2
By William Faden   18180
    David, R.I. Chaplain, 43, 6 1/8 x 5 3/4, 10 7/8 x 16 1/2

Lundin, Cockpit, 336, 3 1/2 x 3 1/4
By Francois de Fleury   18185
  Kimball, Fleury in Am. Rev., 6, 6 3/8 x 5 1/4
  Winsor, America, 6:432-433, 8 x 6 1/2; 434-435,
    6 x 8 1/2
American camps near Philadelphia, Oct. - Dec., 1777   18190
  Freeman, Washington, 4:531, 6 1/4 x 4 3/4
American encampment and operations at Whitemarsh, Pa.,   18195
    Nov. 2 - Dec. 11, 1777
  Reed, Campaign to Valley Forge, 373, 4 3/4 x 6 5/8
British positions, Chestnut Hill, Pa., Dec. 4, 1777, by   18200
  Maj. John André
  André, Journal, 1:124, 7 7/8 x 5 1/2 col.
Marches of the British army, Dec. 4-7, 1777, by Maj. John André   18205
  André, Journal, 1:126, 6 1/4 x 11 1/4 col.
Whitemarsh, Pa., Battle of, Dec. 5-8, 1777   18210
  Pa. Mag. Hist. and Biog., 26(Apr. 1902):36, 7 1/4 x 10 1/2,
    German map
  Rosengarten, Am. Hist. from Ger. Archives, 18, 7 1/4 x 10 1/4,
    by Stephan Popp
British attack on American advanced guard, Dec. 6, 1777, by   18215
  Maj. John André
  André, Journal, 1:126, 6 1/4 x 11 1/4 col.
Cornwallis' foraging expedition, Dec. 11-12, 1777   18220
  Reed, Campaign to Valley Forge, 389, 4 7/8 x 5 3/4
Route of American army from Whitemarsh to Valley Forge,   18225
  Dec. 11-19, 1777
  Reed, Campaign to Valley Forge, 389, 4 7/8 x 5 3/4
Area from Valley Forge to Philadelphia   18227
  Reed, Valley Forge, 33, 8 7/8 x 8 1/4, from Clinton Papers
American encampment, Valley Forge, Pa., Dec. 19, 1777   18230
    June 17, 1778
  Adams, Lexington, 17, 5 3/4 x 8 1/2, from Clinton papers
  Avery, Hist. of U.S., 6:164, 2 3/4 x 3 3/4 col.
  Bean, Washington, frontis., 22 1/4 x 30 1/2
  Bill, Valley Forge, 95, 3 1/8 x 4
  Brown, Oration at Valley Forge, 107, 3 1/2 x 5 1/2
  Carrington, Battles, 402, 4 5/8 x 6 5/8
  Carrington, Washington, 211, 3 1/2 x 5 7/8
  Duncan, Medical Men, 226, 4 3/8 x 4 1/8
  Egleston, John Paterson, 92, 4 1/4 x 6 1/2
  Ewing, Geo. Ewing, 56, 4 x 5 1/2
  Fast, Conceived in Liberty, lining papers, 7 7/8 x 10 1/2
  Fiske, Am. Rev., 2:53, 4 5/8 x 3 3/8
  Futhey, Hist. of Chester Co., 98, 5 1/8 x 7 1/8
  Garner, Hist. of U.S., 2:460, 2 7/8 x 1 7/8
  Greene, Revolutionary War, 132, 2 3/4 x 3 3/4 col.
  Guizot, Atlas, pl.15, 7 1/4 x 4 1/8
  Hart, Sleeping Sentinel, 11, 4 1/8 x 6 1/4
  Haycox, Winds of Rebellion, 175, 2 1/2 x 3 5/8
  Heathcote, Chester Co., 52, 3 7/8 x 6
  Hist. Soc. Montgomery Co., Bul., 4(Oct. 1943): front,
    7 5/8 x 10 1/2
  Hist. Soc. Montgomery Co., Historical Sketches, 2:346, 7 1/2
    x 11 1/8

Kinnaird, Geo. Washington, 125, 4 1/8 x 6 3/8, by
    "Mr. Parker," a British spy
Lossing, Field-Book of Rev., 2:128, 4 x 2 5/8
MacNeill, Valley Forge Landmarks, 18-19, 8 1/8 x 11
Mag. of Am. Hist., 8(Feb. 1882):112, 4 5/8 x 7 5/8
Montross, Rag, Tag and Bobtail, 244, 3 1/4 x 4 1/4
Pennypacker, Pa., the Keystone, 97, 3 1/2 x 5 1/2
Pennypacker, Valley Forge, end, 15 5/8 x 11, by French
    engineer
Picket Post, Apr. 1954, 4, 3 1/2 x 4 7/8
Reade, Dedication Exercises, 19, 5 3/4 x 8, by French
    engineer
Scharf, Hist. of Phila., 1:360, 8 5/8 x 8 1/8
Scribner's Mag., 23(1898):718, 1 3/8 x 1 3/8
Sparks, Washington's Writings, 5:196, 4 1/4 x 7 1/4
Stoudt, Ordeal at Valley Forge, 103, 6 1/2 x 5 3/8; 184,
    5 x 7, by French engineer
Wildes, Valley Forge, lining papers, 8 1/2 x 11 1/4 col.
Winsor, America, 6:439, 3 3/8 x 4 5/8
By Brig. Gen. Louis Lebêque de Presle Duportail   18235
Chidsey, Valley Forge, 75, 4 7/8 x 6 1/2
Freeman, Washington, 4:567, 4 5/8 x 6 1/4
Gurney, Pict. Hist. U.S. Army, 54, 5 1/4 x 7 1/8
Meredith, Am. Wars, 61, 3 5/8 x 4 1/4; 62, 4 7/8 x 6 5/8
Mil. Engineer, 41(Sept.-Oct. 1949):360, 5 x 6 7/8
Pag. Am., 6:182, 3 3/8 x 4 3/4
Pa. Mag. Hist. and Biog., 56(Oct. 1932):344, 4 x 5 5/8
Picket Post, Apr. 1954, 27, 4 3/8 x 6; Feb. 1959, 21,
    4 3/8 x 6
Reade, Dedication Exercises, 19, 4 1/4 x 7 1/4
Reed, Valley Forge, 20, 6 1/4 x 8 3/8; interpretation of map,
    21, 6 1/2 x 8 1/4
Stoudt, Ordeal at Valley Forge, lining papers, 8 1/4 x 11
Taylor, Valley Forge, 52, 4 1/2 x 7
Valley Forge Park   18240
Burk, Valley Forge, front, 8 1/8 x 12 3/8; 7, 3 1/8 x 5 3/4
Pa. Mag. Hist. and Biog., 21, no.3(1897):299, 7 1/2 x
    11 1/4 col.
Sons of Am. Rev., Maine at Valley Forge, 1, 7 3/4 x 12 col.
Taylor, Valley Forge, 120, 11 5/8 x 16 col.
Valley Forge Park Commn., Report for 1906, 16, 15 1/8 x 24 7/8
    col; Report for 1908, end, 15 x 24 3/4 col.
Woodman, Hist. of Valley Forge, end, 7 5/8 x 10 1/2
Col. Dewees' Upper Forge, Valley Forge, Pa., 1770   18245
Picket Post, Oct. 1946, 17, 4 5/8 x 4; 18, 5 5/8 x 3 1/2
British positions near Darby, Pa., Dec. 22-27, 1777, by Maj.   18250
    John André
André, Journal, 1:131, 5 1/2 x 7 1/8; 132, 5 5/8 x 7 1/4;
    133, 5 1/2 x 7; 134, 5 1/2 x 7
British defenses around Philadelphia, 1777-1778   18255
André, Journal, 1:135, 11 x 7 col., by Maj. John André
Avery, Hist. of U.S., 6:173, 2 1/4 x 3 5/8 col.
Greene, Revolutionary War, 132, 2 1/4 x 3 5/8 col.
Scharf, Hist. of Phila., 1:360, 8 5/8 x 8 1/8
Taylor, Valley Forge, 20, 4 3/4 x 7 1/2

Washington Bicentennial, 1:395, 3 1/2 x 5, annotated by
   Washington
Winsor, America, 6:440, 3 5/8 x 6 3/4; 441, 7 x 5 by
   Capt. John Montrésor
Raids and skirmishes around Philadelphia, 1777-1778   18260
   Picket Post, July 1955, 24-25, 8 1/8 x 10
Military movements, Montgomery Co., Pa., 1777-1778   18265
   Alderfer, Montgomery Co. Story, 127, 5 3/4 x 4 1/4
Washington's movements, Montgomery Co., Pa., Sept 19, 1777-   18270
   June 19, 1778
   Picket Post, Jan. 1946, end, 12 1/2 x 19 3/4

1778

Crooked Billet, Pa., Battle of, May 1, 1778   18275
   Hist. Soc. Montgomery Co., Bul., 2(Apr. 1941):261,
      6 7/8 x 4 1/2
Barren Hill, Pa., Battle of, May 20, 1778   18280
   Avery, Hist. of U.S., 6:176, 3 x 4 1/2 col.
   Bean, Washington, 40, 8 1/8 x 5 1/8
   Carrington, Battles, 408, 8 x 4 3/4
   Gottschalk, Lafayette Joins Am. Army, 190, 7 x 9 1/4
   Greene, Revolutionary War, 146, 3 x 4 1/2 col.
   Hist. Soc. Montgomery Co., Bul., 4(Oct. 1943):6, 5 1/4 x 5
   Ingles, Queen's Rangers, 78, 4 1/8 x 6 1/4
   Lossing, Field-Book of Rev., 2:122, 3 x 2 5/8
   Seelye, Story of Washington, 238, 2 1/2 x 3 3/8
   Serle, Am. Journal, 294, 2 3/8 x 2, by Ambrose Serle
   Sparks, Washington's Writings, 5:378, 7 x 4
   Stedman, Am. War, 1:377, 8 3/8 x 6 3/4
   Tower, La Fayette, 1:328, 7 1/8 x 9 3/4, Lafayette's map
By Maj. Michel Capitaine du Chesnoy   18285
   Guthorn, Am. Maps, 10, 6 3/8 x 8 1/2; 11, 6 1/4 x 8 3/8
   Reed, Valley Forge, 60, 6 1/4 x 8 3/8; interpretation of
      map, 61, 4 x 4
   Stoudt, Ordeal at Valley Forge, 300, 4 x 6 1/2
   Winsor, America, 6:443, 4 x 4 3/4

1781

Route of French army, Red Lion Tavern, Pa., to Philadelphia,   18290
   Sept. 3, 1781, on way to Yorktown, by Louis-Alexandre
   Berthier
   Chastellux, Travels, 1:136, 5 1/4 x 8
   Maggs Bros., Berthier, 10, 5 1/8 x 7 3/4
Twenty-Seventh French camp, Philadelphia, Sept. 3, 1781   18295
   Maggs Bros., Berthier, 17, 7 3/8 x 4 7/8, by Louis-Alexandre
   Berthier
Camp of Hessian prisoners, Reading, Pa., 1781-1783   18300
   Berks Co. Hist. Soc., Trans., 3(1910-1916):24,
      6 5/8 x 3 1/2

NORTHEASTERN PENNSYLVANIA

Connecticut claims to lands in Pennsylvania   19010
    Pa. Archives, 2d series, 18:125, 5 3/4 x 9 3/4
    Weyburn, Following Conn. Trail, 18, 3 1/2 x 4 1/2
    See also 10015
Wyoming and Lackawanna Valleys, Pa.   19015
    Fiske, Am. Rev., 2:88-89, 2 3/4 x 7 1/2
    Tubbs, Wyo. Military Establishment, frontis., 4 x 8
Wyoming Valley, Pa.   19020
    Avery, Hist. of U.S., 6:185, 4 1/8 x 3 7/8 col.
Courses of Northeast Branch, Susquehanna River, from Wyoming,   19025
    Pa., to mouth of the Tioga, by Lt. Col. Adam Hubley, Jr.
    Pa. Mag. Hist. and Biog., 33(Apr. 1909):144, 9 x 5 1/2
Cayuga or Tioga Branch of Susquehanna River, by George   19030
    Washington
    N.Y. State Hist. Assn., Quar. Jl., 10(July 1929):205, 3 1/2 x 4
Northumberland County, Pa.
    1772   19035
        Godcharles, Chronicles, 2:237, 2 x 3 1/4
    1785   19040
        Godcharles, Chronicles, 2:237, 2 x 4 1/2
Easton, Pa., 1776   19045
    Chidsey, Frontier Village, 262, 7 7/8 x 15 7/8
Nazareth, Pa., 1771   19050
    Frontier Forts, 1:256, 3 1/4 x 2 1/2 col.
Sunbury, Pa., and vicinity, 1775   19055
    Godcharles, Chronicles, 2:245, 1 1/4 x 4, by Philip
        Vickers Fithian

DEFENSES

Fort Augusta, Sunbury, Pa., built 1756   19060
    Frontier Forts, 1:347, 10 3/4 x 17 1/8 col.; 354, 8 x 5 col.
Fort Muncy, on West Branch of Susquehanna, erected Sept. 1778   19065
    Northumberland Co. Hist. Soc., Proc., 6(1934):217,
    3 7/8 x 2 7/8; 222, 3 3/8 x 4 3/4
Pittston Fort, Pittston, Pa., 1772-1779   19070
    Frontier Forts, 1:446, 4 1/2 x 7 1/4
Fort Potter, site, Centre County, Pa., built 1777   19075
    Frontier Forts, 1:505, 8 x 5 col.
Wyoming Valley forts   19080
    Lossing, Field-Book of Rev., 1:353, 1 3/4 x 2
    Rogers, Journal, 51, 1 5/8 x 1 7/8

MILITARY OPERATIONS

Col. John Butler's raid on Wyoming Valley, Pa., July 1778   19085
    Clarke, Bloody Mohawk, 243, 3 x 4 3/8
    Faulkner, Am. Political & Social Hist., 133, 4 5/8 x 2 1/2
    Pag. Am., 6:214, 4 1/8 x 8 1/2
Col. Thomas Hartley's route, autumn 1778   19090
    Stevens, Exploring Penna., 181, 3 5/8 x 5 3/4
Maj. Gen. John Sullivan's expedition into country of the Six
        Nations, June - Oct. 1779
    See 14395-14410

WESTERN PENNSYLVANIA

Western Pennsylvania
  1760-1776   20005
    Billington, W. Expansion, 2d ed., 155, 2 x 3 3/4
  1775, by Nicholas Scull   20010
    Brown, Early Maps, pl.49, 9 1/2 x 7 1/8
  By Samuel Lewis   20015
    Kellogg, Frontier Retreat, 55, 8 1/4 x 6 3/4
  Pennsylvania-Virginia boundary dispute, 1774-1779   20020
    Adams, Atlas, pl.57, 9 1/2 x 6 3/8
    Buck, Planting of Civ., 165, 3 3/8 x 4 3/8
    Miller, W.Va. and Its People, 1:155, 6 1/4 x 4 3/4;
      161, 6 x 4 5/8
    Paullin, Atlas, pl.97G, 4 1/4 x 7 3/8 col.
    Winsor, Westward Movement, 197, 2 7/8 x 3 3/4
  Washington County, Pa., 1784   20023
    Hulbert, Washington and West, 48, 6 1/4 x 3 1/2
  Logstown, Beaver County, Pa., Aug. 1785   20025
    Darlington, Col. Bouquet, 9, 4 x 6 5/8
  Pittsburgh, Pa., lots, 1764   20030
    Fleming, Hist. of Pittsburgh, 1:520, 4 5/8 x 7 7/8
    Fleming, Views, 10, 4 5/8 x 7 7/8
    Jenkins, Pa. Colonial & Federal, 1:467, 3 5/8 x 5 1/2
  Lands purchased from the Indians by George Croghan
  200,000 acres in vicinity of Pittsburgh, 1749, 1768   20035
    Lewis, Indiana Co., 144, 2 1/4 x 3 3/4
  In Western Pennsylvania, 1773   20040
    Lewis, Indiana Co., 144, 5 1/2 x 9 3/8
  George Washington's farm at Great Meadows, near Farmington, Pa.   20042
    Hulbert, Washington and West, 137, 4 1/2 x 3

DEFENSES

Site of Fort McIntosh, Beaver, Pa., erected 1778   20045
  Frontier Forts, 2:496, 8 x 5 col.
Fort Palmer, Westmoreland County, Pa.   20050
  Frontier Forts, 2:358, 10 3/4 x 8 col.; 359, 8 x 5 col.
Fort Pitt, Pittsburgh, Pa., 1776   20055
  Jenkins, Pa. Colonial & Federal, 1:472, 3 5/8 x 4 1/8

MILITARY OPERATIONS

Col. Daniel Brodhead's expedition, Aug. 11 - Sept. 14, 1779   20060
  Am. Heritage Atlas, 101, 4 3/4 x 7 1/2 col.
  Avery, Hist. of U.S., 6:187, 4 1/2 x 6 3/4 col.
  Commager, Spirit of '76, 2:1004, 4 5/8 x 6 1/2
  Eyres, Sullivan Trail, 9, 5 x 5 1/8; 20-21, 7 x 10 1/2 col.
  Greene, Revolutionary War, 156, 4 1/2 x 6 3/4 col.
  Mag. of Am. Hist., 3(Nov. 1879):655, 5 7/8 x 7 1/2
  N.Y. State Hist. Assn., Quar. Jl., 9(Apr. 1928):217, 5 1/8 x
    4; 10(Oct. 1929):280, 4 1/4 x 7 col.
  N.Y., Sullivan-Clinton Campaign, 18, 4 1/4 x 7 col.
  Pag. Am., 6:217, 4 3/8 x 6 7/8
  Pa. Mag. Hist. and Biog., 48(July 1924):215, 4 7/8 x 3 3/4

Rayback, Richards Atlas, 32, 15 1/2 x 20 col.
Stevens, Exploring Penna., 181, 3 5/8 x 5 3/4
W. Pa. Hist. Mag., 7(Apr. 1924):88, 9 x 8 7/8
Hannastown, Pa., at time of destruction by Indians, July 13, 1782   20065
    Frontier Forts, 2:320, 17 x 21 3/4 col.
    Fed. Writers' Proj., Bid for Liberty, 27, 6 7/8 x 5 3/4

DELAWARE

Delaware
    See 11090, 11105
Delaware counties at time of the Revolution   21010
    Brown, King's Friends, 157, 3 1/8 x 2 3/4

MILITARY OPERATIONS

Area of operations
    See 11140, 11145, 11155
Washington's headquarters in Delaware   21015
    Washington Atlas, pl. 37, 15 1/2 x 11 col.
    Washington Bicentennial, 1:410, 5 3/4 x 10 1/8
American encampments along White Clay Creek and Red Clay Creek,   21020
    Del., Aug. 28-29, 1777
    Cooch, Cooch's Bridge, 19, 6 x 4 1/4, by S. Lewis
British camp near Carson's Tavern, Del., Sept. 2, 1777   21025
    André, Journal, 1:79, 7 x 5 5/8, by Maj. John André
Movements of British and American troops before and after   21030
    Battle of Cooch's Bridge
    Cooch, Cooch's Bridge, 55, 15 1/2 x 13, British Army map
Cooch's Bridge, Del., Battle of, Sept. 3, 1777   21035
    Cooch, Cooch's Bridge, 41, 9 x 6 3/4
    Reed, Campaign to Valley Forge, 101, 5 1/2 x 4 7/8
Position of British army near Aikens' Tavern, Del., Sept. 5,   21040
    1777, by Maj. John André
    André, Journal, 1:80, 5 5/8 x 7
    Cooch, Cooch's Bridge, 49, 5 1/2 x 4 1/8
Position of Washington's army between Newport and Marshallton,   21045
    Del., Sept. 6-9, 1777
    Nields, Washington's Army in Del., front, 13 5/8 x 7 3/8

MARYLAND

Maryland
  1777
    See 11090
  1780   22010
    Gipson, Br. Empire, 2:49, 7 3/4 x 5 5/8
Maryland counties at time of the Revolution   22015
    Brown, King's Friends, 165, 3 1/8 x 4 5/8
  1776-1779   22020
    Crowl, Maryland, frontis., 4 3/8 x 6
Road from Bladensburg, Md., through Georgetown, to near   22025
    Alexandria, Va., 1781?
    Guthorn, Am. Maps, 14, 6 1/2 x 3 3/4, by Simeon DeWitt

MILITARY OPERATIONS

Area of operations
  See 11155
British landing place at head of Chesapeake Bay, Aug. 25, 1777   22029
  Seelye, Story of Washington, 204, 4 x 2 1/4
Encampment of Sir William Howe's army upon landing at Head of   22030
  Elk River, Md., Aug. 26, 1777
  André, Journal, 1:70, 5 5/8 x 7, by Maj. John André
Encampment of Lt. Gen. Knyphausen's division along Elk River,   22035
  Aug. 29, 1777
  André, Journal, 1:73, 5 5/8 x 7, by Maj. John André
Position of Lt. Gen. Knyphausen's division, Cecil Church, Md.,   22040
  Sept. 1, 1777
  André, Journal, 1:78, 7 x 5 5/8, by Maj. John André
Lafayette's route to and through Harford County, Md., Apr. 1781   22043
  Shriver, Lafayette in Harford Co., 22, 4 1/8 x 4 1/4
Thirty-fourth camp of French army on march to Yorktown,   22045
  Baltimore, Md., Sept. 12, 1781
    Maggs Bros., Berthier, 18, 7 3/8 x 4 5/8, by Louis-Alexandre
    Berthier
Twentieth camp of French army on march from Yorktown to Boston,   22050
  Baltimore, Md., July 24, 1782
    Maggs Bros., Berthier, 28, 7 1/2 x 5, by Louis-Alexandre
    Berthier

THE SOUTH

Southern states during the Revolution	23000

Adams, Atlas, pl.74, 9 1/4 x 6 1/4
Am. Heritage, Revolution, 338, 9 1/8 x 7 col.
Baurmeister, Revolution, 446, 7 3/8 x 5
Billias, Washington's Opponents, xxxi, 7 1/2 x 4 3/4
Boatner, Enc. of Am. Rev., end lining paper, 7 5/8 x 4 3/4
Bolton, Colonization, 526, 3 7/8 x 3 7/8
Botta, War of Ind., 2:257, 6 1/2 x 4 1/8
Carrington, Battles, 555, 7 5/8 x 4 5/8
Channing, Hist. of U.S., 3:316, 5 x 4
Chitwood, Colonial America, 569, 3 1/2 x 4
Duncan, Medical Men, 311, 5 3/8 x 4 1/8
Dupuy, Compact Hist., end, 6 3/4 x 5 5/8
Fite, Book of Old Maps, 282, 12 x 8 5/8, by S. Lewis
Frothingham, Washington, 282, 5 1/4 x 4 5/8
Garner, Hist. of U.S., 2:499, 7 x 4 1/4
Hart, Am. Nation, 9:290, 6 1/2 x 4 1/8 col.
Kinnaird, Geo. Washington, 172, 9 1/2 x 5 3/4
Mackesy, War for America, 340, 4 5/8 x 4 1/4
Marshall, Atlas, map 8, 9 3/8 x 6 3/4, by S. Lewis
Montross, Rag, Tag and Bobtail, 376, 6 3/8 x 4 1/4
Peckham, War for Independence, end, 10 5/8 x 8
Rankin, Am. Rev., 231, 5 3/4 x 4
Scheer, Rebels and Redcoats, 391, 7 3/8 x 4 1/2
Ward, Revolution, 2:657, 7 1/8 x 4 3/8
See also 23045

North and South Carolina	23005

Pratt, 11 Generals, 16, 3 x 4

1771-1775	23010

Carroll, Hist. Coll. of S.C., 1:frontis., 17 1/4 x 22
See also 25125-25140
North Carolina, South Carolina and Georgia

1776	23015

Naval Docs. of Am. Rev., 2:458, 5 1/2 x 7 3/8, engr. by
Robert Aitken

1782	23020

Hilliard d'Auberteuil, Essais, 1:265, 9 x 12 3/4 col.
North Carolina, South Carolina, Georgia, and Florida

1762, by J. Gibson	23025

Gipson, Br. Empire, 12:195, 5 x 6 1/4

By Bernard Romans	23030

Naval Docs. of Am. Rev., 2:773, 5 1/4 x 6 5/8, pub. by
Robert Sayer and John Bennett

Coasts of South Carolina, Georgia, and Florida at time of	23032

Revolutionary War
Butler, King's Royal Rifle Corps, 1:318, 8 5/8 x 5 5/8

Georgia and Florida, 1763	23035

Howell, Hist. of Ga., 1:169, 6 1/4 x 5, by Thomas Wright

Northern Florida and Southern Georgia	23040

Barrs, East Fla., 14-15, 9 1/4 x 6 3/8

MILITARY OPERATIONS

Southern theatre of operations   23045
    Alden, Hist. of Am. Rev., 399, 8 5/8 x 8 5/8
    Clarke, Am. Revolution, end lining paper, 4 1/4 x 2 7/8 col.
    Churchill, English-Speaking Peoples, 3:209, 6 1/4 x 4
    Gewehr, United States, 77, 4 3/4 x 4
    Hall, School History, 108, 7 1/2 x 6 1/8
    Hall-Quest, From Colony to Nation, 201, 6 1/8 x 3 3/4
    Lossing, Life of Washington, 2:711, 8 7/8 x 5 1/2
    Lossing, Washington and Am. Republic, 2:711, 8 7/8 x 5 1/2
    Matloff, Am. Military History, 86, 5 7/8 x 4 3/8
    Miers, Yankee Doodle Dandy, 180-181, 5 1/4 x 8
    Mitchell, Discipline and Bayonets, 134, 6 3/8 x 4 1/4
    Nettels, Roots of Am. Civ., 710, 6 3/8 x 4
    Scharf, Hist. of Md., 2:359, 7 1/2 x 4 5/8
    Sloane, French War and Rev., 312, 5 1/4 x 3 1/4 col.
    Sobel, Am. Revolution, 117, 3 3/4 x 6 1/2
    Sosin, Revolutionary Frontier, 127, 7 1/2 x 5 1/8
Southern campaigns
1776-1781   23050
    Hicks, Federal Union, 4th ed., 193, 4 x 5 1/2
1778-1779   23055
    Paullin, Atlas, pl.160E, 3 5/8 x 2 5/8 col.
1778-1780   23060
    Am. Heritage Atlas, 102, 5 1/4 x 7 1/2 col.
    Avery, Hist. of U.S., 6:212, 6 3/4 x 5 3/8 col.
    Greene, Revolutionary War, 192, 6 3/4 x 5 3/8 col.
1778-1781   23065
    Chron Am., 12:250, 7 x 5 7/8 col.
    Dupuy, Mil. Heritage of Am., 102, 4 5/8 x 3 1/2
    Esposito, Am. Wars Atlas, 1:map 8a., 9 1/2 x 6 1/4 col.
    Esposito, Civil War Atlas, map 8a, 9 1/2 x 6 1/4 col.
    World Book, 16:261, 3 x 4 5/8 col.
1779-1781   23070
    Faulkner, Am. Political & Social Hist., 138, 3 1/4 x 3 5/8
    Morison, Growth of Am. Republic, 5th ed., 222, 6 x 4 1/2
1780   23075
    Avery, Hist. of U.S., 6:210, 6 3/4 x 4 3/4 col.
    Pag. Am., 6:236, 6 3/8 x 5 3/8
    Paullin, Atlas, pl. 160F, 3 5/8 x 3 1/8 col.
1780-1781   23080
    Am. Heritage Atlas, 103, 5 3/4 x 7 1/2 col.
    Baldwin, Adult's History, 110, 5 7/8 x 5 5/8
    Callahan, Daniel Morgan, 188, 5 3/4 x 3 7/8
    Cook, Golden Bk. of Am. Revolution, 166, 8 5/8 x 6 5/8 col.
    Hofstadter, Am. Republic, 188, 4 x 3 1/4
    Kraus, U.S. to 1865, 235, 5 1/4 x 4 1/8
    Malone, Am. Origins, 182, 7 1/8 x 4 1/2
    Morison, Hist. of Am. People, 252, 7 1/4 x 4 1/2
    Tarleton, Campaigns, 1, 25 5/8 x 19 1/4 col., by William Faden
    Todd, America's Hist., 143, 4 1/2 x 5 1/8
1781   23085
    Avery, Hist. of U.S., 6:283, 5 1/4 x 4 1/2 col.; 284,
      7 x 5 7/8 col.
    Greene, Revolutionary War, 226, 7 x 5 7/8 col.; 232,
      5 1/4 x 4 1/2 col.

Landers, Va. Campaign, map 1, 12 1/2 x 13 5/8
Mitchell, Battles Am. Rev., 195, 7 1/2 x 5 col.
Pag. Am., 6:242, 6 5/8 x 5 5/8

VIRGINIA

Virginia
  1770   24005
    Abernethy, Western Lands, 292, 18 3/8 x 24, by John Henry
  1779   24010
    Gipson, Br. Empire, 2:48, 5 3/4 x 6 1/2
  1781   24013
    Naval Docs. of Am. Rev., 3:1208, 5 x 7 7/8, by Jacques
      Nicolas Bellin
  1782   24015
    Chastellux, Travels, 1:back lining paper, 8 x 11 5/8;
      2:front lining paper, 8 x 11 5/8
Maritime parts of Virginia, 1776   24020
    Naval Docs. of Am. Rev., 2:124, 5 1/8 x 7 3/4, engr. by
      Nicholas Pocock
Tidewater Virginia
  1775   24025
    Noel Hume, 1775, xxiv-xxv, 7 1/8 x 8 1/2
  At close of the Revolution   24030
    Madison, Papers, 1:212, 7 3/4 x 6 1/8
Virginia Peninsula, 1781   24035
    Johnston, Yorktown, 103, 4 5/8 x 7 7/8
    Stevens, Yorktown Handbook, 9, 2 1/2 x 2 1/4
Virginia piedmont and mountain areas   24040
    Madison, Papers, 1:212, 7 3/4 x 6 1/8
Valley of Virginia, physical map   24045
    Hart, Valley of Va., 4, 5 x 3 7/8
Western Virginia
  1768   24050
    De Vorsey, Indian Boundary, 72, 3 3/8 x 6 7/8
  1780   24055
    Abernethy, Western Lands, 65, 4 x 7
Disputed boundaries of Pennsylvania and Virginia
See 20020
Virginia counties, 1763   24059
    Morton, Colonial Va., 2:742, 7 5/8 x 4
Virginia county boundaries at time of Revolution   24060
    Brown, King's Friends, 179, 4 x 6 1/4
District of West Augusta, 1775, and original counties formed   24062
    therefrom by Virginia legislature, 1776
    Callahan, Hist. of West Va., 1:191, 7 1/4 x 5
    Callahan, Making of Morgantown, 39, 7 1/8 x 5
Albemarle County, Va., 1777   24065
    Jefferson, Papers, 2:208, 6 3/4 x 4 7/8
Old Botetourt County, Va., 1770, and its subdivisions   24066
    Kegley, Va. Frontier, 380, 5 5/8 x 7 1/2, by Elizabeth
      Waller Wilkins
Norfolk County, Va., part of, c.1781
  Portsmouth to Great Bridge   24070
    Whichard, Lower Tidewater Va., 1:303, 7 5/8 x 4 7/8

Princess Anne County, Va., parts of, c.1781
  Kempsville to Moore's Bridges   24075
    Whichard, Lower Tidewater Va., 1:272, 3 x 4 1/4
  Cape Henry to Little Creek   24080
    Whichard, Lower Tidewater Va., 1:274, 3 1/4 x 7
Washington County, Va., 1780   24083
    Summers, Hist. of Southwest Va., 258, 4 3/8 x 6 3/8
Fincastle, Va., 1770   24084
    Kegley, Va. Frontier, 402, 3 3/4 x 5 1/4
Hampton, Va., and vicinity, about 1775   24085
    Noël Hume, 1775, pl.X, 8 3/8 x 11
Jamestown, Va., 1781   24087
    Garvan, Arch. and Town Planning, 40, 8 7/8 x 6, from Rochambeau
    Papers, Library of Congress
Norfolk and Portsmouth, Va.   24089
    Naval Docs. of Am. Rev., 3:564, 7 1/2 x 5 1/8
Portsmouth and Gosport, Va., at time of the Revolution 24090
    Va. Cavalcade, 2(Autumn 1952):33, 4 1/8 x 5 1/4
Portsmouth, Va., 1788   24095
    Noël Hume, 1775, pl.XIX, 5 x 7 1/2
Williamsburg and Yorktown, Va., 1781   24100
    Arthur, Sieges of Yorktown, 11, 4 1/8 x 7
Williamsburg, Va.   24105
    Miers, Blood of Freedom, 72, 5 1/2 x 3 5/8
  1782   24110
    Adams, Album of Am. Hist., 1:253, 2 1/8 x 3 1/4
    Am. Heritage, 1(Winter 1950):37, 3 1/4 x 7 1/4
    Noël Hume, 1775, pl.V, 4 3/4 x 6 7/8
Yorktown, Va., and vicinity, 1781   24115
    Ingles, Queen's Rangers, 221, 4 3/4 x 7 7/8
    Mil. Engineer, 48(Sept.-Oct. 1956):377, 2 5/8 x 4 1/8
Valley of Virginia population, 1776   24120
    Hart, Valley of Va., 6, 5 x 3 7/8

MILITARY OPERATIONS

Area of operations in Virginia, 1775-1781   24125
    Boatner, Enc. of Am. Rev., 1150, 4 x 6 5/8
    Gordon, Hist. of U.S.A., 4:116, pl.VIII, 7 1/8 x 10 3/8, engr.
    by T. Conder

1775

Great Bridge, Va., Battle of, Dec. 9, 1775   24130
    Noël Hume, 1775, pl.XXI, 4 3/8 x 6 3/4; pl.XXII, 5 x 4 1/4
    Mays, Edmund Pendleton, 2:66, 5 3/4 x 5, Clinton Map 281,
    Wm. L. Clements Library
    Thayne, Virginia Colony, 120, 6 7/8 x 3 3/4

1776

Disposition of British and American forces on and about Gwynn's
    Island, Va., July 1776
    Va. Cavalcade, 2(Spring 1953):41, 4 1/2 x 6 1/2, by Thomas
    Jefferson

1780

Operations in Virginia, 1780   24140
    Palmer, Steuben, 246, 9 7/8 x 13 7/8

1781

Theatre of operations in Virginia, 1781   24145
    Fiske, Am. Rev., 2:283, 6 x 3 3/4
    Ingles, Queen's Rangers, 169, 5 1/4 x 7 7/8
    Miers, Yankee Doodle Dandy, 209, 3 5/8 x 5 3/8
Operations in Virginia, 1781   24150
    Avery, Hist. of U.S., 6:299, 4 1/2 x 7 col.
    Esposito, Am. Wars Atlas, 1:map 9, 9 1/2 x 12 1/4 col.
    Esposito, Civil War Atlas, map 9, 9 1/2 x 12 1/4 col.
    Flexner, Washington in Am. Revolution, 453, 2 3/4 x 4 3/4,
        by Samuel H. Bryant
    Greene, Revolutionary War, 258, 4 1/2 x 7 col.
    Gurney, Pict. Hist. U.S. Army, 71, 6 1/8 x 3 5/8
    Hicks, Federal Union, 4th ed., 195, 3 3/4 x 2 5/8
    Hofstadter, Am. Republic, 189, 4 1/4 x 3 1/4
    Landers, Va. Campaign, map 2, 12 3/8 x 15 3/8
    N.Y. Hist. Soc. Quar., 45(Jan. 1961):38, 2 3/4 x 4 1/4
    Pag. Am., 6:247, 7 x 5 7/8
    Palmer, Steuben, 246, 9 7/8 x 13 7/8
    Perkins, U.S. of Am., 165, 3 3/4 x 4 5/8
    Vestal, Washington, 44, 3 x 4
    Wallace, Appeal to Arms, 249, 4 3/4 x 7 1/8
    Washington Bicentennial, 1:119, 4 x 4
Movements of American commanders in Virginia, 1781
  Marquis de Lafayette   24155
    Am. Heritage Atlas, 103, 5 3/4 x 7 1/2 col.
    Avery, Hist. of U.S., 6:299, 4 1/2 x 7 col.
    Boatner, Enc. of Am. Rev., 1153, 3 1/2 x 4 1/8;
        1154, 2 3/4 x 4 1/8; 1155, 3 4 x 4 1/8
    Carrington, Battles, 616, 4 3/4 x 7 3/4
    Carrington, Washington, 339, 3 1/2 x 5 3/4
    Chron. Am., 12:250, 7 x 5 5/8 col.
    Coast Artillery Jl., 72(Apr. 1930):321, 3 1/2 x 4 1/2
    Esposito, Am. Wars Atlas, 1:map9, 9 1/2 x 12 1/4 col.
    Esposito, Civil War Atlas, map 9, 9 1/2 x 12 1/4 col.
    Faulkner, Am. Political & Social Hist., 138, 3 1/4 x 3 5/8
    Fleming, Beat the Last Drum, front, 7 7/8 x 10 5/8
    Freeman, Washington, 5:303, 4 1/2 x 6 1/2
    Frothingham, Washington, 338, 7 x 4 1/8
    Gottschalk, Lafayette and Close of Am. Rev., 238, 8 x 10,
        by Maj. Capitaine
    Greene, Revolutionary War, 258, 4 1/2 x 7 col.
    Hatch, Yorktown, 5, 5 3/8 x 8 5/8
    Johnston, Yorktown, 57, 4 3/4 x 6 1/8
    Journal of Am. Hist., 25(1931):109, 3 x 5 1/8
    Landers, Va. Campaign, map 1, 12 1/2 x 13 5/8; map 2,
        12 3/8 x 15 3/8
    Mag. of Am. Hist., 6(May 1881):344, 4 3/4 x 7 3/4
    N.Y. Hist. Soc. Quar., 45(Jan. 1961):38, 2 3/4 x 4 1/4
    Pag. Am., 6:247, 7 x 5 7/8

Paullin, Atlas, pl.160H, 7 5/8 x 4 7/8 col.; pl.160H inset,
   1 3/4 x 2 1/2 col.
Perkins, U.S. of Am., 165, 3 3/4 x 4 5/8
Sparks, Washington's Writings, 8:158, 7 x 4 1/4
Steele, Am. Campaigns, 2:28, 3 5/8 x 6 1/4 col.
Tower, La Fayette, 2:244, 10 1/4 x 6 3/4 col.; 288,
   9 1/4 x 7 3/8 col.; 342, 7 1/2 x 9 1/2 col.
U.S.N. Inst. Proc., 57(June 1931):729, 4 1/4 x 5 1/2
Vestal, Washington, 44, 3 x 4
Wallace, Appeal to Arms, 249, 4 3/4 x 7 1/8
Washington Bicentennial, 1:119, 3 x 4

Brig. Gen. Daniel Morgan   24160
Landers, Va. Campaign, map 1, 12 1/2 x 13 5/8

Maj. Gen. Friedrich von Steuben   24165
Avery, Hist. of U.S., 6:299, 4 1/2 x 7 col.
Doyle, Von Steuben, 194, 4 1/2 x 7
Esposito, Am. Wars Atlas, 1:map 9, 9 1/2 x 12 1/4 col.
Esposito, Civil War Atlas, map 9, 9 1/2 x 12 1/4 col.
Greene, Revolutionary War, 258, 4 1/2 x 7 col.
Pag. Am., 6:247, 7 x 5 7/8
Vestal, Washington, 44, 3 x 4
Wallace, Appeal to Arms, 249, 4 3/4 x 7 1/8
Washington Bicentennial, 1:119, 3 x 4

Brig. Gen. Anthony Wayne   24170
Avery, Hist. of U.S., 6:299, 4 1/2 x 7 col.
Esposito, Am. Wars Atlas, 1:map 9, 9 1/2 x 12 1/4 col.
Esposito, Civil War Atlas, map 9, 9 1/2 x 12 1/4 col.
Greene, Revolutionary War, 258, 4 1/2 x 7 col.
Journal of Am. Hist., 25(1931), 109, 3 x 5 1/8
Pag. Am., 6:247, 7 x 5 7/8
Paullin, Atlas, pl.160H, 7 5/8 x 4 7/8 col.; pl.160H inset,
   1 3/4 x 2 1/2 col.
Vestal, Washington, 44, 3 x 4

Movements of British commanders in Virginia, 1781
Brig. Gen Benedict Arnold   24175
Avery, Hist. of U.S., 6:299, 4 1/2 x 7 col.
Greene, Revolutionary War, 258, 4 1/2 x 7 col.
Pag. Am., 6:247, 7 x 5 7/8
Vestal, Washington, 44, 3 x 4

Lt. Gen. Charles Cornwallis   24180
Am. Heritage Atlas, 103, 5 3/4 x 7 1/2 col.
Am. Heritage, Revolution, 352, 2 1/4 x 2
Army, Am. Military Hist., 96, 7 1/4 x 4 3/8
Avery, Hist. of U.S., 6:299, 4 1/2 x 7 col.
Barck, Colonial Am., 643, 7 x 4 5/8
Barck, Colonial Am., 2d ed., 617, 4 5/8 x 7
Billias, Washington's Opponents, xxxi, 7 1/2 x 4 3/4;
   xxxii, 7 1/4 x 4 5/8
Boatner, Enc. of Am. Rev., 1153, 3 1/2 x 4 1/8; 1154,
   2 3/4 x 4 1/8; 1155, 3 x 4 1/8
Carrington, Battles, frontis., 7 1/2 x 4 1/2; 616, 4 3/4 x
   7 3/4
Chron. Am., 12:250, 7 x 5 5/8 col.
Coast Artillery Jl., 72(Apr. 1930):321, 3 1/2 x 4 1/2
Cook, Golden Bk. of Am. Rev., 166, 8 5/8 x 6 5/8 col.

Current, Am. Hist., 2d ed., 114, 3 1/2 x 2 1/2
Dupuy, Compact Hist., end, 6 3/4 x 5 5/8
Esposito, Am. Wars Atlas, 1:map 9, 9 1/2 x 12 1/4 col.
Esposito, Civil War Atlas, map 9, 9 1/2 x 12 1/4 col.
Faulkner, Am. Political & Social Hist., 138, 3 1/4 x 3 5/8
Fisher, Struggle for Am. Ind., 2:468, 6 x 3 1/2
Fleming, Beat the Last Drum, front, 7 7/8 x 10 5/8 col.
Freeman, Washington, 5:303, 4 1/2 x 6 1/2
Frothingham, Washington, 338, 7 x 4 1/8
Gottschalk, Lafayette and Close of Am. Rev., 238, 8 x 10,
  by Maj. Capitaine
Greene, Revolutionary War, 258, 4 1/2 x 7 col.
Harper's Mag., 63(Aug. 1881):324, 5 1/4 x 4 3/4
James, Br. Navy in Adversity, 276, 6 1/8 x 4
Hart, Am. Nation, 9:290, 6 1/2 x 4 1/8 col.
Hatch, Yorktown, 5, 5 3/8 x 8 5/8
Johnston, Yorktown, 27, 5 1/4 x 4 3/4; 57, 4 3/4 x 6 1/8
Journal of Am. Hist., 25(1931):109, 3 x 5 1/8
Landers, Va. Campaign, map 1, 12 1/2 x 13 5/8; map 2,
  12 3/8 x 15 3/8
Lowell, Hessians, 265, 5 1/2 x 3 3/8
Matloff, Am. Military History, 95, 7 3/8 x 4 3/8
N.Y. Hist. Soc. Quar., 45(Jan. 1961):38, 2 3/4 x 4 1/4
Pag. Am., 6:247, 7 x 5 7/8
Paullin, Atlas, pl. 160H, 7 5/8 x 4 7/8 col.; pl.160H inset,
  1 3/4 x 2 1/2 col.
Perkins, U.S. of Am, 165, 3 3/4 x 4 5/8
Sparks, Washington's Writings, 8:158, 7 x 4 1/4
Steele, Am. Campaigns, 2:28, 3 5/8 x 6 1/4 col.
Tarleton, Campaigns, 1, 25 5/8 x 19 1/4 col., by William
  Faden
Tower, La Fayette, 2:288, 9 1/4 x 7 3/8 col.; 342, 7 1/2 x
  9 1/2 col.
Vestal, Washington, 44, 3 x 4
Wallace, Appeal to Arms, 249, 4 3/4 x 7 1/8
Washington Bicentennial, 1:119, 3 x 4
Wells, Am. War of Independence, 169, 5 3/8 x 4
Whitton, Am. War of Ind., 318, 6 x 3 1/2
Wickwire, Cornwallis, 327, 6 x 4 1/8
Whitton, Am. War of Ind., 318, 6 x 3 1/2

Brig. Gen. Charles O'Hara   24185
  Tarleton, Campaigns, 1, 25 5/8 x 19 1/4 col., by William
    Faden
Maj. Gen. William Phillips   24190
  Avery, Hist. of U.S., 6:299, 4 1/2 x 7 col.
  Greene, Revolutionary War, 258, 4 1/2 x 7 col.
  Pag. Am., 6:247, 7 x 5 7/8
  Vestal, Washington, 44, 3 x 4
Lt. Col. John Graves Simcoe   24195
  Pag. Am., 6:247, 7 x 5 1/8
  Wallace, Appeal to Arms, 249, 4 3/4 x 7 1/8
Lt. Col. Banastre Tarleton   24200
  Am. Heritage Atlas, 103, 5 3/4 x 7 1/2 col.
  Avery, Hist. of U.S., 6:299, 4 1/2 x 7 col.
  Boatner, Enc. of Am. Rev., 1154, 2 3/4 x 4 1/8

Carrington, Battles, 616, 4 3/4 x 7 3/4
Carrington, Washington, 339, 3 1/2 x 5 3/4
Esposito, Am. Wars Atlas, 1:map 9, 9 1/2 x 12 1/4 col.
Esposito, Civil War Atlas, map 9, 9 1/2 x 12 1/4 col.
Fleming, Beat the Last Drum, front, 7 7/8 x 10 5/8 col.
Greene, Revolutionary War, 258, 4 1/2 x 7 col.
Journal of Am. Hist., 25(1931):109, 3 x 5 1/8
Landers, Va. Campaign, map 1, 12 1/2 x 13 5/8; map 2,
    12 3/8 x 15 3/8
Mag. of Am. Hist., 6(May 1881):344, 4 3/4 x 7 3/4
Pag. Am., 6:247, 7 x 5 7/8
Paullin, Atlas, pl. 160H, 7 5/8 x 4 7/8 col.
Perkins, U.S. of Am., 165, 3 3/4 x 4 5/8
Tarleton, Campaigns, 1, 25 5/8 x 19 1/4 col., by William
    Faden
Vestal, Washington, 44, 3 x 4
Wallace, Appeal to Arms, 249, 4 3/4 x 7 1/8
Washington Bicentennial, 1:119, 3 x 4
Richmond, Va., skirmish, Jan. 5, 1781   24205
    Avery, Hist. of U.S., 6:298, 3 x 3 3/4 col.
    Carrington, Battles, 533, 4 1/8 x 4 5/8
    Greene, Revolutionary War, 260, 3 x 3 3/4 col.
    Lossing, Field-Book of Rev., 2:229, 2 3/4 x 2 1/4
  By Lt. Allang of Queen's Rangers   24210
    Ingles, Queen's Rangers, 172, 4 3/8 x 5 7/8
    Jefferson, Papers, 4:267, 4 3/4 x 5 7/8
    Pag. Am., 6:246, 3 1/8 x 3 7/8
    Simcoe, Military Jl., 162, 6 1/4 x 8
Brig. Gen. Benedict Arnold's picket line, Richmond, Va.,   24215
    Jan. 5, 1781
    Sons of Rev. in Va., Mag., 3(July 1924):16, 4 1/4 x 4 1/8
Burrell's Va., skirmish, Apr. 19, 1781, by Lt. George Spencer 24220
    Ingles, Queen's Rangers, 185, 4 7/8 x 6 1/4
    Simcoe, Military Jl., 192, 6 1/2 x 8 1/4
Petersburg, Va., Battle of, Apr. 25, 1781   24225
    Avery, Hist. of U.S., 6:302, 1 7/8 x 2 5/8 col.
    Carrington, Battles, 533, 3 1/2 x 4 5/8
    Greene, Revolutionary War, 260, 1 7/8 x 2 5/8 col.
    Lossing, Field-Book of Rev., 2:338, 2 1/4 x 2 3/4
  By Lt. George Spencer and Lt. John Hills   24230
    Ingles, Queen's Rangers 189, 4 7/8 x 6 7/8
    Simcoe, Military Jl., 198, 6 1/2 x 8
Osburne's (or Osborne's), Va., skirmish, Apr. 27, 1781   24235
    Lossing, Field-Book of Rev., 2:339, 2 5/8 x 2 5/8
  By Lt. George Spencer   24240
    Ingles, Queen's Rangers, 191, 5 x 5 3/4
    Jefferson, Papers, 5:417, 4 3/8 x 5 5/8
    Simcoe, Military Jl., 202, 6 1/2 x 8 3/8
Spencer's Ordinary, Va., skirmish, June 26, 1781   24245
    Lossing, Field-Book of Rev., 2:258, 3 1/8 x 2 1/8
  By Lt. George Spencer   24250
    Ingles, Queen's Rangers, 209, 5 1/8 x 5 5/8
    Simcoe, Military Jl., 236, 8 x 8 3/4
Green Spring (or Jamestown Ford), Va., Battle of, July 6, 1781 24255
    Gottschalk, Lafayette and Close of Am. Rev., 264, 8 x 8 3/8,
        prob. by Maj. Michel Capitaine du Chesnoy

Miers, Blood of Freedom, 127, 5 5/8 x 3 5/8, after Col.
Desandrouins
Mil. Engineer, 48(July-Aug. 1956):262, 3 5/8 x 3 1/4
Va. Mag. Hist. and Biog., 53(July 1945):172, 5 3/4 x 4 3/8,
by Col. Desandrouins
James River crossing used by Cornwallis, July 6-7, 1781   24260
Mil. Engineer, 48(July-Aug. 1956):262, 3 5/8 x 3 1/4
Routes of Washington's and Rochambeau's forces from King's   24265
Ferry, N.Y., to Yorktown, Va., Aug.-Sept. 1781
Adams, Atlas, pl.80, 9 1/4 x 6 1/4
Army, Am. Military Hist., 96, 7 1/4 x 4 3/8
Avery, Hist. of U.S., 6:299, 4 1/2 x 7 col.
Balch, French in Am., end, 5 x 10 1/8
Buchser, Yorktown, 16, 2 7/8 x 2 3/8
Clarke, Am. Revolution, end lining paper, 4 1/4 x 3 1/2 col.
Closen, Journal, lining papers, 11 3/4 x 9 col.
Coast Artillery Jl., 72(Apr. 1930):327, 5 x 2 3/8
Davis, Yorktown, 106, 7 x 5 1/4
Dupuy, Mil. Heritage of Am., 109, 5 3/8 x 2 1/2
Eckenrode, Yorktown, 26, 7 3/4 x 19
Esposito, Am. Wars Atlas, 1:map 9 inset, 4 1/4 x 1 7/8 col.
Esposito, Civil War Atlas, map 9 inset 4 1/4 x 1 7/8 col.
Faulkner, Am. Political & Social Hist., 138, 3 1/4 x 3 5/8
Fish, Washington in Highlands, 24, 5 3/8 x 3 3/4
Flexner, Washington in Am. Rev., lining papers, 6 5/8 x 4 7/8,
by Samuel H. Bryant
Freeman, Washington, abridgment, 47, 7 3/4 x 5 1/2
Greene, Revolutionary War, 258, 4 1/2 x 7 col.
Harper's Mag., 63(Aug. 1881):328, 5 x 2 3/8
Johnston, Yorktown, 89, 5 x 2 3/8
Kinnaird, Geo. Washington, 179, 5 x 2 3/8
Landers, Va. Campaign, map 3, 12 3/8 x 15 3/8
Mag. of Am. Hist., 4(July 1880):17, 6 1/2 x 21, by Lt. John
Hills; 7(July 1881):12, 4 3/4 x 7; 17, 5 3/4 x 5 1/8
Mass. Hist. Soc., Proc., 67(1941-1944)152, 7 1/4 x 16, from
Rochambeau papers
Matloff, Am. Military History, 95, 7 3/8 x 4 3/8
Montmort, Vioménil, lining papers, 6 1/2 x 8 3/4
Pag. Am., 6:247, 7 x 5 7/8; 252, 2 x 5 7/8, French chart
Paullin, Atlas, pl.160H, 7 5/8 x 4 7/8 col.
Perkins, U.S. of Am., 165, 3 3/4 x 4 5/8
Reeder, Story of Rev. War, 233, 4 1/2 x 4 1/8
Steele, Am. Campaigns, 2:29, 6 x 3 3/4 col.
U.S.N. Inst. Proc., 57(June 1931):731, 6 1/4 x 3
Vestal, Washington, 44, 3 x 4
Wallace, Appeal to Arms, 249, 4 3/4 x 7 1/8
Washington Atlas, pl.39, 15 1/2 x 11 col., 5 3/8 x 3 5/8 col.
Washington Bicentennial, 1:119, 3 x 4
Whitridge, Rochambeau, 157, 7 3/4 x 5
See also 04065, 16573-16575, 18290
French encampments en route to Yorktown, by Louis-Alexandre
Berthier
Archer's Hope, Va., Sept. 25, 1781   24270
Weelen, Rochambeau, 218, 4 3/8 x 3 3/4
Thirty-ninth camp, Williamsburg, Va., Sept. 26, 1781   24275
Jefferson, Papers, 2:304, 7 3/8 x 4 3/4

Madison, Papers, 2:165, 8 1/4 x 5 1/4
Maggs Bros., Berthier, 19, 7 1/2 x 4 7/8
Weelen, Rochambeau, 226, 5 1/8 x 3 3/4
Yorktown campaign, 1781   24280
   Boatner, Enc. of Am. Rev., 1238, 6 3/4 x 4 1/8
Yorktown, Va., siege, Sept. 28 - Oct. 19, 1781   24285
   Adams, Atlas, pl.81, 6 1/4 x 9 1/4
   Alden, Am. Revolution, 246, 4 3/4 x 4 1/4
   Alden, Rise of Am. Republic, 155, 3 3/8 x 4 3/8
   Am. Heritage, Revolution, 258, 2 3/8 x 1 3/4
   Armstrong, 15 Battles, 81, 6 3/8 x 4
   Army, Am. Military Hist., 96, 1 3/4 x 2 1/4
   Arthur, Sieges of Yorktown, 18, 11 1/8 x 11 3/4
   Avery, Hist. of U.S., 6:314, 7 1/8 x 7 3/4 col.,
     5 1/8 x 4 1/2 col.
   Balch, French in Am., 1:end, 9 x 12
   Bland, Yorktown Sesquicentennial, 342, 10 7/8 x 8
   Boatner, Enc. of Am. Rev., 1243, 4 3/4 x 4 1/8
   Botta, War of Ind., 2:385, 4 1/8 x 6 5/8
   Boyd, Wayne, 192, 6 1/2 x 4
   Britt, Hungry War, pl.v, 4 1/8 x 4 1/2
   Buchser, Yorktown, 20, 6 x 5
   Callahan, Henry Knox, 182, 4 7/8 x 4 1/4
   Carrington, Battles, 646, 7 3/4 x 4 5/8
   Carrington, Washington, 357, 5 7/8 x 3 1/2
   Channing, Hist. of U.S., 3:337, 3 3/8 x 4
   Chidsey, Yorktown, 134-135, 6 1/4 x 9 7/8; 146-147, 8 7/8 x
     7 1/2
   Clarke, Am. Revolution, 58, 2 1/8 x 4
   Close, Yorktown, front lining papers, 8 3/4 x 12; 12, 4 x
     3 1/4; 18, 4 x 3 1/4; end lining papers, 8 3/4 x 12
   Closen, Journal, 144, 6 3/4 x 4 1/4
   Coast Artillery Jl., 72(Apr. 1930):331, 4 7/8 x 4 1/2
   Coffin, Boys of '76, 387, 4 1/2 x 4 3/4
   Coggins, Boys in Revolution, 87, 5 3/8 x 5 5/8
   Commager, Spirit of '76, 2:1211, 5 x 4 5/8
   Cugnac, Yorktown, 30, 6 1/8 x 6 1/2, French map
   DuHamel, Surrender of British Forces, frontis., 4 x 6 7/8
   Duncan, Medical Men, 349, 3 1/2 x 6
   Dupuy, Compact Hist., 445, 5 1/4 x 4 1/2
   Dupuy, Enc. of Mil. History, 722, 3 5/8 x 3
   Dupuy, Mil. Heritage of Am., 110, 4 1/4 x 3 5/8
   Eckenrode, Yorktown, 46, 10 7/8 x 7 7/8
   Enc. Americana, 29:689, 3 x 2 3/4
   Falls, Great Mil. Battles, 105, 6 1/2 x 8 1/2, French map;
     106, 6 1/4 x 8 1/2 col.
   Fite, Book of Old Maps, 286, 11 5/8 x 12 7/8, by J. F. Renault
   Fiske, Am. Rev., 2:296, col.
   Fleming, Battle of Yorktown, 72-73, 8 1/2 x 9 3/8 col.,
     French map; 90, 10 x 7 col.
   Fleming, Beat the Last Drum, frontis., 5 3/8 x 4 3/4
   Flexner, Washington in Am. Rev., 453, 4 7/8 x 4 3/4, by
     Samuel H. Bryant
   Fortescue, British Army, 3:pl.IV, 3 x 2 1/2 col.

Freeman, Washington, 5:329, 4 1/4 x 4 1/2; 346, 4 1/2 x 5 1/4;
    348, 3 3/8 x 5 1/4; 367, 3 7/8 x 4 1/2; end, 8 5/8 x 8 3/4
    col.
Freeman, Washington, abridgment, 481, 5 1/2 x 7 3/4
Frothingham, Washington, 356, 3 7/8 x 4 1/2
Fuller, Battles, 87, 4 7/8 x 4
Fuller, Decisive Battles of W. World, 2:335, 6 x 4 3/4
Garner, Hist. of U.S., 509, 4 x 6 7/8
Gordon, Hist. of U.S.A., 4:196, pl.IX, 11 1/4 x 8 3/8
Greene, Revolutionary War, 274, 5 1/8 x 4 1/2 col.
Guizot, Atlas, pl.19, 7 x 4 3/8
Gurney, Pict. Hist. U.S. Army, 71, 1 1/2 x 1 7/8
Hall, School History, 265, 3 3/8 x 6 1/8
Hamilton, Hist. of Republic, 2:264, 7 1/8 x 9 7/8
Harper's Mag., 63(Aug. 1881):333, 5 1/4 x 4 7/8
Hughes, Washington, 3:665, 3 7/8 x 6 1/4
Ingles, Queen's Rangers, 234, 5 3/4 x 5 1/4
Irving, Life of Washington, 4:356, 4 5/8 x 7 7/8
Johnston, Yorktown, 133, 5 1/4 x 4 3/4; 144, 3 7/8 x 3
Keim, Rochambeau, 438, 4 x 5 1/8
Kinnaird, Geo. Washington, 181, 4 1/4 x 7 1/4
Landers, Va. Campaign, map 6, 12 1/2 x 12 7/8; map 7,
    15 1/2 x 12 1/2
Leake, John Lamb, 278, 5 x 8 1/2
Lee, Memoirs, 500, 4 5/8 x 7 1/2
Lossing, Field-Book of Rev., 2:312, 4 1/2 x 4 3/4
Lowell, Hessians, 278, 3 7/8 x 3 1/2
McDowell, Revolutionary War, 174-175, 6 7/8 x 8 1/4 col.,
    French map
McKown, Am. Revolution, 83, 5 1/4 x 3 3/8
Mag. of Am. Hist., 4(June 1880):448, 9 x 10 1/4; 6(Jan. 1881):8,
    6 7/8 x 8 1/8; 7(Oct. 1881):288, 11 1/8 x 8; 339, 10 3/4 x
    8 1/2
Marshall, Atlas, map 9, 7 5/8 x 9
Matloff, Am. Military History, 95, 1 3/4 x 2 1/4
Miers, Blood of Freedom, 116, 5 5/8 x 3 5/8
Mil. Engineer, 23(Sept.-Oct. 1931):439, 5 1/4 x 3 3/8; 441,
    2 5/8 x 3 1/4; 443, 5 5/8 x 6 3/4, French map; 31(Nov.-Dec.
    1939):415, 6 1/8 x 4 1/2; 48(Nov.-Dec. 1956):448, 4 1/2 x
    4 7/8; 450, 5 x 4 7/8
Miller, Triumph of Freedom, 611, 4 1/4 x 7
Mitchell, Battles Am. Rev., 203, 7 1/2 x 5 col.
Montross, Rag, Tag and Bobtail, 431, 5 7/8 x 4 1/4
Niles, Chronicles, XXVII, 5 1/4 x 5 3/4
Pag. Am., 6:247, 2 1/8 x 2 1/8; 253, 5 3/4 x 6 3/4
Patton, Yorktown, 34, 11 x 8
Paullin, Atlas, pl.160H inset, 1 3/4 x 2 1/2 col.
Ramsay, Revolution in S.C., 2:326, 8 1/2 x 7 5/8
Rankin, Am. Rev., 327, 4 1/4 x 4
Reeder, Story of Rev. War, 233, 1 5/8 x 4 1/8
Revel, Journal, 152-153, 6 x 7
Ridpath, New Complete Hist., 7:3080, 4 1/2 x 4 7/8
Rouse, Virginia, 128, 7 1/2 x 7 1/8
Royaumont, La Fayette et Rochambeau, 127, 6 5/8 x 4 5/8,
    engr. by Ch. Schreiber

Sanderlin, 1776:Journals, 240-241, 8 1/8 x 10, French
  map in Library of Congress
Scheer, Rebels and Redcoats, 479, 7 5/8 x 4 1/2
Scott, De Grasse, 304, 4 1/4 x 5
Scribner's Mag., 24(1898):602, 1 1/2 x 1 1/2; 606,
  2 1/8 x 1 3/4
Seelye, Story of Washington, 301, 4 3/4 x 3 1/2
Soc. for Army Hist. Res., Jl., 17(Summer 1938):72,
  3 1/4 x 4 1/2
Sons of Rev. in Va. Mag., 9(Jan.-June 1931):5, 4 x 5
Soulés, Histoire des Troubles, 4:end, 11 1/4 x 15 col.
Sparks, Washington's Writings, 8:186, 4 1/2 x 7
Stedman, Am. War, 2:412, 10 3/4 x 12 3/4
Steele, Am. Campaigns, 2:31, 6 1/4 x 3 3/4 col.
Stephenson, Washington, 166, 5 3/8 x 4
Stone, Our French Allies, 424, 4 7/8 x 4
Tarleton, Campaigns, 394, 11 3/4 x 12 5/8 col.
U.S.N. Inst. Proc., 57(June 1931):733, 5 1/2 x 5;
  57(Oct. 1931):1305, 5 3/4 x 5 1/2
Va. Cavalcade, 1(Autumn 1951):47, 4 3/8 x 4 1/4; 7(Autumn
  1957):19, 8 1/2 x 6 1/2 col.; 13(Autumn 1963):17, 3 7/8
  x 6 1/2
Vestal, Washington, 48, 4 3/4 x 4
Wallace, Appeal to Arms, 257, 6 1/4 x 4 1/8
Ward, Revolution, 2:891, 5 1/8 x 4 1/2
Washington Bicentennial, 1:120, 4 3/4 x 4
Whitridge, Rochambeau, 199, 7 5/8 x 5
Wickwire, Cornwallis, 367, 3 5/8 x 4 1/8
Willcox, Portrait, 425, 5 1/2 x 6 7/8
Winsor, America, 6:550, 7 x 5; 551, 5 1/4 x 4 3/4;
  552, 6 1/8 x 5
By Sebastian Bauman   24290
  Am. Heritage, Revolution, 370, 10 1/4 x 7 1/2 col.
  Close, Yorktown, 28, 4 1/4 x 3 1/4
  Comstock, Enc. of Am. Antiques, 2:pl.281, 7 1/2 x 5 3/4
  Cook, Golden Book of Am. Rev., 182, 9 1/4 x 6 5/8 col.
  Cunliffe, Washington, 101, 8 1/4 x 6 1/8
  Delaware Hist., 4(Sept. 1950):116, 4 1/4 x 5 3/8
  Mag. of Am. Hist., 6(Jan. 1881):54, 11 3/8 x 8
  Mil. Engineer, 23(Sept.-Oct. 1931):442, 9 1/8 x 6 3/4
  Roscoe, Picture Hist., no.233, 5 7/8 x 7 1/2
  Stevens, Yorktown Handbook, 20, 4 5/8 x 3 3/8
  Trudell, Colonial Yorktown, 179, 6 1/8 x 4 3/8
  Washington Atlas, pl.41, 14 3/4 x 10 5/8
  Washington Bicentennial, 1:421, 9 5/8 x 6 7/8
  Wm. and Mary Quar., 19(July 1939):264, 3 7/8 x 6 1/2
  Yale Library Gaz., 21(July 1946):15, 5 7/8 x 4 1/2
Pub. by Esnauts et Rapilly   24292
  Am. Heritage, 12(Oct. 1961):58-59, 8 3/8 x 10 7/8 col.
  Am. Heritage Atlas, 112, 5 3/4 x 7 3/8 col.
  Am. Heritage, Revolution, 284-285, 7 3/4 x 9 7/8 col.
  Cook, Golden Bk. of Am. Rev, 180-181, 8 1/2 x 10 3/4 col.
  Falls, Great Mil. Battles, 105, 6 1/2 x 8 1/2
  Fleming, Battle of Yorktown, lining paper, 9 7/8 x 12 5/8 col.
  Rouse, Virginia, 127, 5 x 6 3/8

By Capt. Fage of Royal Artillery   24295
    Arthur, Sieges of Yorktown, 14, 9 1/4 x 12 5/8, 3 1/2 x 5 3/4
    Month at Goodspeed's, 29(Oct. 1957):16-17, 5 1/2 x 7
By Jean-Baptiste Gouvion, "Washington's Map"   24300
    Gouvion, Washington's Map, 18 3/4 x 15
    Gurney, Pict. Hist. U.S. Army, 71, 5 1/2 x 4 1/8
By Lt. John Hills, pub. by William Faden   24305
    Bonsal, French Were Here, lining papers, 7 3/4 x 10 5/8
    Davis, Yorktown, 137, 6 7/8 x 5 3/8
    Dearborn, Journals, 218, 8 1/4 x 10 3/8
    Fleming, Battle of Yorktown, 54, 7 3/4 x 5 7/8
    Hamilton, Papers, 2:680, 7 5/8 x 5 3/4
    Pa. Mag. Hist. and Biog., 51(July 1927): 193, 4 3/8 x 5 1/2
    U.S.N. Inst. Proc., 53(Nov. 1927):1171, 5 1/2 x 6 5/8
By Gabriel Joachim du Perron, Comte de Revel   24310
    Revel, Map of Yorktown, 12 1/4 x 13 7/8 col.
By Ezra Stiles   24315
    Stiles, Diary, 2:569, 4 3/4 x 3 1/2
    U.S.N. Inst. Proc., 57(Oct. 1931):1369, 8 x 5
Strategy of the siege of Yorktown   24320
    Hatch, Yorktown, 8, 8 5/8 x 5 3/8
British position between Wormley and Yorktown Creeks, Sept. 28   24322
    and 29, 1781
    Fleming, Battle of Yorktown, 66, 4 7/8 x 6 1/8 col.
British fortifications and disposition of British, French, and   24325
    American troops, Gloucester Point, Va., during siege of
    Yorktown
    Wm. and Mary Quar., 20(Apr. 1940):268, 8 x 8 7/8
French positions near Gloucester, Va., 1781   24330
    Revel, Journal, 146, 4 1/2 x 7 3/8
Storming of British redoubts No.9 and No.10, Yorktown, Va.,   24335
    night of Oct. 14, 1781
    Arthur, Sieges of Yorktown, 21, 3 7/8 x 3
Surrender of Cornwallis, Yorktown, Va., Oct. 19, 1781, by   24340
    Ezra Stiles
    Stiles, Diary, 2:570, 3 3/4 x 4
    U.S.N. Inst. Proc., 57(Oct. 1931):1368, 8 x 5
Yorktown Battlefield Colonial National Historical Park   24345
    Eckenrode, Yorktown Sesquicentennial, end, 16 3/8 x 24
    Hatch, Yorktown, 28-29, 7 5/8 x 9 7/8

1782

Route of French army from Yorktown to Boston, autumn 1782   24350
    Balch, French in Am., 1:end, 4 x 10 1/8, 5 x 10 1/8
    Closen, Journal, lining papers, 11 3/4 x 9 col.
    Mag. of Am. Hist., 7(July 1881):8, 4 7/8 x 7; 12, 4 3/4 x 7;
    17, 5 3/4 x 5 1/8
    Soules, Histoire des Troubles, 4:end, 36 1/8 x 10 3/8 col.
Route from Williamsburg to Alexandria, Va.   24355
    Chastellux, Travels, 2:376, 5 3/8 x 7 3/4
Route from Williamsburg to Connecticut   24360
    Mass. Hist. Soc., Proc., 67(1941-1944):152, 7 1/4 x 16,
    from Rochambeau Papers
See also 04070

NORTH CAROLINA

North Carolina
  1766   25003
    Caruso, Appalachian Frontier, 2 1/2 x 4 1/8
  1770   25005
    Crittenden, Commerce of N.C., end, 8 x 7 7/8
    Meyer, Highland Scots of N.C., 70, 5 5/8 x 4 1/2
  By John A. Collet   25010
    Cumming, Southeast, pls. 63, 64, 65, 66, each 7 1/4 x 9 3/4
    Naval Docs. of Am. Rev., 2:794, 6 1/2 x 5 3/8
  During the Revolution   25015
    Rankin, N.C. in Rev., 17, 4 x 6
  1783   25020
    Ashe, N. Carolina, 1:725, 6 1/2 x 9
    Newsome, Growth of N.C., 82, 2 3/4 x 7
North Carolina coast, from Cape Fear to Ocracoke Inlet, 1770   25023
    Naval Docs. of Am. Rev., 3:758, 5 1/4 x 7 3/4, by
      John A. Collet
North Carolina coastland, 1775   25025
    Brown, Hist. Geog., 61-62, 5 3/4 x 4 5/8, 4 x 4 5/8
North Carolina counties
  1769   25030
    Merrens, Colonial N.C., 73, 2 3/4 x 5 1/8
  1775   25035
    Lonsdale, Atlas of N.C., 39, 4 3/8 x 11 1/8 col.; 43,
      3 1/4 x 8 1/8 col.
  At time of the Revolution   25040
    Brown, King's Friends, 195, 3 3/4 x 6
Lower Cape Fear counties about 1770   25045
    Merrens, Colonial N.C., 128, 4 1/4 x 4 1/4
Mecklenburg County, N.C., 1789   25047
    Graham, Gen. Joseph Graham, 189, 6 3/8 x 7 7/8
Roads, towns, and settlements in North Carolina
  1775   25050
    Lonsdale, Atlas of N.C., 39, 4 3/8 x 11 1/8 col.
    Merrens, Colonial N.C., 144, 3 x 5 1/8
  1783   25055
    Newsome, Growth of N.C., 82, 2 3/4 x 7
Cape Fear River, 1778   25059
    Naval Docs. of Am. Rev., 4:440, 7 3/4 x 5 5/8, French map
Cape Fear River, Brunswick, and Wilmington, N.C., 1781   25060
    Winsor, America, 6:542, 4 3/4 x 3 1/2
Halifax, N.C., Feb. 1781   25065
    Haiman, Kosciusko, 107, 3 3/4 x 4 1/8, by Thaddeus Kosciusko
New Bern, N.C., May 1769, by Claude Joseph Sauthier   25070
    Henderson, N. Carolina, 1:204, 5 x 6 1/4
    Naval Docs. of Am. Rev., 2:185, 5 1/8 x 6 3/8
Salisbury, N.C., 1770   25075
    Cumming, Southeast, pl.62, 7 1/4 x 9, by Claude Joseph
      Sauthier

POPULATION

Distribution of Negro taxables, N.C., 1767   25080
    Merrens, Colonial N.C., 79, 3 1/8 x 5

Distribution of taxables, N.C., 1769   25085
    Merrens, Colonial N.C., 71, 3 1/2 x 5 1/8

COMMERCE

North Carolina trade routes, 1770   25090
    Meyer, Highland Scots of N.C., 80, 5 5/8 x 4 1/2
Distribution of commercial wheat growing in North Carolina,   25100
    c.1765-1775
    Merrens, Colonial N.C., 114, 3 3/8 x 5 1/4
Exports of naval stores from North Carolina ports, 1768-1771   25105
    Merrens, Colonial N.C., 88, 3 1/8 x 4 1/4
Exports of wood products from North Carolina, 1768-1772   25110
    Merrens, Colonial N.C., 97, 4 x 4 1/4
Public warehouses for tobacco inspection in North Carolina, 1767   25115
    Merrens, Colonial N.C., 122, 1 5/8 x 3

MILITARY OPERATIONS

WAR OF THE REGULATION

Alamance, Battle of the, May 16, 1771   25120
    Powell, War of Regulation, end, 7 3/8 x 13 3/8
By Claude Joseph Sauthier   25121
    Fitch, Some Neglected Hist. of S.C., frontis., 4 5/8 x 8
    Haywood, Tryon, 124, 5 1/4 x 9

REVOLUTIONARY WAR GENERAL

Theatre of operations in North and South Carolina   25125
    Mag. of Am. Hist., 5(Oct. 1880):269, 6 x 4 1/2
1778-1781   25130
    Army, Am. Military Hist., 86, 6 x 4 3/8
1780-1781   25135
    Ingles, Queen's Rangers, 141, 6 x 5 1/4
1780-1782   25140
    Madison, Papers, 2:59, 6 x 7 1/8
    Ward, Del. Continentals, end, 11 3/4 x 8 7/8 col.
Jan.-Sept. 1781   25145
    Fiske, Am. Rev., 2:269, 6 x 3 3/4
Revolutionary localities in western portion of North and South   25150
    Carolina
    Boatner, Enc. of Am. Rev., end lining paper, 7 5/8 x 4 3/4
    N.C. Booklet, 8(Apr. 1909):299, 6 1/4 x 4 1/8
Operations in North and South Carolina   25155
    Frothingham, Washington, 336, 4 x 4 5/8
1779-1780   25160
    Avery, Hist. of U.S., 6:212, 6 3/4 x 5 3/8 col.
    Greene, Revolutionary War, 192, 6 3/4 x 5 3/8 col.
1779-1781   25165
    Alden, Am. Rev., 229, 7 x 4 3/4
    Commager, Spirit of '76, 2:1074, 6 5/8 x 4 5/8
    Esposito, Am. Wars Atlas, 1:map 8a, 9 1/2 x 4 1/4 col.
    Esposito, Civil War Atlas, map 8a, 9 1/2 x 6 1/4 col.
    Wallace, Appeal to Arms, 207, 7 x 4 3/4

1780-1781   25170
  Davis, Cowpens, xi, 6 1/4 x 4 1/4
  N.P.S., Guilford, 8-9, 5 3/4 x 7 1/4
  Reid, Guilford, 4, 4 7/8 x 4 5/8
1781   25175
  Ashe, N. Carolina, 1:619, 5 7/8 x 4
  Avery, Hist. of U.S.; 6:283, 5 1/4 x 4 1/2 col.;
    284, 7 x 5 7/8 col.
  Greene, Revolutionary War, 226, 7 x 5 7/8 col.;
    232, 5 1/4 x 4 1/2 col.
  Mitchell, Discipline and Bayonets, 204, 6 1/4 x 4 1/4
  Reid, Guilford, 24, 5 3/8 x 5
1781-1783   25180
  Greene, Gen. Greene, 190, 6 x 4

1776

Moore's Creek Bridge campaign, Feb. 1776   25185
  N.C. Hist. Rev., 30(Jan. 1953):39, 5 x 6 1/4
Moore's Creek Bridge, N.C., Battle of, Feb. 27, 1776   25190
  Adams, Atlas, pl.68, 6 1/4 x 9 1/4
  Bryant, Popular Hist. of U.S., 3:465, 2 x 2 1/2
  N.C. Booklet, 3(Mar. 1904):18, 3 5/8 x 3; 25, 2 1/2 x 3 1/4
  N.C. Hist. Rev., 30(Jan. 1953):51, 5 1/8 x 4 1/2

1780

Movements of American commanders in North Carolina, 1780
  Maj. Gen. Horatio Gates
    See 26165
  Maj. Gen. Nathanael Greene
    See 26170
  Col. Jones
    See 26175
  Maj. Gen. Johann Kalb   25195
    Pag. Am., 6:236, 6 3/8 x 5 3/8
    Paullin, Atlas, pl.160F, 3 5/8 x 3 1/8 col.
  Brig. Gen. Daniel Morgan
    See 26190
Movements of British commanders in North Carolina, 1780
  Lt. Gen. Charles Cornwallis
    See 26250
  Lt. Col. Patrick Ferguson
    See 26255
British advance on Charlotte, N.C., Sept. 1780   25196
  Pugh, Cowpens Campaign, 60
Charlotte, N.C., skirmish, Sept. 26, 1780   25197
  Pugh, Cowpens Campaign, 72
Cornwallis' retreat from Charlotte, Oct. 1780   25198
  Pugh, Cowpens Campaign, 94

1781

Movements of American commanders in North Carolina, 1781
  Maj. Gen. Nathanael Greene
    See 26365

Brig. Gen. Isaac Huger
  See 26380
Lt. Col. Henry Lee
  See 26385
Brig. Gen. Daniel Morgan
  See 26395
Movements of British commanders in North Carolina, 1781
  Lt. Gen. Charles Cornwallis
    See 26415

Brig. Gen. Charles O'Hara   25200
  Tarleton, Campaigns, 1, 25 5/8 x 19 1/4 col., by William
    Faden

Cowan's Ford (or Catawba River), N.C., Battle of, Feb. 1, 1781   25205
  Coffin, Boys of '76, 347, 2 3/8 x 1 7/8
  Graham, Gen. Joseph Graham, 289, 5 5/8 x 3 1/2
  Hamilton, Grenadier Guards, 2:245, 2 3/8 x 4 5/8
  Lossing, Field-Book of Rev., 2:392, 2 3/4 x 2 1/8
  N.C. Booklet, 5(Apr. 1906):237, 5 3/4 x 3 1/2
  Pag. Am., 6:240, 3 x 3
  Stedman, Am. War, 2:329, 6 5/8 x 6 7/8

Guilford Courthouse, N.C., Battle of, Mar. 15, 1781   25210
  Avery, Hist. of U.S., 6:290, 5 x 4 1/4 col.
  Bass, Green Dragoon, 182, 3 3/4 x 5 3/8
  Boatner, Enc. of Am. Rev., 462, 6 5/8 x 4 1/8
  Carrington, Battles, 565, 7 3/4 x 4 5/8
  Coffin, Boys of '76, 357, 2 7/8 x 2 5/8
  Commager, Spirit of '76, 2:1161, 5 1/4 x 4 1/2
  Daves, Md. and N.C., 72, 7 x 4 3/8
  Davis, Cowpens, XIII, 6 1/4 x 4 1/2
  Dupuy, Compact Hist., 396, 5 3/8 x 4 1/2; 401, 5 1/4 x 4 1/2
  Esposito, Am. Wars Atlas, 1:map 8d, 3 3/8 x 2 3/4 col.
  Esposito, Civil War Atlas, map 8d, 3 3/8 x 2 3/4 col.
  Fiske, Am. Rev., 2:270, 6 x 3 3/4 col.
  Fortescue, British Army, 3:pl.IV, 7.1/2 x 3 1/8 col.
  Greene, Gen. Greene, 226, 6 x 4
  Greene, Nathanael Greene, 3:176, 4 1/8 x 2 1/4, 1 7/8 x 2 1/4,
    7/8 x 2 1/4, 1 5/8 x 2 1/4, 1 7/8 x 1 5/8
  Greene, Revolutionary War, 238, 5 x 4 1/4 col.
  Guilford, Memorial Volume, 5, 7 1/8 x 4 3/8
  Hamilton, Grenadier Guards, 2:245, 5 1/8 x 4 5/8
  MacMunn, Am. War, 303, 4 3/4 x 3 1/2
  Mitchell, Battles Am. Rev., 183, 5 x 7 1/2 col.
  Mitchell, Discipline and Bayonets, 192, 4 1/4 x 6 1/4
  Montross, Rag, Tag and Bobtail, 413, 4 1/8 x 4 1/4
  N.P.S., Guilford, 11, 4 5/8 x 3
  Pratt, 11 Generals, 23, 4 7/8 x 4
  Reid, Guilford, 11, 4 7/8 x 4 3/8; 18-19, 7 5/8 x 10 3/8
  Ridpath, New Complete Hist., 7:3034, 5 1/2 x 4 7/8
  Scharf, Hist. of Md., 2:414, 4 5/8 x 6
  Scheer, Rebels and Redcoats, 446, 4 7/8 x 4 3/8
  Schenck, N. Carolina, 320, 7 1/8 x 4 3/8
  Steele, Am. Campaigns, 2:25, 4 7/8 x 3 3/4 col.
  Treacy, Prelude to Yorktown, 172, 5 3/4 x 5 7/8
  Wallace, Appeal to Arms, 231, 6 3/8 x 4 1/8
  Ward, Del. Continentals, 412, 4 5/8 x 4 1/8

Ward, Revolution, 2:789, 5 x 4 1/2
Wickwire, Cornwallis, 295, 6 x 4 1/8
By William Faden   25215
    Caruthers, Rev. Incidents, 2, 8 1/4 x 6 7/8
    Lee, Memoirs of War, 276, 7 1/2 x 4 5/8
    Lossing, Field-Book of Rev., 2:402, 3 1/4 x 2 3/4
    Mag. of Am. Hist., 7(July 1881):44, 3 5/8 x 3 1/4
    Pag. Am., 6:241, 4 x 3 1/2
    Stedman, Am. War, 2:342, 8 3/8 x 7 3/8
    Tarleton, Campaigns, 276, 8 1/4 x 7 3/8 col.
    Winsor, America, 6:540, 5 3/8 x 4 3/4
Guilford Courthouse National Military Park   25220
    N.P.S., Guilford, 15, 6 1/4 x 8 3/8
    Reid, Guilford, 18-19, 7 5/8 x 10 3/8
Rockfish Creek, N.C., attle of, Aug. 2, 1781   25225
    N.C. Booklet, 6(Jan. 1907):181, 4 1/8 x 2 1/2

SOUTH CAROLINA

South Carolina   26000
    Bass, Gamecock, front, 7 5/8 x 10 1/2
    Bass, Swamp Fox, front, 6 1/8 x 10 1/2
1766   26005
    Woodmason, Carolina Backcountry, lining papers, 7 1/2 x
        10 1/4 col.
c.1768-1771   26010
    Brown, S.C. Regulators, 1, 4 3/4 x 7 1/4
1773   26015
    Cumming, Southeast, pl.67, 7 3/8 x 7 7/8, by James Cook
1775   26020
    Wallace, Hist. of S.C., 2:130, 6 x 7 5/8
At time of Revolution   26025
    Drayton, Memoirs, 1:frontis., 16 1/4 x 18 3/4 col.
Geographical sections of South Carolina (low country, middle   26030
        country, and up country), 1750-1790
    Singer, S.C. in Confederation, 1, 4 1/8 x 5 3/8
Coastal South Carolina, 1776   26035
    Brown, Hist. Geog., 64, 4 1/4 x 6 1/2
South Carolina coastline   26037
    Coggins, Ships and Seamen, 103, 5 1/8 x 3 3/4
South Carolina districts at time of the Revolution   26040
    Brown, King's Friends, 213, 4 1/8 x 5 3/8
Charleston, S.C.   26045
    Boatner, Enc. of Am. Rev., 198, 4 1/8 x 6 1/2
1776   26050
    Adams, Atlas, pl.69, 9 1/4 x 6 1/4
1779   26055
    Gérard, Despatches, 777, 7 7/8 x 8 5/8
    McCrady, S. Carolina, 1775-80, 356, 6 1/4 x 4
1780   26060
    Paullin, Atlas, pl.157A, 4 1/2 x 6 1/4 col.
Charleston Harbor, S.C.
Entrance, Dec. 30, 1776   26065
    Naval Docs. of Am. Rev., 2:1212, 5 3/4 x 5 1/2, by Philip

1776-1780   26070
    Allen, Naval Hist. of Am. Rev., 2:492, 3 3/4 x 6
    James, Br. Navy in Adversity, 42, 6 1/8 x 3 7/8
1777   26071
    Naval Docs. of Am. Rev., 4:276, 7 1/4 x 5 3/8, from J.F.W.
    Des Barres, American Neptune
1777-1778   26075
    Clark, Capt. Dauntless, 186, 4 7/8 x 4 5/8
Stateburg, S.C., laid out in 1783   26077
    Gregorie, Thomas Sumter, 204, 3 7/8 x 6 3/8

                           MILITARY OPERATIONS

Area of operations in South Carolina   26080
    Dean, Knight of Rev., 152-153, 6 5/8 x 8 1/4
    See also 25125-25145
Revolutionary localities in western portion of South Carolina
    See 25150
Operations in South Carolina, 1779-1782
    See 25155-25180
Battlefields of South Carolina
  1775-1780   26085
    McCrady, S. Carolina, 1775-80, front, 4 3/8 x 6 col.
  1775-1782   26090
    McCrady, S. Carolina, 1780-83, front, 4 3/8 x 6 col.
  1780-1781   26095
    Boatner, Enc. of Am. Rev., 1028, 6 3/4 x 4 1/8
  In Upper South Carolina   26100
    Landrum, Upper S.C., 106, 4 x 3 1/4

                                 1775

Williamson's Fort, Ninety-Six, S.C., siege, Nov. 19-21, 1775   26105
    Landrum, Upper S.C., 65, 2 1/2 x 4 5/8

                                 1776

Charleston, S.C., siege, June-July 1776   26110
    Garner, Hist. of U.S., 1:408, 2 1/2 x 3
    Journal of South. Hist., 11(Feb. 1945):98, 7 3/8 x 4 1/2
Fort Moultrie, Sullivan's Island, S.C., British attack on,   26115
        June 28, 1776
    Adams, Album of Am. Hist., 1:386, 3 3/4 x 4 3/8, 3 3/4 x 3 1/8
    Adams, Atlas, pl.69, 9 1/4 x 6 1/4
    Alden, Gen. Charles Lee, 125, 3 1/2 x 4 1/8
    Am. Heritage, 6(Oct. 1955):63, 2 1/8 x 4; 9(Feb. 1958):51,
        2 1/4 x 4 col., engr. by T. Conder
    Am. Heritage Atlas, 102, 3 1/4 x 3 3/4, 3 1/4 x 2 5/8
    Am. Heritage, Revolution, 134, 2 1/8 x 4
    Avery, Hist. of U.S., 5:367, 2 3/8 x 2 1/2 col.
    Channing, Hist. of U.S., 3:227, 4 7/8 x 4
    Coffin, Boys of '76, 86, 1 3/4 x 2 1/8; 87, 1 1/8 x 1 1/4
    Commager, Spirit of '76, 2:1066, 4 1/8 x 4 1/2
    Drayton, Memoirs, 2:290, 6 7/8 x 8 1/8, 6 7/8 x 5 5/8
    Dupuy, Compact Hist., 95, 3 3/4 x 4 1/2

Dupuy, Rev. War Naval Battles, 29, 4 3/4 x 5 7/8
Fiske, Am. Rev., 1:211, 3 1/4 x 3 3/4
Gordon, Hist. of U.S.A., 3:358, 3 3/8 x 6 3/8, engr. by
  T. Condor
Greene, Revolutionary War, 186, 2 3/8 x 2 1/2 col.
Johnson, Traditions, 96
Lossing, Field-Book of Rev., 2:546, 1 1/8 x 1 1/4; 548,
  1 3/4 x 2 1/8
McCrady, S. Carolina, 1775-80, 139, 5 1/8 x 4 5/8, 6 1/4 x 7
Mason, Stars on the Sea, front lining paper, 7 3/4 x 10 1/2
Ramsay, Revolution of S.C., 1:144, 6 3/8 x 11 3/8, engr. by
  Abernethie
Reeder, Story of Rev. War, 71, 4 1/4 x 4 1/8
Ridpath, New Complete Hist., 6:2506, 3 1/2 x 4 1/8
Scheer, Rebels and Redcoats, 137, 5 5/8 x 4 3/8, 2 1/2 x 2 5/8
Ward, Revolution, 2:675, 4 3/4 x 4 1/2
Wilson, Am. People, 2:250, 3 1/8 x 3 3/4
Winsor, America, 6:169, 4 1/4 x 4 7/8; 170, 3 3/4 x 7 7/8
By Lt. Col. Thomas James, engr. and pub. by William Faden   26120
  Am. Heritage, Revolution, 127, 1 7/8 x 2 1/4
  Charleston Centennial, 96, 10 3/4 x 14 1/4, 3 5/8 x 7 3/8
  Lee, Hist. of N. America, 6:349, 3 3/4 x 5 col.
  Pag. Am., 6:142, 3 x 3 3/4

1779

Movements of American commanders in South Carolina, 1779
  Brig. Gen. John Ashe   26125
    Esposito, Am. Wars Atlas, 1:map 8a, 9 1/2 x 6 1/4 col.
    Esposito, Civil War Atlas, map 8a, 9 1/2 x 6 1/4 col.
    Paullin, Atlas, pl.160E, 3 5/8 x 2 3/4 col.
  Maj. Gen. Benjamin Lincoln   26130
    Alden, Am. Revolution, 229, 7 x 4 3/4
    Alden, Rise of Am. Republic, 153, 6 5/8 x 4 1/2
    Am. Heritage Atlas, 102, 5 1/4 x 7 1/2 col.
    Avery, Hist. of U.S., 6:212, 6 3/4 x 5 3/8 col.
    Boatner, Enc. of Am. Rev., 1035, 4 1/8 x 4 1/8
    Commager, Spirit of '76, 2:1074, 6 5/8 x 4 5/8
    Esposito, Am. Wars Atlas, 1:map 8a, 9 1/2 x 6 1/4 col.
    Esposito, Civil War Atlas, map 8a, 9 1/2 x 6 1/4 col.
    Greene, Revolutionary War, 192, 6 3/4 x 5 3/8 col.
    Morison, Growth of Am. Republic, 5th ed., 222, 6 x 4 1/2
    Paullin, Atlas, pl.160E, 3 5/8 x 2 3/4 col.
    Wallace, Appeal to Arms, 207, 7 x 4 3/4
  Brig. Gen. William Moultrie   26135
    Paullin, Atlas, pl.160E, 3 5/8 x 2 3/4 col.
  Gov. John Rutledge   26140
    Paullin, Atlas, pl.160E, 3 5/8 x 2 3/4 col.
Movements of British commanders in South Carolina, 1779
  Col. Boyd   26145
    Paullin, Atlas, pl.160E, 3 5/8 x 2 3/4 col.
  Maj. Gen. Augustine Prevost   26150
    Alden, Am. Revolution, 229, 7 x 4 3/4
    Alden, Rise of Am. Republic, 153, 6 5/8 x 4 1/2
    Avery, Hist. of U.S., 6:212, 6 3/4 x 5 3/8 col.

Boatner, Enc. of Am. Rev., 1035, 4 1/8 x 4 1/8
Chron. Am., 12:250, 7 x 5 5/8 col.
Commager, Spirit of '76, 2:1074, 6 5/8 x 4 5/8
Esposito, Am. Wars Atlas, 1:map 8a, 9 1/2 x 6 1/4 col.
Esposito, Civil War Atlas, map 8a, 9 1/2 x 6 1/4 col.
Gordon, Hist. of U.S.A., 3:frontis., 13 7/8 x 14 3/8,
    engr. by T. Conder
Greene, Nathanael Greene, 3:frontis., 7 7/8 x 8 1/4
Greene, Revolutionary War, 192, 6 3/4 x 5 3/8 col.
Paullin, Atlas, pl.160E, 3 5/8 x 2 3/4 col.
Ramsay, Revolution of S. C., 2:frontis., 19 3/8 x 22 1/2
Wallace, Appeal to Arms, 207, 6 x 4 3/4

1780

British occupation of South Carolina   26155
    Fisher, Struggle for Am. Ind., 2:374, 6 x 3 1/2
British fort, Dorchester, S.C. 1780   26160
    Harper's Mag., 52(Dec. 1875):10, 3 x 3
Movements of American commanders in South Carolina (and
    North Carolina when so stated), 1780
Maj. Gen Horatio Gates in North and South Carolina   26165
    Alden, Am. Revolution, 229, 7 x 4 3/4
    Alden, Rise of Am. Republic, 153, 6 5/8 x 4 1/2
    Am. Heritage Atlas, 103, 5 3/4 x 7 1/2 col.
    Avery, Hist. of U.S., 6:212, 6 3/4 x 5 3/8 col.
    Commager, Spirit of '76, 2:1074, 6 5/8 x 4 5/8
    Faulkner, Am. Political & Social Hist., 138, 3 1/4 x 3 5/8
    Greene, Revolutionary War, 192, 6 3/4 x 5 3/8 col.
    N.P.S., Guilford, 8-9, 5 3/4 x 7 1/4
    Pag. Am., 6:236, 6 3/8 x 5 3/8
    Paullin, Atlas, pl.160F, 3 5/8 x 3 1/8 col.
    Wallace, Appeal to Arms, 207, 7 x 4 3/4
Maj. Gen. Nathanael Greene in North and South Carolina   26170
    Am. Heritage Atlas, 103, 5 3/4 x 7 1/2 col.
    Cook, Golden Bk. of Am. Rev., 166, 8 5/8 x 6 5/8 col.
    Esposito, Am. Wars Atlas, 1:map 8a, 9 1/2 x 6 1/4 col.
    Esposito, Civil War Atlas, map 8a, 9 1/2 x 6 1/4 col.
    Faulkner, Am. Political & Social Hist., 138, 3 1/4 x 3 5/8
    Greene, Gen. Greene, 190, 6 x 4
    Lonsdale, Atlas of N.C., 48, 3 1/4 x 8 1/8 col.
    Morison, Growth of Am. Republic, 5th ed., 222, 6 x 4 1/2
    N.P.S., Guilford, 8-9, 5 3/4 x 7 1/4
    Pag. Am., 6:236, 6 3/8 x 5 3/8
    Paullin, Atlas, pl.160F, 3 5/8 x 3 1/8 col.
    Ridpath, New Complete Hist., 6:2914, 4 1/4 x 5 5/8; 2938,
        3 5/8 x 5 1/2
    Schenck, N. Carolina, 16, 14 1/4 x 19
Col. Jones, from Georgia through South Carolina to   26175
    McDowell's Camp, N.C.
    Avery, Hist. of U.S., 6:212, 6 3/4 x 5 3/8 col.
    Greene, Revolutionary War, 192, 6 3/4 x 5 3/8 col.
Lt. Col. Francis Marion   26180
    Avery, Hist. of U.S., 6:212, 6 3/4 x 5 3/8 col.
    Greene, Revolutionary War, 192, 6 3/4 x 5 3/8 col.

Pag. Am., 6:233, 6 3/8 x 5 1/2
Paullin, Atlas, pl.160F, 3 5/8 x 3 1/8 col.
Area of Marion's operations   26185
Am. Heritage, 9(Apr. 1958):45, 4 5/8 x 6 7/8 col.
Athearn, The Revolution, 262, 4 5/8 x 6 5/8 col.
Bass, Swamp Fox, end, 6 1/8 x 10 1/2
Mil. Service Institution Jl., 51(Sept. 1912):256, 4 1/8 x 5
Brig. Gen. Daniel Morgan in North and South Carolina   26190
Am. Heritage Atlas, 103, 5 3/4 x 7 1/2 col.
Esposito, Am. Wars Atlas, 1:map 8a, 9 1/2 x 6 1/4 col.
Esposito, Civil War Atlas, map 8a, 9 1/2 x 6 1/4 col.
Pag. Am., 6:236, 6 3/8 x 5 3/8; 239, 2 3/8 x 2 3/8
Paullin, Atlas, pl.160F, 3 5/8 x 3 1/8 col.
Area of Morgan's operations in North and South Carolina,   26195
    1780-1781
Higginbotham, Morgan, 123, 5 3/8 x 4 1/8
Brig. Gen. Thomas Sumter   26200
Avery, Hist. of U.S., 6:212, 6 3/4 x 5 3/8 col.
Greene, Revolutionary War, 192, 6 3/4 x 5 1/2 col.
Pag. Am., 6:233, 6 3/8 x 5 1/2
Area of Sumter's operations   26202
Gregorie, Thomas Sumter, end, 13 x 10
Sumter's camp on Clem's Branch, S.C., June 1780   26205
Bass, Gamecock, 58, 3 1/4 x 3 7/8
Lt. Col. George Turnbull's camp at Rocky Mount, S.C.,   26210
    July 1780
Bass, Gamecock, 64, 3 1/4 x 3 7/8
British camp at Hanging Rock, S.C., Aug. 1780   26215
Bass, Gamecock, 69, 3 3/8 x 4
Battle sites along Catawba-Wateree River, S.C., May-Aug. 1780   26220
Bass, Gamecock, 81, 4 7/8 x 3 7/8
Battle sites along Broad River, S.C., 1780   26225
Bass, Gamecock, 93, 4 7/8 x 3 7/8
Sumter's camp at Fish Dam Ford, S.C., Nov. 9, 1780   26230
Bass, Gamecock, 97, 4 5/8 x 4
Blackstock's, Battle of. See 26360
Movements of British commanders in South Carolina (and North
    Carolina when so indicated), 1780
Lt. Col. Nisbet Balfour   26235
Avery, Hist. of U.S., 6:212, 6 3/4 x 5 3/8 col.
Greene, Revolutionary War, 192, 6 3/4 x 5 3/8 col.
Pag. Am., 6:236, 6 3/8 x 5 3/8
Paullin, Atlas, pl.160F, 3 5/8 x 3 1/8 col.
Lt. Col. Thomas Brown(e)   26240
Avery, Hist. of U.S., 6:212, 6 3/4 x 5 3/8 col.
Greene, Revolutionary War, 192, 6 3/4 x 5 3/8 col.
Pag. Am., 6:236, 6 3/8 x 5 3/8
Sir Henry Clinton   26245
Avery, Hist. of U.S., 6:212, 6 3/4 x 5 3/8 col.
Esposito, Am. Wars Atlas, 1:map 8a, 9 1/2 x 6 1/4 col.
Esposito, Civil War Atlas, map 8a, 9 1/2 x 6 1/4 col.
Faulkner, Am. Political & Social Hist., 138, 3 1/4 x 3 5/8
Greene, Revolutionary War, 192, 6 3/4 x 5 1/2 col.
Pag. Am., 6:236, 6 3/8 x 5 3/8
Paullin, Atlas, pl.160F, 3 5/8 x 3 1/8 col.
Wickwire, Cornwallis, 83, 3 3/8 x 4 1/8

Lt. Gen. Charles Cornwallis in North and South Carolina   26250
  Alden, Am. Revolution, 229, 7 x 4 3/4
  Alden, Rise of Am. Republic, 153 6 5/8 x 4 1/2
  Am. Heritage Atlas, 102, 5 1/4 x 7 1/2 col.; 103,
    5 3/4 x 7 1/2 col.
  Avery, Hist. of U.S., 6:212, 6 3/4 x 5 3/8 col.
  Barck, Colonial Am., 643, 7 x 4 5/8
  Barck, Colonial Am., 2d ed., 617, 4 5/8 x 7
  Carrington, Battles, frontis., 7 1/2 x 4 1/2
  Chron. Am., 12:250, 7 x 5 5/8 col.
  Commager, Spirit of '76, 2:1074, 6 5/8 x 4 5/8
  Coast Artillery Jl., 72(Apr. 1930), 318, 5 x 4 1/2
  Cook, Golden Bk. of Am. Rev., 166, 8 5/8 x 6 5/8 col.
  Current, Am. Hist., 2d ed., 114, 3 1/2 x 2 1/2
  Esposito, Am. Wars Atlas, 1:map 8a, 9 1/2 x 6 1/4 col.
  Esposito, Civil War Atlas, map 8a, 9 1/2 x 6 1/4 col.
  Faulkner, Am. Political & Social Hist., 138, 3 1/4 x 3 5/8
  Fisher, Struggle for Am. Ind., 2:468, 6 x 3 1/2
  Greene, Revolutionary War, 192, 6 3/4 x 5 3/8 col.
  Harper's Mag., 63(Aug. 1881):324, 5 1/4 x 4 3/4
  Hart, Am. Nation, 9:290, 6 1/2 x 4 1/8 col.
  Johnston, Yorktown, 27, 5 1/4 x 4 3/4
  Lefler, North Carolina, 160, 5 1/8 x 5 1/2 col.
  Lonsdale, Atlas of N.C., 48, 3 1/4 x 8 1/2 col.
  Lowell, Hessians, 265, 5 1/2 x 3 3/8
  MacMunn, Am. War, 299, 3 7/8 x 5 3/4
  Morison, Growth of Am. Republic, 5th ed., 222, 6 x 4 1/2
  Morison, Hist. of Am. People, 252, 7 1/4 x 4 1/2
  N.P.S., Guilford, 8-9, 5 3/4 x 7 1/4
  Newsome, Growth of N.C., 150, 3 1/2 x 3 3/4
  Pag. Am., 6:236, 6 3/8 x 5 3/8
  Paullin, Atlas, pl.160F, 3 5/8 x 3 1/8 col.
  Ridpath, New Complete Hist., 6:2914, 4 1/4 x 5 5/8;
    2938, 3 5/8 x 5 1/2
  Schenck, N.Carolina, 16, 14 1/4 x 19
  Tarleton, Campaigns, 1, 25 5/8 x 19 1/4 col., by William Faden
  Tower, Essays, 130, 5 5/8 x 4 3/4
  Wallace, Appeal to Arms, 207, 7 x 4 3/4
  Warren, N.C. Atlas, 15, 6 1/4 x 15 col.
  Wells, Am. War of Independence, 169, 5 3/8 x 4
  Whitton, Am. War of Ind., 318, 6 x 3 1/2
  Wickwire, Cornwallis, 197, 6 x 4 1/8
Lt. Col. Patrick Ferguson in North and South Carolina   26255
  Am. Heritage Atlas, 102, 5 1/4 x 7 1/2 col.
  Army War College, Kings Mt., 44, 17 3/4 x 13
  Avery, Hist. of U.S., 6:212, 6 3/4 x 5 3/8 col.
  Esposito, Am. Wars Atlas, 1:map 8a, 9 1/2 x 6 1/4 col.
  Esposito, Civil War Atlas, map 8a, 9 1/2 x 6 1/4 col.
  Greene, Revolutionary War, 192, 6 3/4 x 5 3/8 col.
  Pag. Am., 6:236, 6 3/8 x 5 3/8
  Paullin, Atlas, pl.160F, 3 5/8 x 3 1/8 col.
  Reid, Guilford, 4, 4 7/8 x 4 5/8
Brig. Gen. Charles O'Hara   26260
  Tarleton, Campaigns, 1, 25 5/8 x 19 1/4 col., by William Faden
Brig. Gen. James Paterson   26265
  Pag. Am., 6:236, 6 3/8 x 5 3/8

Lt. Col. Francis Rawdon   26270
  Pag. Am., 6:236, 6 3/8 x 5 3/8
Lt. Col. Banastre Tarleton   26275
  Avery, Hist. of U.S., 6:212, 6 3/4 x 5 3/8 col.
  Greene, Revolutionary War, 192, 6 3/4 x 5 3/8 col.
  N.P.S., Guilford, 8-9, 5 3/4 x 7 1/4
  Pag. Am., 6:233, 6 3/8 x 5 1/2
  Paullin, Atlas, pl.160F, 3 5/8 x 3 1/8 col.
  Reid, Guilford, 4, 4 7/8 x 4 5/8
  Tarleton, Campaigns, 1, 25 5/8 x 19 1/4 col., by William Faden
Maj. James Wemyss   26280
  Avery, Hist. of U.S., 6:212, 6 3/4 x 5 3/8 col.
  Greene, Revolutionary War, 192, 6 3/4 x 5 3/8 col.
  Pag. Am., 6:233, 6 3/8 x 5 1/2
  Paullin, Atlas, pl.160F, 3 5/8 x 3 1/8 col.
Charleston, S.C., siege, Feb. 11 - May 12, 1780   26285
  Am. Heritage, 9(Feb. 1958):51, 5 1/8 x 4 col.
  Army, Am. Military Hist., 86, 1 5/8 x 2
  Avery, Hist. of U.S., 6:217, 4 1/8 x 5 1/8 col.
  Botta, War of Ind., 2:257, 1 7/8 x 2 3/8
  Carrington, Battles, 498, 4 5/8 x 7 3/4
  Charleston Year Book, 1880, 264, 7 5/8 x 5 3/4; 1882, 368,
    25 3/4 x 19, 4 5/8 x 8 1/4, Sir Henry Clinton's map
  Clinton, Am. Rebellion, 158, 6 x 8 3/4
  Coffin, Boys of '76, 291, 3 1/4 x 4 5/8
  Commager, Spirit of '76, 2:1098, 3 3/4 x 4 5/8
  Dupuy, Compact Hist., 344, 4 1/2 x 5 5/8
  Fortescue, British Army, 3:pl.IV, 3 5/8 x 3 7/8 col.
  Frothingham, Washington, 310, 4 5/8 x 4 1/2
  Gordon, Hist. of U.S.A., 3:358, pl.VII, 8 x 6 3/8, engr. by
    T. Conder
  Greene, Revolutionary War, 202, 4 1/8 x 5 1/8 col.
  Gurney, Pict. Hist. U.S. Army, 64, 1 1/2 x 2
  Johnson, Traditions, 246
  Lee, Memoirs of War, 146, 4 5/8 x 7 1/2
  Lossing, Field-Book of Rev., 2:537, 1 3/8 x 1 3/8; 559,
    3 1/4 x 4
  McCrady, S. Carolina, 1775-80, 444, 4 x 6 1/4
  Mag. of Am. Hist., 8(Dec. 1882):827, 3 3/4 x 4 3/4
  Marshall, Atlas, 10, 6 1/2 x 9 3/8
  Matloff, Am. Military History, 86, 1 1/2 x 2
  Mitchell, Battles Am. Rev., 161, 7 1/2 x 5
  Montross, Rag, Tag and Bobtail, 355, 6 1/2 x 4 1/4
  Pag. Am., 6:232, 3 1/8 x 4 5/8
  Ramsay, Revolution of S.C., 2:43, 14 1/4 x 11 1/4, by Abernethie
  Ridpath, New Complete Hist., 6:2812, 3 1/4 x 3 1/2
  S.C. Hist. Mag., 66(July 1965):148, 4 1/2 x 6 7/8, 4 7/8 x 5 3/8,
    4 3/4 x 4 1/2, 5 1/8 x 7, four maps from Sir Henry Clinton's
    papers
  Stedman, Am. War, 2:185, 10 x 11 5/8
  Tarleton, Campaigns, 32, 10 x 11 1/2 col.
  Uhlendorf, Siege of Charleston, 40, 7 1/4 x 8 1/2, by Des
    Barres; 180, 7 1/8 x 9, by Sproule
  Vestal, Washington, 42, 3 1/8 x 4
  Ward, Revolution, 2:699, 4 1/2 x 6 5/8
  Washington, Bicentennial, 1:118, 3 1/8 x 4

Wickwire, Cornwallis, 83, 3 7/8 x 4 1/8
Willcox, Portrait of a Gen., 305, 4 5/8 x 7 3/8
Winsor, America, 6:526, 3 3/4 x 4 7/8; 528, 5 7/8 x 5
Fort Moultrie, S.C., attack on, 1780   26290
Ramsay, Revolution of S.C., 2:59, 6 1/2 x 11 1/2
Charleston Neck, S.C., May 21, 1780   26295
Robertson, Diaries, pl.58, 4 1/4 x 7, prob. by Lt. Gen.
Archibald Robertson
Wofford's Iron Works(or Cedar Spring), S.C., skirmish,   26300
Aug. 8, 1780
Draper, King's Mt., 91, 2 7/8 x 3 3/4
Camden campaign, July-Aug. 1780   26305
Boatner, Enc. of Am. Rev., 160, 6 3/4 x 4 1/8
Mag. of Am. Hist., 8(July 1882):497, 4 1/2 x 5
Camden, S.C., and vicinity, 1780-1781   26310
Boatner, Enc. of Am. Rev., 164, 6 5/8 x 4
Gates' camp, Rugeley's Farm, S.C., Aug. 13-15, 1780   26315
Landers, Camden, 20, 4 x 6
Camden, S.C., Battle of, Aug. 16, 1780   26320
Avery, Hist. of U.S., 6:226, 2 1/4 x 1 1/4, 2 5/8 x 2 1/2,
1 1/2 x 2 1/2 col.
Bass, Green Dragoon, 182, 3 7/8 x 5 3/8
Carrington, Battles, 522, 7 5/8 x 4 5/8
Coffin, Boys of '76, 299, 3 7/8 x 2 1/2
Commager, Spirit of '76, 2:1125, 5 x 4 3/4, 2 7/8 x 4 3/4
Dupuy, Compact Hist., 364, 4 3/4 x 4 1/2
Esposito, Am. Wars Atlas, 1:map 8b, 2 3/4 x 3 col.
Esposito, Civil War Atlas, map 8b, 2 3/4 x 3 col.
Fiske, Am. Rev., 2:196, 6 x 3 3/4 col.
Fortescue, British Army, 3:pl.IV, 3 x 2 7/8 col.
Greene, Revolutionary War, 218, 2 1/4 x 1 1/4, 2 5/8 x 2 1/2,
1 1/2 x 2 1/2 col.
Landers, Camden, 40, 4 1/4 x 6 5/8
Lossing, Field-Book of Rev., 2:466, 4 x 2 1/2
McCrady, S. Carolina, 1775-80, 672, 6 1/4 x 4
Mag. of Am. Hist., 5(Oct. 1880):275, 2 1/2 x 2 7/8, 2 1/2 x
2 7/8; 280, 6 1/8 x 5 1/2
Mitchell, Battles Am. Rev., 165, 7 1/2 x 5 col.
Mitchell, Discipline and Bayonets, 146, 6 1/4 x 4 1/4
Pag. Am., 6:235, 3 1/2 x 3 1/8
Ridpath, New Complete Hist., 6:2952, 6 3/4 x 5
Scharf, Hist. of Md., 2:418, 4 5/8 x 6 1/8, 2 3/4 x 2 1/2
Schenck, N. Carolina, 88, 7 5/8 x 4 5/8
Steele, Am. Campaigns, 2:23, 5 3/4 x 3 3/8 col.
Vestal, Washington, 43, 2 x 1 7/8
Ward, Del. Continentals, 346, 4 3/8 x 4 1/8
Ward, Revolution, 2:127, 4 3/4 x 4 1/2
Washington Bicentennial, 1:118, 2 x 1 7/8
Wickwire, Cornwallis, 159, 4 1/8 x 4 1/8
Winsor, America, 6:533, 3 x 4 3/4, by Col. Senff
By William Faden   26325
Lee, Memoirs of War, 182, 7 1/2 x 4 3/4
Stedman, Am. War, 2:210, 8 1/4 x 7 3/8
Tarleton, Campaigns, 108, 8 1/4 x 7 3/8 col.
Winsor, America, 6:531, 5 3/8 x 4 3/4

Musgrove's Mill, S.C., Battle of, Aug. 18, 1780   26330
  Draper's King's Mt., 110, 1 7/8 x 1 3/4
British campaign in the Carolinas before King's Mountain, 1780   26335
  Mackenzie, Kings Mt., 4 3/4 x 4 3/8
King's Mountain campaign, area of operations   26340
  Clark, Frontier America, 123, 5 3/8 x 4 3/4
Route of the Mountain Men, Sycamore Shoals to King's Mountain,   26345
    Sept. 6 - Oct. 7, 1780
  Am. History, 1(Apr. 1966):26, 4 1/4 x 3 1/4
  Army War College, Kings Mt., 44, 17 3/4 x 13
  Caruso, Appalachian Frontier, 236, 3 3/4 x 4 1/8
  Mackenzie, Kings Mt., 14, 5 1/2 x 4 3/8
  Roosevelt, Winning of West, 1:end, 6 1/2 x 8 col.
King's Mountain, S.C., Battle of, Oct. 9, 1780   26350
  Adams, Atlas, pl.75, 9 1/4 x 6 1/4
  Am. History, 1(Apr. 1966):30, 4 1/2 x 6 7/8
  Army War College, Kings Mt., 44, 6 1/2 x 10
  Avery, Hist. of U.S., 6:230, 3 1/2 x 4 1/4 col.
  Boatner, Enc. of Am. Rev., 580, 6 5/8 x 4
  Billington, W. Expansion, 2d ed., 186, 5 1/4 x 4 1/8
  Commager, Spirit of '76, 2:1136, 4 1/4 x 4 5/8
  Draper, King's Mt., 236, 4 1/2 x 7 3/4
  Dupuy, Compact Hist., 369, 3 1/2 x 4 1/2
  Greene, Revolutionary War, 218, 3 1/2 x 4 1/4 col.
  Kings Mt., Sesquicentennial, 14, 8 1/2 x 9 3/4; 24,
    3 1/4 x 5 1/4
  Landrum, Upper S.C., 208, 3 x 5 1/8
  McCrady, S. Carolina, 1775-80, 780, 3 5/8 x 6 1/4
  Mackenzie, Kings Mt., 22-23, 7 5/8 x 9 1/2
  N.C. Booklet, 8(Apr. 1909):299, 6 1/4 x 4 1/8; 309,
    3 3/4 x 6 3/8
  Pag. Am., 6:237, 2 1/2 x 4 1/8
  Ridpath, New Complete Hist., 7:3000, 4 3/4 x 8, 3 1/4 x 3 3/8
  Scheer, Rebels and Redcoats, 415, 5 7/8 x 4 3/8
  Schenck, N. Carolina, 164, 4 3/8 x 7 5/8
  Ward, Revolution, 2:743, 7 1/8 x 4 1/2
  Wickwire, Cornwallis, 213, 2 3/4 x 4 1/8
  By Gen. Joseph Graham   26355
    Am. Heritage Atlas, 104, 3 3/8 x 5 5/8
    Graham, Gen. Joseph Graham, 272, 3 3/8 x 5 7/8
    Mag. of Am. Hist., 5(Dec. 1880):415, 4 1/8 x 4 3/4
    Ramsay, Annals of Tenn., 238, 4 3/4 x 7 3/4
Blackstock's, S.C., Battle of, Nov. 21, 1780   26360
  Bass, Gamecock, 105, 2 3/4 x 3 7/8
  Bass, Green Dragoon, 182, 3 3/4 x 5 3/8
  Pugh, Cowpens Campaign, 126
Movement of American army to the Cheraws, S.C., Dec. 1780   26362
  Pugh, Cowpens Campaign, 163

1781

Movements of American commanders in South Carolina (and North
    Carolina when so stated), 1781
  Maj. Gen. Nathanael Greene in North and South Carolina   26365
    Alden, Am. Revolution, 229, 7 x 4 3/4

Alden, Rise of Am. Republic, 153, 6 5/8 x 4 1/2
Am. Heritage Atlas, 103, 5 3/4 x 7 1/2 col.
Ashe, N. Carolina, 1:619, 5 7/8 x 4
Avery, Hist. of U.S., 6:283, 5 1/4 x 4 1/2 col; 284,
   7 x 5 7/8 col.
Boatner, Enc. of Am. Rev., 1024, 6 3/4 x 4 1/8
Caruthers, Rev. Incidents, front, 9 5/8 x 18 1/4
Chron. Am., 12:250, 7 x 5 5/8 col.
Commager, Spirit of '76, 2:1074, 6 5/8 x 4 5/8
Cook, Golden Bk. of Am. Rev., 166, 8 5/8 x 6 5/8 col.
Davis, Ragged Ones, frontis., 7 5/8 x 5
Esposito, Am. Wars Atlas, 1:map 8a, 9 1/2 x 6 1/4 col.
Esposito, Civil War Atlas, map 8a, 9 1/2 x 6 1/4 col.
Gordon, Hist. of U.S.A., 3:frontis., 13 7/8 x 14 3/8, engr.
   by T. Conder
Greene, Gen. Greene, 190, 6 x 4
Greene, Nathanael Greene, 3:frontis., 7 7/8 x 8 1/4
Greene, Revolutionary War, 226, 7 x 5 7/8 col.; 232,
   5 1/4 x 4 1/2 col.
Journal of Am. Hist., 25(1931):112, 4 7/8 x 3
Landers, Va. Campaign, map 1, 12 1/2 x 13 5/8
Lonsdale, Atlas of N.C., 48, 3 1/4 x 8 1/8 col.
Morison, Growth of Am. Republic, 5th ed., 222, 6 x 4 1/2
Pag. Am., 6:242, 6 5/8 x 5 5/8
Passano, Hist. of Md., 109, 4 7/8 x 3
Paullin, Atlas, pl.160 inset, 3 5/8 x 3 1/8 col.
Ramsay, Revolution of S.C., 2:frontis., 19 3/8 x 22 1/2
Reeder, Story of Rev. War, 208, 5 1/4 x 4 1/8
Ridpath, New Complete Hist., 6:2914, 4 1/4 x 5 5/8; 2938,
   3 5/8 x 5 1/2
Schenck, N. Carolina, 16, 14 1/4 x 19
Steele, Am. Campaigns, 2:22, 6 1/8 x 3 3/4 col.
Wallace, Appeal to Arms, 207, 7 x 4 3/4
Warren, North Carolina, 115, 4 1/8 x 4 1/8
Area of Greene's operations   26370
   Freeman, Washington, 5:253, 3 5/8 x 4 1/2
   Scribner's Mag., 24(1898):335, 5 3/4 x 4 1/2
   Treacy, Prelude to Yorktown, 15, 4 7/8 x 5 1/8
Col. William Harden   26375
   Avery, Hist. of U.S., 6:284, 7 x 5 7/8 col.
   Greene, Revolutionary War, 226, 7 x 5 7/8 col.
Brig. Gen. Isaac Huger in North and South Carolina   26380
   Avery, Hist. of U.S., 6:284, 7 x 5 7/8 col.
   Boatner, Enc. of Am. Rev., 1024, 6 3/4 x 4 1/8
   Caruthers, Rev. Incidents, front, 9 5/8 x 18 1/4
   Esposito, Am. Wars Atlas, 1:map 8a, 9 1/2 x 6 1/4 col.
   Esposito, Civil War Atlas, map 8a, 9 1/2 x 6 1/4 col.
   Greene, Revolutionary War, 226, 7 x 5 7/8 col.
   Pag. Am., 6:242, 6 5/8 x 5 5/8
   Paullin, Atlas, pl.160H inset, 3 5/8 x 3 1/8 col.
   Steele, Am. Campaigns, 2:22, 6 1/8 x 3 3/4 col.
Lt. Col. Henry Lee in North and South Carolina   26385
   Ashe, N. Carolina, 1;619, 5 7/8 x 4
   Avery, Hist. of U.S., 6:284, 7 x 5 7/8 col.
   Gordon, Hist. of U.S.A., 3:frontis., 13 7/8 x 14 3/8,
      engr. by T. Conder

Greene, Gen. Greene, 190, 6 x 4
Greene, Nathanael Greene, 3:frontis., 7 7/8 x 8 1/4
Greene, Revolutionary War, 226, 7 x 5 7/8 col.
Pag. Am., 6:242, 6 5/8 x 5 5/8
Paullin, Atlas, pl.160H inset, 3 5/8 x 3 1/8 col.
Brig. Gen. Francis Marion   26390
  Avery, Hist. of U.S., 6:284, 7 x 5 7/8 col.
  Greene, Revolutionary War, 226, 7 x 5 7/8 col.
  Pag. Am., 6:242, 6 5/8 x 5 5/8
Brig. Gen. Daniel Morgan in North and South Carolina   26395
  Am. Heritage Atlas, 103, 5 3/4 x 7 1/2 col.
  Ashe, N. Carolina, 1:619, 5 7/8 x 4
  Avery, Hist. of U.S., 6:284, 7 x 5 7/8 col.
  Boatner, Enc. of Am. Rev., 1024, 6 3/4 x 4 1/8
  Cook, Golden Bk. of Am. Rev., 166, 8 5/8 x 6 5/8 col.
  Davis, Ragged Ones, frontis., 7 5/8 x 5
  Esposito, Am. Wars Atlas, 1:map 8a, 9 1/2 x 6 1/4 col.
  Esposito, Civil War Atlas, map 8a, 9 1/2 x 6 1/4 col.
  Gordon, Hist. of U.S.A., 3:frontis., 13 7/8 x 14 3/8, engr.
    by T. Conder
  Greene, Gen. Greene, 190, 6 x 4
  Greene, Nathanael Greene, 3:frontis., 7 7/8 x 8 1/4
  Greene, Revolutionary War, 226, 7 x 5 7/8 col.
  Landers, Va. Campaign, map 1, 12 1/2 x 13 5/8
  Pag. Am., 6:239, 2 3/8 x 2 3/8; 242, 6 5/8 x 5 5/8
  Paullin, Atlas, pl. 160H inset, 3 5/8 x 3 1/8 col.
  Ramsay, Revolution of S.C., 2:frontis., 19 3/8 x 22 1/2
  Steele, Am. Campaigns, 2:22, 6 1/8 x 3 3/4 col.
Brig. Gen. Thomas Sumter   26400
  Avery, Hist. of U.S., 6:284, 7 x 5 7/8 col.
  Bass, Gamecock, 132, 2 3/8 x 4
  Greene, Revolutionary War, 226, 7 x 5 7/8
  Pag. Am., 6:242, 6 5/8 x 5 5/8
 Area of Sumter's operations   26402
  Gregorie, Thomas Sumter, end, 13 x 10
 Region around Fort Granby, S.C., Apr.-May 1781   26405
  Bass, Gamecock, 169, 5 7/8 x 4
 Region around Monck's Corner, S.C., July 1781   26410
  Bass, Gamecock, 196, 2 3/8 x 4
 See also 26475
Movements of British commanders in South Carolina (and North
    Carolina when so stated), 1781
  Lt. Gen. Charles Cornwallis in North and South Carolina   26415
  Alden, Am. Revolution, 229, 7 x 4 3/4
  Alden, Rise of Am. Republic, 153, 6 5/8 x 4 1/2
  Am. Heritage Atlas, 103, 5 3/4 x 7 1/2 col.
  Army, Am. Military Hist., 96, 7 1/4 x 4 3/8
  Ashe, N. Carolina, 1:619, 5 7/8 x 4
  Avery, Hist. of U.S., 6:283, 5 1/4 x 4 1/2 col.; 284,
    7 x 5 7/8 col.
  Barck, Colonial Am., 643, 7 x 4 5/8
  Barck, Colonial Am., 2d ed., 617, 4 5/8 x 7
  Billias, Washington's Opponents, xxxi, 7 1/2 x 4 3/4;
    xxxii, 7 1/4 x 4 5/8
  Boatner, Enc. of Am. Rev., 1024, 6 3/4 x 4 1/8
  Carrington, Battles, frontis., 7 1/2 x 4 1/2

Caruthers, Rev. Incidents, front, 9 5/8 x 18 1/4
Chron. Am., 12:250, 7 x 5 5/8 col.
Commager, Spirit of '76, 2:1074, 6 5/8 x 4 5/8
Cook, Golden Bk. of Am. Rev., 166, 8 5/8 x 6 5/8 col.
Current, Am. Hist., 2d ed., 114, 3 1/2 x 2 1/2
Davis, Ragged Ones, frontis., 7 5/8 x 5
Dupuy, Compact Hist., end, 6 3/4 x 5 5/8
Esposito, Am. Wars Atlas, 1:map 8a, 9 1/2 x 6 1/4 col.
Esposito, Civil War Atlas, map 8a, 9 1/2 x 6 1/4 col.
Faulkner, Am. Political & Social Hist., 138, 3 1/4 x 3 5/8
Fisher, Struggle for Am. Ind., 2:468, 6 x 3 1/2
Gordon, Hist. of U.S.A., 3:frontis., 13 7/8 x 14 3/8,
   engr. by T. Conder
Greene, Gen. Greene, 190, 6 x 4
Greene, Nathanael Greene, 3:frontis., 7 7/8 x 8 1/4
Greene, Revolutionary War, 226, 7 x 5 7/8 col.; 232,
   5 1/4 x 4 1/2 col.
Hamilton, Grenadier Guards, 2:243, 7 3/8 x 4 5/8
Harper's Mag., 63(Aug. 1881):324, 5 1/4 x 4 3/4
Hart, Am. Nation, 9:290, 6 1/2 x 4 1/8 col.
James, Br. Navy in Adversity, 276, 6 1/8 x 4
Johnston, Yorktown, 27, 5 1/4 x 4 3/4
Journal of Am. Hist., 25(1931):112, 4 7/8 x 3
Landers, Va. Campaign, map 1, 12 1/2 x 13 5/8
Larrabee, Decision, 99, 7 5/8 x 4 3/4
Lefler, North Carolina, 160, 5 1/8 x 5 1/2 col.
Lonsdale, Atlas of N.C., 48, 3 1/4 x 8 1/2 col.
Lowell, Hessians, 265, 5 1/2 x 3 3/8
MacMunn, Am. War., 299, 3 7/8 x 5 3/4
Morison, Growth of Am. Republic, 5th ed., 222, 6 x 4 1/2
Morison, Hist. of Am. People, 252, 7 1/4 x 4 1/2
N.P.S., Guilford, 8-9, 5 3/4 x 7 1/4
Newsome, Growth of N.C., 150, 3 1/2 x 3 3/4
Pag. Am., 6:242, 6 5/8 x 5 5/8
Passano, Hist. of Md., 109, 4 7/8 x 3
Paullin, Atlas, pl.160H, 7 5/8 x 4 7/8 col.; pl.160H inset,
   3 5/8 x 3 1/8 col.
Ramsay, Revolution of S.C., 2:frontis., 19 3/8 x 22 1/2
Reeder, Story of Rev. War, 208, 5 1/4 x 4 1/8
Ridpath, New Complete Hist., 6:2914, 4 1/4 x 5 5/8; 2938,
   3 5/8 x 5 1/2
Schenck, N. Carolina, 16, 14 1/4 x 19
Steele, Am. Campaigns, 22, 6 1/8 x 3 3/4 col.
Tarleton, Campaigns, 1, 25 5/8 x 19 1/4 col., by
   William Faden
Tower, Essays, 130, 5 5/8 x 4 3/4
U.S.N. Inst. Proc., 57(June 1931):725, 5 5/8 x 5
Wallace, Appeal to Arms, 207, 7 x 4 3/4
Warren, N.C. Atlas, 15, 6 1/4 x 15 col.
Wells, Am. War of Independence, 169, 5 3/8 x 4
Whitton, Am. War of Ind., 318, 6 x 3 1/2
Wickwire, Cornwallis, 197, 6 x 4 1/8
Col. Welbore Doyle   26420
   Avery, Hist. of U.S., 6:284, 7 x 5 7/8 col.
   Greene, Revolutionary War, 226, 7 x 5 7/8 col.

Maj. Gen. Alexander Leslie   26425
    Avery, Hist. of U.S., 6:284, 7 x 5 7/8 col.
    Boatner, Enc. of Am. Rev., 1024, 6 3/4 x 4 1/8
    Greene, Revolutionary War, 226, 7 x 5 7/8 col.
Lt. Col. Francis Rawdon   26430
    Alden, Am. Revolution, 229, 7 x 4 3/4
    Alden, Rise of Am. Republic, 153, 6 5/8 x 4 1/2
    Ashe, N. Carolina, 1:619, 5 7/8 x 4
    Avery, Hist. of U.S., 6:283, 5 1/4 x 4 1/2 col.;
      284, 7 x 5 7/8 col.
    Commager, Spirit of '76, 2:1074, 6 5/8 x 4 5/8
    Esposito, Am. Wars Atlas, 1:map 8a, 9 1/2 x 6 1/4 col.
    Esposito, Civil War Atlas, map 8a, 9 1/2 x 6 1/4 col.
    Greene, Gen. Greene, 190, 6 x 4
    Greene, Nathanael Greene, 3:frontis., 7 7/8 x 8 1/4
    Greene, Revolutionary War, 226, 7 x 5 7/8 col.; 232,
      5 1/4 x 5 1/2 col.
    Pag. Am., 6:242, 6 5/8 x 5 5/8
    Paullin, Atlas, pl.160H inset, 3 5/8 x 3 1/8 col.
    Wallace, Appeal to Arms, 207, 7 x 4 3/4
Lt. Col. Alexander Stewart   26435
    Esposito, Am. Wars Atlas, 1:map 8a, 9 1/2 x 6 1/4 col.
    Esposito, Civil War Atlas, map 8a, 9 1/2 x 6 1/4 col.
    Greene, Nathaniel Greene, 3:frontis., 7 7/8 x 8 1/4
    Pag. Am., 6:242, 6 5/8 x 5 5/8
    Paullin, Atlas, pl.160H inset, 3 5/8 x 3 1/8 col.
Lt. Col. Banastre Tarleton   26440
    Alden, Am. Revolution, 229, 7 x 4 3/4
    Alden, Rise of Am. Republic, 153, 6 5/8 x 4 1/2
    Am. Heritage Atlas, 103, 5 3/4 x 7 1/2 col.
    Avery, Hist. of U.S., 6:284, 7 x 5 7/8 col.
    Boatner, Enc. of Am. Rev., 1024, 6 3/4 x 4 1/8
    Commager, Spirit of '76, 2:1074, 6 5/8 x 4 5/8
    Cook, Golden Bk. of Am. Rev., 166, 8 5/8 x 6 5/8 col.
    Davis, Ragged Ones, frontis., 7 5/8 x 5
    Esposito, Am. Wars Atlas, 1:map 8a, 9 1/2 x 6 1/4 col.
    Esposito, Civil War Atlas, map 8a, 9 1/2 x 6 1/4 col.
    Greene, Revolutionary War, 226, 7 x 5 7/8 col.
    Landers, Va. Campaign, map 1, 12 1/2 x 13 5/8
    N.P.S., Guilford, 8-9, 5 3/4 x 7 1/4
    Pag. Am., 6:239, 2 3/8 x 2 3/8; 242, 6 5/8 x 5 5/8
    Reid, Guilford, 4, 4 7/8 x 4 5/8
    Tarleton, Campaign, 1, 25 5/8 x 19 1/4 col., by William Faden
    Wallace, Appeal to Arms, 207, 7 x 4 3/4
Lt. Col. John Watson Tadwell Watson   26445
    Avery, Hist. of U.S., 6:284, 7 x 5 7/8 col.
    Greene, Revolutionary War, 226, 7 x 5 7/8 col.
Locale of Cowpens campaign   26447
    Pugh, Cowpens Campaign, 10
Maneuvers preliminary to Battle of Cowpens, Jan. 1781   26448
    Pugh, Cowpens Campaign, 191
Cowpens, S.C., Battle of, Jan. 17, 1781   26450
    Am. Heritage, 7(Apr. 1956):36-37, four diagrams, each
      1 7/8 x 1 7/8 col.
    Am. Heritage Atlas, 110-111, 9 5/8 x 17 col.

Army, Am. Military Hist., 94, 5 1/8 x 4 1/2
Army War College, Kings Mt., 78, 13 3/4 x 12, 12 x 7 7/8
Avery, Hist. of U.S., 6:286, 3 3/4 x 2 1/2 col.
Boatner, Enc. of Am. Rev., 295, 6 1/4 x 4 1/8
Callahan, Daniel Morgan, 209, 4 7/8 x 3 3/4
Carrington, Battles, 546, 7 3/4 x 4 5/8
Commager, Spirit of '76, 2:1154, 4 x 4 1/8, 3 7/8 x 4 1/8
Cowpens, Centennial Committee, Battle Monument, 71,
    6 5/8 x 3 7/8
Davis, Cowpens, XII, 3 1/2 x 4 1/4, 2 3/4 x 4 1/4
Dean, Fighting Dan, 280, 6 1/2 x 4
Dupuy, Brave Men and Great Captains, 48, 4 1/4 x 4 1/8
Dupuy, Compact Hist., 381, 6 3/8 x 4 1/2
Dupuy, Mil. Heritage of Am., 105, 3 3/4 x 3 7/8
Esposito, Am. Wars Atlas, 1:map 8d, 3 1/2 x 2 3/4 col.
Esposito, Civil War Atlas, map 8d, 3 1/2 x 2 3/4 col.
Fiske, Am. Rev., 2:266, 3 x 3 3/4 col., 3 x 3 3/4 col.
Fortescue, British Army, 3:pl.IV, 4 1/2 x 2 7/8 col.
Greene, Revolutionary War, 238, 3 3/4 x 2 1/2 col.
Gurney, Pict. Hist. U.S. Army, 68, 4 1/4 x 3 7/8
Higginbotham, Morgan, 138, 6 5/8 x 4 1/8
Johnson, Traditions, 529, 530
McDowell, Revolutionary War, 166, 167, 10 x 13 1/2 col.
Matloff, Am. Military History, 92, 5 1/8 x 4 3/8
Military Review, 30(Dec. 1950):49, two maps each 2 1/8 x 2 1/8
Mitchell, Battles Am. Rev., 177, 7 1/2 x 5 col.
Mitchell, Discipline and Bayonets, 168, 6 1/4 x 4 1/4
Montross, Rag, Tag and Bobtail, 405, 5 x 4 1/4
N.C. Hist. Rev., 31(July 1954):357, 5 1/8 x 4 1/4
Pag. Am., 6:239, 3 5/8 x 3
Pratt, 11 Generals, 18, 5 1/2 x 4
Pugh, Cowpens Campaign, 244, 260, 268, 274
Ridpath, New Complete Hist., 7:3018, 7 3/8 x 2 5/8, 3 7/8 x
    2 7/8, 3 1/2 x 2 7/8
Roberts, Cowpens, lining papers, 6 5/8 x 5 1/4 col., 1 1/8 x
    4 3/4 col., 7 3/8 x 4 3/4 col.
Scheer, Rebels and Redcoats, 429, 5 5/8 x 4 3/8
Schenck, N. Carolina, 210, 7 3/4 x 4 5/8
Steele, Am. Campaigns, 2:24, 5 3/4 x 3 col.
Treacy, Prelude to Yorktown, 95, 6 3/8 x 4 7/8
Ward, Del. Continentals, 374, 5 3/8 x 4 1/8
Ward, Revolution, 2:759, 5 3/4 x 4 1/2
Wickwire, Cornwallis, 261, 4 1/8 x 4 1/8
British posts in South Carolina, Apr. 1781   26455
    Scheer, Rebels and Redcoats, 454, 4 1/4 x 4 1/2
Hobkirk's Hill, S.C., Battle of (also known as Second Battle
    of Camden), Apr. 25, 1781
    Avery, Hist. of U.S., 6:293, 4 x 3 3/4 col.
    Boatner, Enc. of Am. Rev., 164, 6 5/8 x 4
    Carrington, Battles, 576, 7 5/8 x 4 1/2
    Commager, Spirit of '76, 2:1174, 4 3/4 x 4 5/8
    Dupuy, Compact Hist., 409, 4 3/8 x 4 1/2
    Esposito, Am. Wars Atlas, 1:map 8e, 4 1/2 x 3 col.
    Esposito, Civil War Atlas, map 8e, 4 1/2 x 3 col.
    Fortescue, British Army, 3:pl.IV, 3 3/4 x 3 1/8 col.
    Greene, Gen. Greene, 242, 6 x 4

Greene, Nathanael Greene, 3:239, 6 1/8 x 4 1/8, 2 3/4 x 2 1/2
Greene, Revolutionary War, 246, 4 x 3 3/4 col.
Gunby, Col. John Gunby, 77, 5 7/8 x 4
Lossing, Field-Book of Rev., 2:473, 3 x 2 1/8
McCrady, S. Carolina, 1780-83, 182, 5 3/4 x 3 5/8
Pag. Am., 6:244, 2 5/8 x 3 5/8
Pratt, 11 Generals, 27, 4 x 4
Ridpath, New Complete Hist., 7:3042, 5 x 8
Schenck, N. Carolina, 402, 7 5/8 x 4 1/2
Steele, Am. Campaigns, 2:26, 6 x 3 1/2 col.
Ward, Del. Continentals, 432, 3 3/8 x 4 1/8
Ward, Revolution, 2:805, 3 5/8 x 4 1/2
 By Capt. C. Vallancey, pub. by William Faden   26465
  Lee, Memoirs of War, 336, 7 3/8 x 4 5/8
  Stedman, Am. War, 2:358, 17 x 11 1/2
  Winsor, America, 6:543, 7 x 4 3/4
Ninety-Six, S.C., siege, May 22-June 19, 1781   26470
  Am. Heritage, Revolution, 334, 2 1/4 x 2 col.
  Avery, Hist. of U.S., 6:294, 2 3/4 x 2 1/4 col.
  Commager, Spirit of '76, 2:1180, 5 3/8 x 4 5/8
  Dupuy, Compact Hist., 414, 6 x 4 1/2
  Greene, Gen. Greene, 258, 4 x 4
  Greene, Nathanael Greene, 3:299, 6 1/8 x 4 1/8
  Greene, Revolutionary War, 246, 2 3/4 x 2 1/4 col.
  Landrum, Upper S.C., 329, 3 1/4 x 3
  Lossing, Field-Book of Rev., 2:485, 2 1/2 x 2 1/4
  McCrady, S. Carolina, 1780-83, 278, 4 3/4 x 3 5/8
  Ward, Del. Continentals, 446, 5 1/2 x 4 1/8
  Ward, Revolution, 2:819, 6 x 4 1/2
Quinby Plantation, S.C., Battle of. July 17, 1781   26475
  Bass, Gamecock, 199, 2 3/8 x 4
  Gregorie, Thomas Sumter, 177, 5 1/4 x 3 7/8, by Joseph
    Purcell, 1791
Eutaw Springs, S.C., Battle of, Sept. 8, 1781   26480
  Am. Heritage Atlas, 104, 5 7/8 x 3 3/4, 5 7/8 x 3 3/4
  Avery, Hist. of U.S., 6:295, 3 1/4 x 4 col.
  Boatner, Enc. of Am. Rev., 352, 5 1/8 x 4 1/8
  Carrington, Battles, 582, 4 3/4 x 7 3/4
  Commager, Spirit of '76, 2:1186, 3 7/8 x 4 5/8
  Dupuy, Compact Hist., 418, 4 1/2 x 5 3/4
  Esposito, Am. Wars Atlas, 1:map 8f, 2 3/8 x 5 7/8 col.
  Esposito, Civil War Atlas, map 8f, 2 3/8 x 5 7/8 col.
  Fortescue, British Army, 3:pl.IV, 3 x 2 1/2 col.
  Greene, Gen. Greene, 276, 4 x 6
  Greene, Nathanael Greene, 3:384, 4 5/8 x 6 1/8
  Greene, Revolutionary War, 254, 3 1/4 x 4 col.
  McCrady, S. Carolina, 1775-80, 441, 3 5/8 x 4 3/4
  Montross, Rag, Tag and Bobtail, 442, 3 3/4 x 4 1/4
  Pag. Am., 6:245, 3 x 4
  Pratt, 11 Generals, 31, 3 5/8 x 4
  Ridpath, New Complete Hist., 7:3074, 5 1/2 x 8
  Scharf, Hist. of Md., 2:424, 4 5/8 x 6
  Scheer, Rebels and Redcoats, 463, 5 3/4 x 4 3/8
  Schenck, N. Carolina, 446, 4 5/8 x 7 5/8
  Steele, Am. Campaigns, 2:27, 3 3/4 x 6 1/8 col.

Ward, Del. Continentals, 460, 5 1/8 x 4 1/8
Ward, Revolution, 2:829, 5 x 4 1/2
Seat of war in South Carolina after Eutaw Springs, 1781   26485
   McCrady, S. Carolina, 1780-83, 480, 4 7/8 x 3 5/8

GEORGIA

Georgia   27005
 1763
   Cumming, Southeast, pl.60, 7 1/8 x 8 7/8
   Smith, School Hist. of Ga., 4 x 6
 1765   27010
   Coleman, Am. Rev. in Ga., vi, 4 5/8 x 7 1/8
   Science Res. Assoc., Story of Ga., 130, 3 1/8 x 4
Georgia coast, 1780   27015
   Brown, Hist. Geog., 71, 4 5/8 x 4 5/8
Coast, rivers, and inlets of Georgia, 1780   27017
   Naval Docs. of Am. Rev., 4:387, 5 3/8 x 7 1/8, by Joseph
    Avery and others, from J.F.W. Des Barres, Atlantic Neptune
Northern frontiers of Georgia, 1778   27020
   Ga. Hist. Soc. Coll., 8(1913):32, by Lt. Col. Archibald
    Campbell
Upper Savannah River Valley, 1778   27025
   Fleming, Autobiog. of Colony, 126, 7 7/8 x 4, after Lt. Col.
    Archibald Campbell
Indian Land cessions
 1763   27030
   Fleming, Autobiog. of Colony, 82, 4 5/8 x 4
 1783   27035
   Fleming, Autobiog. of Colony, 155, 4 5/8 x 4
Georgia parishes
 1763   27040
   De Vorsey, Indian Boundary, 147, 6 1/8 x 4 3/8
 At time of the Revolution   27045
   Brown, King's Friends, 231, 4 x 4 3/4
   Evans, First Lessons in Ga. Hist., 95, 4 3/8 x 3 5/8
Georgia counties, 1777   27050
   Evans, First Lessons in Ga. Hist., 133, 4 3/8 x 3 5/8
   Science Res. Assoc., Story of Ga., 147, 4 3/8 x 4 col.
County of Savannah, Ga.   27055
   Ga. Hist. Soc. Coll., 8(1913):96, 7 1/2 x 6 7/8
Augusta, Ga.
 1778   27060
   Fleming, Autobiog. of Colony, lining papers, 9 x 12 1/8,
    after Lt. Col. Archibald Campbell
 1780   27065
   Fleming, Autobiog. of Colony, 134, 3 5/8 x 4
Savannah, Ga., 1772, by William Gerard De Brahm   27070
   Gipson, Br. Empire, 12:238, 5 3/8 x 5
   Pag. Am., 6:229, 3 7/8 x 3

MILITARY OPERATIONS

Operations in Georgia   27075
 1778
   Pag. Am., 6:210-211, 10 7/8 x 8 1/2

1779   27080
    Avery, Hist. of U.S., 6:212, 6 3/4 x 5 3/8 col.
    Boatner, Enc. of Am. Rev., 1035, 4 1/8 x 4 1/8
    Esposito, Am. Wars Atlas, 1:map 8a, 9 1/2 x 6 1/4 col.
    Esposito, Civil War Atlas, map 8a, 9 1/2 x 6 1/4 col.
    Greene, Revolutionary War, 192, 6 3/4 x 5 3/8 col.
    Pag. Am., 6:220-221, 10 7/8 x 8 1/2
    Paullin, Atlas, pl.160E, 3 5/8 x 2 3/4 col.
1780   27085
    Avery, Hist. of U.S., 6:212, 6 3/4 x 5 3/8 col.
    Greene, Revolutionary War, 192, 6 3/4 x 5 3/8 col.
Area of operations in Georgia, 1782   27090
    Wildes, Anthony Wayne, 273, 6 5/8 x 4
Movements of American commanders in Georgia
  Brig. Gen. John Ashe, 1779   27100
    Boatner, Enc. of Am. Rev., 1035, 4 1/8 x 4 1/8
    Esposito, Am. Wars Atlas, 1:map 8a, 9 1/2 x 6 1/4 col.
    Esposito, Civil War Atlas, map 8a, 9 1/2 x 6 1/4 col.
    Morison, Growth of Am. Republic, 5th ed., 222, 6 x 4 1/2
    Paullin, Atlas, pl.160E, 3 5/8 x 2 3/4 col.
  Col. Elijah Clarke, 1780   27105
    Avery, Hist. of U.S., 6:212, 6 3/4 x 5 3/8 col.
    Greene, Revolutionary War, 192, 6 3/4 x 5 3/8 col.
  Maj. Gen. Benjamin Lincoln, 1779   27110
    Alden, Am. Revolution, 229, 7 x 4 3/4
    Am. Heritage Atlas, 102, 5 1/4 x 7 1/2 col.
    Avery, Hist. of U.S., 6:212, 6 3/4 x 5 3/8 col.
    Boatner, Enc. of Am. Rev., 1035, 4 1/8 x 4 1/8
    Commager, Spirit of '76, 2:1074, 6 5/8 x 4 5/8
    Esposito, Am. Wars Atlas, 1:map 8a, 9 1/2 x 6 1/4 col.
    Esposito, Civil War Atlas, map 8a, 9 1/2 x 6 1/4 col.
    Greene, Revolutionary War, 192, 6 3/4 x 5 3/8 col.
    Paullin, Atlas, pl.160E, 3 5/8 x 2 3/4 col.
    Wallace, Appeal to Arms, 207, 7 x 4 3/4
  Col. Andrew Pickens, 1779   27115
    Paullin, Atlas, pl.160E, 3 5/8 x 2 3/4 col.
Movements of British Commanders in Georgia
  Col. Boyd, 1779   27120
    Paullin, Atlas, pl.160E, 3 5/8 x 2 3/4 col.
  Lt. Col. Archibald Campbell, Jan.-Feb. 1779   27125
    Esposito, Am. Wars Atlas, 1:map 8a, 9 1/2 x 6 1/4 col.
    Esposito, Civil War Atlas, map 8a, 9 1/2 x 6 1/4 col.
  Maj. Gen. Augustine Prevost, 1779   27130
    Alden, Am. Revolution, 229, 7 x 4 3/4
    Am. Heritage Atlas, 102, 5 1/4 x 7 1/2 col.
    Avery, Hist. of U.S., 6:212, 6 3/4 x 5 3/8 col.
    Boatner, Enc. of Am. Rev., 1035, 4 1/8 x 4 1/8
    Chron. Am., 12:250, 7 x 5 5/8 col.
    Commager, Spirit of '76, 2:1074, 6 5/8 x 4 5/8
    Esposito, Am. Wars Atlas, 1:map 8a, 9 1/2 x 6 1/4 col.
    Esposito, Civil War Atlas, map 8a, 9 1/2 x 6 1/4 col.
    Greene, Revolutionary War, 192, 6 3/4 x 5 3/8 col.
    Pag. Am., 6:220-221, 10 7/8 x 8 1/2
    Paullin, Atlas, pl.160E, 3 5/8 x 2 3/4 col.
    Wallace, Appeal to Arms, 207, 7 x 4 3/4

Lt. Col. Marc Prevost, 1779   27135
   Avery, Hist. of U.S., 6:212, 6 3/4 x 5 3/8 col.
   Greene, Revolutionary War, 192, 6 3/4 x 5 3/8 col.
Kettle Creek, Ga., Battle of, Feb. 14, 1779   27140
   Ga. Hist. Quar., 10(June 1926):87, 6 1/8 x 2 3/8; 90, 5 x 4
Briar Creek, Ga., Battle of, Mar. 3, 1779   27145
   Ga. Hist. Quar., 10(June 1926):87, 6 1/8 x 2 3/8; 107,
    6 1/8 x 3 3/4
Route of Lt. Col. John Maitland from Dawfuskie to Savannah, Ga.,   27150
   Sept. 16?-17, 1779
   Steward, St. Domingo Legion, 5, 2 x 3 1/2
Savannah, Ga., siege, Sept. 23 - Oct. 28, 1779   27155
   Avery, Hist. of U.S., 6:215, 3 7/8 x 3 3/4 col.
   Boatner, Enc. of Am. Rev., 983, 4 7/8 x 4 1/8
   Butler, King's Royal Rifle Corps, 1:318, 3 7/8 x 3 3/4
   Carrington, Battles, 484, 4 5/8 x 7 3/4
   Commager, Spirit of '76, 2:1091, 4 5/8 x 4 5/8
   Coggins, Ships and Seamen, 145, 5 7/8 x 7 1/2
   Dupuy, Compact Hist., 328, 4 1/4 x 4 1/2
   Fleming, Autobiog. of Colony, 131, 2 7/8 x 4
   Fortescue, British Army, 3:pl.IV, 3 7/8 x 3 7/8 col.
   Garner, Hist. of U.S., 2:486, 2 7/8 x 4
   Grant, British Battles, 2:157, 6 3/8 x 5 5/8
   Greene, Revolutionary War, 202, 3 7/8 x 3 3/4 col.
   Jones, Savannah, end, 17 1/2 x 25 3/8, from Hessian sources
   Lawrence, Storm over Savannah, front, 7 x 10 3/4, by Capt.
    Antoine O'Connor; end, 8 x 10 3/4, by John Wilson
   Lossing, Field-Book of Rev., 2:520, 1 x 1 3/8
   Montross, Rag, Tag and Bobtail, 339, 5 1/8 x 4 1/4
   Moore, Diary of Am. Rev., 2:224, 7 x 9 7/8
   N.Y. Hist. Soc. Quar., 36(July 1952):262, 5 3/4 x 8 7/8
   Ridpath, New Complete Hist., 6:2812, 3 1/4 x 3 1/2; 2828,
    5 1/2 x 6 1/2
   Steward, St. Domingo Legion, 6, 3 x 4 3/8
   Ward, Revolution, 2:691, 4 1/2 x 5 3/4
   Winsor, America, 6:521, 4 1/2 x 4 3/4, French map
By Capt.-Lt. James Moncrieff, pub. by William Faden   27160
   Lossing, Field-Book of Rev., 2:530, 3 1/2 x 4 5/8
   Pag. Am., 6:231, 4 5/8 x 5 7/8
   Stedman, Am. War, 2:132, 20 x 22 1/4
By Ozanne   27162
   Am. Heritage, Revolution, 322, 2 3/8 x 2 1/8
   Cook, Golden Bk. of Am. Rev., 164, 3 1/2 x 3 1/8

FLORIDA

British Florida, 1763-1783   28005
   Adams, Atlas, pl.50, 6 1/4 x 9 1/4
   Boatner, Enc. of Am. Rev., 372, 4 1/8 x 6 3/4
   Hanna, Florida, 78, 3 x 4
   Sosin, Revolutionary Frontier, 63, 5 1/8 x 7 1/2
1763   28010
   De Vorsey, Indian Boundary, 183, 4 3/4 x 5 7/8, from
    Gentleman's Mag.
   Gentleman's Mag., 33(Nov. 1763):552, 7 1/2 x 9 7/8, engr. by
    J. Gibson

Gipson, Br. Empire, 4:12, 4 3/4 x 6 3/4, by Thomas Wright
1765
28012
    Cole, Pict. Hist. of Pensacola, 11, 4 7/8 x 6 5/8
1768
28015
    Gipson, Br. Empire, 9:182, 6 3/4 x 5 5/8, by Thomas Jefferys
East Florida
1776
28020
    Mowat, East Fla., 11, 5 x 4 3/8, 2 x 1 3/4, by Bernard Romans
    Siebert, Loyalists in E. Fla., 44, 10 1/8 x 8, pub. by
      R. Sayer and J. Bennett
During American Revolution
28025
    Hanna, Florida, 92, 5 1/4 x 4
General surveys of East Florida, 1766-1770
28030
    Gipson, Br. Empire, 9:183, 7 x 5 1/2, by William Gerard
      De Brahm
West Florida
1763
28035
    Lord, Atlas, map 60, 3 1/8 x 4 7/8
    Philbrick, Rise of West, 214, 3 5/8 x 4 1/8
1763-1780
28040
    Hart, Am. Nation, 12:142, 2 1/8 x 4 1/8
1763-1787
28045
    Lord, Atlas, map 61, 3 1/8 x 3 3/4
1783-1795
28050
    Hanna, Florida, 97, 3 1/4 x 4
    Philbrick, Rise of West, 214, 3 5/8 x 4 1/8
Coast line from Mississippi Delta to Pensacola, 1773
28055
    Brun, Guide, 160, 5 1/4 x 7 5/8, by Bernard Romans
Lower Mississippi River
1773
28060
    Putnam, Memoirs, 90, 4 x 5 1/4, by Rufus Putnam; 92,
      5 3/4 x 7 1/2
1776
28065
    Gipson, Br. Empire, 9:208, 6 1/4 x 5 5/8, by Thomas Jefferys
Lands in West Florida located for Company of Military Adventurers, 28070
    1773
    Putnam, Memoirs, 51, 5 5/8 x 4
Mobile Bay and River
28075
    Hamilton, Colonial Mobile, 250, 15 3/4 x 7 7/8
Mobile Bay, 1771
28080
    Hamilton, Colonial Mobile, 260, 6 3/4 x 7, British Admiralty
      chart
Mobile
1765
28085
    Hamilton, Colonial Mobile, 230, 3 1/4 x 6 3/8
1770
28090
    Gipson, Br. Empire, 9:208, 4 3/4 x 7 1/8, by Thomas Kitchin
Pensacola Bay, 1766
28095
    Hamilton, Colonial Mobile, 234, 4 3/8 x 3 1/2
Pensacola
1763
28097
    Gentleman's Mag., 33(Nov. 1763):552, 3 1/4 x 4 1/4
1765
28100
    Hamilton, Colonial Mobile, 258, 3 7/8 x 5 3/8
1767
28105
    Gipson, Br. Empire, 9:231, 5 x 8 1/8

1773   28107
  Cole, Pict. Hist. of Pensacola, 15, 4 1/8 x 6 1/2
St. Augustine
1769   28110
  Reynolds, Old St. Augustine, 91, 4 x 5 1/2, engr. by
    Thomas Jefferys
1777   28115
  Naval Docs. of Am. Rev., 2:632, 3 7/8 x 5 1/2, engr. by
    Thomas Jefferys, pub. by William Faden
1782   28120
  Siebert, Loyalists in E. Fla., 102, 5 3/4 x 8 1/4, pub. by
    J. Bew
c. 1784   28125
  Siebert, Loyalists in E. Fla., 120, 5 7/8 x 7 1/2
Trans-Florida road or trail, St. Augustine to Apalachee Bay, 1776 28130
  Brown, Hist. Geog., 74, 2 1/2 x 4 5/8

MILITARY OPERATIONS

Gen. Robert Howe's campaign against East Florida, May-July 1778   28132
  Fla. Hist. Quar., 29(Apr. 1951):255, 7 x 3 5/8
Campaigns of Bernardo de Galvez, 1779-1782   28135
  Caughey, Hist. of U.S., 105, 1 3/8 x 2 3/4
Operations of Galvez from Havana against Mobile and Pensacola,   28140
  1780-1781
  Morales Padron, Spanish Help, 16, 5 x 5 1/2
Defenses of Pensacola
 Fort, 1763   28145
  Robertson, Diaries, pl.10, 4 3/8 x 5 3/4
 Fort, 1764   28150
  Robertson, Diaries, pl.11, 4 3/8 x 5 1/2
 Stockade Fort, 1768   28155
  Gipson, Br. Empire, 9:230, 4 5/8 x 5 7/8, by E. Durnford

THE WEST FROM THE ALLEGHENY MOUNTAINS
TO THE MISSISSIPPI RIVER

Cook, Golden Book of Am. Rev., 152, 5 5/8 x 4
Fite, Book of Old Maps, 278, 8 1/2 x 12 1/4
Hutchins, Topo. Description, 112, 7 1/8 x 5
James, Life of Clark, 69, 5 x 3 1/2
Johnson, Papers, 6:90, 7 1/2 x 4 1/2
Parkman, Pontiac, 2:155, 5 3/4 x 3 1/2
Va. Cavalcade, 2(Winter 1952):35, 4 3/8 x 3 1/8
Winsor, America, 6:700, 5 3/8 x 3 3/4
Winsor, Westward Movement, 27, 5 3/8 x 3 3/4
Kaskaskia and environs, 1778   29081
  Sinclair, Westward the Tide, 149, 6 x 4 1/8
Fort Sackville, Vincennes   29085
  English, Conquest, 1:323, 3 7/8 x 2 7/8; 378, 2 7/8 x 2 1/2
  Ill. State Hist. Soc., Trans for 1907, 62, 6 1/8 x 4
Ground around St. Xavier's Church, Vincennes   29090
  English, Conquest, 1:378, 2 1/2 x 2 1/2
Upper Ohio Monongahela frontier   29092
  Sosin, Revolutionary Frontier, 59, 7 1/2 x 5 1/8
Upper Ohio Valley in 18th Century   29095
  Downes, Council Fires, end, 8 1/4 x 11
Allegheny and Ohio frontier   29096
  De Gruyter, Kanawha Spectator, 1:lining papers, 7 3/4 x 11 1/2
The Old Southwest (the region south of the Ohio River, from the
    Alleghenies to the Mississippi)
  1740-1790   29100
    Henderson, Conquest of Old S.W., 192, 5 1/4 x 8
Southwestern Pennsylvania, Western Virginia, and Kentucky   29105
  Mason, James Harrod, 140, 7 7/8 x 18 3/4
Southwest Virginia, prob. by Daniel Smith   29110
  Kellogg, Frontier Retreat, 402, 8 3/4 x 18 3/8
Washington's Ohio River journey, 1770   29115
  Ambler, Washington and West, 143, 4 1/2 x 4
  Ambler, West Va., 109, 4 1/2 x 4
  Ambler, West Va. Stories and Biogs., 67, 4 1/4 x 4
  Cleland, Washington in Ohio Valley, 258, 4 7/8 x 7 3/8
  Freeman, Washington, 3:259, 4 x 5
  Washington Atlas, pl.31, 11 x 15 1/2 col.
  Washington Bicentennial, 1:411, 7 1/8 x 10 1/8
Washington's grant on Great Kanawha River, 1774   29116
  Paullin, Atlas, pl.51B, 3 7/8 x 9 col.
Washington's western tour to Ohio Basin, Sept. 1784   29118
  Ambler, Washington and West, 179, 3 7/8 x 5 7/8
  Ambler, West Va., 181, 2 3/4 x 4
  Ambler, West Va. Stories and Biogs., 96, 2 3/4 x 4
  Cleland, Washington in Ohio Valley, 258, 4 7/8 x 7 3/8; 300,
    4 7/8 x 7 5/8
  Hulbert, Washington and West, 32, 6 x 9
  Washington Atlas, pl.31, 11 x 5 1/2 col.
  Washington Bicentennial, 1:411, 7 1/8 x 10 1/8
Western lands claimed by States and ceded to Congress, 1781-1802   29120
  Alden, Rise of Am. Republic, 163, 5 3/4 x 4 1/2
  Am. Heritage Atlas, 118, 9 3/4 x 7 1/2 col.
  Avery, Hist. of U.S., 6:388, 6 3/4 x 5 col.
  Baldwin, Adult's History, 115, 6 1/2 x 5 5/8
  Barck, Colonial Am., 687, 7 x 4 5/8

Barck, Colonial Am., 2d ed., 658, 7 x 4 5/8
Billington, W. Expansion, 2d ed., 203, 4 1/2 x 4 1/8
Caughey, Hist. of U.S., 119, 3 1/2 x 5 3/4
Chitwood, Colonial America, 3rd ed., 611, 6 3/4 x 4 1/4
Craven, U.S. 123, 6 1/8 x 4 1/2
Gerson, Franklin, 59, 6 1/2 x 4 1/2
Harlow, United States, 133, 4 7/8 x 4 5/8
Hart, Am. Nation, 10:108, 6 3/8 x 4 1/8 col.
Hawke, Colonial Experience, 652, 5 1/4 x 4 1/2
Hicks, Federal Union, 4th ed., 209, 7 1/2 x 5 1/2
Lefler, North Carolina, 183, 5 1/8 x 5 1/2 col.
Morison, Growth of Am. Republic, 5th ed., 259, 5 1/4 x 4 1/2
Newsome, Growth of N.C., 168, 2 3/4 x 3
Palmer, Atlas of World Hist., 151, 5 5/8 x 4 3/8 col.
Passano, Hist. of Md., 121, 7 3/4 x 5 3/8 col.
Perkins, U.S. of Am., 167 4 7/8 x 4 1/2
Philbrick, Rise of West, 118, 5 1/2 x 4 1/8
Roosevelt, Winning of West, 3:end, 7 7/8 x 6 3/8 col.
Todd, Am. Hist., 117, 6 5/8 x 5 1/8
Proposed division of the West into states according to Thomas   29125
    Jefferson's first territorial ordinance, Apr. 23, 1784
Hart, Am. Nation, 10:116, 6 1/2 x 4
Kinnaird, Geo. Washington, 198, 4 3/4 x 6 1/4, pub. by
    Francis Bailey
Paullin, Atlas, pl.46B, 3 5/8 x 3 3/8 col.
Paxson, Am. Frontier, 62, 4 1/8 x 4 1/4
Turner, Sections in Am. Hist., 94, 5 5/8 x 4 col.
Winsor, Westward Movement, 259, 6 3/4 x 3 3/4, from Crevecour's
    Letters, 1787
Public land survey system established by Ordinance of 1785   29130
    Alden, Rise of Am. Republic, 177, 1 3/4 x 3 3/8
Current, Am. Hist., 123, 5 3/4
Todd, America's Hist., 159, 2 1/2 x 5 1/8
See also 42035 and 42045
Boundary of Northwest Territory, organized in 1787   29135
Chron. Am., 19:24, 7 x 9 1/4 col.

WESTERN RIVERS

Beaver Creek, by J. Hector St. John Crèvecoeur   30005
    Hanna, Wilderness Trail, 2:386, 7 3/4 x 4 3/4
Thwaites, Rev. on Upper Ohio, frontis., 9 x 5 5/8
Headwaters of the Clinch and Holston Rivers, 1774?, by   30010
    Daniel Smith
Thwaites, Dunmore's War, 30, 4 7/8 x
Little Kanawha River, 1773, by George Washington   30015
    Brown, Early Maps, pl.48, 5 7/8 x 10
Mouth of Little Miami River, 1766, by Thomas Hutchins   30020
Bond, Foundations of Ohio, 197, 1 7/8 x 4 3/8
Mississippi and Ohio Valleys   30025
    Pag. Am., 2:108, 4 5/8 x 2 5/8, from Crèvecoeur's
    "Lettres d'un Cultivateur Americain," Paris, 1787
Source of the Mississippi River
1766-1767, by Jonathan Carver   30030
    Winsor, Westward Movement, 215, 6 3/4 x 3 7/8

1774, by Samuel Dunn   30035
  Winsor, Westward Movement, 214, 2 5/8 x 3 7/8
1785, by Peter Pond
  Winsor, Westward Movement, 471, 2 x 2
Muskingum River and Beaver Creek, by J. Hector St. John   30045
  Crèvecoeur
  Hanna, Wilderness Trail, 2:386, 7 3/4 x 8 5/8
  Thwaites, Rev. on Upper Ohio, frontis., 9 x 10
Ohio River
 1766, by Capt. Harry Gordon   30050
  Brown, Early Maps, pl.42, 4 3/4 x 9 3/4
  Hutchins, Courses of Ohio R., 75, 22 x 10 3/8
Upper Ohio River, c.1776, by John Montrésor   30055
  Brown, Early Maps, pl.50, 9 1/8 x 7 1/4
Falls of the Ohio
 c.1766, by William Brazier   30060
  Brown, Early Maps, pl.43, 7 x 10
 1778, by Thomas Hutchins   30065
  Hutchins, Courses of Ohio R., frontis., 5 5/8 x 7 1/8
  Hutchins, Topo. Description, 80, 5 3/4 x 7 1/4
Divide between the Potomac and the Youghiogheny, 1784, by   30070
  George Washington
  Hulbert, Washington and West, 184, 4 x 6 3/8, after Washington
  Winsor, Westward Movement, 253, 3 3/4 x 6
Scioto River, by J. Hector St. John Crèvecoeur   30075
  Hanna, Wilderness Trail, 2:386, 7 3/4 x 3 5/8
  Thwaites, Rev. on Upper Ohio, frontis., 9 x 4 1/8
  Winsor, Westward Movement, 67, 7 x 3 7/8
Wabash River, c.1766, by Thomas Hutchins   30080
  Brown, Early Maps, pl.44, 8 x 7
  Hulbert, Military Roads, 35, 6 3/8 x 6

ROADS AND TRAILS TO AND IN THE WEST

Mountain passes through the Appalachians   31005
  Lefler, North Carolina, 179, 3 3/8 x 5 1/2
Routes between Fort Venango, Fort Pitt, and Fort Cumberland,   31010
  c.1766
  Brown, Early Maps, pl.40, 9 3/4 x 6 3/4
Pioneer roads to Kentucky through Cumberland Gap   31015
  Pusey, Wilderness Rd., 50, 9 x 15 3/4
Early settlers' roads and trails, Kentucky-Tennessee frontier   31020
  Van Every, Co. of Heroes, 297, 3 5/8 x 4
Braddock's Road   31025
  Adams, Atlas, pl.43, 9 1/4 x 6 1/4; pl.57, 9 1/4 x 6 1/4
  Am. Heritage Atlas, 78-79, 9 3/4 x 11 7/8 col.; 80, 9 3/4 x
    7 1/2 col.
  Baldwin, Adult's History, 78, 5 1/4 x 5 5/8
  Barck, Colonial Am., 636, 4 5/8 x 7
  Barck, Colonial Am., 2d ed., 609, 4 5/8 x 7
  Havighurst, Geo. Rogers Clark, lining papers, 7 1/2 x 10 3/8
  Lord, Atlas, map 58, 4 1/2 x 6 1/2 col.
  Mason, James Harrod, 140, 7 7/8 x 18 3/4; 176, 8 x 16 3/4
Cumberland-Wheeling Road   31030
  Mason, James Harrod, 140, 7 7/8 x 18 3/4; 176, 8 x 16 3/4

Forbes' Road 31035
   Adams, Atlas, pl.43, 9 1/4 x 6 1/4; pl.57, 9 1/4 x 6 1/4
   Am. Heritage Atlas, 80, 9 3/4 x 7 1/2 col.
   Baldwin, Adult's History, 78, 5 1/4 x 5 5/8; 162, 5 5/8 x 8 1/2
   Barck, Colonial Am., 636, 4 5/8 x 7
   Barck, Colonial Am., 2d ed., 609, 4 5/8 x 7
   Craven, U.S., 259, 6 3/8 x 4 1/2
   Lord, Atlas, map 58, 4 1/2 x 6 1/2 col.
   Mason, James Harrod, 140, 7 7/8 x 18 3/4; 176, 8 x 16 3/4
Wilderness Road 31037
   Adams, Atlas, pl.62, 6 1/4 x 9 1/4; pl.84, 6 1/4 x 9 1/4
   Am. Heritage Atlas, 78-79, 9 3/4 x 11 7/8 col.; 80, 9 3/4 x
     7 1/2 col.
   Baldwin, Adult's History, 88, 5 5/8 x 8 1/2
   Barck, Colonial Am., 636, 4 5/8 x 7
   Barck, Colonial Am., 2d ed., 609, 4 5/8 x 7
   Bruce, Boone, end, 3 5/8 x 5 3/8
   Caruso, Appalachian Frontier, 160, 5 1/2 x 4 1/8
   Clark, Exploring Kentucky, 35, 3 7/8 x 4; 174, 4 1/4 x 4
   Craven, U.S. 259, 6 3/8 x 4 1/2
   Havighurst, Geo. Rogers Clark, lining papers, 7 1/2 x 10 3/8
   Hicks, Federal Union, 4th ed., 151, 3 7/8 x 5 3/8
   Jillson, Bibliog. of Clark, 11, 3 5/8 x 6 1/2
   Kincaid, Wilderness Rd., lining papers, 5 3/8 x 9 1/2
   Lefler, North Carolina, 178, 2 3/4 x 5 1/2 col.
   Lord, Atlas, map 58, 4 1/2 x 6 1/2 col.
   Mason, James Harrod, 140, 7 7/8 x 18 3/4
   Newsome, Growth of N.C., 162, 1 5/8 x 3 7/8
   Pag. Am., 4:52, 4 3/4 x 3 5/8
   Pusey, Wilderness Rd., 70-83, six maps each approx. 9 x 7 1/8
   Roosevelt, Winning of West, 1:end, 6 1/2 x 8 col.
   Rouse, Virginia, 165, 5 1/2 x 7 1/4
   Speed, Wilderness Rd., frontis., 9 5/8 x 7 1/2
   Van Every, Co. of Heroes, 297, 3 5/8 x 4
Avery's Trace 31040
   Adams, Atlas, pl.84, 6 1/4 x 9 1/4
Chickasaw Trail (Natchez Trace) 31045
   Adams, Atlas, pl.84, 6 1/2 x 9 1/2
   Am. Heritage Atlas, 78-79, 9 3/4 x 11 7/8 col.
Great Buffalo Trace 31050
   Van Every, Co. of Heroes, 297, 3 5/8 x 4
Great Trading Path 31055
   Am. Heritage Atlas, 78-79, 9 3/4 x 11 7/8 col.; 80,
     9 3/4 x 7 1/2 col.
Great Trail, Pittsburgh to Detroit 31060
   Am. Heritage Atlas, 78-79, 9 3/4 x 11 7/8 col.; 80,
     9 3/4 x 7 1/2 col.
   Bond, Foundations of Ohio, 202, 3 1/2 x 4 1/4
Hunters' Trails 31065
   Mason, James Harrod, 176, 8 x 16 3/4
Lake Shore Trail, Presque Isle to Detroit 31070
   Bond, Foundations of Ohio, 202, 3 1/2 x 4 1/4
Mahoning Trail, Pittsburgh to Mouth of Cuyahoga River 31075
   Bond, Foundations of Ohio, 202, 3 1/2 x 4 1/4
Nickajack Trail 31080
   Adams, Atlas, pl. 84, 6 1/4 x 9 1/4

Am. Heritage Atlas, 78-79, 9 3/4 x 11 7/8 col.
Scioto Trail   31085
    Am. Heritage Atlas, 78-79, 9 3/4 x 11 7/8 col.; 80,
      9 3/4 x 7 1/2 col.
Route of Col. Alexander Lowrey and other Indian traders from   31090
    the Scioto to Detroit, by way of Rocher de Bout
    Butterfield, Washington-Irvine Corr., 354, 16 3/4 x 7 1/4
Shawnee-Cherokee Trail   31095
    Van Every, Co. of Heroes, 297, 3 5/8 x 4
Trade paths to Catawba and Cherokee towns, c.1776   31097
    Atkin, Indians, 34, 5 3/8 x 4
Warrior's Path   31100
    Am. Heritage Atlas, 78-79, 9 3/4 x 11 7/8 col.; 80,
      9 3/4 x 7 1/2 col.
    Caruso, Appalachian Frontier, 66, 3 1/8 x 4 1/8; 160, 5 1/2 x
      4 1/8; 254, 3 3/4 x 4 1/8
    Mason, James Harrod, 140, 7 7/8 x 18 3/4; 176, 8 x 16 3/4

INDIAN TRIBES

Indian nations east of the Mississippi, 1775, by James Adair   32010
    Atkin, Indians, frontis., 6 1/8 x 4 5/8
    Greene, Rev. Generation, 174, 8 3/4 x 7
    Pag. Am., 2:25, 5 1/2 x 4

Six Nations (Iroquois)
    See 14005-14025
Indians on the western frontier   32012
    Clarke, Am. Revolution, end lining paper, 4 1/4 x 3 3/8 col.
Location of Indian tribes of the Old Northwest   32015
    Pag. Am., 2:75, 3 1/2 x 3 1/4
Great Lakes Indian country, 1776   32020
    Gipson, Br. Empire, 9:96, 5 x 6 3/8, by Thomas Jeffreys
Location of principal Indian tribes in Ohio at time of the   32025
    Revolution
    Bond, Foundations of Ohio, 202, 3 1/2 x 4 1/4
Indian towns on Muskingum and Scioto Rivers and Beaver Creek,   32030
    from Crèvecoeur's "Lettres d'un Cultivateur Americain," 1787
    Hanna, Wilderness Trail, 2:386, 7 3/4 x 8 5/8, 7 3/4 x 3 5/8,
      7 3/4 x 4 3/4
    Thwaites, Rev. on Upper Ohio, frontis., 9 x 10, 9 x 4 1/8,
      9 x 5 1/8
Moravian Indian Mission villages in Ohio, 1772-1782   32035
    Morrison, Ohio in Maps, 14, 4 1/8 x 6 5/8
County of the Southern Indians, 1764   32040
    Hamilton, Colonial Mobile, 240, 3 7/8 x 6 3/4
Southern Indian District, 1764   32045
    De Vorsey, Indian Boundary, 15, 4 1/4 x 5 1/4, after John
    Stuart
Indian nations in the Southern Department, 1766, by John Gerar   32050
    William De Brahm
    Alden, John Stuart, end, 18 1/8 x 22 3/8
    Cumming, Southeast, pl.61, 7 1/4 x 8 7/8
    De Vorsey, Indian Boundary, lining papers, 8 7/8 x 10 7/8
Cherokee-Creek country, 1760-1781   32055
    Adams, Atlas, pl.76, 9 1/4 x 6 1/4

Cherokee country   32060
    Alden, John Stuart, 102, 5 1/4 x 4 1/8
    Caruso, Appalachian Frontier, 104, 4 1/8 x 4 1/8
    Malone, Cherokees, front, 5 1/2 x 6 1/4
  1762, by Lt. Henry Timberlake   32065
    Avery, Hist. of U.S., 4:346, 7 1/4 x 4 1/2
    Gipson, Br. Empire, 9:76, 7 1/2 x 4 3/4
    Pag. Am., 6:109, 4 x 2 1/2
    Timberlake, Memoirs, 27
  1772   32070
    Gipson, Br. Empire, 9:56, 5 1/4 x 7 1/2
  1776, by Thomas Jefferys   32075
    Gipson, Br. Empire, 9:57, 5 x 8 1/8
Cherokee settlements, 1762-1776   32077
    Gilbert, Eastern Cherokees, 179, 4 x 4 3/8
Situation of western Indian nations, 1785   32078
    Johnson, Papers, 6:524, 6 1/8 x 4 1/2
Distribution of major Indian tribes, 1787   32080
    Avery, Hist. of U.S., 6:410, 16 x 14 col.

INDIAN BOUNDARY LINES

Proclamation line of 1763   33005
    Adams, Atlas, pl.47, 9 1/4 x 6 1/4; pl.61, 9 1/4 x 6 1/4
    Alden, Hist. of Am. Rev., 40, 8 5/8 x 5 5/8
    Alden, Rise of Am. Republic, 115, 5 x 4 3/8
    Alvord, Lord Shelburne, end, 1 1/2 x 1 3/4 col.
    Am. Heritage Atlas, 76, 9 3/4 x 7 1/2 col.
    Baldwin, Adult's History, 88, 5 5/8 x 8 1/2
    Barck, Colonial Am., 624, 7 x 4 5/8; 636, 4 5/8 x 7
    Barck, Colonial Am., 2d ed., 475, 5 x 4 1/2; 598, 7 x 4 5/8;
      609, 4 5/8 x 7
    Billington, W. Expansion, 2nd ed., 147, 5 1/8 x 4 1/4
    Caughey, Hist. of U.S., 79, 3 1/2 x 5 7/8
    Chitwood, Colonial America, 501, 3 3/4 x 4 1/8
    Chron. Am., 19:24, 7 x 9 1/4 col.
    Clark, Frontier America, 85, 5 1/2 x 4 3/4; 93, 4 x 4 3/4
    Craven, U.S., 48, 5 3/8 x 4 1/2
    Current, Am. Hist., 2nd ed., 73, 8 x 5 1/4
    Dupuy, Compact Hist., front, 8 7/8 x 11 1/2
    Enc. Americana, 1:721, 9 3/8 x 6 1/4
    Flexner, Mohawk Baronet, 325, 4 1/8 x 5 1/2
    Flexner, Washington in Am. Rev., lining papers, 8 1/2 x
      11 3/4, by Samuel H. Bryant
    Freeman, Washington, abridgment, 151, 7 3/4 x 5 1/2
    Gewehr, United States, 69, 4 1/2 x 5 1/4
    Gipson, Br. Empire, 9:47, 4 3/4 x 5 1/2
    Gipson, Coming of Rev., 122-123, 8 1/2 x 6 1/2; 130-131,
      8 1/2 x 6 1/2
    Greene, Foundations, 389, 4 x 6 col.
    Harlow, United States, 74, 7 x 4 3/4
    Hart, Am. Nation, 7:268, 6 1/2 x 4 1/8 col.; 8:4, 8 1/2 x
      6 1/2 xol.; 224, 6 1/2 x 4 1/8 col.; 298, 8 1/2 x 6 1/2 col.
    Hawke, Colonial Experience, 524, 5 x 4 1/2; 527, 3 5/8 x 4 1/2
    Henderson, Conquest of Old S.W., 192, 5 1/4 x 8

Kerr. Hist. Atlas of Canada, 31, 6 3/8 x 8 5/8 col.
Lanctot, Canada and Am. Revolution, 210, 7 x 5
McDowell, Revolutionary War, 26, 9 3/8 x 6 3/4 col.
Malone, Am. Origins, 107, 6 3/4 x 4 1/4; 125, 6 1/2 x 4 1/2
Mason, James Harrod, 140, 7 7/8 x 18 3/4
Morison, Hist. of Am. People, 213, 4 1/2 x 4 1/2
Morris, Enc. of Am. Hist., 66, 7 1/2 x 5
Nettels, Roots of Am. Civ., 645, 3 7/8 x 4 1/8
Newsome, Growth of N.C., 69, 4 x 3 3/4
Pag. Am., 6:105, 3 7/8 x 3; 261, 7 5/8 x 5 7/8
Palmer, Atlas of World Hist., 150, 5 5/8 x 5 col.
Paxson, Am. Frontier, 9, 7 x 4 1/4
Perkins, U.S. of Am., 128, 7 1/8 x 4 5/8
Rice, Allegheny Frontier, 60, 4 1/4 x 7 1/4
Sosin, Whitehall and Wilderness, 64, 5 x 5 3/8
Todd, America's Hist., 117, 6 5/8 x 5 1/8
World Book, 16:254, 3 3/8 x 3 1/8
Engr. by J. Gibson   33012
  De Vorsey, Indian Boundary, 37, 5 3/8 x 6 1/4
  Fite, Book of Old Maps, 218, 9 3/8 x 11 1/4
  Gentleman's Mag., 33(Oct. 1763):477, 8 x 9 1/4
Indian boundary line, 1763-1771   33010
  Savelle, Foundations, 617, 4 x 4
Southern Indian boundary line
    Preliminary Board of Trade proposal, 1763   33015
  De Vorsey, Indian Boundary, 33, 4 1/2 x 3 1/2
Board of Trade map showing line in 1768   33020
  De Vorsey, Indian Boundary, 63, 5 1/2 x 4
The line in 1775   33025
  De Vorsey, Indian Boundary, 231, 6 3/8 x 5 1/2; 232, 6 x 6 1/2
Virginia-Cherokee section   33030
  De Vorsey, Indian Boundary, 82, 1 1/8 x 5 1/4, 1 3/8 x 5 1/4,
    1 5/8 x 3 1/2
North Carolina-Cherokee section   33035
  De Vorsey, Indian Boundary, 103, 4 1/8 x 1 1/8, 4 1/8 x
    1 1/8, 4 1/8 x 1 1/4, 1 7/8 x 4; 104, 7 5/8 x 3 3/4 ;
    106, 5 1/2 x 5 1/2
South Carolina-Cherokee section   33040
  De Vorsey, Indian Boundary, 114, 7 x 4 7/8, 1 1/2 x 1 1/2;
    131, 1 5/8 x 7 1/4, 2 x 7 1/4
Georgia-Creek section, 1768   33045
  De Vorsey, Indian Boundary, 154, 3 5/8 x 2 1/2, 5 x 1 3/8,
    4 3/4 x 1 3/8, 1 3/4 x 1 3/4; 158, 4 x 7 3/8
Georgia section, 1773   33050
  De Vorsey, Indian Boundary, 164, 3 1/2 x 2 1/2, 4 x 7/8,
    4 3/8 x 7/8, 4 3/8 x 1 1/4; 176, 6 x 5 3/8; 177, 3 1/4
    x 7 3/8
East Florida-Creek section   33055
  De Vorsey, Indian Boundary, 185, 3 3/4 x 2 1/8, 5 3/4 x 2,
    2 1/4 x 2 3/8; 196, 4 3/4 x 3 7/8
West Florida section   33060
  De Vorsey, Indian Boundary, 211, 5 7/8 x 1 5/8, 6 7/8 x 7/8,
    4 1/8 x 1, 5 3/4 x 1 1/2, 1 1/4 x 2 3/8
North and South Carolina Indian boundary lines, 1766-1767   33065
  De Vorsey, Indian Boundary, 96, 6 5/8 x 4 1/2

Barck, Colonial Am., 2d ed., 475, 5 x 4 1/2
Billington, W. Expansion, 2d ed., 147, 5 1/8 x 4 1/4
Buell, Sir Wm. Johnson, 244, 4 1/4 x 3 1/4
Chalmers, West to Setting Sun, lining papers, 10 5/8 x 7 3/4,
    10 5/8 x 7 3/4
Clarke, Bloody Mohawk, 181, 3 x 4 1/4
Downes, Council Fires, end, 8 1/4 x 11
Flexner, Mohawk Baronet, 325, 4 1/8 x 5 1/2
Freeman, Washington, abridgment, 151, 7 3/4 x 5 1/2
Halsey, Old N.Y. Frontier, 1, 4 5/8 x 6 3/8
Hart, Am. Nation, 8:224, 6 1/2 x 4 1/8 col.
Hofstadter, Am. Republic, 153, 6 5/8 x 5 1/2
Kerr, Hist. Atlas of Canada, 31, 6 3/8 x 8 5/8 col.
Mason, James Harrod, 140, 7 7/8 x 18 3/4
Sosin, Whitehall and Wilderness, 176, 5 1/8 x 7
By Guy Johnson   33135
Hamilton, Johnson and Indians, 30, 3 3/4 x 5 3/4
Johnson, Papers, 6:450, 7 3/8 x 11 1/4
Lee, Hist. of N. America, 5:445, 4 x 6 1/8 col.
Lydekker, Faithful Mohawks, 116, 5 x 7 1/2
O'Callaghan, Doc. Hist. of N.Y., 1:376, 11 x 17 1/8 col.,
    4 1/2 x 5 1/2 col.
Pound, Johnson of Mohawks, front lining paper, 5 7/8 x 9
Seymour, Lords of the Valley, 234, 3 3/4 x 5 3/4
Winsor, Westward Movement, 15, 2 5/8 x 3 7/8
Creek Treaty line, Nov. 18, 1768   33140
Billington, W. Expansion, 2d ed., 147, 5 1/8 x 4 1/4
Hart, Am. Nation, 8:224, 6 1/2 x 4 1/8 col.
Hofstadter, Am. Republic, 153, 6 5/8 x 5 1/2
Treaty of Lochaber line, Oct. 18, 1770   33145
Abernethy, Western Lands, 65, 4 x 7
Adams, Atlas, pl.61, 9 1/4 x 6 1/2
Am. Heritage Atlas, 77, 5 1/8 x 7 1/2 col.
Avery, Hist. of U.S., 5:285, 6 7/8 x 4 7/8 col.
Barck, Colonial Am., 2d ed., 475, 5 x 4 1/2
Billington, W. Expansion, 2d ed., 147, 5 1/8 x 4 1/4
Caruso, Appalachian Frontier, 104, 4 1/8 x 4 1/8
Clark, Frontier America, 93, 4 x 4 3/4
De Vorsey, Indian Boundary, 70, 4 3/8 x 5
Freeman, Washington, abridgment, 151, 7 3/4 x 5 1/2
Hart, Am. Nation, 8:224, 6 1/2 x 4 1/8 col.
Henderson, Conquest of Old S.W., 192, 5 1/4 x 8
Rice, Allegheny Frontier, 60, 4 1/4 x 7 1/4
By John Stuart, 1771, 1773   33150
De Vorsey, Indian Boundary, 69, 4 1/4 x 5 1/4
Sosin, Whitehall and Wilderness, 188, 5 x 6 3/4
Col. John Donelson's line, 1771   33155
Abernethy, Western Lands, 65, 4 x 7
Adams, Atlas, pls.60-61, 9 1/4 x 13
Am. Heritage Atlas, 77, 5 1/8 x 7 1/2 col.
Billington, W. Expansion, 2d ed., 147, 5 1/8 x 4 1/4
De Vorsey, Indian Boundary, 80, 4 1/2 x 5
Freeman, Washington, abridgment, 151, 7 3/4 x 5 1/2
Henderson, Conquest of Old S.W., 192, 5 1/4 x 8
Philbrick, Rise of West, 88, 3 1/4 x 4 1/8

Rice, Allegheny Frontier, 60, 4 1/4 x 7 1/4
Sosin, Whitehall and Wilderness, 194, 6 3/8 x 5 1/2
By John Stuart   33160
    Abernethy, Western Lands, 54, 11 1/2 x 14 5/8
Cherokee-Creek Treaty line, June 1, 1773   33165
    Avery, Hist. of U.S., 5:285, 6 7/8 x 4 7/8 col.
Treaty of Sycamore Shoals line, 1775   33170
    Adams, Atlas, pl.60-61, 9 1/4 x 13
Treaty of Dewitt's Corner line, May 20, 1777   33175
    Billington, W. Expansion, 2d ed., 176, 4 1/8 x 4 1/8
Treaty of Long Island line, July 20, 1777   33180
    Billington, W. Expansion, 2d ed., 176, 4 1/8 x 4 1/8
Cherokee boundary, 1783   33185
    Billington, W. Expansion, 2d ed., 205, 4 x 4 5/8
    Malone, Cherokees, front, 5 1/2 x 6 1/4
Treaty of Augusta line, Nov. 1, 1783   33190
    Billington, W. Expansion, 2d ed., 229, 5 1/4 x 4 3/8
Second Treaty of Fort Stanwix line, Oct. 22, 1784   33195
    Adams, Atlas, pl.90, 6 1/4 x 9 1/4
    Billington, W. Expansion, 2d ed., 209, 2 7/8 x 4 1/8
    Van Every, Ark of Empire, 186, 3 3/8 x 4
Treaty of Fort McIntosh line, Jan. 21, 1785   33200
    Billington, W. Expansion, 2d ed., 209, 2 7/8 x 4 1/8
    Van Every, Ark of Empire, 186, 3 3/8 x 4
Treaty of Dumpling Creek proposed line, May 1785   33205
    Billington, W. Expansion, 2d ed., 205, 4 x 4 5/8
Treaty of Hopewell line, Nov. 28, 1785   33210
    Adams, Atlas, pl.90, 6 1/4 x 9 1/4
    Billington, W. Expansion, 2d ed., 205, 4 x 4 5/8
Treaty of Fort Finney line, Jan. 31, 1786   33215
    Billington, W. Expansion, 2d ed., 209, 2 7/8 x 4 1/8
    Van Every, Ark of Empire, 186, 3 3/8 x 4
Treaty of Fort Harmar line, Jan. 9, 1789   33220
    Van Every, Ark of Empire, 186, 3 3/8 x 4
Boundary accepted by Creeks and Cherokees, 1789   33225
    Billington, W. Expansion, 2d ed., 234, 4 3/4 x 4 5/8

PROPOSED WESTERN COLONIES AND STATES, 1763-1785

Charlotiana or Charlotina, 1763   34005
    Alvord, Miss. Valley, 1:97, 4 1/2 x 7 3/8 col.
    Avery, Hist. of U.S., 5:174, 7 5/8 x 10 3/8 col.
    Billington, W. Expansion, 2d ed., 135, 2 7/8 x 3 3/4
    Bolton, Colonization, 405, 1 1/8 x 1 3/8
    Hart, Am. Nation, 8:230, 6 1/2 x 8 1/4 col.
    Lord, Atlas, map 53, 6 1/2 x 4 1/2
    Morison, Growth of Am. Republic, 5th ed., 1:139, 4 1/8 x 7
    Nettels, Roots of Am. Civ., 605, 4 1/8 x 6 5/8
Mississippi Company, petition of 1763   34010
    Alvord, Miss. Valley, 1:97, 4 1/2 x 7 3/8 col.
    Billington, W. Expansion, 2d ed., 135, 2 7/8 x 3 3/4
New Wales, 1763   34015
    Alvord, Miss. Valley, 1:97, 4 1/2 x 7 3/8 col.
    Billington, W. Expansion, 2d ed., 135, 2 7/8 x 3 3/4

Illinois Company, 1766   34020
    Alvord, Miss. Valley, 1:317, 7 1/2 x 4 1/2 col.
    Billington, W. Expansion, 2d ed., 144, 3 3/4 x 3 5/8
    Savelle, Foundations, 617, 4 x 4
Phineas Lyman's Military Associates plan, 1766   34025
    Alvord, Miss. Valley, 1:317, 7 1/2 x 4 1/2 col.
    Billington, W. Expansion, 2d ed., 144, 3 3/4 x 3 5/8
Amherst's Detroit plan, 1767   34027
    Alvord, Miss. Valley, 1:317, 7 1/2 x 4 1/2 col.
Indiana Company   34030
    Alvord, Miss. Valley, 2:frontis., 4 1/2 x 4 7/8 col.
    Ambler, West Va., 140, 3 3/8 x 3
    Baldwin, Adult's History, 88, 5 5/8 x 8 1/2
    Billington, W. Expansion, 2d ed., 144, 3 3/4 x 3 5/8;
      147, 5 1/8 x 4 1/4; 203, 4 1/2 x 4 1/8
    Lewis, Indiana Co., frontis., 6 1/4 x 8 3/8; 144, 5 1/2 x 9 3/8
    Philbrick, Rise of West, 88, 3 1/4 x 4 1/8
    Rice, Allegheny Frontier, 74, 5 1/8 x 7 1/2
    Savelle, Foundations, 617, 4 x 4
  By Thomas Hutchins   34032
    Ambler, West Va., 137, 5 1/8 x 4
    Winsor, Westward Movement, 17, 3 7/8 x 5 1/8
Mississippi Company, petition of 1768   34035
    Alvord, Miss. Valley, 2:frontis., 4 1/2 x 4 7/8 col.
    Billington, W. Expansion, 2d ed., 144, 3 3/4 x 3 5/8
Vandalia, 1769   34040
    Abernethy, Western Lands, 39, 3 3/4 x 7
    Adams, Atlas, pl.61, 9 1/4 x 6 1/2
    Alvord, Miss. Valley, 2:frontis., 4 1/2 x 4 7/8 col.
    Ambler, West Va., 140, 3 3/8 x 3
    Am. Heritage Atlas, 77, 5 1/8 x 7 1/2 col.
    Avery, Hist. of U.S., 5:174, 7 5/8 x 10 3/8 col.
    Baldwin, Adult's History, 88, 5 5/8 x 8 1/2
    Billington, W. Expansion, 2d ed., 144, 3 3/4 x 3 5/8
    Bolton, Colonization, 405, 1 1/8 x 1 3/8
    Clark, Frontier America, 93, 4 x 4 3/4
    Hart, Am. Nation, 8:230, 6 1/2 x 8 1/4 col.
    Hicks, Federal Union, 4th ed., 151, 3 7/8 x 5 3/8
    Lewis, Indiana Co., frontis., 6 1/4 x 8 3/8
    Lord, Atlas, map 53, 6 1/2 x 4 1/2
    Morison, Growth of Am. Republic, 5th ed., 1:139, 4 1/8 x 7
    Nettels, Roots of Am. Civ., 605, 4 1/8 x 6 5/8
    Philbrick, Rise of West, 88, 3 1/4 x 4 1/8
    Rice, Allegheny Frontier, 74, 5 1/8 x 7 1/2
    Turner, Sections in Am. Hist., 94, 5 5/8 x 4 col.
    Savelle, Foundations, 617, 4 x 4
    Sosin, Whitehall and Wilderness, 188, 5 x 6 3/4
  By John Stuart, 1772, 1773   34045
    Abernethy, Western Lands, 54, 11 1/2 x 14 5/8
    Brown, Early Maps, pl.47, 7 1/8 x 9
  Western boundary of Vandalia grant   34050
    Mason, James Harrod, 140, 7 7/8 x 18 3/4
Georgiana   34055
    Alvord, Miss. Valley, 2:frontis., 4 1/2 x 4 7/8 col.
Mississippi Colony   34060
    Alvord, Miss. Valley, 2:frontis., 4 1/2 x 4 7/8 col.

Walpole Company grant, 1772   34065
   Philbrick, Rise of West, 88, 3 1/4 x 4 1/8
Illinois purchase, July 5, 1773   34070
   Alvord, Miss. Valley, 2:frontis., 4 1/2 x 4 7/8 col.
   Baldwin, Adult's History, 88, 5 5/8 x 8 1/2
   Billington, W. Expansion, 2d ed., 144, 3 3/4 x 3 5/8
Wabash Land Company, 1774-1775   34075
   Alvord, Miss. Valley, 2:frontis., 4 1/2 x 4 7/8 col.
   Baldwin, Adult's History, 88, 5 5/8 x 8 1/2
   Billington, W. Expansion, 2d ed., 144, 3 3/4 x 3 5/8
   Savelle, Foundations, 617, 4 x 4
John Cartwright's plan for division of Trans-Allegheny region   34080
   into territories, 1775
   Williams, Dawn of Tenn. Valley, 424, 4 x 5 1/4
Transylvania, 1775
   See 40055
Westsylvania, proposed state, 1776   34085
   Ambler, West Va., 140, 3 3/8 x 3
   Avery, Hist. of U.S., 6:402, 7 1/8 x 4 1/2 col.
   Billington, W. Expansion, 2d ed., 203, 4 1/2 x 4 1/2
   Bolton, Colonization, 405, 1 1/8 x 1 3/8
   Hart, Am. Nation, 9:278, 4 1/8 x 6 1/2
   Morison, Growth of Am. Republic, 5th ed., 1:139, 4 1/8 x 7
   Paullin, Atlas, pl.410, 4 7/8 x 5 1/4 col.
   Rice, Allegheny Frontier, 74, 5 1/8 x 7 1/2
   Turner, Sections in Am. Hist., 94, 5 5/8 x 4 col.
Thomas Paine's plan for new state, Dec. 1780   34090
   Turner, Sections in Am. Hist., 94, 5 5/8 x 4 col.
Washington County, Va. petitions to Congress for new state, 1784   34095
   and 1785
   Turner, Sections in Am. Hist., 94, 5 5/8 x 4 col.
Franklin, state of, established 1784
   See 41045
Fourteen proposed colonies or states to be laid out along the   34100
   Ohio and Mississippi Rivers, 1783-1784, by David Hartley
   Brown, Early Maps, pl.52, 7 1/4 x 9 3/8

MILITARY OPERATIONS IN THE WEST

PONTIAC'S WAR, 1763-1764

Theatre of war   35005
   Adams, Atlas, pl.47, 9 1/2 x 6 1/2
   Hawke, Colonial Experience, 526, 3 5/8 x 4 1/2
   Parkman, Pontiac, 1:11-12, 5 3/4 x 7 1/4
1764, by Thomas Hutchins   35010
   Clark, Frontier America, 24, 6 x 7 3/4
   Stotz, Ft. Ligonier, 32, 5 1/4 x 3 1/2
Forts in the West, 1763-1764   35011
   Kingsford, Hist. of Canada, 5:1, 6 3/4 x 6 7/8
Fort Michilimackinac, near present Mackinaw City, Mich.,
   captured by Indians, June 2, 1763
 From Crown Collection of Maps, British Museum   35012
   Clements, Jl. of Maj. Robt. Rogers, 4, 4 1/8 x 5 7/8
                                                       35013

1766, By Lt. Perkins Magra   35013
   Clements Library, Old Ft. Michilimackinac, 5, 7 3/4 x
     11 3/4 col.
   Cuneo, Robert Rogers, 85, 4 3/4 x 5 1/4
   Johnson, Papers, 12:438, 6 1/2 x 7 1/4
1769, by Lt. John Nordberg   35014
   Clements Library, Old Ft. Michilimackinac, 9, 7 1/4 x
     8 5/8
Events in the Lake Erie region, 1763-1764   35015
   Peckham, Pontiac, 162, 4 3/8 x 7
Detroit River
1763   35020
   Ohio Arch. and Hist. Soc. Pub., 12(Oct. 1903):423, 4 x 4
   Parkman, Pontiac, 1:155, 5 3/4 x 3 1/2
1763, by Lt. John Montrésor, drawn during Pontiac's siege   35021
   Goodrich, First Michigan Frontier, front lining paper,
     9 1/8 x 11 3/4
   Johnson, Papers, 10:870, 4 1/4 x 6 3/8
   Peckham, Pontiac, 61, 4 3/8 x 6 3/4
July 17, 1764   35025
   Johnson, Papers, 4:486, 4 5/8 x 4
Pub. by Jacques Nicolas Bellin, 1764   35030
   Brown, Hist. Geo r., 280, 3 x 4 5/8
   Gipson, Br. Empire, 9:97, 4 7/8 x 7 3/8
   Goodrich, First Michigan Frontier, end lining paper,
     7 5/8 x 11 3/4
   Peckham, Pontiac, 45, 4 x 6
   Trudel, Atlas of New France, 212, 7 x 10 1/4
Events along the Detroit River, 1763   35035
   Peckham, Pontiac, 118, 6 7/8 x 4 3/8
Detroit and vicinity, 1763-1764   35040
   Adams, Atlas, pl.46, 9 1/4 x 6 1/4
Fort Detroit, pub. by Jacques Nicolas Bellin, 1764   35045
   Brown, Hist. Geog., 280, 1 5/8 x 2 5/8
   Gipson, Br. Empire, 9:97, 2 5/8 x 4
   Goodrich, First Michigan Frontier, end lining paper,
     4 1/8 x 6 3/4
   Peckham, Pontiac, 45, 2 1/8 x 3 1/2
   Trudel, Atlas of New France, 212, 3 3/4 x 6
Niagara district   35050
   Webster, Life of John Montrésor, 13, 6 x 4 1/4
Fort Erie, on Niagara River, opposite site of present Buffalo,   35052
   built by Capt. John Montrésor in 1764
   Adams, Album of Am. Hist., 1:356, 2 1/2 x 3 5/8
   Porter, Landmarks on Niagara Frontier, 37, 1 5/8 x 2 1/4
Fort Niagara   35055
   Johnson, Papers, 4:466, 4 1/8 x 5 3/4, from Rocque, Set of
     Plans and Forts in America, pub. 1763
Col. John Bradstreet's route, 1764   35060
   Bolton, Colonization, 373, 6 1/2 x 4 1/8
   Hart., Am. Nation, 7:256, 6 1/2 x 4 1/8
Forks of the Ohio region at time of Pontiac's War   35065
   Darlington, Col. Bouquet, 104, 6 1/2 x 4
Fort Pitt, 1763   35067
   Swanson, Unconquered, end lining paper, 8 x 10 3/4

Col. Henry Bouquet's expeditions, 1763, 1764   35070
  Am. Heritage, 8(June 1957):61, 3 1/8 x 4 7/8 col.
  Am. Heritage Atlas, 78-79, 9 3/4 x 11 7/8 col.
  Am. History, 4(Oct. 1969):18-19, 3 1/8 x 9 7/8
  Bolton, Colonization, 373, 6 1/2 x 4 1/8
  Butler, King's Royal Rifle Corps, 1:195, 8 1/2 x 12 3/8
  Hart, Am. Nation, 7:256, 6 1/2 x 4 1/8
  Hutton, Col. Henry Bouquet, 40, 7 5/8 x 9 7/8 col.
  Infantry Jl., 36(Jan. 1930):, 40, 3 3/4 x 4 7/8
  Ridpath, New Complete Hist., 5:2320, 5 x 7 3/8
 By Thomas Hutchins   35075
  Avery, Hist. of U.S., 4:374, 1 5/8 x 4 1/2, 7 x 9 1/4
  Bond, Foundations of Ohio, 172, 3 3/8 x 4 1/4, 1 7/8 x 4 1/4
  Bouquet, Orderly Book, 11, 9 x 4 1/4
  Brown, Early Maps., pl.45, 2 5/8 x 7 1/4
  Gipson, Br. Empire, 9:124, 4 3/4 x 5 3/4
  Hannah, Wilderness Trail, 2:202, 6 x 7 5/8, 2 3/4 x 7 5/8
  Johnson, Papers, 11:866, 6 1/8 x 8, 2 7/8 x 8
  McIver, Washington in French and Indian War, 26-27, 7 1/8 x 10
  Pag. Am., 6:113, 4 1/4 x 2 3/4
  Parkman, Pontiac, 2:126, 5 3/4 x 7 1/4
  West Pa. Hist. Mag., 42(June 1959):180, 8 3/4 x 4 1/8
  Winsor, America, 6:696, 3 3/4 x 4 3/4
 By Lt. Bernard Ratzer   35080
  Brown, Early Maps, pl.39, 6 1/2 x 10 3/8
Col. Henry Bouquet's march from Fort Pitt to the Forks of   35085
    the Muskingum, 1764, shown on a modern highway map
  Bouquet, Orderly Book, 10, 5 7/8 x 11 3/4
  West Pa. Hist. Mag., 42(Mar. 1959)16, 5 7/8 x 10 3/4
Country traversed by Bouquet's expedition, 1764   35090
  Buck, Planting of Civ., 108, 4 1/2 x 5 7/8
Bushy Run, Pa., Battle of, Aug. 5-6, 1763
  Avery, Hist. of U.S., 4:367, 3 3/8 x 3 3/8
  Bomberger, Bushy Run, 13, 5 x 3 3/4
  Fleming, Hist. of Pittsburgh, 1:497, 1 1/2 x 4 1/8,
    5 1/4 x 4 1/8
  Fortescue, British Army, 3:pl.I, 2 5/8 x 2 3/4
  Frontier Forts, 2:512, 10 3/4 x 8 col.
  Pag. Am., 6:114, 4 1/2 x 3 3/8
  Sipe, Fort Ligonier, 206, 5 x 3
  Sipe, Indian Wars of Pa., 448, 5 x 3
  West Pa. Hist. Mag., 46(July 1963):213, 4 7/8 x 4 7/8
 By Thomas Hutchins   35100
  Am. History, 4(Oct. 1969):20, 3 7/8 x 3 7/8
  Bomberger, Bushy Run, 5, 5 1/4 x 5 1/2
  Buck, Planting of Civ., 100, 4 1/4 x 4 3/8
  Gipson, Br. Empire, 9:124, 5 3/8 x 5 1/2
  Hutton, Col. Henry Bouquet, 26, 5 5/8 x 5 7/8
  O'Meara, Guns at the Forks, 237, 3 5/8 x 6
  Pag. Am., 6:113, 3 5/8 x 4
  Winsor, America, 6:693, 4 5/8 x 4 3/4
Disposition of Pennsylvania troops in the western district for 35105
    the winter season, 1764
  Frontier Forts, 1:466, 8 x 10 3/4 col.

LORD DUNMORE'S WAR, 1774

Area of operations   36005
    Adams, Atlas, pl.63, 6 1/4 x 9 1/4
    Avery, Hist. of U.S., 5:174, 7 5/8 x 10 3/8 col.
Maj. Angus McDonald's route   36010
    Avery, Hist. of U.S., 5:174, 7 5/8 x 10 3/8 col.
    Morison, Growth of Am. Republic, 4th ed., 1:141, 4 5/8 x 6 1/2
Lord Dunmore's route   36015
    Am. Heritage Atlas, 78-79, 9 3/4 x 11 7/8 col.
    Avery, Hist. of U.S., 5:174, 7 5/8 x 10 3/8 col.
    Caruso, Appalachian Frontier, 122, 4 3/8 x 4 1/8
    De Gruyter, Kanawha Spectator, 1:lining papers, 7 3/4 x 11 1/2
    Mason, James Harrod, 140, 7 7/8 x 18 3/4
    Morison, Growth of Am. Republic, 4th ed., 1:141, 4 1/8 x 6 3/8
    Morrison, Ohio in Maps, 13, 7 7/8 x 6 5/8
Dunmore's form of March   36020
    Pag. Am., 2:30, 4 7/8 x 3 3/4
Col. Andrew Lewis' route   36025
    Am. Heritage Atlas, 78-79, 9 3/4 x 11 7/8 col.
    Avery, Hist. of U.S., 5:174, 7 5/8 x 10 3/8 col.
    Caruso, Appalachian Frontier, 122, 4 3/8 x 4 1/8
    De Gruyter, Kanawha Spectator, 1:lining papers, 7 3/4 x 11 1/2
    Mason, James Harrod, 140, 7 7/8 x 18 3/4
    Morison, Growth of Am. Republic, 4th ed., 1:141, 4 1/8 x 6 3/8
    Morrison, Ohio in Maps, 13, 7 7/8 x 6 5/8
Col. Lewis' form of march   36030
    Thwaites, Dunmore's War, 280, 5 1/2 x 3 1/4, by Col. William
        Fleming
Point Pleasant, Battle of, Oct. 10, 1774   36035
    Atkinson, Kanawha Co., 36, 2 7/8 x 2 3/8
    Avery, Hist. of U.S., 5:183, 5 x 1 3/4 col.
    Lewis, Hist. and Govt. of W. Va., 91, 1 7/8 x 2 5/8
    Miller, W. Va. and Its People, 1:97, 4 1/2 x 3
    Myers, Hist. of W. Va., 1:145, 3 5/8 x 3 7/8
    Pag. Am., 2:30, 2 1/2 x 3 7/8
    Randall, Dunmore War, 18, 3 1/4 x 3 1/8
    Thwaites, Dunmore's War, 5 3/8 x 8 5/8
Pickaway Plains, 1774   36040
    Randall, Dunmore War, 24, 4 x 4
    Randall, Hist. of Ohio, 2:104, 3 3/4 x 3 3/4
Shawnee town on Scioto River (near Circleville, O.), 1774   36045
    Lossing, Field-Book of Rev., 2:282, 1 1/2 x 1 5/8

CHEROKEE WAR, 1776

Col. Andrew Williamson's marches against the Cherokee Nation   37005
    Drayton, Memoirs, 2:343, 7 x 11
    Winsor, America, 6:675, 4 1/2 x 4 3/4
    Winsor, Westward Movement, 94-95
Col. William Christian's map of his march against the Cherokees   37010
    Williams, Tenn. druing Rev. War, 54, 4 x 5 1/2

THE REVOLUTIONARY WAR IN THE WEST

Western theatre of operations   38005
    Adams, Atlas, pl.77, 9 1/4 x 6 1/4

Alden, Hist. of Am. Rev., 426, 8 5/8 x 5 5/8
Boatner, Enc. of Am. Rev., 1189, 4 1/8 x 6 5/8
Roosevelt, Winning of West, 1:end, 6 1/2 x 8 col.
Sosin, Revolutionary Frontier, 139, 7 1/2 x 5 1/8

The Frontier during the Revolution
1780-1783   38010
   Billington, W. Expansion, 2d ed., 186, 5 1/4 x 4 1/8
Northwest Virginia   38015
   Thwaites, Frontier Defense, frontis., 11 3/4 x 9 3/4
Southern, 1776-1780   38020
   Billington, W. Expansion, 2d ed., 176, 4 1/8 x 4 1/8
North Carolina-Tennessee   38025
   Gilmore, Rear-Guard, front, 5 x 8 3/4
Ohio Valley in the Revolution   38030
   Clark, Frontier America, 113, 2 1/2 x 4 3/4
Frontier posts and forts, 1750-1781   38035
   Clark, Frontier America, 31, 3 7/8 x 4 3/4
Revolutionary War forts in West Virginia   38037
   Rice, The Allegheny Frontier, 48, 5 3/8 x 6 1/8
Campaigns in the West, 1778-1781   38040
   World Book, 16:261, 3 x 4 5/8 col.
Indian operations in the West, 1778-1782   38045
   Avery, Hist. of U.S., 6:192, 4 7/8 x 7 col.
Operations in Ohio during the Revolutionary War   38050
   Morrison, Ohio in Maps, 13, 7 7/8 x 6 5/8

1775

Route of Col. Richard Butler, envoy of the Continental Congress,   38060
   from Fort Pitt to the Ohio Indian towns, Aug.-Sept. 1775
   West Pa. Hist. Mag., 47(Apr. 1964):144, 6 3/8 x 11 1/8

1778

Brig. Gen. Edward Hand's "Squaw Campaign," Feb. 1778   38075
   Morrison, Ohio in Maps, 13, 7 7/8 x 6 5/8
Lt. Col. George Rogers Clark's campaign, from Redstone, Pa.,   38080
   to the Falls of the Ohio, Kaskaskia, and Vincennes, May 12,
   1778 - Feb. 25, 1779
   Am. Heritage, 13(Oct. 1962):61, 4 x 2 3/8 col.
   Am. Heritage Atlas, 100, 4 3/4 x 7 1/2 col.
   Am. Heritage, Revolution, 315, 6 3/8 x 4 1/2 xol., by Thomas
      Hutchins
   Avery, Hist. of U.S., 6:196, 3 1/2 x 3 7/8 col.
   Barck, Colonial Am., 636, 4 5/8 x 7
   Barck, Colonial Am., 2d ed., 609, 4 5/8 x 7
   Billington, W. Expansion, 2d ed., 178, 3 x 4 1/8
   Bodley, First Great West, 1, 7 1/2 x 10 1/4 col.
   Caruso, Gt. Lakes Frontier, 48, 5 3/8 x 8
   Chitwood, Colonial America, 3rd ed., 501, 3 3/4 x 4 1/8
   Chron. Am., 19:24, 7 x 9 1/4 col.
   Clark, Frontier America, 113, 2 1/2 x 4 3/4
   Commager, Spirit of '76, 2:1036, 4 5/8 x 6 1/4
   Current, Am. Hist., 2d ed., 112, 2 5/8 x 3 1/4
   English, Conquest, 1:290, 7 1/8 x 9 1/8

Faulkner, Am. Political & Social Hist., 137, 2 1/4 x 3 5/8
Hart, Am. Nation, 9:270, 4 1/8 x 6 1/2; 26:324, 4 1/8 x 6 1/2
Havighurst, Geo. Rogers Clark, lining papers, 2 1/2 x 3 1/4
Hicks, Federal Union, 4th ed., 192, 2 5/8 x 2 3/4
Hofstadter, Am. Republic, 186, 2 1/2 x 2 5/8
Hulbert, Military Roads, 21, 11 3/4 x 12 1/4
James, Life of Clark, 116, 3 7/8 x 5 1/4
James, Oliver Pollock, 84, 5 7/8 x 4
Jillson, Bibliog. of Clark, 11, 3 5/8 x 6 1/2
Lancaster, Big Knives, lining papers, 7 3/4 x 10 3/8
McDowell, Revolutionary War, 142, 2 5/8 x 2 7/8 col.
Mason, James Harrod, 140, 7 7/8 x 18 3/4
Miers, Yankee Doodle Dandy, 160, 2 7/8 x 3 5/8
Mitchell, Battles Am. Rev., 151, 5 x 6 1/2 col.
Montross, Rag, Tag and Bobtail, 303, 4 3/8 x 4 1/4
Morrison, Indiana, 12, 5 3/4 x 7 1/4
Pag. Am., 2:46, 3 1/2 x 6; 6:219, 4 1/8 x 6 7/8
Palmer, Clark of the Ohio, 202, 3 7/8 x 6 1/4
Paullin, Atlas, pl.160D, 3 x 4 1/8 col.
Perkins, U.S. of Am., 163, 3 x 4 5/8
Quaife, Capture, 126, 4 x 6 1/4
Reeder, Story of Rev. War, 180, 3 5/8 x 4 1/8
Roosevelt, Winning of West, 1:end, 6 1/2 x 8 col.
Schlarman, From Quebec to New Orleans, 496, 4 x 5 3/8
Scribner's Mag., 24(1898):62, 3 x 4 3/4
Thwaites, Clark, 26, 3 1/8 x 3 3/8
Todd, America's Hist., 143, 4 1/2 x 5 1/8
Van Every, Co. of Heroes, 137, 4 x 4
Ward, Revolution, 2:857, 4 3/8 x 6 1/8
Wright, Fabric of Freedom, 114, 1 1/8 x 1 7/8
See also 38105
Capt. John Bowman's route, Kaskaskia to Cahokia, July 1778   38085
English, Conquest, 1:196, 5 x 2 5/8; 290, 7 1/8 x 9 1/8
Morrison, Indiana, 12, 5 3/4 x 7 1/4
Capt. Leonard Helm's march to occupy Vincennes, July 1778   38090
Morrison, Indiana, 12, 5 3/4 x 7 1/4
Lt. Col. Henry Hamilton's route, Detroit to Vincennes, Oct. 7 -   38095
Dec. 17, 1778
Am. Heritage Atlas, 100, 4 3/4 x 7 1/2 col.
Barck, Colonial Am., 636, 4 5/8 x 7
Barck, Colonial Am., 2d ed., 609, 4 5/8 x 7
Billington, W. Expansion, 2d ed., 178, 3 x 4 1/8
Caruso, Gt. Lakes Frontier, 48, 5 3/8 x 8
Chron. Am., 19:24, 7 x 9 1/4 col.
Clark, Frontier America, 113, 3 1/2 x 4 3/4
Commager, Spirit of '76, 2:1036, 4 5/8 x 6 1/4
Faulkner, Am. Political & Social Hist., 137, 2 1/4 x 3 5/8
Havighurst, Proud Prisoner, 88-89, 8 3/8 x 10 5/8
Hicks, Federal Union, 4th ed., 192, 2 5/8 x 2 3/4
Hofstadter, Am. Republic, 186, 2 1/2 x 2 5/8
James, Life of Clark, 116, 3 7/8 x 5 1/4
James, Oliver Pollock, 84, 5 7/8 x 4
Lancaster, Big Knives, lining papers, 7 3/4 x 10 3/8
McDowell, Revolutionary War, 142, 2 5/8 x 2 7/8 col.
Montross, Rag, Tag and Bobtail, 303, 4 3/8 x 4 1/4

Morrison, Indiana, 12, 5 3/4 x 7 1/4
Palmer, Clark of the Ohio, 202, 3 7/8 x 6 1/4
Paullin, Atlas, pl.160D, 3 x 4 1/8 col.
Perkins, U.S. of Am., 163, 3 x 4 5/8
Quaife, Capture, 126, 4 x 6 1/4
Roosevelt, Winning of West, 1:end, 6 1/2 x 8 col.
Todd, America's Hist., 143, 4 1/2 x 5 1/8
Van Every, Co. of Heroes, 137, 4 x 4
Brig. Gen. Lachlan McIntosh's campaign, Oct.-Dec. 1778   38100
  Bond, Foundations of Ohio, 202, 3 1/2 x 4 1/4
  Caruso, Gt. Lakes Frontier, 84, 8 x 5 3/8
  Morrison, Ohio in Maps, 13, 7 7/8 x 6 5/8
  W. Pa. Hist. Mag., 43(Mar. 1960):8, 6 x 10 1/2

1779

George Rogers Clark's route through the over-flowed lands, from   38105
  mouth of Embarrass River to Vincennes, Feb. 20-23, 1779
  English, Conquest, 1:313, 4 1/4 x 7
  Palmer, Clark of the Ohio, 354, 5 5/8 x 4
  Quaife, Capture, 182, 3 3/4 x 6 1/8
  Schlarman, From Quebec to New Orleans, 354, 5 5/8 x 4
Capt. Leonard Helm's march up the Wabash from Vincennes   38110
  to capture British supply party, Feb. 1779
  Morrison, Indiana, 12, 5 3/4 x 7 1/4
Hamilton's route as a prisoner from Vincennes to Williamsburg,   38111
  Va., March 8-15, 1779
  Havighurst, Proud Prisoner, 88-89, 8 3/8 x 10 5/8
Capt. John Bowman's expedition against Chillicothe, May 1779   38115
  Morrison, Indiana, 12, 5 3/4 x 7 1/4
Col. David Rogers' route up the Ohio River with supplies from   38120
  New Orleans, summer 1779
  Morrison, Indiana, 12, 5 3/4 x 7 1/4
Fort Lernoult, Detroit, completed Apr. 1779   38125
  Mason, Ft. Lernoult, 1, 6 1/8 x 5 1/8, by John J. Rivardi, 1799

1780

British offensive in Northwest, 1780   38130
  Van Every, Co. of Heroes, 243, 4 x 4
Capt. Henry Bird's route, Detroit to Kentucky, Apr.-June 1780   38135
  Billington, W. Expansion, 2d ed., 186, 5 1/4 x 4 1/8
  Caruso, Gt. Lakes Frontier, 48, 5 3/8 x 8
  Morrison, Indiana, 12, 5 3/4 x 7 1/4
  Morrison, Ohio in Maps, 13, 7 7/8 x 6 5/8
  Van Every, Co. of Heroes, 243, 4 x 4
Capt. Emanuel Hesse's route, Mackinac to St. Louis and Cahokia,   38140
  May 1780
  Billington, W. Expansion, 2d ed., 186, 5 1/4 x 4 1/8
  Bolton, Colonization, 399, 4 x 5 5/8
  Caruso, Gt. Lakes Frontier, 48, 5 3/8 x 8
  Morrison, Indiana, 12, 5 3/4 x 7 1/4
  Van Every, Co. of Heroes, 243, 4 x 4
St. Louis, 1780   38145
  Houck, Hist. of Mo., 1:312, 2 3/4 x 5 1/8, by Cruzat

Fortifications of St. Louis, 1780   38150
    Winsor, Westward Movement, 172-173, 7 3/4 x 4 3/8
British-Indian attack on St. Louis, May 26, 1780
    Mo. Hist. Rev., 55(Oct. 1960):40, 6 3/8 x 4 3/8
Capt. Charles Michel de Langlade's route, May 1780   38160
    Van Every, Co. of Heroes, 243, 4 x 4
    Morrison, Indiana, 12, 5 3/4 x 7 1/4
Col. John Montgomery's pursuit of Hesse, June 1780   38165
    Morrison, Indiana, 12, 5 3/4 x 7 1/4
George Rogers Clark's expedition into the Shawnee Country,   38170
    Aug. 1780
    Bond, Foundations of Ohio, 202, 3 1/2 x 4 1/4
    Caruso, Gt. Lakes Frontier, 84, 8 x 5 3/8
    Morrison, Indiana, 12, 5 3/4 x 7 1/4
    Morrison, Ohio in Maps, 13, 7 7/8 x 6 5/8
Augustin Mottin de La Balme's expedition against Detroit,   38175
    fall 1780
    Morrison, Indiana, 12, 5 3/4 x 7 1/4

1781

Route of Spanish force under Capt. Eugenio Pourré, from St. Louis 38180
    to Fort St. Joseph and return, Jan. 2 - Mar. 1781
    Billington, W. Expansion, 2d ed., 186, 5 1/4 x 4 1/8
    Bolton, Colonization, 399, 4 x 5 5/8
    Chron, Am., 19:24, 7 x 9 1/4 col.
    Morrison, Indiana, 12, 5 3/4 x 7 1/4
    Paullin, Atlas, pl.160D, 3 x 4 1/8 col.
Fort St. Joseph and vicinity, 1781   38185
    Mich. Hist. Mag., 14(Summer 1930):398, 5 3/8 x 4
Col. Daniel Brodhead's Coshocton expedition, Apr. 1781   38190
    Morrison, Ohio in Maps, 13, 7 7/8 x 6 5/8
Camp of Joseph Brant, George Girty, and Indians, Great Miami   38195
    River, Hamilton County, O., Aug. 1781, after defeat of
    Col. Archibald Lochry
    Hist. and Philos. Soc. Ohio, Bul., 10(July 1952):229,
    5 5/8 x 4 1/2
Frontier defense on the Upper Ohio, 1781-1782   38200
    Van Every, Co. of Heroes, 259, 3 1/4 x 4

1782

Col. William Crawford's campaign, May-June 1782   38205
    Bond, Foundations of Ohio, 202, 3 1/2 x 4 1/4
    Caruso, Gt. Lakes Frontier, 84, 8 x 5 3/8
    Morrison, Indiana, 12, 5 3/4 x 7 1/4
    Morrison, Ohio in Maps, 13, 7 7/8 x 6 5/8
Crawford's proposed line of march, May 24, 1782   38210
    Rose, Journal, 10, 5 1/8 x 2 3/4
Crawford's line of march, June 1, 1782   38215
    Rose, Journal, 17, 3 1/8 x 2 5/8
Plan of encampment   38220
    Rose, Journal, 29, 5 x 3 3/4
Upper Indian settlements on Sandusky River, June 30, 1782,   38225
    by a Delaware Indian
    Rose, Journal, 65, 5 1/4 x 4 1/2

Capt. William Caldwell's and Alexander McKee's route   38230
    Detroit to Kentucky, July-Aug. 1782
    Billington, W. Expansion, 2d ed., 186, 5 1/4 x 4 1/8
    Morrison, Indiana, 12, 5 3/4 x 7 1/4
    Morrison, Ohio in Maps, 13, 7 7/8 x 6 5/8
Blue Licks, Ky., Battle of the, Aug. 19, 1782   38235
    Blue Licks Commission, Monument, 88, 5 7/8 x 5 1/2
    Kentucky, Blue Licks Sesqui-Cent., 114, 5 7/8 x 5 3/8
    Wilson, Blue Licks, frontis., 4 x 5, by Col. Benjamin Logan

1783

Territory in West actually gained by U.S. during Revolutionary War 38240
    Roosevelt, Winning West, 3:end, 7 7/8 x 6 3/8 col.

SETTLEMENT OF THE TRANS-ALLEGHENY REGION

Approximate limit of settlement
 in Pennsylvania, Virginia, and North Carolina, 1760   39005
    Hofstadter, Am. Republic, 154, 4 7/8 x 5 1/2
 in Old Southwest, 1784-1794   39010
    Van Every, Ark of Empire, 257, 3 5/8 x 4
 See also 02290-02310
Western settlements
 1760-1776   39013
    Hofstadter, Am. Republic, 154, 4 7/8 x 5 1/2
 During the Revolution   39015
    Barck, Colonial Am., 636, 4 5/8 x 7
 1775-1782   39020
    Hart, Am. Nation, 9:278, 4 1/8 x 6 1/2
 1775-1785   39025
    Paullin, Atlas, pl.41C, 4 7/8 x 5 1/4 col.
 1777-1786   39030
    Avery, Hist. of U.S., 6:402, 7 1/8 x 4 1/2 col.
 1783   39035
    Becker, Beginnings of Am. People, 272, 5 3/4 x 3 3/8
Patterns of settlement on the Allegheny frontier   39037
    Rice, Allegheny Frontier, 68, 5 x 7 3/8
Kentucky-Tennessee frontier, 1782   39040
    Van Every, Co. of Heroes, 297, 3 5/8 x 4
Territory in Old Northwest opened to settlement by Indian   39045
    treaties, 1784-1786
    Billington, W. Expansion, 2d ed., 209, 2 7/8 x 4 1/8

KENTUCKY

Exploration of Kentucky.   Routes of:
 Capt. James Smith, 1766   40005
    Billington, W. Expansion, 2d ed., 161, 3 1/4 x 4 5/8
 Isaac Lindsey, 1766   40010
    Billington, W. Expansion, 2d ed., 161, 3 1/4 x 4 5/8
 James Harrod and Michael Stoner, 1766   40015
    Billington, W. Expansion, 2d ed., 161, 3 1/4 x 4 5/8
 Daniel Boone
  1767-1768, 1769-1771   40020

Billington, W. Expansion, 2d ed., 161, 3 1/4 x 4 5/8
Chron. Am., 18:56, 7 x 6 1/4 col.
1767-1775   40025
  Am. Heritage Atlas, 78-79, 9 3/4 x 11 7/8 col.
1769-1771   40027
  Caruso, Appalachian Frontier, 66, 3 1/8 x 4 1/8
The Long Hunters, 1769-1772   40030
  Am Heritage Atlas, 78-79, 9 3/4 x 11 7/8 col.
Kentucky
1774-1785   40035
  Adams, Atlas, pl.62, 6 1/4 x 9 1/4
1780, showing forts, stations, and licks   40037
  Fed. Writers Proj., Mil. Hist. of Ky., front lining paper,
    7 7/8 x 10
1782   40040
  Paullin, Atlas, pl.41C, 4 7/8 x 5 1/4 col.
1784, by John Filson   40045
  Abernethy, Western Lands, 124, 17 1/2 x 16
  Brown, Blue Licks Oration, 13 5/8 x 12 3/8, French edition,
    pub. 1785
  Hanna, Wilderness Trail, 2:212, 8 5/8 x 7 7/8
  Hulbert, Boone's Wilderness Rd., 118, 10 x 9
  Ky. Hist. Soc., Reg., 54(Oct. 1956):308, 5 5/8 x 5
  Pusey, Wilderness Rd., 4, 8 1/4 x 7 1/2
  Mason, James Harrod, 208, 9 x 7 7/8
  Winsor, Westward Movement, 332-333, 6 3/4 x 7 1/2
Ohio Company of Virginia survey of approximately 400,000 acres   40050
  in Kentucky, 1775
  James, Ohio Co., 162, 4 3/4 x 6 1/2
Transylvania, proposed state, 1775   40055
  Alvord, Miss. Valley, 2:frontis., 4 1/2 x 4 7/8 col.
  Am. Heritage Atlas, 77, 5 1/8 x 7 1/2 col.
  Avery, Hist. of U.S., 5:174, 7 5/8 x 10 3/8 col.
  Baldwin, Adult's History, 88, 5 5/8 x 8 1/2
  Bolton, Colonization, 405, 1 1/8 x 1 3/8
  Caruso, Appalachian Frontier, 144, 3 3/4 x 4 1/8
  Hart, Am. Nation, 8:230, 6 1/2 x 8 1/4 col.; 9:278,
    4 1/8 x 6 1/2
  Henderson, Conquest of Old S.W., 192, 5 1/4 x 8
  Hicks, Federal Union, 4th ed., 151, 3 7/8 x 5 3/8
  Lord, Atlas, map 53, 6 1/2 x 4 1/2
  Morison, Growth of Am. Republic, 4th ed., 1:141, 4 1/8 x 6 3/8
  Morison, Growth of Am. Republic, 5th ed., 1:139, 4 1/8 x 7
  Nettels, Roots of Am. Civ., 605, 4 1/8 x 6 5/8
  Paullin, Atlas, pl.41C, 4 7/8 x 5 1/4 col.
  Philbrick, Rise of West, 88, 3 1/4 x 4 1/8
  Savelle, Foundations, 617, 4 x 4
  Turner, Sections in Am. Hist., 94, 5 5/8 x 4 col.
Transylvania boundary at greatest extent   40060
  Mason, James Harrod, 140, 7 7/8 x 18 3/4
Early settlements in Kentucky   40065
  Billington, W. Expansion, 2d ed., 170, 4 5/8 x 4 5/8
  Bruce, Boone, end, 3 5/8 x 5 3/8
  Caruso, Appalachian Frontier, 160, 5 1/2 x 4 1/8
  Clark, Exploring Kentucky, 35, 3 7/8 x 4

Drake, Ohio Valley States, 111, 2 3/8 x 3 5/8
Hicks, Federal Union, 4th ed., 151, 3 7/8 x 5 3/8
Lefler, North Carolina, 178, 2 3/4 x 5 1/2 col.
Newsome, Growth of N.C., 162, 1 5/8 x 3 7/8
Boonesborough, Ky.   40070
   Hulbert, Boone's Wilderness Rd., 97, 5 1/2 x 3 1/2
   Winsor, Westward Movement, 83, 2 1/4 x 1 1/2

TENNESSEE

Valley of East Tennessee   41005
   Chron. Am., 18:56, 2 3/4 x 4 1/2
Eastern Tennessee frontier, 1760-1776   41010
   Billington, W. Expansion, 2d ed., 157, 2 1/8 x 4 1/8
Early settlements in Tennessee   41015
   Lefler, North Carolina, 178, 2 3/4 x 5 1/2 col.
   Newsome, Growth of N.C., 162, 1 5/8 x 3 7/8
Watauga Purchase, 1772, and settlements   41020
   Abernethy, Frontier to Plantation, 5, 4 x 5 3/4
   Caruso, Appalachian Frontier, 104, 4 1/8 x 4 1/8
   Garrett, Hist. of Tenn., 52, 3 1/8 x 4 col.
   Henderson, Conquest of Old S.W., 192, 5 1/4 x 8
   Hicks, Federal Union, 4th ed., 151, 3 7/8 x 5 3/8
Brown's Purchase, 1775, and settlements   41025
   Garrett, Hist. of Tenn., 52, 3 1/8 x 4 col.
   Henderson, Conquest of Old S.W., 192, 5 1/4 x 8
James Robertson's overland route to Nashboro, 1779   41030
   Barck, Colonial Am., 636, 4 5/8 x 7
   Barck, Colonial Am., 2d ed., 609, 4 5/8 x 7
   Billington, W. Expansion, 2d ed., 176, 4 1/8 x 4 1/8
   Chitwood, Colonial America, 501, 3 3/4 x 4 1/8
   Chron. Am., 18:56, 7 x 6 1/4 col.
   Roosevelt, Winning of West, 1:end, 6 1/2 x 8 col.
   Van Every, Co. of Heroes, 221, 4 1/4 x 4
Col. John Donelson's river route to Nashboro, 1780   41035
   Billington, W. Expansion, 2d ed., 1176, 4 1/8 x 4 1/8
   Caruso, Appalachian Frontier, 254, 3 3/4 x 4 1/8
   Roosevelt, Winning of West, 1:end, 6 1/2 x 8 col.
   Van Every, Co. of Heroes, 221, 4 1/4 x 4
Cumberland settlements   41040
   Adams, Atlas, pl.84, 6 1/4 x 9 1/4
   Caruso, Appalachian Frontier, 254, 3 3/4 x 4 1/8
   Hicks, Federal Union, 4th ed., 219, 4 x 5 1/2
State of Franklin, 1784-1789   41045
   Abernethy, Western Lands, 292, 3 3/4 x 4 1/4
   Adams, Atlas, pl.84, 6 1/4 x 9 1/4
   Am. Heritage Atlas, 125, 9 3/4 x 7 1/2 col.
   Avery, Hist. of U.S., 6:402, 7 1/8 x 4 1/2 col.
   Baldwin, Adult's History, 157, 5 5/8 x 5 5/8
   Billington, W. Expansion, 2d ed., 203, 4 1/2 x 4 1/8;
      205, 4 x 4 5/8
   Caruso, Appalachian Frontier, 282, 2 5/8 x 4 1/8
   Gerson, Franklin, 4 1/8 x 6 1/2
   Henderson, Conquest of Old S.W., 192, 5 1/4 x 8
   Hicks, Federal Union, 4th ed., 219, 4 x 5 1/2

Lord, Atlas, map 53, 6 1/2 x 4 1/2
Pag. Am., 2:106, 2 1/8 x 3 3/4
Philbrick, Rise of West, 88, 3 1/4 x 4 1/8
Turner, Sections in Am. Hist., 94, 5 5/8 x 4 col.
Van Every, Ark of Empire, 92, 4 x 4
Wright, Fabric of Freedom, 158, 6 1/4 x 4

OHIO

The Ohio country (between the Ohio River and Lake Erie)   42005
  c.1763
    Brown, Early Maps, pl.38, 6 1/4 x 10, by Guy Johnson
  1766   42010
    Brown, Early Maps, pl.41, 7 1/4 x 10, after Lewis Evans;
      pl.45, 5 3/4 x 7 1/4, by Thomas Hutchins
  1778   42015
    Bond, Foundations of Ohio, 198, 4 1/2 x 4 3/8, by Thomas
      Hutchins
  1787   42020
    Winsor, Westward Movement, 294-295, 6 7/8 x 7 5/8, by
      Crèvecoeur
  c.1787, following Northwest Ordinance   42025
    Brown, Hist. Geog., 216, 6 x 4 3/8
Territory in Ohio demanded of the western Indians in the treaties   42030
    of Fort Stanwix, Oct. 22, 1784, Fort McIntosh, Jan. 21, 1785,
    Fort Finney, Jan. 31, 1786, and Fort Harmar, Jan. 9, 1789
    Van Every, Ark of Empire, 186, 3 3/8 x 4
Geographer's Line, 1785   42035
    Adams, Atlas, pl.86, 9 1/4 x 6 1/4
    Am. Heritage Atlas, 126, 6 3/8 x 4 1/2 col.
    Bond, Foundations of Ohio, 276, 4 1/2 x 4 1/4
Ohio land divisions
  Virginia Military District, 1784   42040
    Adams, Atlas, pl.85, 9 1/4 x 6 1/4
    Avery, Hist. of U.S., 7:96, 7 x 10 col.
    Baldwin, Adult's History, 155, 6 x 5 5/7
    Barck, Colonial Am., 2d ed., 679, 4 x 4 1/2
    Billington, W. Expansion, 2d ed., 214, 4 1/8 x 4 5/8; 262,
      4 5/8 x 4 5/8
    Bond, Foundations of Ohio, 276, 4 1/2 x 4 1/4
    Boyd, Wayne, 263, 3 3/4 x 3 5/8
    Caruso, Gt. Lakes Frontier, 112, 8 x 5 3/8
    Hinsdale, Old Northwest, 290, 4 1/8 x 4 1/4
    Lord, Atlas, map 53, 6 1/2 x 4 1/2
    McMaster, Hist. of People of U.S., 3:89, 7 1/2 x 7 3/4 col.
    Pag. Am., 2:93, 3 1/4 x 3 1/8
    Randall, Hist. of Ohio, 2:486, 4 5/8 x 4 1/2
    Roseboom, Hist. of Ohio, 35, 4 3/4 x 4 3/8
  Seven Ranges   42045
    Adams, Atlas, pl.85, 9 1/4 x 6 1/4; pl.86, 9 1/4 x 6 1/4
    Am. Heritage Atlas, 125, 9 3/4 x 7 1/2 col.; 126, 6 3/8 x
      4 1/2 col.
    Avery, Hist. of U.S., 6:406, 6 3/4 x 12 col., by Thomas
      Hutchins; 7:96, 7 x 10 col.
    Baldwin, Adult's History, 155, 6 x 5 5/8

Barck, Colonial Am., 2d ed., 679, 4 x 4 1/2
Billington, W. Expansion, 2d ed., 214, 4 1/8 x 4 5/8; 262,
    4 5/8 x 4 5/8
Caruso, Gt. Lakes Frontier, 112, 8 x 5 3/8
Hawke, Colonial Experience, 658, 3 1/2 x 4 3/8
Hinsdale, Old Northwest, 290, 4 1/8 x 4 1/4
Lord, Atlas, map 53, 6 1/2 x 4 1/2
Pag. Am., 2:93, 3 1/4 x 3 1/8
Randall, Hist. of Ohio, 2:486, 4 5/8 x 4 1/2
Roseboom, Hist. of Ohio, 35, 4 3/4 x 4 3/8
Connecticut Western Reserve, 1786   42050
Adams, Atlas, pl.85, 9 1/4 x 6 1/4
Avery, Hist. of U.S., 7:96, 7 x 10 col.
Baldwin, Adult's History, 155, 6 x 5 5/8
Barck, Colonial Am., 2d ed., 679, 4 x 4 1/2
Billington, W. Expansion, 2d ed., 214, 4 1/8 x 4 5/8; 262,
    4 5/8 x 4 5/8
Bond, Foundations of Ohio, 276, 4 1/2 x 4 1/4
Boyd, Wayne, 263, 3 3/4 x 3 5/8
Hinsdale, Old Northwest, 290, 4 1/4 x 4 1/4
Lord, Atlas, map 53, 6 1/2 x 4 1/2
McMaster, Hist. of People of U.S., 3:89, 7 1/2 x 7 3/4 col.
Pag. Am., 2:91, 3 1/4 x 4 1/8; 93, 3 1/4 x 3 1/8
Randall, Hist. of Ohio, 2:486, 4 5/8 x 4 1/2
Roseboom, Hist. of Ohio, 35, 4 3/4 x 4 3/8
Ohio Company of Associates purchase, 1787   42055
Adams, Atlas, pl.85, 9 1/4 x 6 1/4
Am. Heritage Atlas, 125, 9 3/4 x 7 1/2 col.
Avery, Hist. of U.S., 7:96, 7 x 10 col.
Baldwin, Adult's History, 155, 6 x 5 5/8
Barck, Colonial Am., 2d ed., 679, 4 x 4 1/2
Billington, W. Expansion, 2d ed., 214, 4 1/8 x 4 5/8; 262,
    4 5/8 x 4 5/8
Bond, Foundations of Ohio, 276, 4 1/2 x 4 1/4
Boyd, Wayne, 263, 3 3/4 x 3 5/8
Brown, Hist. Geog., 216, 6 x 4 3/8
Caruso, Gt. Lakes Frontier, 112, 8 x 5 3/8
Hinsdale, Old Northwest, 290, 4 1/8 x 4 1/4
Lord, Atlas, map 53, 6 1/2 x 4 1/2
McMaster, Hist. of People of U.S., 3:89, 7 1/2 x 7 3/4 col.
Pag. Am., 2:79, 2 x 3 1/2; 93, 3 1/4 x 3 1/8
Paullin, Atlas, pl.50B, 6 x 9 col.
Randall, Hist. of Ohio, 2:486, 4 5/8 x 4 1/2
Roseboom, Hist. of Ohio, 35, 4 3/4 x 4 3/8
Winsor, Westward Movement, 291, 5 1/8 x 3 7/8, by Collot
Scioto Company purchase, 1787   42060
Avery, Hist. of U.S., 7:96, 7 x 10 col.
Baldwin, Adult's History, 155, 9 x 5 5/8
Barck, Colonial Am., 2d ed., 679, 4 x 4 1/2
Billington, W. Expansion, 2d ed., 214, 4 1/8 x 4 5/8
Ohio and Scioto Companies' lands, 1788, engr. by P.F. Tardieu   42065
    for Joel Barlow
Hulbert, Ohio River, 266, 5 3/8 x 4
Pag. Am., 2:81, 4 7/8 x 4
Winsor, Westward Movement, 300-301, 6 3/4 x 7 3/4

Symmes (or Miami) purchase, 1788   42070
  Adams, Atlas, pl.85, 9 1/4 x 6 1/4
  Am. Heritage Atlas, 125, 9 3/4 x 7 1/2 col.
  Avery, Hist. of U.S., 7:96, 7 x 10 col.
  Baldwin, Adult's History, 155, 6 x 5 5/8
  Barck, Colonial Am., 2d ed., 679, 4 x 4 1/2
  Billington, W. Expansion, 2d ed., 214, 4 1/8 x 4 5/8; 262,
    4 5/8 x 4 5/8
  Bond, Foundations of Ohio, 276, 4 1/2 x 4 1/4
  Boyd, Wayne, 263, 3 3/4 x 3 5/8
  Caruso, Gt. Lakes Frontier, 112, 8 x 5 3/8
  Hinsdale, Old Northwest, 290, 4 1/8 x 4 1/4
  Lord, Atlas, map 53, 6 1/2 x 4 1/2
  McMaster, Hist. of People of U.S., 3:89, 7 1/2 x 7 3/4 col.
  Pag. Am., 2:93, 3 1/4 x 3 1/8
  Randall, Hist. of Ohio, 2:486, 4 5/8 x 4 1/2
  Roseboom, Hist. of Ohio, 35, 4 3/4 x 4 3/8
Fort Steuben (Steubenville, Ohio), 1787   42075
  Ohio Arch. and Hist. Soc., Pub., 6(1898):189, 5 x 3 1/2
Fort Harmar and Indian earthworks on site of Marietta, Ohio,   42080
    at mouth of Muskingum River
  Winsor, Westward Movement, 300-301, 6 5/8 x 7 3/4, from
    Crèvecoeur's "Voyage," 1801
Earliest Ohio settlements, 1788-1790   42085
  Bond, Foundations of Ohio, 276, 4 1/2 x 4 1/4
  Roseboom, Hist. of Ohio, 35, 4 3/4 x 4 3/8

CANADA

Northern British colonies (Quebec, Nova Scotia, Newfoundland,   45025
    New England, and New York), 1776
        Naval Docs. of Am. Rev., 2:1126, 5 1/4 x 7, by Maj. Holland
        et al., pub. by Robert Sayer and John Bennett
Eastern Canada and Nova Scotia, 1782   45050
    Hilliard d'Auberteuil, Essais, 1:199, 9 x 12 7/8 col.
British possessions in North America after peace of 1783   45075
    Graham, Br. Policy and Canada, 41, 5 1/4 x 4 1/4
See also 01005-01040

QUEBEC

Boundaries of Province of Quebec as established by Proclamation   46005
    of Oct. 7, 1763
    Am. Heritage Atlas, 76, 9 3/4 x 7 1/2 col.
    Current, Am. Hist., 2d ed., 86, 3 5/8 x 5 1/4
    Gipson, Coming of Rev., 122-123, 8 1/2 x 6 1/2
    Greene, Foundations, 389, 4 x 6 col.
    Kerr, Hist. Atlas of Canada, 31, 6 3/8 x 8 5/8 col.
    Morrison, Indiana, 11, 6 5/8 x 9 1/2
    Morrison, Ohio in Maps, 12, 6 5/8 x 9 1/2
    Neatby, Quebec, 5, 4 3/8 x 7 1/4
 By Capt. Jonathan Carver, pub. by Robert Sayer and John   46007
    Bennett, 1776
    Burt, Old Province of Quebec, 84-85, 7 1/8 x 9 3/4
    Fite, Book of Old Maps, 222, 9 3/8 x 13
Province of Quebec, 1764   46010
    Gipson, Br. Empire, 9:162, 5 x 6 1/4, by Thomas Kitchin
Boundaries of Province of Quebec as established by Quebec Act,   46015
    May 20, 1774
    Am. Heritage Atlas, 76, 9 3/4 x 7 1/2 col.
    Baldwin, Adult;s History, 88, 5 5/8 x 8 1/2
    Burt, Old Province of Quebec, 192-193, 6 7/8 x 9 3/4
    Chron. Am., 19:24, 7 x 9 1/4 col.
    Current, Am. Hist., 2d ed., 86, 3 5/8 x 5 1/4
    Gipson, Coming of Rev., 130-131, 8 1/2 x 6 1/2
    Greene, Foundations, 389, 4 x 6 col.
    Kerr, Hist. Atlas of Canada, 32, 8 3/8 x 8 7/8 col.
    McDowell, Revolutionary War, 26, 9 3/8 x 6 3/4 col.
    Morrison, Indiana, 11, 6 5/8 x 9 1/2
    Morrison, Ohio in Maps, 12, 6 5/8 x 9 1/2
    Neatby, Quebec, 131, 4 3/8 x 7 1/4
    Perkins, U.S. of Am., 141, 3 1/4 x 4 5/8
    Savelle, Foundations, 617, 4 x 4
    Todd, America's Hist., 124, 6 5/8 x 5 1/8
Western boundary of Province of Quebec as defined by Carleton's   46020
    commission, 1774
    Am. Heritage Atlas, 76, 9 3/4 x 7 1/2 col.
Province of Quebec, July 1781   46025
    Naval Docs. of Am. Rev., 2:237, 5 1/2 x 6 5/8, from Universal
    Mag.
Western boundary of Province of Quebec by Treaty of 1783   46027
    Neatby, Quebec, 131, 4 3/8 x 7 1/4

Montreal   46028
  Neatby, Quebec, 28, 4 3/8 x 7 1/4
  From Rocque, Set of Plans and Forts in America, pub, 1763   46029
    Johnson, Papers, 4:222, 4 1/4 x 5 1/4
    Winsor, America, 5:555, 3 3/4 x 4 3/4
  By Capt. Jonathan Carver, pub. by Robert Sayer and John Bennett,   46030
    1776
    Burt, Old Province of Quebec, 84, 2 5/8 x 2 1/2, 1 1/8 x 2 1/2
    Fite, Book of Old Maps, 222, 3 1/2 x 3 1/4, 1 5/8 x 3 1/4
    Lucas, Appendiculae, 124, 7 1/2 x 7 1/4
    Smith, Struggle for 14th Colony, 1:479, 3 3/8 x 6
Quebec (City)
  From Rocque, Set of Plans and Forts in America, pub. 1763   46035
    Johnson, Papers, 4:746, 4 1/8 x 5 5/8
    Winsor, America, 5:553, 3 1/2 x 3 3/4
  By Capt. Jonathan Carver, pub. by Robert Sayer and John Bennett,   46040
    1776
    Burt, Old Province of Quebec, 8, 4 x 4; 84, 3 1/2 x 2 1/2
    Fite, Book of Old Maps, 222, 4 1/2 x 3 1/8

MILITARY OPERATIONS

Area of operations   46045
  Alden, Am. Revolution, 53, 4 1/4 x 3 3/4
  Baldwin, Adult's History, 108, 4 7/8 x 5 5/8
  Boatner, Enc. of Am. Rev., 175, 5 1/2 x 4 1/8
  Carrington, Battles, 170, 7 3/4 x 4 5/8
  Commager, Spirit of '76, 1:193, 5 1/8 x 4 5/8
  Duncan, Medical Men, 83, 5 1/2 x 4 1/8
  Freeman, Washington, 3:531, 6 1/4 x 4 1/2
  French, First Year, end, 8 1/2 x 11 3/4
  Hart, Am. Nation, 26:324, 4 1/8 x 6 1/2
  Jacobs, Tarnished Warrior, 8, 11 1/2 x 7 3/8
  Lanctot, Canada and Am. Revolution, 211, 6 1/4 x 5
  Montross, Rag, Tag and Bobtail, 53, 5 5/8 x 4 1/4
  Naval Docs. of Am. Rev., 2:1386, 6 3/8 x 5 1/2
  Ridpath, New Complete Hist., 5:2444, 6 1/2 x 3
  Smith, Arnold's March, 7, 3 7/8 x 6 1/4, by Capt. Jonathan
    Carver, pub. by Robert Sayer and John Bennett, 1776
  Wildes, Anthony Wayne, 59, 6 5/8 x 4
Albany to Quebec   46050
  Vose, Journal, 10, 11 x 4
Ticonderoga to Montreal, 1775   46055
  Naval Docs. of Am. Rev., 2:868, 7 7/8 x 3 1/4, engr. by
    Robert Aitken
Country between Crown Point and Albany, 1776   46060
  Smith, Struggle for 14th Colony, 1:112, 5 5/8 x 3 3/8
Lake Champlain
  Middle portion, 1776   46065
    Smith, Struggle for 14th Colony, 1:146, 5 3/8 x 1 1/2, by
      William Faden
  Lower portion, 1776   46070
    Smith, Struggle for 14th Colony, 1:306, 3 3/4 x 2 3/8, by
      William Faden
  Richelieu River, from Sorel to Ft. St. John   46075

Wilkinson, Diagrams, No. 1, 4 3/8 x 7 5/8
Winsor, America, 6:215, 2 7/8 x 5
St. Lawrence River
From the Cedars to Montreal, 1777   46080
   Smith, Struggle for 14th Colony, 2:359, 2 3/4 x 3 1/2,
     by William Faden
From La Valterie to Quebec, by Capt. Jonathan Carver,   46085
   pub. by Robert Sayer and John Bennett, 1776
   Burt, Old Province of Quebec, 85, 2 3/8 x 2 3/4
   Fite, Book of Old Maps, 222, 3 1/4 x 3 5/8
From Montreal to Quebec   46090
   Smith, Struggle for 14th Colony, 2:311, 2 7/8 x 2 1/2
From Montreal to Three Rivers, 1777   46095
   Smith, Struggle for 14th Colony, 2:397, 5 1/2 x 3 1/2,
     by William Faden
From Quebec to Lake St. Francis   46100
   Beebe, Journal, frontis., 2 1/2 x 7 1/2, French map
From Tadousac to Lake St. Francis   46102
   Burt, Old Province of Quebec, 3, 4 x 4
From Trois Rivieres to Lake St. Francis   46105
   Decker, Arnold, 152, 4 3/4 x 4
From Sorel to La Prairie   46110
   Wilkinson, Diagrams, No. 1, 4 3/8 x 7 5/8
   Winsor, America, 6:215, 2 7/8 x 5
Sources of the Chaudière, Penobscot, and Kennebec Rivers,   46115
   1761, by John Montrésor
   Meredith, Am. Wars, 44, 6 5/8 x 6 5/8
   Todd, Real Arnold, 38, 4 3/4 x 4
   Winsor, America, 6:224, 7 1/8 x 4 3/4
Lower Chaudière River   46120
   Smith, Struggle for 14th Colony, 1:601, 4 1/2 x 3 1/2
Dead River-Lake Megantic region, 1761, by John Montrésor   46125
   Roberts, March to Quebec, 5, 7 7/8 x 5 1/2
   Smith, Struggle for 14th Colony, 1:584, 6 x 3 1/2
Lake Megantic region   46130
   Roberts, March to Quebec, 45, 7 7/8 x 10 5/8 col.
Chain of Ponds   46135
   Smith, Struggle for 14th Colony, 1:565, 3 1/4 x 3 1/2

1775-1776

Movements of American and British commanders, Sept. 1775 -   46140
   Oct. 1776
   Burt, U.S., G.B., and Br. No. Am., 7, 4 x 4 1/2
Brig. Gen. Richard Montgomery's expedition to Quebec, Aug. 28 -   46145
   Dec. 2, 1775
   Adams, Atlas, pl.67, 9 1/4 x 6 1/4
   Am. Heritage Atlas, 96, 6 1/2 x 4 5/8 col.
   Am. Heritage, Revolution, 131, 4 7/8 x 4 col.
   Armstrong, 15 Battles, 37, 6 3/8 x 4
   Army, Am. Military Hist., 42, 5 1/2 x 4 1/2
   Avery, Hist. of U.S., 5:326-327, 5 1/8 x 9 col.
   Barck, Colonial Am., 2d ed., 598, 7 x 4 5/8
   Chron. Am., 12:180, 7 x 5 3/4 col.
   Clarke, Am. Revolution, 16, 2 3/8 x 1 1/2

Coggins, Boys in Revolution, 34, 7 1/8 x 6 1/8
Cook, Golden Bk. of Am. Rev., 33, 4 3/4 x 4
Current, Am. Hist., 2d ed., 105, 4 1/4 x 2 1/2
Esposito, Am. Wars Atlas, 1:map 4a, 9 1/2 x 8 3/8 col.
Esposito, Civil War Atlas, map 4a, 9 1/2 x 8 3/8 col.
Faulkner, Am. Political & Social Hist., 121, 4 5/8 x 2 1/2
Freeman, Washington, 3:531, 6 1/4 x 4 1/2
Freeman, Washington, abridgment, 239, 7 3/4 x 5 1/2
Greene, Revolutionary War, 20, 5 1/8 x 9 col.
Gurney, Pict. Hist. U.S. Army, 29, 5 3/8 x 4 3/8
Hart, Am. Nation, 9:26, 6 1/2 x 2 5/8 col.
Hofstadter, Am. Republic, 173, 4 3/4 x 3 1/4
James, Br. Navy in Adversity, 20, 6 1/2 x 4
Kerr, Hist. Atlas of Canada, 33, 6 1/2 x 8 1/2 col.
Matloff, Am. Military History, 51, 5 1/2 x 4 3/8
Morison, Hist. of Am. People, 213, 4 1/2 x 4 1/2
Perkins, U.S. of Am., 146, 4 5/8 x 2 1/2
Rayback, Richards Atlas, 28, 15 7/8 x 9 3/8 col.
Reeder, Story of Rev. War, 57, 4 x 4 1/8
Scheer, Rebels and Redcoats, 116, 5 7/8 x 4 1/2
Vestal, Washington, 10, 6 1/2 x 3 5/8
Washington Bicentennial, 1:109, 6 1/2 x 3 5/8

Col. Benedict Arnold's expedition to Quebec, Sept. 13 -   46150
   Nov. 9, 1775
Adams, Atlas, pl.67, 9 1/4 x 6 1/4
Alden, Am. Revolution, 53, 4 1/4 x 3 3/4
Alden, Rise of Am. Republic, 139, 3 3/8 x 3 5/8
Am. Heritage Atlas, 96, 6 1/2 x 4 5/8 col.
Am. Heritage, Revolution, 131, 4 7/8 x 4 col.
Armstrong, 15 Battles, 37, 6 3/8 x 4
Army, Am. Military Hist., 42, 5 1/2 x 4 1/2
Avery, Hist. of U.S., 5:332, 6 x 4 1/2 col.
Barck, Colonial Am., 2d ed., 598, 7 x 4 5/8
Bryant, Popular Hist. of U.S., 3:441, 3 x 2
Chron. Am., 12:180, 7 x 5 3/4 col.
Clarke, Am. Revolution, 17, 2 3/8 x 1 1/2
Codman, Arnold's Exped., 58, 13 x 4 3/8
Coffin, Boys of '76, 75, 2 7/8 x 1
Coggins, Boys in Revolution, 34, 7 1/8 x 6 1/8
Commager, Spirit of '76, 1:193, 5 1/8 x 4 5/8
Cook, Golden Book of Am. Rev., 33, 4 3/4 x 4
Crist, Capt. Wm. Hendricks, 21, 7 3/8 x 4 3/4
Current, Am. Hist., 2d ed., 105, 4 1/4 x 2 1/2
Decker, Arnold, 96, 5 3/8 x 2 1/2
Esposito, Am. Wars Atlas, 1:map 4a, 9 1/2 x 8 3/8 col.
Esposito, Civil War Atlas, map 4a, 9 1/2 x 8 3/8 col.
Faulkner, Am. Political & Social Hist., 121, 4 5/8 x 2 1/2
Field Artillery Jl., 23 (Sept.-Oct. 1933):434, 5 3/8 x 2 1/8;
   435, 6 1/4 x 2 1/2
Freeman, Washington, 3:531, 6 1/4 x 4 1/2
Freeman, Washington, abridgment, 239, 7 3/4 x 5 1/2
Greene, Revolutionary War, 22, 6 x 4 1/2 col.
Higginbotham, Morgan, 31, 5 3/8 x 4 1/8
Hofstadter, Am. Republic, 173, 4 3/4 x 3 1/4
James, Br. Navy in Adversity, 20, 6 1/2 x 4

Kerr, Hist. Atlas of Canada, 33, 6 1/2 x 8 1/2 col.
Kingsford, Hist. of Canada, 5:476, 6 3/4 x 4 7/8
Lossing, Field-Book of Rev., 1:193, 3 x 1
McDowell, Revolutionary War, 68, 6 1/4 x 3 1/2 col.
Marshall, Atlas, map 6, 10 x 7 1/4
Matloff, Am. Military History, 51, 5 1/2 x 4 3/8
Miers, Yankee Doodle Dandy, 63, 4 1/4 x 3 5/8
Morison, Growth of Am. Republic, 5th ed., 210, 5 1/2 x 4 1/2
Morison, Hist. of Am. People, 213, 4 1/2 x 4 1/2
Nettels, Washington, 162, 6 3/4 x 5
Pag. Am., 6:131, 5 3/4 x 3
Perkins, U.S. of Am., 146, 4 5/8 x 2 1/2
Rayback, Richards Atlas, 28, 15 7/8 x 9 3/8
Ridpath, New Complete Hist., 5:2476, 6 1/2 x 2 3/8
Roberts, Arundel, lining papers, 7 x 9 1/2 col.
Scheer, Rebels and Redcoats, 116, 5 7/8 x 4 1/2
Sherwin, Arnold, 64, 5 1/4 x 3 1/2
Smith, Arnold's March, frontis., 5 3/4 x 3 1/4; 59, 3 7/8 x
    3 1/4; 67, 6 x 2 7/8; 95, 5 3/8 x 2 1/4; 119, 3 1/4 x 5 3/4;
    137, 5 3/4 x 3 1/4; 165, 3 1/2 x 3 3/4; 171, 4 5/8 x 3 1/2;
    201, 6 x 3 1/2, by John Montrésor; 223, 5 3/4 x 3 1/4; 237,
    4 1/2 x 3 5/8
Smith, Struggle for 14th Colony, 1:512, 5 3/8 x 2 1/2; 572,
    4 5/8 x 3 1/2; 582, 6 1/4 x 2 1/2
Trevelyan, Am. Revolution, 2:end, 11 x 8 5/8
Vestal, Washington, 10, 6 1/2 x 3 5/8
Wallace, Appeal to Arms, 79, 4 3/8 x 4
Wallace, Traitorous Hero, 62, 4 5/8 x 4 1/8
Ward, Revolution, 1:171, 7 1/8 x 3 3/8
Washington Bicentennial, 1:109, 6 1/2 x 3 5/8
Fort Western, Augusta, Me.   46155
    Smith, Arnold's March, 307, 2 1/4 x 2 1/8
Arnold's Hospital, Oct. 1775   46160
    Duncan, Medical Men, 88, 3 5/8 x 6 1/8
Motor routes over trail followed by Arnold in 1775, Augusta, Me.,   46165
    to Quebec
    Roberts, March to Quebec, lining papers, 7 3/8 x 4 7/8
Capt. William Hendrick's route from Carlisle to Easton, Pa., July   46170
    1775, en route to Canada
    Crist, Capt. Wm. Hendricks, 16, 7 5/8 x 11 3/4
Capt. Daniel Morgan's route from Winchester, Va., to Quebec, 1775   46175
    Callahan, Daniel Morgan, 62-63, 6 1/8 x 8 1/2
    Heth, Diary, 36, 7 x 4, 7 x 4
    Winchester Va. Hist. Soc., Annual Papers, 1:36, 7 x 4, 7 x 4
Quebec, siege, Dec. 5, 1775 - May 6, 1776   46180
    Avery, Hist. of U.S., 5:335, 4 7/8 x 6 3/4 col.
    Carrington, Battles, 138, 4 3/4 x 7 3/4
    Codman, Arnold's Exped., 158, 9 3/8 x 13
    Decker, Arnold, 122, 3 3/4 x 4
    Duncan, Medical Men, 90, 4 1/8 x 5 1/2
    Field Artillery Jl., 23(Sept.-Oct. 1933):440, 5 1/4 x 8
    Greene, Revolutionary War, 24, 4 7/8 x 6 3/4 col.
    Lossing, Field-Book of Rev., 183, 1 7/8 x 1 1/4
    R.I. Hist. Soc., Collections, 6:xvii, 5 x 7 3/4
    Roberts, Arundel, lining papers, 7 x 9 5/8 col.

Sherwin, Arnold, 81, 3 1/2 x 5 1/8
Stanley, Canada's Soldiers, 111, 4 5/8 x 7 1/2
Ward, Revolution, 1:189, 5 3/8 x 4 1/2
By Edward Antill   46185
  Smith, Struggle for 14th Colony, 2:247, 3 3/8 x 4 3/4
  Winsor, America, 6:226, 3 3/8 x 4 5/8
Engraved by William Faden   46190
  Dearborn, Journals, 66, 7 5/8 x 10 1/2
  French, First Year, 600, 8 1/2 x 5 5/8
  Frothingham, Washington, 90, 4 3/8 x 6
  Naval Docs. of Am. Rev., 4:1453, 5 3/8 x 7 5/8
  Pag. Am., 6:132, 4 1/8 x 4 1/8
  Smith, Struggle for 14th Colony, 2:78, 3 3/8 x 3 3/4
Assault on Quebec, Dec. 31, 1775   46195
  Crist, Capt. Wm. Hendricks, 28, 2 1/2 x 4 1/8; 30,
    2 3/8 x 4 1/8
  Stiles, Diary, 2:80, 4 x 4, by Ezra Stiles
Lower Barricades, Quebec   46200
  Smith, Struggle for 14th Colony, 2:129, 1 3/4 x 2 3/8
American retreat from Quebec to Ft. Chambly, May 7 - June 10,   46205
  1776
  Rayback, Richards Atlas, 28, 15 7/8 x 9 3/8 col.
Maj. Gen. Guy Carleton's route, 1776   46210
  Am. Heritage Atlas, 96, 6 1/2 x 4 5/8 col.
  James, Br. Navy in Adversity, 36, 6 5/8 x 4
  Kerr, Hist. Atlas of Canada, 33, 6 1/2 x 8 1/2 col.

1778

Proposed American northern campaign, 1778   46215
  Smith, Struggle for 14th Colony, 2:523, 2 1/2 x 3 1/2
Fort Haldimand, built by British on Carleton Island in St.   46220
  Lawrence River in 1778
  Ontario History, 52(Mar. 1960):3, 4 x 5

NOVA SCOTIA AND NEW BRUNSWICK

Nova Scotia and Cape Breton Island
  1775   47005
    Naval Docs. of Am. Rev., 1:1150, 5 1/4 x 8
  1776   47010
    Gipson, Br. Empire, 9:134, 5 x 5 3/8, by Thomas Jefferys;
      135, 4 1/4 x 7 1/2, by Thomas Jefferys
Nova Scotia at time of the Revolution   47015
  Brebner, Neutral Yankees, end, 8 1/8 x 13 3/8
  Burt, U.S., G.B., and Br. N. Am., 14, 8 1/8 x 13 3/8
Nova Scotia and Eastern Maine, 1775-1776   47020
  Ahlin, Maine Rubicon, 29, 3 7/8 x 6
Halifax Harbor, Nova Scotia, 1781   47025
  Naval Docs. of Am. Rev., 1:994, 4 1/2 x 8; 3:289, 7 3/8 x
    5 1/2, from J.F.W. Des Barres, Atlantic Neptune

MILITARY OPERATIONS

Military exercise of Gen. Howe's army, Halifax, May 1776   47027
    Am. Heritage, 20(Aug. 1969):32, 5 1/8 x 6 3/4, by Capt.
      Edward Barron
Capt. Jonathan Eddy's expedition to Fort Cumberland, Aug.-   47030
    Nov. 1776
    Ahlin, Maine Rubicon, 43, 3 7/8 x 6
    Kerr, Hist. Atlas of Canada, 33, 2 3/8 x 2 7/8 col.
    Stanley, Canada's Soldiers, 119, 4 5/8 x 6 7/8
Fort Cumberland   47035
    Royal Soc. Canada, Proc., 2d series, 5(1899):329, 4 1/4 x
      6 7/8
John Allen's expedition to the St. John River, May 30-Aug. 2,   47040
    1777
    Ahlin, Maine Rubicon, 75, 5 7/8 x 3 3/4
Naval Yard, Halifax, c.1784   47045
    Naval Docs. of Am. Rev., 4:1247, 4 1/4 x 7 3/4

LOYALIST SETTLEMENTS

Upper and Lower Canada and the Maritime Provinces at the time   48005
    of the Loyalist settlements
    Wallace, United Empire Loyalists, 52, 5 3/4 x 9 1/8 col.
Loyalist settlements in Nova Scotia, New Brunswick, Lower Canada, 48010
    and Upper Canada
    Kerr, Hist. Atlas of Canada, 36-37, 6 x 15 5/8 col.
Loyalist settlements in Maritime Provinces, 1777-1788   48015
    Burpee, Hist. Atlas of Canada, 22, map 61, 4 3/4 x 7 3/8 col.
Loyalist grants in New Brunswick   48020
    Royal Soc. Canada, Proc., 2d series, 5(1899):344, 7 1/4 x
      7 3/8
Loyalist settlements in New Brunswick
  Original settlements   48025
    Ganong, Origins, 53, 4 3/8 x 4 1/2
  1783-1812   48030
    Ganong, Origins, 60, 4 1/2 x 4 1/2
  On Passamaquoddy Bay   48035
    New Brunswick Hist. Soc., Coll., 36, no.9(1914):507,
      5 5/8 x 4
  Military settlements   48040
    Kerr, Hist. Atlas of Canada, 37, 3 3/8 x 2 1/2 col.
Loyalist refugee cantonments and garrisons in Lower Quebec   48042
    Province during the Revolutionary War
    Vt. Hist. Soc., Proc., new series, 6(June 1938):111, 6 5/8 x 4
Areas in Province of Quebec recommended for, and forbidden to,   48043
    Loyalist settlement by Governor General Frederick
    Haldimand, 1783
    Vt. Hist. Soc., Proc., new series, 6(June 1938):96, 6 3/8 x 4
Loyalist settlement, Missisquoi Bay, Quebec   48044
    Vt. Hist. Soc. Proc., new series, 6(June 1938):111, 6 5/8 x 4
Loyalist settlements in Upper Canada before 1800   48045
    Burpee, Hist. Atlas of Canada, 23, map 63, 4 3/4 x 7 3/8 col.
Settlements of Loyalists and Six Nation Indians in Niagara   48050
    Peninsula and adjacent regions of Ontario
    Siebert, Loyalists and Six Nation Indians, end, 4 1/4 x 6 1/4

NAVAL OPERATIONS

Atlantic Ocean
  1775   49005
    Naval Docs. of Am. Rev., 1:321, 5 1/4 x 7 5/8, by Thomas
      Jefferys
  1779   49007
    Naval Docs. of Am. Rev., 3:XIV, 5 1/2 x 6 1/2, pub. by
      Carington Bowles
North Atlantic Ocean   49010
    Mahan, Influence of Sea Power, 532, 6 3/4 x 11
    Mahan, Navies, 280, 6 5/8 x 11
Gulf Stream
  1769, by Benjamin Franklin   49015
    Am. Heritage Atlas, 8-9, 3 1/2 x 4 1/4
  1786   49020
    Comstock, Enc. of Am. Antiques, 2:pl.279A, 3 1/2 x 4 1/4
Trinidada Island, 1782, off Brazil   49025
    Pasley, Sea Journals, 186, 6 x 9 1/2, by Capt. P. D'Auverne
North Atlantic area, 1775-1783   49030
    Van Alstyne, Empire and Independence, 58-59, 6 1/2 x 8 1/2
Naval Battles, 1776-1782   49035
    Paullin, Atlas, pl.160J, 3 5/8 x 4 1/8 col.
Naval warfare on British shipping by American Naval vessels and   49040
    privateers, 1775-1782
    Pag. Am., 6:264, 4 3/4 x 7 1/4
American logistics lifeline, France to St. Eustatius to   49045
    Philadelphia, 1777
    Roscoe, Picture Hist., no.114, 4 x 6 3/8, 1 1/2 x 1 7/8
British naval warfare with French, Dutch, and Spanish, 1780-1782   49050
    Pag. Am., 6:271, 5 x 8 3/8, 2 x 1 3/8, 1 7/8 x 1 5/8
Major British, French, and Spanish naval movements across the   49052
    Atlantic and in West Indies, 1780-1781
    Coggins, Ships and Seamen, 192-193, 6 1/2 x 11 3/8
Location of British-French and British-Spanish naval battles in   49055
    European waters
    James, Br. Navy in Adversity, 82, 4 x 6 1/4
Principal British, French, and Spanish naval bases   49060
    James, Br. Navy in Adversity, 82, 4 x 6 1/4
Atlantic voyages of British Naval vessels
  HMS Glasgow, July-Oct. 1778, and HMS Jupiter, May-Sept. 1782   49065
    Pasley, Sea Journals, 278, 6 3/4 x 9 1/4
  HMS Sybil, Feb.-Aug. 1780, and HMS Jupiter, Mar. 1781 -   49070
    Mar. 1782
    Pasley, Sea Journals, 238, 6 3/4 x 4

NORTH AMERICAN WATERS

Eastern North America and West Indies   50005
    Clowes, Royal Navy, 3:377, 7 3/8 x 4 1/2
    Mahan, Royal Navy, 377, 7 3/8 x 4 5/8
Atlantic Coast of North America
  From Banks of Newfoundland to New York   50010
    Serle, Am. Journal, 17, 3 3/4 x 5 1/2
  From Banks of Newfoundland to Delaware Bay   50012
    Allen, Naval Hist. of Am. Rev., 1:1, 3 3/4 x 6

From Cape Breton Island to New York   50013
   Dupuy, Rev. War Naval Battles, 2, 6 3/4 x 5 7/8
From Boston to Delaware Bay   50015
   Mahan, Royal Navy, 381, 4 3/8 x 7 3/8
From Nantucket Is. to New York, 1778   50020
   André, Journal, 2:32, 7 3/8 x 25 5/8, by Maj. John André
From Delaware Bay to Albemarle Sound, 1775   50025
   Naval Docs. of Am. Rev., 1:867, 7 5/8 x 5 1/2, by Joshua Fry
     and Peter Jefferson
From Delaware Bay to Savannah   50026
   Dupuy, Rev. War Naval Battles, 4, 5 1/2 x 5 3/8
From Cape May to the mouth of the Mississippi River   50027
   Allen, Naval Hist. of Am. Rev., 2:367, 6 x 4
Coast of North and South Carolina, 1770   50030
   Naval Docs. of Am. Rev., 2:103, 5 3/8 x 6 7/8
Bermuda, 1778   50034
   Naval Docs. of Am. Rev., 3:539, 4 3/8 x 4 1/8, pub. by
     Antonio Zatta

1776

Commodore Esek Hopkins' fleet vs. HMS *Glasgow*, Apr. 6, 1776   50035
   Morison, Jones, 49, five diagrams, each 1 5/8 x 2
Operations of HMS *Phoenix* and HMS *Rose* on the Hudson
   River, July 12 - Aug. 18, 1776
  Breakthrough to the Tappan Zee, July 12, 1776   50040
   N.Y. Hist. Soc. Quar, 40(Apr. 1956):124, 6 1/2 x 3
  In the Tappan Zee and Haverstraw Bay, July 12-25, 1776   50045
   N.Y. Hist. Soc. Quar., 40(Apr. 1956):133, 6 3/8 x 2 3/4
  In the Tappan Zee and Haverstraw Bay, July 25-Aug. 2, 1776 50050
   N.Y. Hist. Soc. Quar., 40(Apr. 1956):144, 6 3/8 x 2 3/4
  American row galley attack, Aug. 3, 1776   50055
   N.Y. Hist. Soc. Quar., 40(Apr. 1956):147, 6 3/8 x 2 5/8
  American fireship attack   50060
   N.Y. Hist. Soc. Quar., 40(Apr. 1956):154, 6 3/8 x 2 1/2
Naval operations on Lake Champlain, Oct. 1776   50065
   Clowes, Royal Navy, 3:355, 2 x 7 3/8
   Mahan, Navies, 8, 7 1/2 x 4
   Scribner's Mag., 23(Feb. 1898):149, 7 3/8 x 1 5/8
Valcour Island, Battles of, Lake Champlain, Oct. 11, 1776   50070
   Alden, U.S. Navy, 20, 6 5/8 x 4 1/8
   Am. Heritage Atlas, 96, 4 3/8 x 2 1/2
   Am. Heritage, Revolution, 132, 4 1/2 x 3 1/2
   Am. Historical Rec., 3(1874):501, 2 1/8 x 2 1/4
   Avery, Hist. of U.S., 6:6, 5 1/4 x 1 3/4 col.
   Bird, Navies in the Mts., 120, 6 1/2 x 3 7/8, 2 3/8 x 1 7/8
   Coffin, Boys of '76, 124, 2 5/8 x 2 5/8
   Coggins, Ships and Seamen, 56, 6 1/8 x 3 3/4
   Cook, Golden Bk. of Am. Rev., 35, 4 x 3 1/8
   Drake, Burgoyne's Invasion, 23, 3 1/2 x 3
   Dupuy, Compact Hist., 107, 4 1/2 x 4 1/2
   Dupuy, Rev. War Naval Battles, 41, 5 5/8 x 5 7/8
   Greene, Revolutionary War, 96, 5 1/4 x 1 3/4 col.
   Hadden, Journal, 23, 14 x 4 5/8
   Harper's Mag., 23(Nov. 1861):726, 2 1/8 x 2 5/8
   Kimball, Vermont, 132, 3 5/8 x 3

Krafft, Sea Power, 24, 5 1/2 x 2 1/4
Lossing, Field-Book of Rev., 1:163, 2 5/8 x 2 5/8
Maclay, Hist. of U.S. Navy, 1:54, 1 3/4 x 1 1/2
Mahan, Navies, 8, 2 5/8 x 1 7/8
Mahan, Royal Navy, 355, 2 x 7 3/8
Pag. Am., 6:135, 4 7/8 x 3 3/4
Palmer, L. Champlain, 128, 2 7/8 x 2 1/4
Rayback, Richards Atlas, 28, 8 x 2 5/8 col.
Sherwin, Arnold, 113, 4 3/8 x 4
Smith, Struggle for 14th Colony, 2:463, 1 1/8 x 1 1/4
Spears, Hist. of Our Navy, 92, 5 3/4 x 2; 93, 2 1/4 x 1 3/4;
  94, 2 5/8 x 2 3/8
Todd, Real Arnold, 104, 3 1/4 x 2 3/4
Ward, Revolution, 1:391, 7 1/8 x 3 1/2
Winsor, America, 6:347, 5 1/2 x 4 3/4
Engraved by William Faden   50075
Avery, Hist. of U.S., 6:7, 4 3/8 x 6 3/4
Brown, Br. Maps of Am. Rev., frontis., 5 3/4 x 4
Roscoe, Picture Hist., no. 111, 8 x 13 7/8
Lake Champlain, Second Battle of, Oct. 13, 1776   50080
Coffin, Boys of '76, 125, 2 3/8 x 2 3/8
Lossing, Field-Book of Rev., 1:164, 2 3/8 x 2 3/8
Alfred and *John* vs. HMS *Milford*, Dec. 8-9, 1776   50085
Morison, Jones, 83, five diagrams, one 1 5/8 x 4 1/4,
  four 1 5/8 x 2
Operations on Chesapeake Bay, 1776-1781   50090
Carrington, Battles, 596, 7 5/8 x 4 5/8
Carrington, Washington, 355, 5 7/8 x 3 1/2

1777

Hancock vs. HMS *Fox*, June 7, 1777, location of engagement   50092
  near Grand Banks
Allen, Naval Hist. of Am. Rev., 1:1, 3 3/4 x 6
Hancock vs. HMS *Fox*, July 7-8, 1777, location of engagement   50093
  off Cape Sable
Allen, Naval Hist. of Am. Rev., 1:1, 3 3/4 x 6
Operations on the Delaware River, Oct.-Nov. 1777
See 18160

1778

Operations of Richard, Admiral Lord Howe's fleet, 1778   50095
James, Br. Navy in Adversity, 96, 6 1/8 x 4
Adm. Howe's defense of New York, 1778   50100
Fisher, Struggle for Am. Ind., 2:208, 6 x 3 1/2
Adm. Howe's defensive line at New York, July 1778
James, Br. Navy in Adversity, 99, 4 1/2 x 4, 1 7/8 x 3 7/8
Howe vs. D'Estaing, off Sandy Hook, July 22, 1778   50110
N.Y. Hist. Soc., Coll., 14:505, 7 1/8 x 9 1/2, by Capt. John
  Montrésor
Maneuvers of Howe and D'Estaing off Rhode Island, Aug. 11, 1778 50115
Clowes, Royal Navy, 3:407, 3 3/4 x 4 3/8
Mahan, Royal Navy, 407, 3 3/4 x 4 3/8
Robison, Hist. of Naval Tactics, 278, 3 7/8 x 4 1/2

1779

Penobscot expedition, Maine, July-Aug. 1779   50120
 Avery, Hist. of U.S., 6:237, 3 3/4 x 1 3/4 col.
 Coffins, Ships and Seamen, 164, 4 1/2 x 3 7/8; 167, 5 1/4 x
  7 1/2
 Goold, Mitchell's Regt., frontis., 3 7/8 x 4 3/4
 Gould, Storming the Heights, 7, 6 1/2 x 4
 Greene, Revolutionary War, 152, 3 3/4 x 1 3/4 col.
 Lovell, Journal, 53, 6 7/8 x 3 7/8
 Mil. Affairs, 17(Summer 1953):84, 6 7/8 x 5 1/2; 86, 5 3/4 x
  4 3/4
 Pag. Am., 6:268, 4 1/4 x 3 7/8
 Winsor, America, 6:604, 4 1/2 x 2 3/4
 By John Calef   50125
 Ahlin, Maine Rubicon, 123, 6 x 3 7/8
 Allen, Naval Hist. of Am. Rev., 2:424, 5 7/8 x 3 1/2, after
  Calef
 Calef, Siege of Penobscot, frontis., 7 1/4 x 8 3/4, 3 3/4 x
  8 3/4
 Essays in Mod. Eng. Hist., 250, 4 x 3 7/8
 Wheeler, Castine, 75, 3 7/8 x 4 3/4
 Wheeler, Castine, Penobscot, and Brooksville, 42, 4 3/8 x 5 3/8
American attack on Fort Penobscot, Aug. 14, 1779, by an officer   50130
 present
 Am. Heritage, Revolution, 290, 4 x 3 5/8
 Cook, Golden Bk. of Am. Rev., 142, 4 3/8 x 3 7/8
 O.P.S. Portfolio, 7(Jan. 1948):92, 3 1/2 x 3 3/4
 Roscoe, Picture Hist., no.217, 8 x 8 1/2
 Spears, Hist. of Our Navy, 288-289, 5 7/8 x 6
Location in North Atlantic where *Confederacy* was dismasted,   50132
 Nov. 7, 1779, while conveying John Jay and French Minister
 Gérard to Europe
 Howard, Seth Harding, 106, 4 5/8 x 6

1780

Trumbull vs. HMS *Watt*, June 2, 1780, location of engagement,   50135
 200 miles north of Bermuda
 Maclay, Hist. of U.S. Navy, 1:84, 4 1/8 x 3 1/8
 Spears, Hist. of Our Navy, 161, 5 3/4 x 3 1/4
Capt. William Cornwallis vs. De Ternay, June 20, 1780, in   50137
 vicinity of Bermuda
 Clowes, Royal Navy, 3:475, 3 5/8 x 4 1/4
 James, Br. Navy in Adversity, 220, 6 3/8 x 3 7/8
 Mahan, Navies, 156, 3 x 3 3/4
 Mahan, Royal Navy, 475, 3 3/4 x 4 3/8
 Weelen, Rochambeau, 200, 201, two charts, each 5 1/8 x 3 3/4,
  by the Vicomte de Rochambeau
French naval dispositions at Newport, R.I., latter half of   50140
 July 1780
 Journal of Mod. Hist., 17(Dec. 1945):311, 5 3/8 x 5 1/4

1781

Delaware and Chesapeake Bays, 1781   50145
 Naval Docs. of Am. Rev., 1:1360, 7 1/2 x 4 1/8

Chesapeake Bay   50150
   Allen, Naval Hist. of Am. Rev., 2:396, 6 x 3 5/8
   Coggins, Ships and Seamen, 101, 6 3/4 x 3 3/4
   Cugnac, Yorktown, 9, 5 x 4 1/8
1780
 Upper Bay   50151
   Naval Docs. of Am. Rev., 4:423, 7 1/2 x 5 3/8, from
     Atlantic Neptune
 Lower Bay   50152
   Naval Docs. of Am. Rev., 4:1208, 7 3/8 x 5 1/2, from
     Atlantic Neptune
1781   50153
   Naval Docs. of Am. Rev., 3:1208, 5 x 7 7/8, by Jacques
     Nicolas Bellin
Capes of Chesapeake Bay area, c.1781   50154
   Naval Docs. of Am. Rev., 3:243, 6 7/8 x 5 3/8
Operations on Chesapeake Bay, Mar. 1781   50155
   Avery, Hist. of U.S., 6:300, 2 5/8 x 3 1/8 col.
Cape Henry, Battle of, Arbuthnot vs. Destouches, Mar. 16, 1781   50160
   Clowes, Royal Navy, 3:491, 3 5/8 x 4 3/8
   Coggins, Ships and Seamen, 197, 2 1/2 x 3 3/4, 2 1/2 x 3 3/4,
    2 1/2 x 3 3/4, 2 1/2 x 3 3/4
   James, Br. Navy in Adversity, 271, 6 3/8 x 4; 273, 6 3/8 x 4
   Mahan, Influence of Sea Power, 386, 3 3/4 x 6 5/8
   Mahan, Navies, 172, 3 3/4 x 6 1/8
   Mahan, Royal Navy, 491, 3 5/8 x 4 3/8
   Robison, Hist. of Naval Tactics, 328, 3 7/8 x 4 1/2
Routes of French and British fleets approaching Chesapeake Bay,   50165
    Aug. - Sept. 1781
   Adams, Atlas, pl.80, 9 1/4 x 6 1/4
   Antier, De Grasse, 135, 6 3/8 x 4; 209, 6 1/4 x 4
   Billias, Washington's Opponents, xxxii, 7 1/4 x 4 5/8
   Buchser, Yorktown, 16, 7 1/2 x 4 3/4
   Clarke, Am. Revolution, end lining paper, 4 1/4 x 3 1/2 col.
   Coast Artillery Jl., 72(Apr. 1930):329, 6 1/4 x 4 1/2
   Davis, Yorktown, 106, 7 x 5 1/4
   Dupuy, Rev. War Naval Battles, 95, 4 7/8 x 5 7/8
   Flexner, Washington in Am. Rev., lining papers, 6 5/8 x 4 7/8,
    by Samuel H. Bryant
   Freeman, Washington, abridgment, 471, 7 3/4 x 5 1/2
   Larrabee, Decision, 151, 7 5/8 x 4 3/4
Operations on Chesapeake Bay, Sept. 1781   50170
   Avery, Hist. of U.S., 6:310, 2 3/4 x 3 1/4 col.
   Davis, Yorktown, 106, 7 x 5 1/4
   Greene, Revolutionary War, 260, 2 3/4 x 3 1/4 col.
   Steele, Am. Campaigns, 2:30, 6 1/4 x 3 3/4 col.
Chesapeake Capes, Battle of, Graves vs. De Grasse, Sept. 5, 1781   50175
   Adams, Atlas, pl.80, 9 1/4 x 6 1/4
   Am. Heritage, Revolution, 284-285, 7 3/4 x 9 7/8 col.
   Buchser, Yorktown, 18, 5 x 6 7/8
   Channing, Hist. of U.S., 3:344, 6 3/8 x 4
   Clowes, Royal Navy, 3:498, 3 3/4 x 4 3/8
   Coggins, Ships and Seamen, 201, 3 1/2 x 3 3/4, 3 1/2 x 3 3/4
   Cugnac, Yorktown, 19, 3 7/8 x 6 7/8
   Dupuy, Rev. War Naval Battles, 98, 4 1/2 x 5 7/8
   Fleming, Battle of Yorktown, 46-47, pub. by William Graves, 1781

Fuller, Battles, 83, 3 1/4 x 4
Fuller, Decisive Battles of W. World, 2:329, 2 3/4 x 4 1/4
James, Br. Navy in Adversity, 289, 6 1/2 x 4; 291, 6 3/8 x 4
Kinnaird, Geo. Washington, 180, 3 7/8 x 5 3/4, from Political
   Magazine, 1782
Knox, Navy, 39, 4 x 6 1/4
Landers, Va. Campaign, map 5, 12 1/2 x 15 3/8
Larrabee, Decision, 187, 7 5/8 x 4 3/4
Lewis, Adm. De Grasse, 160, 3 1/8 x 3 7/8
Lossing, Field-Book of Rev., 2:306, 2 x 2
Macintyre, Admiral Rodney, 192, 6 x 3 7/8; 193, 5 7/8 x 3 7/8
Mag. of Am. Hist., 7(Nov. 1881):368, 5 3/8 x 6 1/2
Mahan, Navies, 180, 3 x 3 3/4
Mahan, Royal Navy, 498, 3 3/4 x 4 3/8
Pag. Am., 6:251, 3 7/8 x 5 3/4
Stedman, Am. War, 2:400, 8 1/4 x 9 7/8
Tornquist, Naval Campaigns, 175, 4 1/2 x 7 1/2
U.S.N. Inst. Proc., 53(Nov. 1927):1177, 5 1/8 x 7; 1179,
   5 1/8 x 7 3/4
Winsor, America, 6:548, 5 x 2
Pub. by Esnauts et Rapilly   50176
Am. Heritage, 12(Oct. 1961):58-59, 8 3/8 x 10 7/8 col.
Am. Heritage Atlas, 112, 5 3/4 x 7 3/8 col.
Am. Heritage, Revolution, 284-285, 7 3/4 x 9 7/8 col.
Cook, Golden Bk. of Am. Rev., 180-181, 8 1/2 x 10 3/4 col.
Falls, Great Mil. Battles, 105, 6 1/2 x 8 1/2
Fleming, Battle of Yorktown, lining paper, 9 7/8 x 12 5/8 col.
Rouse, Virginia, 127, 5 x 6 3/8
Position of French naval units during siege of Yorktown,   50178
   Sept. 28 - Oct. 17, 1781
Coggins, Ships and Seamen, 202, 3 1/8 x 6 1/8

1782

Cagey's (or Kedges) Straits, Battle of, Chesapeake Bay, Nov. 30,   50180
   1782
Va. Cavalcade, 4(Autumn 1954):36, 5 5/8 x 4 col.

BRITISH ISLES AND VICINITY

British Isles
1774   51000
   Naval Docs. of Am. Rev., 3:332, 8 1/4 x 6 1/8, by Samuel Dunn
1779-1780   51003
   Clark, Privateers, lining papers, 10 5/8 x 8 1/2 col.
Southern England and English Channel   51005
   Serle, Am. Journal, 3, 3 3/4 x 5 1/2
English Channel and North Sea   51010
   Mahan, Influence of Sea Power, 107, 4 x 7 1/8
English Channel
1773   51013
   Naval Docs. of Am. Rev., 3:428, 5 3/8 x 7 1/2, French map
1775, by Thomas Jefferys   51015
   Naval Docs. of Am. Rev., 1:1348, 3 3/4 x 5 1/8; 4:898-899,
      7 3/4 x 9 1/2

Coast of Flanders, Picardy, and Normandy, 1773   51017
   Naval Docs. of Am. Rev., 3:508, 5 1/2 x 7 1/4
Ports of the British Isles, France, Holland, and Spain   51018
   Allen, Naval Hist. of Am. Rev., 1:252, 6 x 3 3/4
The Downs, roadstead off East coast of Kent, 1785   51019
   Naval Docs. of Am. Rev., 3:493, 5 1/2 x 6 3/4
Portsmouth Harbor, Eng., 1774   51020
   Naval Docs. of Am. Rev., 2:746, 5 7/8 x 5 1/2
River Thames from London to the Buoy of the Noure, 1785   51022
   Naval Docs. of Am. Rev., 3:447, 4 7/8 x 7 3/4
Cork Harbor, Ireland, 1764   51023
   Naval Docs. of Am. Rev., 4:90, 5 3/8 x 6 3/4, by John Lindsay

1777

Commodore Lambert Wickes' raid around Ireland, May-June 1777   51025
   Coggins, Ships and Seamen, 88, 5 7/8 x 3 7/8
   Knox, Navy, 33, 7 x 4 1/8
   Spears, Hist. of Our Navy, 139, 5 3/4 x 3 3/8

1778-1780

John Paul Jones' cruises in British waters, 1778-1780   51030
   Alden, U.S. Navy, 32, 6 3/4 x 4 1/8
   Avery, Hist. of U.S., 6:264, 7 3/8 x 5 1/2 col.; 365,
     7 3/8 x 5 1/2 col.
   Brown, Jones, 144, 4 1/2 x 3 1/2
   Knox, Navy, 33, 7 x 4 1/8
   Krafft, Sea Power, 40, 4 1/4 x 3 5/8
   Miers, Yankee Doodle Dandy, 149, 4 3/4 x 4
   Pag. Am., 6:270, 6 1/8 x 4 3/8
Cruise of the Ranger, Apr. 10 - May 8, 1778   51035
   Avery, Hist. of U.S., 6:263, 3 3/8 x 4 1/2 col.
   Coggins, Ships and Seamen, 112, 10 1/8 x 7 3/8, 2 1/2 x 3 3/4
   Dupuy, Rev. War Naval Battles, 55, 7 x 5 7/8; 59, 4 x 5 7/8
   Frost, We Build a Navy, front, 12 x 8 1/4; 25, 4 x 5 3/8
   Maclay, Hist. of U.S. Navy, 1:75, 3 1/2 x 2 1/4
   Morison, Jones, 136, 5 1/2 x 4 1/2
   Roscoe, Picture Hist., no.141, 2 1/8 x 3 7/8
   Scribner's Mag., 24(1898):205, 6 1/4 x 4 7/8
   Spears, Hist. of Our Navy, 139, 5 3/4 x 3 3/8
Probable layout of Whitehaven Harbor, Eng., at time of Jones'   51040
   raid, Apr. 27-28, 1778
   Frost, We Build a Navy, 31, 3 3/4 x 6
Cruise of Bonhomme Richard, 1779, Aug. 14 - Sept. 23, 1779   51045
   Avery, Hist. of U.S., 6:268-269, 6 5/8 x 5 1/4, 1 5/8 x
     1 3/8 col.
   Bailey, Fighting Sailor, 71, 6 1/2 x 4
   Coggins, Ships and Seamen, 112, 10 1/8 x 7 3/8
   DeKoven, John Paul Jones, 1:432, 5 3/8 x 4
   Dupuy, Compact Hist., 304, 6 5/8 x 4 1/2
   Dupuy, Rev. War Naval Battles, 55, 7 x 5 7/8
   Frost, We Build a Navy, front, 12 x 8 1/4; 71, 6 x 3 3/4
   Maclay, Hist. of U.S. Navy, 1:107, 3 1/4 x 2
   Morison, Jones, 211, 6 1/8 x 4 1/8

Roscoe, Picture Hist., no.182, 4 1/4 x 2 7/8
Scribner's Mag., 24(1898):205, 6 1/4 x 4 7/8
Spears, Hist. of Our Navy, 139, 5 3/4 x 3 7/8
 Bonhomme Richard vs. *Serapis*, off Flamborough Head, Eng.,   51050
    Sept. 23, 1779
  Allen, Naval Hist. of Am. Rev., 2:459, 2 5/8 x 3 1/8
  Avery, Hist. of U.S., 6:266, 5 x 4 1/2 col.; 267, 3 3/8 x
    4 1/2 col.
  Coggins, Ships and Seamen, 117, 3 3/4 x 3 3/8, 4 1/8 x 3 3/4
  DeKoven, John Paul Jones, 451, 4 x 5 3/4
  Dupuy, Rev. War Naval Battles, 79, 4 7/8 x 5 7/8
  Frost, We Build a Navy, 77, 6 x 3 3/4
  Krafft, Sea Power, 43, 2 7/8 x 3 5/8
  Maclay, Hist. of U.S. Navy, 119, 1 3/4 x 3 3/4
  Morison, Jones, 224, 5 7/8 x 4 1/8; 231, eight diagrams,
    seven 1 1/2 x 1 3/8, one 1 7/8 x 1 3/8
  Roscoe, Picture Hist., no.188, 2 5/8 x 1 5/8
  Scribner's Mag., 24(1898):208, 2 5/8 x 3 1/2
  Spears, Hist. of Our Navy, 249, 2 x 3 3/8
 Cruise of *Alliance*, Dec. 26, 1779 - Feb. 10, 1780   51051
  Coggins, Ships and Seamen, 112, 10 1/8 x 7 3/8
Ushant, Battle of, Keppel vs. D'Orvilliers, July 27, 1778   51055
  Allen, Battles of Br. Navy, 1:236, 2 7/8 x 2 3/4
  Antier, De Grasse, 113, 6 1/4 x 4
  Clowes, Royal Navy, 3:419, 3 3/4 x 4 3/8; 421, 3 3/4 x 4 3/8
  James, Br. Navy in Adversity, 128, 6 1/4 x 4; 130, 6 3/8 x 4;
    131, 6 3/8 x 4; 133, 6 1/2 x 4
  Lewis, Adm. De Grasse, 65, 3 1/8 x 3 7/8
  Mahan, Influence of Sea Power, 351, 3 3/4 x 6 5/8
  Mahan, Navies, 86, 3 3/4 x 6 1/8; 90, 3 x 3 3/4, 3 x 3 3/4
  Mahan, Royal Navy, 419, 3 3/4 x 4 3/8; 421, 3 3/4 x 4 3/8
  Robison, Hist. of Naval Tactics, 281, 3 3/4 x 4 1/2
Positions of British fleet and combined French-Spanish fleet   51060
    threatening to invade England, July 1779
  Pag. Am., 6:273, 2 x 3 1/2
Cruises in British waters of American privateers commissioned   51065
    by Benjamin Franklin
 Black Prince, June-Sept. 1779   51070
  Clark, Privateers, 89, 6 5/8 x 4
 Black Prince and *Black Princess*, Dec. 1779 - Apr. 1780   51075
  Clark, Privateers, 111, 6 3/8 x 4
 Fearnot, Mar. - Aug. 1780   51080
  Clark, Privateers, 161, 6 1/2 x 4
 Black Princess, May - Aug. 1780   51085
  Clark, Privateers, 153, 6 1/2 x 4

1781-1782

Cruise of *Count de Guichen*, Mar. 23 - Aug. 1, 1781   51090
  Bailey, Fighting Sailor, 122, 3 1/4 x 4
First cruise of cutter *Eclipse*, Dec. 10, 1781 - Mar. 6, 1782   51095
  Bailey, Fighting Sailor, 134, 3 1/4 x 4
Second cruise of cutter *Eclipse*, June 6 - end of Aug. 1782   51100
  Bailey, Fighting Sailor, 161, 6 1/2 x 4
Cruise of *Ranger*, Oct. 23 - 27, 1782   51105
  Bailey, Fighting Sailor, 202, 3 1/4 x 4

WEST INDIES AND THE CARIBBEAN

West Indies   52000
    Allen, Naval Hist. of Am. Rev., 1:196, 3 1/2 x 5 7/8
    Billias, Washington's Opponents, xxxiii, 4 1/2 x 7 3/8
    Boatner, Enc. of Am. Rev., 1183, 4 1/8 x 6 1/4
    Dupuy, Rev. War Naval Battles, 23, 3 7/8 x 5 7/8
    Fisher, Struggle for Am. Ind., 2:224, 3 1/2 x 6
    Fortescue, British Army, 3:pl.vii, 11 1/2 x 16 5/8 col.
    Hargreaves, The Bloodybacks, 283, 4 5/8 x 7 5/8
    Landers, Va. Campaign, map 4, 12 1/8 x 15 3/8
    Mackesy, War for America, 226, 4 1/4 x 7 1/8
1774   52005
    Naval Docs. of Am. Rev., 2:615, 5 1/4 x 7 5/8, by Samuel
      Dunn, pub. by Robert Sayer
1775   52010
    Naval Docs. of Am. Rev., 1:209, 3 7/8 x 5 1/2, by Emanuel
      Bowen
1776   52015
    James, Br. Navy in Adversity, 84, 4 x 6 1/4
c.1780   52017
    Robertson, Spanish Town Papers, front lining paper, 6 x 9 3/4
Gulf of Mexico and Caribbean   52020
    Leboucher, Histoire, 71, 7 3/4 x 11 5/8, after Bellin
Bahamas, 1775   52022
    Naval Docs. of Am. Rev., 4:154, 5 1/8 x 6 7/8, by Thomas
      Jefferys
Barbados, 1777   52023
    Naval Docs. of Am. Rev., 3:989, 7 1/4 x 5 3/8
Dominica, 1773   52025
    Gipson, Br. Empire, 9:239, 5 5/8 x 7 1/8
Grenada   52030
    Gipson, Br. Empire, 9:238, 5 1/8 x 6 1/2, by Thos. Jefferys
Leeward Islands, 1782   52035
    Am. Heritage, 9(June 1958):9, 3 3/4 x 4 7/8
Lesser Antilles (Iles du Vent)   52040
    Leboucher, Historie, end, pl.III, 24 x 14 1/4
    Macintyre, Admiral Rodney, frontis., 5 1/8 x 3 1/4
1764   52045
    Gipson, Br. Empire, 2:217, 5 3/8 x 7 5/8, by J.N. Bellin
1777   52047
    Naval Docs. of Am. Rev., 3:707, 7 3/4 x 5 3/8, by Delarochette,
      engr. by Thomas Jefferys, pub. by William Faden
Martinique   52050
    Mahan, Navies, 164, 4 3/8 x 6 1/8
    Mahan, Royal Navy, 485, 4 1/2 x 6 1/8, pub. by J. Gold
Nevis, 1777   52055
    Gipson, Br. Empire, 2:224, 5 5/8 x 7, by Thomas Jefferys
New Providence I., Bahamas
c.1762   52056
    Naval Docs. of Am. Rev., 4:226, 3 3/4 x 7 3/4
1765   52057
    Naval Docs. of Am. Rev., 4:176, 5 1/8 x 6 5/8, by
      Capt. Thomas Foley
Port Royal and Harbor, Jamaica, 1772   52058
    Naval Docs. of Am. Rev., 3:947, 7 7/8 x 6 5/8, by Geo. Gould

Naval campaigns in the West Indies, 1780-1782   52122
    Coggins, Ships and Seamen, 195, 11 1/8 x 7 3/4
British-French naval engagements in the West Indies
  Grenada, Battle of, Byron vs. D'Estaing, July 6, 1779   52125
      Allen, Battles of Br. Navy, 1:247, 1 5/8 x 3 1/8
      Clowes, Royal Navy, 3:436, 3 3/4 x 4 3/8
      James, Br. Navy in Adversity, 148, 6 1/2 x 4; 150, 6 1/2 x 4;
        151, 6 3/8 x 4
      Mahan, Influence of Sea Power, 368, 4 x 6 5/8
      Mahan, Navies, 106, 3 3/4 x 6 1/8
      Mahan, Royal Navy, 436, 3 3/4 x 4 3/8
      Matthews, Twenty-One Plans, 8, 7 x 10 3/8 col., 7 x 10 3/8
        col., 7 x 10 3/8 col., 7 x 10 3/8 col., 7 1/4 x 10 3/4
        col., 7 1/4 x 10 3/4 col., all by John Matthews
      Robison, Hist. of Naval Tactics, 284, 3 7/8 x 4 1/2
  Confrontation off Basseterre, St. Christopher, July 22, 1779   52127
      Matthews, Twenty-One Plans, 9, 7 1/8 x 10 1/2 col., by John
        Matthews
  Martinique, Battle of, Rodney vs. De Guichen, Apr. 17, 1780   52130
      Clowes, Royal Navy, 3:455, 3 3/4 x 4 3/8; 457, 3 3/4 x 4 3/8
      Coggins, Ships and Seamen, 192, 3 3/8 x 3 7/8
      James, Br. Navy in Adversity, 200, 6 1/2 x 4; 202, 6 1/2 x 4
      Lewis, Adm. De Grasse, 86, 3 1/4 x 3 7/8
      Macintyre, Admiral Rodney, 190, 5 7/8 x 3 7/8; 191, 6 x 3 7/8
      Mahan, Influence of Sea Power, 378, 3 3/4 x 6 5/8
      Mahan, Navies, 132, 3 x 3 3/4, 3 x 3 3/4
      Mahan, Royal Navy, 455, 3 3/4 x 4 3/8; 457, 3 3/4 x 4 3/8
      Robison, Hist. of Naval Tactics, 304, 3 7/8 x 4 1/2; 306,
        3 7/8 x 4 1/2
  St. Lucia Channel, Battle of, Rodney vs. De Guichen, May 15, 1780 52135
      Clowes, Royal Navy, 3:465, 3 3/4 x 4 3/8
      James, Br. Navy in Adversity, 210, 6 3/8 x 4; 212, 6 3/8 x 4
      Mahan, Navies, 143, 3 x 3 3/4
      Mahan, Royal Navy, 465, 3 3/4 x 4 3/8
  Hood vs. De Grasse, off Martinique, Apr. 29, 1782   52145
      Johnson, Swedish Contrib., 1:400, 5 1/8 x 14
      Matthews, Twenty-One Plans, 13, 7 1/4 x 10 3/4 col.,
        7 1/4 x 10 5/8 col., by John Matthews
      Revel, Journal, 56, 4 1/2 x 7 3/8; 63, 4 5/8 x 4 3/8; 65,
        5 1/2 x 4 1/4; 66, 4 1/8 x 4 1/4; 67, 4 1/4 x 7 3/8
      Tornquist, Naval Campaigns, 173, 4 1/2 x 7 1/2
  St. Kitts, Battle of, Hood vs. De Grasse, Jan. 25-26, 1782   52150
      Clowes, Royal Navy, 3:514, 3 5/8 x 4 3/8; 515, 3 5/8 x
        4 3/8; 517, 3 3/4 x 4 3/8
      James, Br. Navy in Adversity, 324, 6 1/2 x 4
      Lewis, Adm. De Grasse, 211, 3 1/4 x 3 7/8
      Mahan, Influence of Sea Power, 470, 3 3/4 x 6 5/8; 472,
        6 5/8 x 3 3/4
      Mahan, Navies, 201, 3 x 3 3/4, 3 x 3 3/4; 203, 3 x 3 3/4
      Mahan, Royal Navy, 514, 3 5/8 x 4 3/8; 515, 3 5/8 x 4 3/8;
        517, 3 3/4 x 4 3/8
      Matthews, Twenty-One Plans, 18, 7 1/4 x 10 5/8 col., 7 1/4 x
        10 5/8 col., 7 1/8 x 10 5/8 col., by John Matthews
      Revel, Journal, 208, 7 1/2 x 4 1/4; 209, 5 1/4 x 4 1/4
      Robison, Hist. of Naval Tactics, 335, 3 3/4 x 4 1/2; 336,
        3 3/4 x 4 1/2; 339, 3 7/8 x 4 1/2

Tornquist, Naval Campaigns, 177, 4 1/2 x 7 1/2
Saints, Battle of the, Rodney vs. De Grasse, Apr. 9, 1782   52155
   Allen, Battles of Br. Navy, 1:303, 2 x 2 7/8
   Clowes, Royal Navy, 3:522, 3 5/8 x 4 3/8; 523, 3 5/8 x 4 3/8
   James, Br. Navy in Adversity, 334, 6 1/2 x 4
   Macintyre, Admiral Rodney, 22, 5 5/8 x 3 3/4
   Mahan, Influence of Sea Power, 482, 3 3/4 x 3 3/8, 3 3/4 x 3 3/8
   Mahan, Navies, 210, 3 x 3 3/4, 3 x 3 3/4
   Mahan, Royal Navy, 522, 3 5/8 x 4 3/8; 523, 3 5/8 x 4 3/8
   Matthews, Twenty-One Plans, 20, 7 x 10 7/8 col., 7 1/8 x
      10 7/8 col., 7 1/8 x 10 7/8 col., by John Matthews
   Revel, Journal, 244, 7 1/2 x 3 7/8; 247, 7 1/2 x 4 7/8;
      251, 7 1/2 x 4 7/8
   Shea, French Fleet, 117, 2 x 2 7/8
   Tornquist, 179, 4 3/8 x 7 3/8
Saints, Battle of the, Rodney vs. De Grasse, Apr. 12, 1782   52160
   Allen, Battles of Br. Navy, 1:305, 2 3/4 x 3 1/8
   Antier, De Grasse, 319, 3 1/8 x 4, 3 1/8 x 4
   Chatterton, Battles by Sea, 144, 3 1/2 x 5 5/8
   Clowes, Royal Navy, 3:526, 3 3/4 x 4 3/8; 527, 3 3/4 x 4 3/8;
      528, 3 3/4 x 4 3/8; 529, 3 3/4 x 4 3/8
   Coggins, Ships and Seamen, 131, 4 1/4 x 4
   De Grasse, Memoire, pl.I, 15 7/8 x 20; pl.II, 16 x 19 3/4
      pl. III, 16 x 19 5/8; pl.IV, 16 x 19 5/8; pl.V, 16 3/8
      x 19 5/8; pl.VI, 16 1/8 x 19 3/4; pl.VII, 16 1/8 x 19 3/4;
      pl.VIII, 16 1/4 x 19 7/8
   Dupuy, Rev. War Naval Battles, 107, 6 x 2 7/8, 6 x 2 1/2
   James, Br. Navy in Adversity, 338, 6 1/2 x 4; 339, 6 1/2 x 4;
      341, 6 3/8 x 4
   Lewis, Adm. De Grasse, 241, 3 1/4 x 3 7/8
   Macintyre, Admiral Rodney, 223, 6 x 3 7/8; 224, 5 7/8 x 3 7/8;
      225, 5 3/4 x 3 7/8
   Mahan, Influence of Sea Power, 486, 3 3/4 x 2 3/4, 3 3/4 x
      7/8, 3 3/4 x 1 1/4, 3 3/4 x 2
   Mahan, Navies, 212, 3 3/4 x 6 1/8; 215, 3 3/4 x 3, 3 3/4 x 3;
      218, 3 3/4 x 6
   Mahan, Royal Navy, 526, 3 3/4 x 4 3/8; 527, 3 3/4 x 4 3/8;
      528, 3 3/4 x 4 3/8; 529, 3 3/4 x 4 3/8
   Matthews, Twenty-One Plans, 24, 7 1/8 x 10 7/8 col., 7 1/4 x
      11 col., 7 1/8 x 10 7/8 col., 7 1/8 x 10 7/8 col., 7 x
      10 7/8 col., 7 1/4 x 11 col., by John Matthews
   Revel, Journal, 256, 3 3/8 x 7 1/2; 260, 3 1/4 x 7 3/4; 262
      3 x 7 1/2; 264, 5 3/8 x 4 1/4; 268, 6 3/4 x 4 1/4
   Revue Maritime, new series, No.195(March 1936):335, 4 1/4 x
      7, by a Swedish naval officer
   Robison, Hist. of Naval Tactics, 344, 4 x 4 1/2; 345, 3 7/8 x
      4 1/2
   Shea, French Fleet, 117, 2 3/4 x 3 1/8
   Tornquist, Naval Campaigns, 181, 4 5/8 x 7 1/2; 183, 4 5/8 c
      7 1/2; 185, 4 1/2 x 7 1/2; 187, 4 5/8 x 7 1/2
British naval operations on the coast of Central America
Luttrell and Dalrymple, 1779   52165
   James, Br. Navy in Adversity, 157, 2 7/8 x 2
Nelson and Polson, 1780   52170
   James, Br. Navy in Adversity, 157, 2 7/8 x 2

AFRICAN WATERS

Capture of Senegal by Marquis de Vaudreuil, Jan. 30, 1779   53000
    Johnson, Swedish Contrib., 1:252, 5 1/8 x 18 7/8
Porto Praya, Battle of, Johnstone vs. Suffren, Cape Verde Is.,   53005
    Apr. 16, 1781
      Clowes, Royal Navy, 3:547, 3 5/8 x 4 3/8
      James, Br. Navy in Adversity, 384, 6 1/2 x 4
      Mahan, Influence of Sea Power, 423, 3 3/4 x 6 5/8
      Mahan, Navies, 237, 3 x 3 3/4
      Mahan, Royal Navy, 547, 3 5/8 x 4 3/8

INDIAN OCEAN

India and Ceylon   54000
      Clowes, Royal Navy, 3:544, 7 3/8 x 4 5/8
      James, Br. Navy in Adversity, 379, 6 1/8 x 4
      Mahan, Influence of Sea Power, 257, 7 1/8 x 4 1/8
      Mahan, Navies, 234, 7 1/8 x 4 1/8
      Mahan, Royal Navy, 544, 7 3/8 x 4 5/8
British territory in India, 1763   54002
    Coggins, Ships and Seamen, 19, 4 3/8 x 4 3/8
Gulf of Bengal   54005
    Leboucher, Histoire, end, pl.IV, 14 7/8 x 16 1/2
Trincomalee Bay   54010
    Leboucher, Histoire, 317, 8 3/8 x 6 3/4, after Bellin
British-French naval engagements
 Sadras, Battle of, Hughes vs. Suffren, south of Madras,   54015
    Feb. 17, 1782
      Clowes, Royal Navy, 3:551, 3 3/4 x 4 3/8
      James, Br. Navy in Adversity, 390, 6 3/8 x 4
      Mahan, Influence of Sea Power, 431, 3 3/4 x 6 5/8
      Mahan, Navies, 240, 3 3/4 x 6 1/8
      Mahan, Royal Navy, 551, 3 3/4 x 4 3/8
 Providien, Battle of, Hughes vs. Suffren, near Trincomalee,   54020
    Apr. 12, 1782
      Clowes, Royal Navy, 3:553, 3 3/4 x 4 3/8
      James, Br. Navy in Adversity, 392, 6 3/8 x 4
      Mahan, Influence of Sea Power, 438, 3 3/4 x 6 5/8
      Mahan, Navies, 243, 3 x 3 3/4
      Mahan, Royal Navy, 553, 3 3/4 x 4 3/8
 Negapatam, Battle of, Hughes vs. Suffren, off Cuddalore,   54025
    July 6, 1782
      Clowes, Royal Navy, 3:555, 3 3/4 x 4 3/8
      James, Br. Navy in Adversity, 396, 6 3/8 x 4
      Mahan, Influence of Sea Power, 447, 3 3/4 x 6 5/8
      Mahan, Navies, 243, 3 x 3 3/4
      Mahan, Royal Navy, 555, 3 3/4 x 4 3/8
 Trincomalee, Battle of, Hughes vs. Suffren, Sept. 3, 1782   54030
      Clowes, Royal Navy, 3:559, 3 3/4 x 4 3/8
      James, Br. Navy in Adversity, 399, 6 3/8 x 4
      Mahan, Influence of Sea Power, 454, 3 3/4 x 6 5/8
      Mahan, Navies, 249, 3 x 3 3/4
      Mahan, Royal Navy, 559, 3 3/4 x 4 3/8

PEACE NEGOTIATIONS, 1779-1783

George III's personal copy of John Mitchell's map of North America used by the King during the peace negotiations   56005
  Am. Heritage Atlas, 113, 7 7/8 x 7 7/8
  Am. Heritage, Revolution, 362-363, 10 1/4 x 14 3/4
  Fite, Book of Old Maps, 290-291, 13 x 18 7/8
Northwestern corner of Mitchell's map used by peace negotiators   56010
  Channing, Hist. of U.S., 3:360, 5 1/2 x 4
Proposed boundaries of the United States
 Line proposed by Committee of Continental Congress, Feb. 23, 1779 56015
   Paullin, Atlas, pl.89, 12 1/4 x 18 3/8 col.; pl.90,
    9 x 12 1/4 col.
 Instructions of Congress to American Peace Commissioners,   56020
   Aug. 14, 1779 and June 15, 1781
  Am. Heritage Atlas, 114, 9 3/4 x 7 1/2 col.
  Bemis, Diplomacy of Am. Rev., 228, 7 5/8 x 10 3/4
  Commager, Spirit of '76, 2:1256, 4 5/8 x 6 3/8
  Hart, Am. Nation, 10:14, 8 3/8 x 6 3/8 col.
  Hinsdale, Old Northwest, 180, 4 1/4 x 5 3/4 col.
  Morris, Enc. of Am. Hist., 69, 4 7/8 x 6 5/8
  Morris, Peacemakers, 350, 4 3/4 x 5 1/4
  Paullin, Atlas, pl.89, 12 1/4 x 18 3/8 col.; pl.90,
   9 x 12 1/4 col.
Minimum boundary for U.S. acceptable to Gouverneur Morris and   56025
  Robert R. Livingston, 1781-1782
  Bemis, Diplomacy of Am. Rev., 238, 7 5/8 x 10 3/4
Northeast boundary proposals
 1779-1783
                              56030
  Burt, U.S., G.B., and Br. No. Am., 36, 5 x 4 1/2
  Paullin, Atlas, pl.90, 9 x 12 1/4 col.
 Northeast line according to Shelburne's instructions to   56035
  British agent Henry Oswald, Apr. 28, 1782
  Am. Heritage Atlas, 114, 9 3/4 x 7 1/2 col.
  Commager, Spirit of '76, 2:1256, 4 5/8 x 6 3/8
  Lord, Atlas, map 52, 7 1/4 x 6
  Morris, Enc. of Am. Hist., 69, 4 7/8 x 6 5/8
  Morris, Peacemakers, 350, 4 3/4 x 5 1/4
  Paullin, Atlas, pl.89, 12 1/4 x 18 3/8 col.; pl.90,
   9 x 12 1/4 col.
  United Empire, new series, 2(Oct. 1911):683, 9 3/8 x 7 3/4 col.
 Northeast boundary as shown on successive editions of William   56040
  Faden's map, 1777, 1783 (first state), 1783 (second state),
  and 1785
  United Empire, new series, 2(Oct. 1911):712, 4 maps, each
   3 5/8 x 3 1/8 col.
Western boundary proposals
 West line proposed to Congress by French Minister La Luzerne,   56045
  Jan. 1780
  Am. Heritage Atlas, 114, 9 3/4 x 7 1/2 col.
  Lord, Atlas, map 52, 7 1/4 x 6
  Morris, Peacemakers, 350, 4 3/4 x 5 1/4
  Paullin, Atlas, pl.89, 12 1/4 x 18 3/8 col.
 West line proposed by Count Aranda, Spanish ambassador to   56050
  France, Aug. 3, 1782
  Am. Heritage Atlas, 114, 9 3/4 x 7 1/2 col.

Becker, Beginnings of Am. People, 272, 5 3/4 x 3 3/8
Bemis, Diplomacy of Am. Rev., 216, 7 5/8 x 10 3/4
Commager, Spirit of '76, 2:1256, 4 5/8 x 6 3/8
Hinsdale, Old Northwest, 180, 4 1/4 x 5 3/4 col.
Lord, Atlas, map 52, 7 1/4 x 6
Morris, Enc. of Am. Hist., 69, 4 7/8 x 6 5/8
Morris, Peacemakers, 350, 4 3/4 x 5 1/4
Paullin, Atlas, pl.89, 12 1/4 x 18 3/8 col.
Winsor, Westward Movement, 211, 6 7/8 x 3 7/8, by Bonne
Northwest line proposed by French Minister of Foreign Affairs　　56055
　　Vergennes, Aug. 25, 1782
　Am. Heritage Atlas, 114, 9 3/4 x 7 1/2 col.
　Bemis, Diplomacy of Am. Rev., 218, 12 5/8 x 18 1/4
　Lord, Atlas, map 52, 7 1/4 x 6
　Morris, Peacemakers, 350, 4 3/4 x 5 1/4
　Paullin, Atlas, pl.89, 12 1/4 x 18 3/8 col.
Northwest line proposed by Count Aranda, Aug. 25, 1782　　56060
　Am. Heritage Atlas, 114, 9 3/4 x 7 1/2 col.
　Bemis, Diplomacy of Am. Rev., 218, 12 5/8 x 18 1/4
　Lord, Atlas, map 52, 7 1/4 x 6
　Morris, Peacemakers, 350, 4 3/4 x 5 1/4
　Paullin, Atlas, pl.89, 12 1/4 x 18 3/8 col.
Division of the West among U.S., England, and Spain proposed　　56065
　　by Gérard Rayneval, Vergennes' secretary, Sept. 6, 1782
　Am. Heritage Atlas, 114, 9 3/4 x 7 1/2 col.
　Bemis, Diplomacy of Am. Rev., 218, 12 5/8 x 18 1/4
　Billington, W. Expansion, 192, 5 1/4 x 4 5/8
　Commager, Spirit of '76, 2:1256, 4 5/8 x 6 3/8
　Drake, Ohio Valley States, 129, 3 3/4 x 2 7/8
　Fitzmaurice, Life of Shelburne, 2:115, 6 3/4 x 4 1/8 col.
　Hart, Am. Nation, 10:14, 8 3/8 x 6 3/8 col.
　Hinsdale, Old Northwest, 176, 4 1/4 x 5 3/4 col.; 180,
　　4 1/4 x 5 3/4 col.
　Lord, Atlas, map 52, 7 1/4 x 6
　Morris, Enc. of Am. Hist., 69, 4 7/8 x 6 5/8
　Morris, Peacemakers, 350, 4 3/4 x 5 1/4
　Nettels, Roots of Am. Civ., 718, 5 3/4 x 3 7/8
　Paullin, Atlas, pl.89, 12 1/4 x 18 3/8 col.
　Ridpath, New Complete Hist., 7:3094, 7 3/8 x 4 1/2 col.
　Wilson, Am. People, 3:34, 5 1/2 x 3 3/8
　Winsor, America, 7:148, 8 x 4 3/4 col.
Boundaries proposed in U.S.-British negotiations of 1782
　According to Mitchell's map of 1755　　56070
　　Avery, Hist. of U.S., 6:350, 4 1/2 x 7 col.
　According to a modern map　　56075
　　Avery, Hist. of U.S., 6:351, 4 3/4 x 6 3/4 col.
Boundary proposed in John Jay's provisional treaty draft, Oct. 5,　56080
　　1782
　Am. Heritage Atlas, 114, 9 3/4 x 7 1/2 col.
　Lord, Atlas, map 52, 7 1/4 x 6
　Morris, Peacemakers, 350, 4 3/4 x 5 1/4
　Paullin, Atlas, pl.89, 12 1/4 x 18 3/8 col.; pl.90, 9 x 12 1/4
　　col.
Alternative lines proposed by British agent Henry Strachey,　　56085
　　Oct. 20, 1782
　Am. Heritage Atlas, 114, 9 3/4 x 7 1/2 col.

Lord, Atlas, map 52, 7 1/4 x 6
Morris, Peacemakers, 350, 4 3/4 x 5 1/4
Paullin, Atlas, pl.89, 12 1/4 x 18 3/8 col.; pl.90, 9 x 12 1/4
   col.
Great Lakes and alternative 45th Parallel lines agreed upon by   56090
   British and American commissioners, Nov. 5 and 30, 1782
   Bemis, Diplomacy of Am. Rev., 228, 7 5/8 x 10 3/4
   Billington, W. Expansion, 192, 5 1/4 x 4 5/8
   Commager, Spirit of '76, 2:1256, 4 5/8 x 6 3/8
   Fitzmaurice, Life of Shelburne, 2:200, 4 1/8 x 6 3/4 col.
   Hinsdale, Old Northwest, 180, 4 1/4 x 5 3/4 col.
   Kerr, Hist. Atlas of Canada, 35, 5 1/8 x 7 1/4 col.
   Morris, Enc. of Am. Hist., 69, 4 7/8 x 6 5/8
   Morris, Peacemakers, 350, 4 3/4 x 5 1/4
   Paullin, Atlas, pl.89, 12 1/4 x 18 3/8 col.
   Philbrick, Rise of West, 69, 3 3/8 x 4 1/8
Alternate northern boundary of West Florida, if England retained 56095
   the Floridas, agreed upon by British and American commission-
   ers, Nov. 5 and 30, 1782
   Am. Heritage Atlas, 114, 9 3/4 x 7 1/2 col.
   Commager, Spirit of '76, 2:1256, 4 5/8 x 6 3/8
   Lord, Atlas, map 52, 7 1/4 x 6
   Morris, Enc. of Am. Hist., 69, 4 7/8 x 6 5/8
   Morris, Peacemakers, 350, 4 3/4 x 5 1/4
   Paullin, Atlas, pl.89, 12 1/4 x 18 3/8 col.
   Philbrick, Rise of West, 214, 3 5/8 x 4 1/8
Boundaries of the United States as finally established by   56100
   Provisional Treaty of Peace, Nov. 30, 1782, and Definitive
   Treaty of Peace, Sept. 3, 1783
   Adams, Pilgrims, Indians, and Patriots, 203, 5 x 6 1/8, pub.
     by J. Fielding, 1785
   Alden, Rise of Am. Republic, 216, 4 x 3 5/8
   Am. Heritage Atlas, 114, 9 3/4 x 7 1/2 col.
   Becker, Beginnings of Am. People, 272, 5 3/4 x 3 3/8
   Bemis, Diplomacy of Am. Rev., 228, 7 5/8 x 10 3/4
   Billington, W. Expansion, 192, 5 1/4 x 4 5/8
   Commager, Spirit of '76, 2:1256, 4 5/8 x 6 3/8
   Craven, U.S., 123, 6 1/8 x 4 1/2
   Faulkner, Am. Political & Social Hist., 149, 7 x 4 1/2
   Hart, Am. Nation, 10:108, 6 3/8 x 4 1/8 col.
   Hinsdale, Old Northwest, 180, 4 1/4 x 5 3/4 col.
   Lacy, Meaning of Am. Rev., frontis., 6 3/8 x 4
   Morris, Enc. of Am. Hist., 69, 4 7/8 x 6 5/8
   Morris, Peacemakers, 350, 4 3/4 x 5 1/4
   Nettels, Roots of Am. Civ., 719, 5 3/4 x 3 7/8
   Pag. Am., 6:261, 7 5/8 x 5 7/8
   Paullin, Atlas, pl.89, 12 1/4 x 18 3/8 col.; pl.90,
     9 x 12 1/4 col.
   Roosevelt, Winning of West, 3:end, 7 7/8 x 6 3/8 col.
   See also 57010
Boundaries of British North America as defined by Treaty of   56105
   Versailles (Britain and France) and Paris (Britain and U.S.)
   Kerr, Hist. Atlas of Canada, 45, 8 1/4 x 8 5/8 col.
   See also 01025, 45075
Boundary between Canada and the United States by Treaty of 1783 56107
   Bourinot, Canada under Br. Rule, 75, 3 1/2 x 5 7/8

Fisheries in the negotiations for peace, 1782   56110
  Burt, U.S., G.B., and Br. No. Am., 41, 4 3/8 x 7
Northeastern fisheries, 1783   56115
  Adams, Atlas, pl.83, 6 1/4 x 9 1/4

THE POST REVOLUTIONARY WAR YEARS

United States of America
1781-1789   57005
  Hicks, Federal Union, 4th ed., 209, 7 1/2 x 5 1/2
1783   57010
  Adams, Atlas, pl.82, 9 1/4 x 6 1/4
  Alden, Rise of Am. Republic, 163, 5 3/4 x 4 3/8
  Caughey, Hist. of U.S., 142, 3 1/2 x 5 3/4
  Coggins, Boys in Revolution, 93, 6 3/8 x 5 1/2
  Craven, U.S., 123, 6 1/8 x 4 1/2
  DeConde, Foreign Policy, 36, 5 1/2 x 4 5/8
  Hinsdale, Old Northwest, 200, 4 1/4 x 5 3/4
  Hofstadter, Am. Republic, 191, 5 5/8 x 5 1/2
  Kraus, U.S. to 1965, 243, 5 3/4 x 4 1/2
  Miller, Triumph of Freedom, front, 9 x 11 3/4 col.
  Niles, Chronicles, XXX, 5 x 5 1/2, by Robert Sayer and
    John Bennett
  Palmer, Atlas of World Hist., 151, 5 5/8 x 4 3/8 col.
  Perkins, U.S. of Am., 180, 4 7/8 x 4 1/2
  Savelle, Foundations, 690, 4 7/8 x 4 1/8
  Sosin, Revolutionary Frontier, lining paper, 8 1/4 x 5 1/8
  United Empire, new series, 2(Oct. 1911):712, 8 3/8 x 10 col.,
    engr. by William Faden
  Wilson, Am. People, 3:47, 4 7/8 x 3 3/4; 48, 7 x 4 3/8 col.
  World Book, 16:264, 6 1/4 x 5 1/4 col.
  Wright, Fabric of Freedom, 6 1/4 x 4
1783-1802   57015
  Clark, Am. Revolution, front lining paper, 9 1/8 x 5 7/8 col.
  Faulkner, Am. Political & Social Hist., 149, 7 x 4 1/2
1784   57020
  Channing, Hist. of U.S., 3:538, 4 x 5 3/4, engr. by H.D.
    Pursell
  Lunny, Early Maps of N. Am., 43, 6 5/8 x 7 1/2, by Abel Buell
1785, by Abel Buell   57023
  Roscoe, Picture Hist., no.1, 11 x 11 3/4
  Rouse, Virginia, 142, 6 1/2 x 7 1/8
1787   57025
  Avery, Hist. of U.S., 6:410, 16 x 14 col.
  Clark, Exploring Kentucky, 42, 6 1/8 x 4
1788   57030
  Gordon, Hist. of U.S.A., 1:frontis., pl.I, 11 1/4 x 11 7/8,
    engr. by T. Conder
Northern Part of the United States, 1783   57035
  Leboucher, Histoire, end, pl.I, 19 3/4 x 23
Southern part of the United States, 1783   57040
  Leboucher, Histoire, end, pl.II, 21 x 17 5/8
Territory now comprising the 48 Contiguous States after peace   57045
  of 1783
  Hinsdale, Old West, 188, 4 1/4 x 5 3/4
  Sloane, French War and Rev., end, 5 1/2 x 8 1/2 col.
Counties of the United States, 1786   57050
  Avery, Hist. of U.S., 6:410, 16 x 14 col.
Settled area, 1787   57055
  Avery, Hist. of U.S., 6:410, 16 x 14 col.

Frontier line, 1787   57060
    Avery, Hist. of U.S., 6:410, 16 x 14 col.
Posts held by British in U.S. territory after 1783   57065
    Baldwin, Adult's History, 115, 6 1/2 x 5 5/8
    Burt, U.S., G.B., and Br. No. Am., 22, 2 3/4 x 4
    DeConde, Foreign Policy, 45, 1 7/8 x 2 3/8
Spanish-American relations in the Old Southwest
  1783-1788   57070
    Billington, W. Expansion, 2d ed., 229, 5 1/4 x 4 3/8
  1783-1795   57075
    Van Every, Ark of Empire, 17, 4 5/8 x 4
Border War in the Old Southwest, 1784-1794   57080
    Van Every, Ark of Empire, 257, 4 x 4
Distribution of votes in ratification of the Constitution,   57085
    1787-1790
    Alden, Rise of Am. Republic, 192, 5 3/8 x 4 3/8
    Am. Heritage Atlas, 116, 9 3/4 x 7 1/2 col.
    Craven, U.S., 142, 5 1/4 x 4 1/2
    Lord, Atlas, map 57, 7 5/8 x 6
    Morris, Enc. of Am. Hist., 118, 7 5/8 x 4 7/8
New England, 1787-1790   57090
    Chitwood, Colonial America, 3rd ed., 6 1/2 x 4 1/8
    Hart, Am. Nation, 10:300, 6 1/2 x 4 1/8
    Wilson, Am. People, 3:80, 10 x 7 col.
Middle and Southern States, 1787-1789   57095
    Chitwood, Colonial America, 3rd ed., 636, 6 1/2 x 4 1/8
    Hart, Am. Nation, 10:278, 6 1/2 x 4
    Wilson, Am. People, 3:78, 10 x 7 col.
Pennsylvania, 1787   57100
    Stevens, Exploring Penna., 191, 3 1/2 x 5
Washington's inaugural journey, 1789   57105
    Freeman, Washington, 6:front, 11 3/4 x 9 5/8 col.

PART II
SUBJECT AND NAME INDEX TO MAP REFERENCES

The five digit numbers refer to entries in Part I

Abernethie, maps engraved by
Charleston, S.C., siege, 1780,
26285
Ft. Moultrie, S.C., British
attack, 1776, 26115
Adair, James, map by
Indian nations east of the Mississippi, 1775, 32010
Agriculture
commercial wheat growing, N.C.,
c.1765-75, 25110
principal grain, tobacco, rice,
indigo, and cattle producing
areas in 13 colonies, 1775,
02705
Aikens Tavern, Del.
British position, 1777, 21040
Aitken, Robert, map engraved by
N.C., S.C., and Ga., 1776, 23015
Alamance, battle of the, N.C.,
1771, 25120
Albany, N.Y.:1763, 12090; c.1770,
12095; 1786, 12097
to Corlear Bay, 1774, 14087
to Crown Point: 14090; 1776,
46060
to Ft. Miller, 14115
to Ft. Ticonderoga, 14105
to Kinderhook, 1779, 14145
to Oswego: 14125; 1775, 14127
to Quebec, 46050
water route from Canada to,
14060
Albany-Schenectady region, N.Y.,
1779, 12085
Albemarle County, Va., 1777, 24065
Albemarle Sound, N.C.
to Delaware Bay, 1775, 50025
Alexander, Maj. Gen. William, Lord
Stirling
route thru N.J. to Pa., 1777,
16300
Alexandria, Va.
road to Bladensburg, Md., via
Georgetown, 1781?, 22025
Alfred and *John* vs. *Milford,*
1776, 50085
Allang, Lt., of Queen's Rangers,
map by
Richmond, Va., skirmish, 1781,
24210

Allegheny frontier
and Ohio frontier, 29096
patterns of settlement on, 39037
Allen, Ethan, route to Ft. Ticonderoga, 1775, 14160
Allentown, N.J.
British position, 1778, 16385
Alliance, cruise of, 1779-80,
51051
Amboy, N.J., roads, 16140
American navy
warfare on British shipping,
1775-82, 49040
Amherst, Jeffery
Detroit plan, 1767, 34027
André, Maj. John
maps by
battles
1776: Harlem Heights, 13426
1777: Brandywine, 18075; Ft.
Mifflin siege, 18175; Germantown, 18150; Paoli, 18110;
Whitemarsh (preliminary marches and attack), 18205, 18215
1778: Monmouth, 16415; Old
Tappan massacre, 13560
British camps, 1777: Carson's
Tavern, Del., 21025; Elk River,
Md., 22030, 22035; Trudruffrin, Pa., 18100
British defenses around Philadelphia, 1777-78, 18255
British positions
1777: Aikens Tavern, Del.,
21040; Cecil Church, Md.,
22040; Charlestown, Pa.,
18125; Chestnut Hill, Pa.,
18200; Darby, Pa., 18250;
after Germantown, Pa., battle,
18155; Middlebush, N.J., 16285;
New Garden, Pa., 18060; New
Brunswick, N.J., 16295; Nor-
rington, Pa., 18130
1778: Allentown, N.J., 16385;
Black Horse, N.J., 16375;
Crosswicks, N.J., 16380;
Evesham, N.J., 16365;
Freehold, N.J., 16395
Middletown, N.J. 16405;
Mt. Holly, N.J., 16370;

from Williamsburg to Alexandria,
Va., 24355; to Conn.,
24360
from Crompond, N.Y., to Hartford,
Conn., 10155
across Conn., R.I., and Mass.,
04070
French camps
en route to Yorktown, Va., 1781
1st, Providence, R.I., 09210
Phillipsburg, N.Y., 13610, 13630
Suffern, N.Y., 13635
24th, Princeton, N.J., 16580
Trenton, N.J., 16590
27th, Philadelphia, Pa., 18295
34th, Baltimore, Md., 22045
Archer's Hope, Va., 24270
39th, Williamsburg, Va., 24275
en route from Yorktown to
Boston, Mass., 1782
20th, Baltimore, Md., 22050
44th, Farmington, Conn., 10165
45th, East Hartford, Conn., 10170
46th, Bolton, Conn., 10175
47th, Windham, Conn., 10180
48th, Canterbury, Conn., 10185
49th, Voluntown, Conn., 10190
50th, Waterman's Tavern, R.I.,
09225
51st, Providence, R.I., 09230
52nd, Providence, R.I., 09235
53rd, Wrentham, Mass., 08275
54th, Dedham, Mass., 08280
North Providence, R.I., 1780-82,
09025
French navy
principal bases, 49060
positions of French-Spanish
fleet threatening to invade
England, 1779, 51060
at Yorktown, Va., siege, 1781,
50178
See also Naval engagements, Naval
movements
French ovens near Odell House,
Westchester Co., N.Y., 13625
French Protestant churches, 1775-76,
02430
Friends meetings: 1775-76, 02435
in New England, 1782, 02495
Frog's Neck or Point (now known as
Throgs Neck), N.Y., 1781,
13220
survey of and route of British
army to, 1776, 13475

Frontier line (approximate limit
of settlement): 1770, 02290;
1774, 02295; 1775, 02300,
39005; 1784, 02305; 1787,
57060
in Old Southwest, 1784-94, 39010
Frontier posts and forts, 1750-81,
38035
Frontiers
Allegheny and Ohio, 29096
Eastern Tenn., 1760-76, 41010
Ga., northern, 1778, 27020
Ky.-Tenn., 1782, 39040
Lake Champlain-Vermont, 07072
N.Y.: northern, 14040; northwest-
ern, 14045
N.C.-Tenn., during Revolution,
38025
Northwest Va., during Revolution,
38015
Pa., 1775, 17025
southern, 1776-80, 38020
Upper Ohio-Monongahela, 29092
western, 1780-83, 38010
See also Frontier line
Fry, Joshua, and Peter Jefferson,
maps by
from Delaware Bay to Albemarle
Sound, 1775, 50025
Virginia and Maryland, with part
of Pa., N.J., and N.C., 1775,
02080

Gage, Maj. Gen Thomas
maps of Massachusetts roads
made by his agents, 1775,
08110, 08115
Galvez, Bernardo de
campaigns, 1779-82, 28135
operations from Havana against
Mobile and Pensacola, 1780-
81, 28140
Gates, Maj. Gen Horatio
camp, Rugeley's Farm, S.C.
1780, 26315
movements in N.C. and S.C., 1780,
26165
Washington Square, N.Y.,
quarters, 1782, 15190
White Plains, N.Y., headquarters,
1778, 13535
Geographer's line, O., 1785, 42035
George III
ground around statue of, New York
City, 1770, 13050

Sullivan's encampments, 1779,
14400-14410
Hudson River and vicinity
from Albany to N.Y. City: 12070;
1779, 12075
from Albany to Tappan Zee, 1779,
12065
from Saratoga to N.Y. City, 12060
from West Point to Stony Point,
1781, 15015
east side: from Fishkill to Dobbs
Ferry, 12080
west side: from King's Ferry,
N.Y., to Bound Brook, N.J.,
11020; from Newburgh to Haverstraw Bay, 15005,15007; from
West Point to Stony Point,
1780, 15010
lower Hudson Valley and N.J.,
11015
operations of *Phoenix* and *Rose* on
Hudson, 1776, 50040-50060
Hudson River Highlands, 1776-83,
15000
American defenses in, 15035-15135
positions of American and French
armies in, 1781-83, 15185
Huger, Brig. Gen. Isaac
movements in N.C. and S.C.,
1781, 26380
Hughes, Adm. Sir Edward
vs. Suffren, 1782
Sadras, 54015
Providien, 54020
Negapatam, 54025
Trincomalee, 54030
Hull, Lt. Col. William
expedition against Morrisiana,
N.Y., 1781, 13595
Hull, Mass., fortifications, 1777,
08255
Hunters' trails, 31065
Hutchins, Thomas, maps by
Bouquet's expeditions, 1763, 1764,
35075
Bushy Run, Pa., battle of, 1763,
35100
Falls of the Ohio, 1778, 30065
Indiana Company, 34030
Kaskaskia and Cahokia, 1778,
29080
Mouth of Little Miami River,
1766, 30020
Ohio country: 1766, 42010; 1778,
42015

Pontiac's War, theatre of, 1764,
35010
Wabash River, c. 1766, 30080
The West, 1778, 29040

Iles du Vent. See Lesser Antilles
Illinois Company, 1766, 34020
Illinois country (from the Missis-
sippi to the Wabash), 1778,
29065
French villages in, 29070-29090
Illinois purchase, 1773, 34070
Imports from England to Thirteen
Colonies, 1765-74, 02715
Independent Battery, N.Y., 13300
Independent churches. See Separatist and Independent churches
India
British territory in, 1763,
54002
and Ceylon, 5400
Indians
boundary lines, 1763-89, 33005-
33225
distribution of tribes: east of
the Mississippi, 1775, 32010;
in Old Northwest, 32015; in
Ohio at time of Revolution,
32025; in Southern Department,
32050; major tribes, 1787,
32080
Cherokee country: 32060; 1762,
32065; 1772, 32070, 1776,
32075
Cherokee-Creek country, 1760-81,
32055
Great Lakes Indian country, 1776,
32020
land cessions in Ga.: 1763, 27030;
1783, 27035
operations: on N.Y. frontier,
1778-81, 14355-14377; in Ohio,
38050; in the West, 1778-82,
38045
Six Nations. See Iroquois
Southern Indian District, 1764,
32040
Southern Indians, country of
1764, 32045
towns: Mohawk, 14025; Moravian in
Ohio, 32035; on Muskingum and
Scioto Rivers and Beaver Creek,
32030; on Sandusky River, 1782,
38225; Shawnee on Scioto River,
1774, 36045

PART III
PUBLICATIONS INDEXED

Listed alphabetically by author's last name and short title, the form in which they appear in Part I. Abbreviations are alphabetized as though spelled out in full. Library of Congress call numbers are given at the end of entries, except in the few instances where the publication, or the particular edition selected for indexing, has not been cataloged.

Abbatt, Crisis of Rev.
  Abbatt, William, *The Crisis of the Revolution: Being the Story of Arnold and André.* New York: William Abbatt, 1899. E236.A12
Abbatt, Pell's Point
  Abbatt, William, *The Battle of Pell's Point (or Pelham), October 18, 1776.* New York: William Abbatt, 1901. E241.P3A2
Abbatt, Youngs' House
  Abbatt, William, *The Attack on Youngs' House (or Four Corners), February 3, 1780.* Tarrytown, N.Y.: William Abbatt, 1926. F127.W5A2
Abbott, N.Y. in Am. Rev.
  Abbott, Wilbur C., *New York in the American Revolution.* New York: Charles Scribner's Sons, 1929. F128.44.A13
Abernethy, Frontier to Plantation
  Abernethy, Thomas Perkins, *From Frontier to Plantation in Tennessee: A Study in Frontier Democracy.* Chapel Hill: The University of North Carolina Press, 1932. F436.A17
Abernethy, Western Lands
  Abernethy, Thomas Perkins, *Western Lands and the American Revolution.* New York: D. Appleton-Century Company, 1937. E210.A15
Adams, Address
  Adams, Josiah, *An Address Delivered at Acton, July 21, 1835, Being the First Centennial Anniversary of the Organization of that Town.* Boston: J.T. Buckingham, 1835. AC901.W3 Vol. 28 no.4 Rare Book Room
Adams, Album of Am. Hist.
  Adams, James Truslow, ed., *Album of American History.* Vol. 1. New York: Charles Scribner's Sons, c1944. E178.A24
Adams, Atlas
  Adams, James Truslow, ed., *Atlas of American History.* New York: Charles Scribner's Sons, 1943. E179.A3
Adams, Hq. Papers
  Adams, Randolph Greenfield, *The Headquarters Papers of the British Army in North America during the War of the American Revolution: A Brief Description of Sir Henry Clinton's Papers in the William L. Clements Library.* Ann Arbor: The William L. Clements Library, 1926. E267.A24
Adams, Letter
  Adams, Josiah, *Letter to Lemuel Shattuck, Esq. . . . in Vindication of the Claims of Capt. Isaac Davis, of Acton, to His Just Share in the Honors of the Concord Fight. . . .* Boston: Damrell & Moore, 1850. E241.C7A2
Adams, Lexington
  Adams, Randolph Greenfield, and Howard H. Peckham, *Lexington to Fallen Timbers, 1775-1794.* Ann Arbor: University of Michigan Press, 1942. E172.M53 no.37 and E181.A23
Adams, Pilgrims, Indians, and Patriots
  Adams, Randolph Greenfield, *Pilgrims, Indians, and Patriots: The Pictorial History of America from the Colonial Age to the Revolution.* Boston: Little, Brown, and Company, 1928. E178.5.A22

Adams, Pilgrims, Indians, and Patriots
    Adams, Randolph Greenfield, *Pilgrims, Indians, and Patriots: The
    Pictorial History of America from the Colonial Age to the Revo-
    lution*. Boston: Little, Brown, and Company, 1928. E178.5A22
Ahlin, Maine Rubicon
    Ahlin, John Howard, *Maine Rubicon: Downeast Settlers during the
    American Revolution*. Calais, Me.: Calais Advertiser Press, 1966.
    E263.M4A37
Alden, Am. Revolution
    Alden, John Richard, *The American Revolution, 1775-1783*. New York:
    Harper & Row, 1962.
Alden, Gen. Chas. Lee
    Alden, John Richard, *General Charles Lee, Traitor or Patriot*. Baton
    Rouge: Louisiana State University Press, c1951. E207.L47A5
Alden, Hist. of Am. Rev.
    Alden, John Richard, *A History of the American Revolution*. New York:
    Alfred A. Knopf, 1969. E208.A38
Alden, Rise of Am. Republic
    Alden, John Richard, *Rise of the American Republic*. New York: Harper
    & Row, c1963. E178.1.A455
Alden, U.S. Navy
    Alden, Carroll Storrs, and Allan Westcott, *The United States Navy, a
    History*. 2nd ed., rev. Chicago: J.B. Lippincott Company, c1945.
    E182.A353 1945
Alderfer, Montgomery Co. Story
    Alderfer, Everett Gordon, *The Montgomery County Story*. Norristown,
    Pa.: The Commissioners of Montgomery County, 1951. F157.M7A6
Allen, Battles of Br. Navy
    Allen, Joseph, *Battles of the British Navy*. Vol. 1. London: A.H.
    Baily & Co., 1842. DA70.A7 1842
Allen, Naval Hist. of Am. Rev.
    Allen, Gardner Weld, *A Naval History of the American Revolution*. 2v.
    New York: Russell & Russell, Inc., 1962. E271.A42 1962
Alvord, Lord Shelburne
    Alvord, Clarence Walworth, *Lord Shelburne and the Founding of British-
    American Goodwill*. London: Oxford University Press, 1926. E249.A48
Alvord, Miss. Valley
    Alvord, Clarence Walworth, *The Mississippi Valley in British Politics:
    A Study of the Trade, Land Speculation and Experiments in Imperial-
    ism Culminating in the American Revolution*. 2v. Cleveland: The
    Arthur H. Clark Company, 1917. F352.A47
Ambler, Washington and West
    Ambler, Charles Henry, *George Washington and the West*. Chapel Hill:
    The University of North Carolina Press, 1936. E312.A62
Ambler, West Va.
    Ambler, Charles Henry, *West Virginia, the Mountain State*. New York:
    Prentice-Hall, Inc., 1940. F241.A523
Ambler, West Va. Stories and Biogs.
    Ambler, Charles Henry, *West Virginia Stories and Biographies*. New
    York: Rand McNally Company, c1942. F241.A528 1942
Am. Heritage
    American Heritage: The Magazine of History. Vols. 6-10, 12, 13. New
    York: American Heritage Publishing Co., Inc. E171.A43
Am. Heritage Atlas
    The American Heritage Pictorial Atlas of United States History. New
    York: American Heritage Publishing Co., Inc.., c1966. G1201.S1A4
    1966

Am. Heritage, Revolution
  The American Heritage Book of the Revolution.   Richard M. Ketchum, ed.
    New York: American Heritage Publishing Co., Inc., c1958. E208.A52
Am. Historical Rec.
  The American Historical Record.   Vol. 3. Philadelphia: John E. Potter
    and Company. E171.P86
Am. History
  American History, Illustrated. Vols. 1,2. Gettysburg, Pa.: Histori-
    cal Times, Incorporated. E171.A574
Am. Scenic Hist. Pres. Soc., Annual Rept.
  American Scenic and Historic Preservation Society, *Annual Report, 1900,
    1902.* Albany, N.Y. E151.A51
Anburey, Travels
  Anburey, Thomas, *Travels through the Interior Parts of America.* 2v.
    Boston: Houghton Mifflin Company, 1923. E163.A53 1923
Anburey, With Burgoyne from Quebec
  Anburey, Thomas, *With Burgoyne from Quebec: An Account of the Life at
    Quebec and of the Famous Battle at Saratoga.* Toronto: Macmillan of
    Canada, 1963. E233.A6
Anderson, Howe Bros.
  Anderson, Troyer Steele, *The Command of the Howe Brothers during the
    American Revolution.* New York: Oxford University Press, 1936.
    E267.A34
André, Journal
  André, John, *Andre's Journal: An Authentic Record of the Movements
    and Engagements of the British Army in America from June 1777 to
    November 1778 as Recorded from Day to Day by Major John André.*
    Henry Cabot Lodge, ed. 2v. Boston: The Bibliophile Society, 1903.
    E280.A5A2 Office
Angell, Diary
  Angell, Israel, *Diary of Colonel Israel Angell, Commanding the Second
    Rhode Island Regiment during the American Revolution, 1778-1781.*
    Edward Field, ed. Providence: Preston and Rounds Company, 1899.
    E263.R4A5
Antier, De Grasse
  Antier, Jean-Jacques, *L'Amiral De Grasse: Heros de l'Independance
    Americaine.* Paris: Plon, c1965. E265.A5
Armstrong, 15 Battles
  Armstrong, Orlando K., *The Fifteen Decisive Battles of the United
    States.* New York: Longmans, Green and Co., 1961. E181.A74
Army, Am. Military Hist.
  U.S. Department of the Army, *American Military History, 1607-1958.*
    (ROTC Manual No.145-20). Washington, D.C.: U.S. Government Print-
    ing Office, 1959. U133.A22 no.145-20 1959
Army War College, Kings Mt.
  Army War College, Historical Section, *Historical Statements concerning
    the Battle of Kings Mountain and the Battle of the Cowpens, South
    Carolina.* Washington, D.C.: U.S. Government Printing Office, 1928.
    (70th Congress, 1st Session, House Document No.328). E241.K5U4
Arthur, Sieges of Yorktown
  Arthur, Robert, *The Sieges of Yorktown, 1781 and 1862.* Fort Monroe,
    Va.: The Coast Artillery School, 1927. E241.Y6A7
Ashe, N. Carolina
  Ashe, Samuel A'court, *History of North Carolina.* Vol. 1. Greensboro,
    N.C.: Charles L. Van Noppen, 1908. F254.A82

Athearn, The Revolution
    Athearn, Robert G., *The Revolution*. (The American Heritage New
    Illustrated History of the United States, Vol. 3). New York: Dell
    Publishing Co., Inc., c1963. E178.A9
Atkin, Indians
    Atkin, Edmond, *Indians of the Southern Colonial Frontier: The Edmond
    Atkin Report and Plan of 1755*. Wilbur R. Jacobs, ed. Columbia,
    S.C.: University of South Carolina Press, c1954. E91.A8 1954
Atkinson, Kanawha Co.
    Atkinson, George W., *History of Kanawha County*. Charleston, W. Va.:
    The West Virginia Journal, 1876. F247.K2A8
Avery, Hist. of U.S.
    Avery, Elroy M., *A History of the United States and Its People*. Vols.
    4, 5, 6. Cleveland: The Burrows Brothers Company, 1908-1909.
    E178.A95
Azoy, Paul Revere's Horse
    Azoy, Anastasio Carlos Mariano, *Paul Revere's Horse*. New York:
    Doubleday & Company, Inc., 1949. E178.A98
Bailey, Brooklyn
    Bailey, J.T., *An Historical Sketch of the City of Brooklyn* . . . .
    Brooklyn, N.Y., 1840. F129.B7B1
Bailey, Fighting Sailor
    Bailey, Ralph Edgar, *Fighting Sailor: The Story of Nathaniel Fanning*.
    New York: William Morrow and Company, 1966. E207.F25B3
Bakeless, Background to Glory
    Bakeless, John Edwin, *Background to Glory: The Life of George Rogers
    Clark*. Philadelphia: J.P. Lippincott Company, 1957. E207.C5B15
Balch, French in Am.
    Balch, Thomas, *The French in America during the War of Independence
    of the United States*. Vol. 1. Philadelphia: Porter & Coates,
    1891. E265.B17
Baldwin, Adult's History
    Baldwin, Leland Dewitt, *The Adult's American History: Pragmatic
    Democracy in Action*. Rindge, N.H.: R.R. Smith, 1955. E178.B16
Barbé-Marbois, Complot d'Arnold
    Barbé-Marbois, Francois, Marquis de, *Complot d'Arnold et de Sir Henry
    Clinton contre les Etats-Unis d'Amerique et contre le General
    Washington*. Paris: P. Didot, 1816. E236.B23
Barck, Colonial Am.
    Barck, Oscar Theodore, Jr., and Hugh Talmage Lefler, *Colonial America*,
    New York: The Macmillan Company, 1958. E118.B26
Barck, Colonial Am., 2d ed.
    Barck, Oscar Theodore, Jr., and Hugh Talmage Lefler, *Colonial America*.
    2nd edition. New York: The Macmillan Company, c1968. E188.B26 1968
Barck, N.Y. City
    Barck, Oscar Theodore, Jr., *New York City during the War for Indepen-
    dence, with Special Reference to the Period of British Occupation*.
    New York: Columbia University Press, 1931. F128.44.B23
Barrs, East Fla.
    Barrs, Burton, *East Florida in the American Revolution*. Jacksonville,
    Fla.: Cooper Press, 1949. F314.B28 1949
Bass, Gamecock
    Bass, Robert D., *Gamecock: The Life and Campaigns of General Thomas
    Sumter*. New York: Holt, Rinehart and Winston, c1961. E207.S95B3

Bass, Green Dragoon

  Bass, Robert D., *The Green Dragoon: The Lives of Banastre Tarleton and Mary Robinson*. New York: Henry Holt and Company, c1957. DA506.T3B3

Bass, Swamp Fox

  Bass, Robert D., *Swamp Fox: The Life and Campaigns of General Francis Marion*. New York: Henry Holt and Comapny, c1959. E207.M3B3

Batchelder, Bits

  Batchelder, Samuel Francis, *Bits of Cambridge History*. Cambridge: Harvard University Press, 1930. F74.C1B29

Batchelder, Burgoyne

  Batchelder, Samuel Francis, *Burgoyne and His Officers in Cambridge, 1777-1778*. Cambridge, Mass., 1926. E281.B32

Baurmeister, Letters

  Baurmeister, Carl Leopold, *Letters from Major Baurmeister to Colonel von Jungkenn Written during the Philadelphia Campaign, 1777-1778*. Bernhard A. Uhlendorf and Edna Vosper, eds. Philadelphia: The Historical Society of Pennsylvania, 1937. E233.B28

Baurmeister, Revolution

  Baurmeister, Carl Leopold, *Revolution in America: Confidential Letters and Journals 1776-1784 of Adjutant General Major Baurmeister of the Hessian Forces*, trans. by Bernhard A. Uhlendorf. New Brunswick, N.J. Rutgers University Press, 1957. E268.B4

Bean, Montgomery Co.

  Bean, Theodore Weber, ed., *History of Montgomery County, Pennsylvania*. Philadelphia: Everts & Peck, 1884. F157.M7B3

Bean, Washington

  Bean, Theodore Weber, *Washington at Valley Forge One Hundred Years Ago*. Norristown, Pa.: C.P. Shreiner, 1876. E234.B36 Toner Coll.

Beauchamp, N.Y. Iroquois

  Beauchamp, William Martin, *A History of the Iroquois, now commonly Called the Six Nations*. (New York State Museum, Bulletin 78). Albany: New York State Education Department, 1905. Q11.N82

Becker, Beginnings of Am. People

  Becker, Carl Lotus, *Beginnings of the American People*. Ithaca, N.Y.: Cornell University Press, 1960. E178.B4 1960

Beebe, Journal

  Beebe, Lewis, *Journal of Lewis Beebe, a Physician on the Campaign against Canada, 1776*. Frederic R. Kirkland, ed. Philadelphia, 1935. E275.B43

Belcher, First Am. Civil War

  Belcher, Henry, *The First American Civil War, First Period, 1775-1778*. Vol.2. London: Macmillan and Co., Limited, 1911. E208.B42

Bell, N.H. at Bunker Hill

  Bell, Charles Henry, *New Hampshire at Bunker Hill*. Cambridge: John Wilson and Son, 1891. E241.B9B4

Bemis, Diplomacy of Am. Rev.

  Bemis, Samuel Flagg, *The Diplomacy of the American Revolution*. New York: D. Appleton-Century Company, c1935. E249.B44 and E183.7.B48 vol. 1

Bemis, Hussey-Cumberland Mission

  Bemis, Samuel Flagg, *The Hussey-Cumberland Mission and American Independence: An Essay in the Diplomacy of the American Revolution*. Gloucester, Mass.: Peter Smith, 1968. E249.B45 1968

Berks Co. Hist. Soc., Trans.
  Berks County Historical Society, *Transactions*. Vol. 3. Reading, Pa.
  F157.B3H5
Bill, N.J. and Rev. War
  Bill, Alfred Hoyt, *New Jersey and the Revolutionary War*. (The New
  Jersey Historical Series, Vol. 11). Princeton: D. Van Nostrand
  Company, Inc., 1964. E263.N5B5
Bill, Princeton
  Bill, Alfred Hoyt, *The Campaign of Princeton, 1776-1777*. Princeton,
  N.J.: Princeton University Press, 1948. E232.B5
Bill, Valley Forge
  Bill, Alfred Hoyt, *Valley Forge: The Making of an Army*. New York:
  Harper & Brothers, c1952. E234.B5
Billias, Gen. John Glover
  Billias, George Athan, *General John Glover and His Marblehead
  Mariners*. New York: Henry Holt and Company, c1960. E207.G56B5
Billias, Washington's Opponents
  Billias, George Athan, ed., *George Washington's Opponents: British
  Generals and Admirals in the American Revolution*. New York:
  William Morrow and Company, Inc., 1969. E267.B56
Billington, W. Expansion
  Billington, Ray Allen, *Westward Expansion, A History of the American
  Frontier*. 2nd edition. New York: The Macmillan Company, c1960.
  E179.5B63 1960
Bird, March to Saratoga
  Bird, Harrison, *March to Saratoga: General Burgoyne and the American
  Campaign, 1777*. New York: Oxford University Press, 1963. E233.B68
Bird, Navies in the Mts.
  Bird, Harrison, *Navies in the Mountains: The Battles on the Waters
  of Lake Champlain and Lake George, 1609-1814*. New York: Oxford
  University Press, 1962. E182.B5
Bland, Yorktown Sesquicentennial
  Bland, Schuyler Otis, *The Yorktown Sesquicentennial: Proceedings of
  the United States Yorktown Sesquicentennial Commission*. Washing-
  ton: U.S. Government Printing Office, 1932. E241.Y6U65
Bliven, Battle for Manhattan
  Bliven, Bruce, *Battle for Manhattan*. New York: Henry Holt and Company,
  c1956. E232.B58
Blue Licks Commission, Monument
  Kentucky, Blue Licks Battle-field Monument Commission, *Blue Licks
  Battle-field Monument*. *Proceedings at the Unveiling and Dedication
  of the Monument on the Site of the Battle of Blue Licks, and Exer-
  cises in Commemoration of the Battle*. At Blue Licks, Ky., Sunday,
  August 19, 1928. Louisville: Westerfield-Bonte Co., 1928.
  E241.B65K32
Boatner, Enc. of Am. Rev.
  Boatner, Mark Mayo, III, *Encyclopedia of the American Revolution*.
  New York: David McKay Company, Inc., c1966. E208.B68
Bodley, First Great West
  Bodley, Temple, *Our First Great West, in Revolutionary War, Diplomacy
  and Politics*. (Filson Club Publications No. 36). Louisville: John
  P. Morton & Co., Incorporated, 1938. F483.B64 and F446.48 no.36
Bolton, Colonization
  Bolton, Herbert Eugene, and Thomas Maitland Marshall, *The Colonization
  of North America, 1492-1783*. New York: The Macmillan Company, 1932.
  E188.B69 1932

Bolton, Washington Hts.
   Bolton, Reginald Pelham, *Washington Heights, Manhattan: Its Eventful
      Past*. New York: Dyckman Institute, 1924. F128.68.W2B6
Bomberger, Bushy Run
   Bomberger, Christian Martin Hess, *The Battle of Bushy Run*. Jeannette,
      Pa.: Jeannette Publishing Company, 1928. E83.76.B69
Bond, Foundations of Ohio
   Bond, Beverly W., Jr., *The Foundations of Ohio*. *(The History of the
      State of Ohio*. Vol. 1)*. Columbus: Ohio State Archaeological and
      Historical Society, 1941. F491.W78
Bonsal, French Were Here
   Bonsal, Stephen, *When the French Were Here: A Narrative of the Sojourn
      of the French Forces in America, and Their Contribution to the
      Yorktown Campaign*. Garden City, N.Y.: Doubleday, Doran and Company,
      Inc., 1945. E265.B7
Boston, Evacuation
   Boston, Mass., *Celebration of the Centennial Anniversary of the Evacu-
      ation of Boston by the British Army, March 17th, 1776*. Boston: A.
      Williams & Company, 1876. E231.B72
Boston, Memorial of Am. Patriots
   Boston, Mass., *A Memorial of the American Patriots Who Fell at the
      Battle of Bunker Hill, June 17, 1775*. 4th ed. Boston: Printed by
      Order of the City Council, 1896. E241.B9B75
Botta, War of Ind.
   Botta, Charles, *History of the War of the Independence of the United
      States of America*. Trans. by George Alexander Otis. 10th ed. 2v.
      Cooperstown, N.Y.: H. & E. Phinney, 1848. E208.B755
Bouquet, Orderly Book
   Bouquet, Henry, *The Orderly Book of Colonel Henry Bouquet's Expedi-
      tion against the Ohio Indians, 1764*. Edward G. Williams, ed.
      Pittsburgh, Pa.: Mayer Press, 1960. E83.76.G7
Bourinot, Canada under Br. Rule
   Bourinot, Sir John George, *Canada under British Rule, 1760-1905*.
      Cambridge, Eng.: Cambridge University Press, 1909. F1026.B765
Boyd, Wayne
   Boyd, Thomas, *Mad Anthony Wayne*. New York: Charles Scribner's Sons,
      1929. E207.W35B78
Boynton, Guide to W.Point
   Boynton, Edward Carlisle, *Guide to West Point and the U.S. Military
      Academy*. New York: D. Van Nostrand, 1867. F129.W7B65
Boynton, West Point
   Boynton, Edward Carlisle, *History of West Point, and Its Military
      Importance during the American Revolution*. New York: D. Van
      Nostrand, 1863. F129.W7B7
Brandow, Saratoga
   Brandow, John Henry, *The Story of Old Saratoga: The Burgoyne Campaign,
      to Which Is Added New York's Share in the Revolution*. 2d ed.
      Albany: The Brandow Printing Company, 1919. F129.S57B7 1919
Brandywine, 150th Anniversary
   Brandywine Memorial Association, *150th Anniversary of the Battle of
      the Brandywine*. 1927. No pagination. E241.B8B7
Brebner, Neutral Yankees
   Brebner, John Bartlet, *The Neutral Yankees of Nova Scotia: A Marginal
      Colony during the Revolutionary Years*. New York: Columbia Univer-
      sity Press, 1937. F1038.B815

Callahan, Daniel Morgan
    Callahan, North, *Daniel Morgan, Ranger of the Revolution.* New York:
      Holt, Rinehart and Winston, c1961. E207.M8C3
Callahan, Henry Knox
    Callahan, North, *Henry Knox, General Washington's General.* New
      York: Rinehart & Company, Inc., c1958. E207.K74C18
Callahan, Hist. of West Va.
    Callahan, James Morton, *History of West Virginia, Old and New.*
      Vol. 1. Chicago: The American Historical Society, Inc., 1923.
      F241.C15
Callahan, Making of Morgantown
    Callahan, James Morton, *History of the Making of Morgantown, West
      Virginia.* Morgantown: West Virginia University Studies in History,
      1926. F249.M8C2
Calver, Hist. with Pick and Shovel
    Calver, William Louis, and Reginald Pelham Bolton, *History Written
      with Pick and Shovel: Military Buttons, Belt-Plates, Badges, and
      Other Relics Excavated from Colonial, Revolutionary, and War of
      1812 Camp Sites by the Field Exploration Committee of the New-York
      Historical Society.* New York: New York Historical Society, 1950.
      F121.C3
Campbell, Annals of Tryon Co.
    Campbell, William W., *Annals of Tryon County, or, The Border Warfare
      of New York, during the Revolution.* New York: Dodd, Mead and
      Company, 1924. E263.N6C28
Campbell, Gen. Wm. Hull
    Campbell, Maria Hull, *Revolutionary Services and Civil Life of General
      William Hull.* New York: D. Appleton & Co., 1848. E353.1.H9C18
      Toner Coll.
Canby, Brandywine
    Canby, Henry Seidel, *The Brandywine.* New York: Farrar & Rinehart,
      Incorporated, c1941. F157.C4C23
Carrington, Battles
    Carrington, Henry B., *Battles of the American Revolution, 1775-1781.*
      5th edition. New York: A.S. Barnes & Company, c1888. E230.C322
Carrington, Washington
    Carrington, Henry B., *Washington the Soldier.* New York: Charles
      Scribner's Sons, 1899. E312.25C32
Carroll, Hist. Coll. of S.C.
    Carroll, Bartholomew Rivers, *Historical Collections of South Carolina.*
      Vol. 1. New York: Harper & Brothers, 1836. F272.C31
Carter, Genuine Detail
    Carter, William, *A Genuine Detail of the Several Engagements, Posi-
      tions, and Movement of the Royal and American Armies. . . .* [London,
      1784?]. E275.C31 Office
Caruso, Appalachian Frontier
    Caruso, John Anthony, *The Appalachian Frontier: America's First Surge
      Westward.* Indianapolis: The Bobbs-Merrill Company, Inc., c1959.
      F396.C32
Caruso, Gt. Lakes Frontier
    Caruso, John Anthony, *Great Lakes Frontier.* Indianapolis: The Bobbs-
      Merrill Company, Inc., c1961. F479.C3
Caruthers, Rev. Incidents
    Caruthers, Rev. Eli Washington, *Interesting Revolutionary Incidents:
      and Sketches of Character, Chiefly in the "Old North State."* 2nd
      series. Philadelphia: Hayes & Zell, 1856. E263.N8C33

Case, Tryon's Raid
  Case, James R., comp., *An Account of Tryon's Raid on Danbury in April,
    1777, also the Battle of Ridgefield and the Career of Gen. David
    Wooster*. Danbury, Conn.: The Danbury Printing Co., 1927. E241.D2C3
Caughey, Hist. of U.S.
  Caughey, John W., and Ernest R. May, *A History of the United States*.
    Chicago: Rand McNally & Company, c1964. E178.C35
Cent. Hist. of West Point
  *The Centennial History of the United States Military Academy at West
    Point, New York, 1802-1902*. Vol. 1. Washington: Government Print-
    ing Office, 1904. U410.L1A2
Chalmers, West to Setting Sun
  Chalmers, Harvey, *West to the Setting Sun*. Toronto: The Macmillan
    Company of Canada, Limited, 1943. PZ3.C3488 We
Channing, Hist. of U.S.
  Channing, Edward, *A History of the United States*. Vol. 3. New York:
    The Macmillan Company, 1930. E178.C442
Charleston, Centennial
  Charleston, S.C., *The Centennial of Incorporation, 1883*. Charleston:
    The News and Courier Book Presses, 1884. F279.C4C32
Charleston, Year Book
  Charleston, S.C., *Year Book*, 1880, 1882, 1883. F279.C4C4
Chastellux, Travels
  Chastellux, Francois Jean, Marquis de, *Travels in North America in the
    Years 1780, 1781, and 1782*. Howard C. Rice, Jr., trans. 2v. Chapel
    Hill: University of North Carolina Press, c1963. E163.C59 1963
Chatterton, Battles by Sea
  Chatterton, Edward Keble, *Battles by Sea*. London: Sidwick and Jackson,
    Ltd., 1925. D27.C5
Chester Co. Hist. Soc., Lafayette
  Chester County Historical Society, *Lafayette at Brandywine*. West
    Chester, Pa., 1896. E241.B8C5
Chidsey, Frontier Village
  Chidsey, Andrew Dwight, *A Frontier Village, Pre-Revolutionary Easton*.
    (The Northampton County Historical and Genealogical Society, Publi-
    cations, Vol. 3). Easton, Pa., 1940. F157.N7N85 vol. 3
Chidsey, Siege of Boston
  Chidsey, Donald Barr, *The Siege of Boston*. New York: Crown Publishers,
    Inc., 1966. E231.C62
Chidsey, Valley Forge
  Chidsey, Donald Barr, *Valley Forge*. New York: Crown Publishers, Inc.,
    c1959. E234.C48
Chidsey, Yorktown
  Chidsey, Donald Barr, *Victory at Yorktown*. New York: Crown Publishers,
    Inc., c1962. E237.C47
Chitwood, Colonial America
  Chitwood, Oliver Perry, *A History of Colonial America*. 3rd edition.
    New York: Harper & Brothers, c1961. E188.C53 1961
Chron. Am.
  Chronicles of America. Allen Johnson, ed. Vols. 12, 18, 19. New
    Haven: Yale University Press, 1919-1921. E173.C555
Churchill, English-Speaking Peoples
  Churchill, Winston S., *A History of the English-Speaking Peoples*.
    Vol. 3. New York: Dodd, Mead & Company, 1957. DA16.C47

Clark, Capt. Dauntless
    Clark, William Bell, *Captain Dauntless: The Story of Nicholas Biddle
    of the Continental Navy.* Baton Rouge: Louisiana State University
    Press, 1949. E207.B48C6
Clark, Exploring Kentucky
    Clark, Thomas Dionysius, and Lee Kirkpatrick, *Exploring Kentucky.*
    Revised edition. New York: American Book Company, c1949.
    F451.C62 1949
Clark, Frontier America
    Clark, Thomas D., *Frontier America: The Story of the Westward Movement.*
    New York: Charles Scribner's Sons, 1959. E179.5.C48
Clark, Privateers
    Clark, William Bell, *Ben Franklin's Privateers, a Naval Epic of the
    American Revolution.* Baton Rouge: Louisiana State University Press,
    c1956. E302.6.F8C55
Clarke, Am. Revolution
    Clarke, Clorinda, *The American Revolution, 1775-83: A British View.*
    New York: McGraw-Hill Book Company, 1967. E208.C55 1967
Cleland, Washington in Ohio Valley
    Cleland, Hugh, *George Washington in the Ohio Valley.* Pittsburgh:
    University of Pittsburgh Press, 1955. E312.C62
Clements, Jl. of Maj. Robt. Rogers
    Clements, William L., *Journal of Maj. Robert Rogers.* Worcester,
    Mass.: The Davis Press, 1918. F572.M16R7
Clements Library, Old Fort Michilimackinac
    Michigan University. William L. Clements Library. *Old Fort
    Michilimackinac.* Ann Arbor: University of Michigan Press, 1938.
    F572.M16M7
Clinton, Am. Rebellion
    Clinton, Sir Henry, *The American Rebellion: Sir Henry Clinton's
    Narrative of His Campaigns, 1775-1782.* William B. Willcox, ed.
    New Haven: Yale University Press, 1954. E267.C63
Clinton, Public Papers
    Clinton, George, *Public Papers of George Clinton, First Governor of
    New York.* Vols. 1, 2, 5, 6, 7. Albany: Oliver A. Quayle, 1899-1904.
    E263.N6N56
Clos, Yorktown
    Clos, Captain Jean Henri, *The Glory of Yorktown.* Yorktown, Va.:
    Yorktown Historical Society, 1924. E241.Y6C6
Closen, Journal
    Closen, Ludwig, Baron von, *The Revolutionary Journal of Baron Ludwig
    von Closen, 1780-1783.* Trans. and ed. by Evelyn M. Acomb. Chapel
    Hill: University of North Carolina Press, c1958. E265.C613
Clowes, Royal Navy
    Clowes, William Laird, *The Royal Navy: A History from the Earliest
    Times to the Present.* Vol. 3. Boston: Little, Brown and Company,
    1898. DA70.C68
Coast Artillery Jl.
    The Coast Artillery Journal. Vols. 72, 81. Washington, D.C.: United
    States Coast Artillery Association. UF1.J86
Coburn, Battle of Apr. 19, 1775
    Coburn, Frank Warren, *The Battle of April 19, 1775 in Lexington, Con-
    cord, Lincoln, Arlington, Cambridge, Somerville and Charlestown,
    Massachusetts.* 2d ed. Lexington: Lexington Historical Society,
    1922. E231.C656

Coburn, Bennington
  Coburn, Frank Warren, *A History of the Battle of Bennington, Vermont*.
    2d ed. Bennington: The Livingston Press, 1912.   E241.B4C62
Cochran, N.Y. in Confed.
  Cochran, Thomas Childs, *New York in the Confederation, An Economic
    Study*. Philadelphia: University of Pennsylvania, 1932.   F123.C66
Codman, Arnold's Exped.
  Codman, John, 2d, *Arnold's Expedition to Quebec*. New York: The
    Macmillan Company, 1901.   E231.C67
Coffin, Boys of '76
  Coffin, Charles Carleton, *The Boys of '76: A History of the Battles
    of the Revolution*. New York: Harper & Brothers, 1877.   E230.C68
    1877
Coggins, Boys in Revolution
  Coggins, Jack, *Boys in the Revolution*. Harrisburg, Pa.: Stackpole
    Books, c1967.   E206.C675
Coggins, Ships and Seamen
  Coggins, Jack, *Ships and Seamen of the American Revolution*. Harris-
    burg, Pa.: Stackpole Books, c1969.   E271.C63
Cole, Pict. Hist. of Pensacola
  Cole, John William, *Pictorial History of Pensacola, City of Five
    Flags*. Pensacola: Fiesta of the Five Flags Association, c1952
    F319.P4C6
Coleman, Am. Rev. in Ga.
  Colemen, Kenneth, *The American Revolution in Georgia, 1763-1789*.
    Athens, Ga.: University of Georgia Press., 1958.   F290.C55
Coles, Washington Hq.
  Coles, Elizabeth G.H., *Historical Sketch of the Washington Head-
    quarters*. White Plains, N.Y.: White Plains Chapter, Daughters of
    the American Revolution, c1923.   F129.W72C6
Collier's Enc.
  Collier's Encyclopedia. Vols. 2, 14. New York: Crowell, Collier
    and Macmillan, Inc., 1967.   AE5.C683 1967
Collins, Hist. of Vermont
  Collins, Edward Day, *A History of Vermont*. Revised edition. Boston:
    Ginn and Company, c1916.   F49.C715
Commager, Spirit of '76
  Commager, Henry Steele, and Richard B. Morris, *The Spirit of 'Seventy-
    Six: The Story of the American Revolution as Told by Participants*.
    2v. Indianapolis: The Bobbs-Merrill Company, Inc., c1958.   E203.C69
Comstock, Enc. of Am. Antiques
  Comstock, Helen, ed., *The Concise Encyclopedia of American Antiques*.
    Vol. 2. New York: Hawthorn Books, Inc., 1958.   NK805.C65
Cooch, Cooch's Bridge
  Cooch, Edward Webb, *The Battle of Cooch's Bridge, Delaware, September
    3, 1777*. Cooch's Bridge, 1940.   E241.C73C7
Cook, Golden Bk. of Am. Rev.
  Cook, Fred J., *The Golden Book of the American Revolution*. New York:
    Golden Press, c1959.   E208.C7
Cookinham, Hist. of Oneida Co.
  Cookinham, Henry J., *History of Oneida County, New York, from 1700
    to the Present Time*. Vol. 1. Chicago: The S.J. Clarke Publishing
    Company, 1912.   F127.05C77
Coolidge, Brochure
  Coolidge, George A., *Brochure of Bunker Hill*. Boston: James R.
    Osgood Company, 1875.   E241.B9C7

Cottrell, Trenton Battle Mon.
  Cottrell, Alden Tucker, *The Trenton Battle Monument and Washington's Campaign, December 26, 1776, to January 3, 1777.* 3rd edition. Trenton: New Jersey Bureau of Forestry, Parks, and Historic Sites, 1951. E241.T7N48 1951
Cowpens Centennial Committee, Battle Monument
  The Cowpens Centennial Committee, *Proceedings at the Unveiling of the Battle Monument in Spartanburg, S.C.* Charleston, S.C., 1896. E241.C9C9
Coxe, Sterling Furnace
  Coxe, Macgrane, *The Sterling Furnace and the West Point Chain.* New York: Privately printed, 1906. E263.N6C8
Crane, West Point
  Crane, John, and James F. Kieley, *West Point, "The Key to America."* New York: McGraw-Hill Book Company, Inc., c1947. U410.L1C7
Craven, U.S.
  Craven, Avery, and Walter Johnson, *The United States, Experiment in Democracy.* Boston: Ginn and Company, c1957. E178.C84 1957
Crist, Capt. Wm. Hendricks
  Crist, Robert Grant, *Capt. William Hendricks and the March to Quebec (1775).* Carlisle, Pa.: The Hamilton Library and Historical Association of Cumberland County, 1960. E231.C7
Crittenden, Commerce of N.C.
  Crittenden, Charles Christopher, *The Commerce of North Carolina, 1763-1789.* New Haven: Yale University Press, 1936. HF3161.N8C7
Crockett, Vermont
  Crockett, Walter Hill, *Vermont, The Green Mountain State.* Vol. 2. New York: The Century History Company, Inc., 1921. F49.C9
Crofut, Guide
  Crofut, Florence S. Marcy, *Guide to the History and the Historic Sites of Connecticut.* Vol. 1. New Haven: Yale University Press, 1937. F94.C88
Crowl, Maryland
  Crowl, Philip A., *Maryland during and after the Revolution, A Political and Economic Study.* Baltimore: The Johns Hopkins Press, 1943. F185.C7
Cugnac, Yorktown
  Cugnac, Gaspar Jean Marie René, Comte de, *Yorktown (1781), Trois Mois d'Opérations Combinées sur Terre et sur Mer dans une Guerre de Coalition.* Nancy: Imprimerie Berger-Levrault, 1932. E241.Y6C84
Cullum, Fortification Defenses
  Cullum, George Washington, *Historical Sketch of the Fortification Defenses of Narraganset Bay, Since the Founding, in 1638, of the Colony of Rhode Island.* Washington, D.C., 1884. UG412.N3C8
Cumming, Southeast
  Cumming, William P., *The Southeast in Early Maps.* Princeton, N.J.: Princeton University Press, 1958. GA405.C8
Cunliffe, Washington
  Cunliffe, Marcus, *George Washington and the Making of a Nation.* New York: American Heritage Publishing Co., 1966. E312.66.C8
Cunningham, N.J. Sampler
  Cunningham, John T., *The New Jersey Sampler: Historic Tales of Old New Jersey.* Upper Montclair: The New Jersey Almanac, Inc., c1964. F134.C86

Current, Am. Hist.
  Current, Richard N., T. Harry Williams, and Frank Freidel, *American History: A Survey.* 2nd edition. New York: Alfred A. Knopf, 1966. E178.1.C93 1966
Cutter, Israel Putnam
  Cutter, William, *The Life of Israel Putnam, Major-General in the Army of the Revolution.* New York: Derby & Jackson, 1861. E207.P9C9
Darlington, Col. Bouquet
  Darlington, Mary Carson, ed., *History of Colonel Henry Bouquet and the Western Frontiers of Pennsylvania, 1747-1764.* Pittsburgh, c1920. E83.76.B95
Darlington, Fort Pitt
  Darlington, Mary Carson, ed., *Fort Pitt and Letters from the Frontier.* Pittsburgh: J.R. Weldin & Co., 1892. F159.P6D2
Daves, Md. and N.C.
  Daves, Edward Graham, *Maryland and North Carolina in the Campaign of 1780-1781.* (Maryland Historical Society, Fund-Publication No. 33). Baltimore, 1893. F176.M37 no.33
David, R.I. Chaplain
  David, Ebenezer, *A Rhode Island Chaplain in the Revolution: Letters of Ebenezer David to Nicholas Brown, 1775-1778.* Jeanette D. Black and William Greene Roelker, eds. Providence: The Rhode Island Society of the Cincinnati, 1949. E275.D25
Davis, Cowpens
  Davis, Burke, *The Cowpens-Guilford Courthouse Campaign.* Philadelphia: J.B. Lippincott Company, c1962. E237.D3
Davis, Ragged Ones
  Davis, Burke, *The Ragged Ones.* New York: Rinehart & Co., Inc., c1951. PZ3.D2908Rag
Davis, Yorktown
  Davis, Burke, *Yorktown: The Winning of American Independence.* New York: Harper & Row, c1969. E241.Y6D3
Dawson, Stony Point
  Dawson, Henry Barton, *The Assault on Stony Point, by General Anthony Wayne, July 16, 1779.* Morrisania, N.Y., 1863. E241.S8D2
Dawson, Westchester Co.
  Dawson, Henry Barton, *Westchester-County, New York, during the American Revolution.* Morrisania, N.Y., 1886. E263.N6D2
Dean, Fighting Dan
  Dean, Sidney Walter, *Fighting Dan of the Long Rifles.* Philadelphia: Macrae-Smith Company, c1942. E207.M8D4
Dean, Knight of Rev.
  Dean, Sidney Walter, *Knight of the Revolution.* Philadelphia: Macrae-Smith Company, c1941. E207.M3D4
Dearborn, Bunker Hill
  Dearborn, Henry, *An Account of the Battle of Bunker Hill.* Philadelphia: Harrison Hall, 1818. E241.B9D2
Dearborn, Journals
  Dearborn, Henry, *Revolutionary War Journals of Henry Dearborn, 1775-1783.* Lloyd A. Brown and Howard H. Peckham, eds. Chicago: The Caxton Club, 1939. E275.D283
Decker, Arnold
  Decker, Malcolm, *Benedict Arnold, Son of the Havens.* Tarrytown, N.Y.: William Abbatt, 1932. E278.A7D3

Decker, Brink of Rev.
  Decker, Malcolm, *Brink of Revolution: New York in Crisis, 1765-1776*
    New York: Argosy-Antiquarian Ltd., c1964. F128.4.D27
DeConde, Foreign Policy
  DeConde, Alexander, *A History of American Foreign Policy*. New York:
    Charles Scribner's Sons, c1963. E183.7.D4
Dedham Hist. Reg.
  Dedham Historical Register. Vol. 12. Dedham, Mass.: Dedham Histori-
    cal Society. F74.D3D8
De Fonblanque, Burgoyne
  De Fonblanque, Edward Barrington, *Political and Military Episodes in
    the Latter Half of the Eighteenth Century, Derived from the Life
    and Correspondence of the Right Hon. John Burgoyne, General, States-
    man, Dramatist*. London: Macmillan and Co., 1876. DA67.1.B8D5
De Grasse, Mémoire
  Grasse-Tilly, Francois Joseph Paul, Marquis de, *Mémoire du Comte de
    Grasse, sur le Combat Naval du 12 Avril 1782*. Paris?, 1782.
    E271.G762 Office
De Gruyter, Kanawha Spectator
  De Gruyter, Julius Allan, *The Kanawha Spectator*. Vol. 1. Charleston,
    W. Va.: Jarrett Printing Company, c1953. F247.K2D4
DeKoven, John Paul Jones
  DeKoven, Anna Farwell, *The Life and Letters of John Paul Jones*. Vol.
    1. New York: Charles Scribner's Sons, 1913. E207.J7D29
DeLancey, Capture of Mt. Washington
  DeLancy, Edward Floyd, *The Capture of Mt. Washington, November 16th,
    1776, the Result of Treason*. New York, 1877. E241.W3D3
Delaware Hist.
  Delaware History. Vol. 4. Wilmington: Historical Society of Dela-
    ware. F161.D37
De Puy, Ethan Allen
  De Puy, Henry Walter, *Ethan Allen and the Green-Mountain Heroes of
    '76*. Buffalo: Phinney & Co., 1859. F52.D45
De Vorsey, Indian Boundary
  De Vorsey, Louis, Jr., *The Indian Boundary in the Southern Colonies,
    1763-1775*. Chapel Hill: The University of North Carolina Press,
    c1966. F212.D4
Dinman, Capture of Gen. Prescott
  Dinman, Jeremiah Lewis, *The Capture of General Richard Prescott by
    Lt. Col. William Barton*. (Rhode Island Historical Tracts No. 1).
    Providence: Sidney S. Rider, 1877. F76.R52
Downes, Council Fires
  Downes, Randolph Chandler, *Council Fires on the Upper Ohio: A Nar-
    rative of Indian Affairs in the Upper Ohio Valley until 1795*.
    Pittsburgh: The University of Pittsburgh Press, 1940. F517.D69
Doyle, Von Steuben
  Doyle, Joseph Beatty, *Frederick William Von Steuben and the American
    Revolution*. Steubenville, O.: The H.C. Cook Co., 1913. E207.S8D75
Drake, Burgoyne's Invasion
  Drake, Samuel Adams, *Burgoyne's Invasion of 1777*. Boston: Lee and
    Shepard, 1889. E233.D76
Drake, Campaign of Trenton
  Drake, Samuel Adams, *The Campaign of Trenton, 1776-77*. Boston: Lee
    and Shepard, 1895. E232.D76

Drake, Historic Fields
  Drake, Samuel Adams, *Historic Fields and Mansions of Middlesex.*
    Boston: James R. Osgood and Company, 1874. F72.M797
Drake, Middlesex Co.
  Drake, Samuel Adams, *History of Middlesex County, Massachusetts.*
    Vol. 2. Boston: Estes and Lauriat, 1880. F72.M7D6
Drake, Ohio Valley States
  Drake, Samuel Adams, *The Making of the Ohio Valley States, 1660-1837.*
    New York: Charles Scribner's Sons, 1894. F516.D76
Drake, Tea Leaves
  Drake, Francis Samuel, *Tea Leaves: Being a Collection of Letters
    and Documents Relating to the Shipment of Tea to the American
    Colonies in the Year 1773, by the East India Company.* Boston:
    A.O. Crane, 1884. E215.7.T25
Draper, King's Mt.
  Draper, Lyman C., *King's Mountain and Its Heroes: History of the
    Battle of King's Mountain, October 7th, 1780, and the Events Which
    Led to It.* Cincinnati: Peter G. Thomson, 1881. E241.K5D7
    (1929 edition E241.K5D73)
Drayton, Memoirs
  Drayton, John, *Memoirs of the American Revolution, from Its Commence-
    ment to the Year 1776, inclusive; as Related to the State of South-
    Carolina: and occasionally Referring to the States of North-Carolina
    and Georgia.* 2v. Charleston: A.E. Miller, 1821. E263.S7D7 Office
Duer, Sterling
  Duer, William Alexander, *The Life of William Alexander, Earl of Ster-
    ling.* (New Jersey Historical Society, Collections, Vol.2). New
    York: Wiley & Putnam, 1847. F131.N62 vol.2
DuHamel, Surrender of British Forces
  DuHamel, William J.C., *A History of the Surrender of the British
    Forces to the Americans and French, at Yorktown, Va.* [Washington,
    D.C.,1881]. E241.Y6D86
Duncan, Medical Men
  Duncan, Louis Caspar, *Medical Men in the American Revolution, 1775-
    1783.* Carlisle Barracks, Pa.: Medical Field Service School, 1931.
    UH201.U6 no.25 or E206.D93
Dunnack, Maine Forts
  Dunnack, Henry E., *Maine Forts.* Augusta, Me.: Charles E. Nash & Sons,
    1924. F19.M25
Dupuy, Brave Men and Great Captains
  Dupuy, Richard Ernest, and Trevor N. Dupuy, *Brave Men and Great
    Captains.* New York: Harper & Brothers, c1959. E181.D77
Dupuy, Compact Hist.
  Dupuy, Richard Ernest, and Trevor N. Dupuy, *The Compact History of the
    Revolutionary War.* New York: Hawthorn Books, Inc., 1963. E230.D8
Dupuy, Enc. of Mil. History
  Dupuy, Richard Ernest, and Trevor N. Dupuy, *The Encyclopedia of
    Military History, from 3500 B.C. to the Present.* New York: Harper &
    Row. c1970. D25.A2D8
Dupuy, Mil. Heritage of Am.
  Dupuy, Richard Ernest, and Trevor N. Dupuy, *Military Heritage of
    America.* New York: McGraw-Hill Company, Inc., 1956. E181.D8
Dupuy, Rev. War Naval Battles
  Dupuy, Trevor N., and Grace P. Hayes, *The Military History of Revolu-
    tionary War Naval Battles.* New York: Franklin Watts, Inc. c1970.
    E271.D85

Dupuy, Where They Have Trod
  Dupuy, Richard Ernest, *Where They Have Trod: The West Point Tradition
  in American Life*. New York: Frederick A. Stokes Company, 1940.
  U410.L1D8
Durant, Hist. of Oneida Co.
  Durant, Samuel W., *History of Oneida County, New York*. Philadelphia
  Everts & Fariss, 1878. F127.05D9
Dutcher, Washington
  Dutcher, George Matthew, *George Washington and Connecticut, in War and
  Peace*. New Haven: Yale University Press, 1933. E312.27.D76
Eckenrode, Yorktown
  Eckenrode, H.J., *The Story of the Campaign and Siege of Yorktown*.
  (71st Congress, 3rd Session, Senate Document 318). Washington, D.C.:
  U.S. Government Printing Office, 1931. E241.Y6E32
Eckenrode, Yorktown Sesquicentennial
  Eckenrode, Hamilton James, and Bryan Conrad, *Official Guidebook of
  the Yorktown Sesquicentennial Celebration, October 16-19, 1931*.
  Richmond: Virginia Yorktown Sesquicentennial Commission, 1931.
  E241.Y6E29
Egle, Journals
  Egle, William Henry, ed., *Journals and Diaries of the War of the
  Revolution, with Lists of Officers and Soldiers, 1775-1783*. Harris-
  burg, Pa.: E.K. Meyers, State Printer, 1893. E263.P4E31 or F146.P41
  2d ser., v.15
Egleston, John Paterson
  Egleston, Thomas, *The Life of John Paterson, Major-General in the
  Revolutionary Army*. New York: G.P. Putnam's Sons, 1894. E207.P3E3
Elizabeth, Rev. Hist.
  Elizabeth, N.J., The Sesquicentennial Committee, *Revolutionary History
  of Elizabeth, New Jersey*. 1926. F144.E4E35
Elizabeth, Souvenir Programme
  Elizabeth, N.J., *Official Souvenir Programme, Celebration of the 125th
  Anniversary of the Battle of Elizabethtown, June 8th, 1905*. [Eliza-
  beth, N.J., 1905.] E241.E39E4
Ellis, Bunker's Hill
  Ellis, George Edward, *History of the Battle of Bunker's (Breed's) Hill,
  on June 17, 1775, from Authentic Sources in Print and Manuscript*.
  Boston: Lockwood, Brooks, and Company, 1875. E241.B9E4 Toner Coll.
Ellis, New York
  Ellis, David M., James A. Frost, and William B. Fink, *New York: The
  Empire State*. 2nd edition. Englewood Cliffs, N.J.: Prentice-Hall,
  Inc., c1964. F119.E45 1964
Ellis, Saratoga Campaign
  Ellis, David M., *The Saratoga Campaign*. New York: McGraw-Hill Book
  Company, c1969. E241.S2E4
Ellis, Short Hist.
  Ellis, David M., James A. Frost, Harold G. Syrett, and Harold J.
  Carman, *A Short History of New York State*. Ithaca: Cornell Univer-
  sity Press, 1957. F119.E46
Elwood, Episode
  Elwood, Mary Cheney, *An Episode of the Sullivan Campaign and Its
  Sequel*. Rochester, N.Y., 1904. E236.E52
Enc. Americana
  The Encyclopedia Americana. International Edition. Vols. 1, 29.
  New York: Americana Corporation, c1967. AE5.E33 1967

English, Conquest
  English, William Hayden, *Conquest of the Country Northwest of the River Ohio, 1778-1783, and Life of Gen. George Rogers Clark.* Vol. 1. Indianapolis: The Bowen-Merrill Company, 1896. E234.E58
Entick, Hist. of Late War
  Entick, John, *The General History of the Late War.* Vol. 1. London: Edward and Charles Dilly, 1766. DD411.E61
Esposito, Am. Wars Atlas
  Esposito, Colonel Vincent J., ed., *The West Point Atlas of American Wars.* Vol. 1. New York: Frederick A. Praeger, 1957. G1201.S1U5 1959
Esposito, Civil War Atlas
  Esposito, Colonel Vincent J., ed., *The West Point Atlas of the Civil War.* New York: Frederick A. Praeger, 1962. G1201.S5U58 1962
Essays in Mod. Eng. Hist.
  Essays in Modern English History in Honor of Wilbur Cortez Abbott. Cambridge: Harvard University Press, 1941. DA300.A2
Essex Inst., Hist. Collections
  The Essex Institute, *Historical Collections.* Vol. 90. Salem, Mass. F72.E7E81
Evans, First Lessons in Ga. Hist.
  Evans, Lawton Bryan, and E.M. Coulter, *First Lessons in Georgia History.* New York: American Book Company, c1938. F286.E89 1938
Ewing, Geo. Ewing
  Ewing, Thomas, *George Ewing, Gentleman, a Soldier of Valley Forge.* Yonkers, N.Y.: Thomas Ewing, 1928. E275.E96
Eyres, Sullivan Trail
  Eyres, Lawrence E., *Along the Sullivan Trail: The Story of Sullivan's Indian Expedition of 1779 that Opened Northern Pennsylvania and the Finger Lakes and Genesee Region of New York for Settlement.* Elmira, N.Y., c1954. E235.E9
Falkner, Forge of Liberty
  Falkner, Leonard, *Forge of Liberty: The Dramatic Opening of the American Revolution.* New York: E.P. Dutton & Co., Inc., 1959. E231.F22
Falls, Great Mil. Battles
  Falls, Cyril Bentham, ed., *Great Military Battles.* New York: The Macmillan Company, c1964. D25.F3
Farrier, Paulus Hook
  Farrier, George H., ed., *Memorial of the Centennial Celebration of the Battle of Paulus Hook, August 19th, 1879.* Jersey City: M. Mulone, 1879. E241.P24F2 Microfilm
Fast, Conceived in Liberty
  Fast, Howard Melvin, *Conceived in Liberty: A Novel of Valley Forge.* New York: Simon and Schuster, 1939. PZ3.F265Co
Fast, The Unvanquished
  Fast, Howard Melvin, *The Unvanquished.* New York: Duell, Sloan and Pearce, c1942. PZ3.F265Un
Faulkner, Am. Political & Social Hist.
  Faulkner, Harold Underwood, *American Political and Social History.* 7th edition. New York: Appleton-Century-Crofts, Inc., c1957. E178.F282 1957
Faust, German Element
  Faust, Albert Bernhardt, *The German Element in the United States.* Vol. 1. Boston: Houghton Mifflin Company, 1909. E184.G3F3

Fed. Writers' Proj., Bid for Liberty
  Federal Writers' Project, *A Bid for Liberty, Being an Account of the Resolutions and Declarations of Independence Adopted in the Colony of Pennsylvania, 1774 to 1776*. Philadelphia: William Penn Association, 1937. E263.P4F4
Fed. Writers Proj., Mil. Hist. of Ky.
  Federal Writers Project, *Military History of Kentucky*. Frankfort, Ky.: The State Journal, c1939. UA210.F4
Field Artillery Jl.
  Field Artillery Journal. Vol. 23, 39. Washington: United States Field Artillery Association. UF1.F6
Field, Battle of L.I.
  Field Thomas W., *The Battle of Long Island, with Preceding and Subsequent Events*. (Memoirs of the Long Island Historical Society, Vol. 2). Brooklyn, N.Y.: The Society, 1869. F116.L954 vol.2
Field, Defences in R.I.
  Field, Edward, *Revolutionary Defences in Rhode Island*. Providence: Preston and Rounds, 1896. E263.R4F4
Field, Esek Hopkins
  Field, Edward, *Esek Hopkins, Commander-in-Chief of the Continental Navy during the American Revolution, 1775 to 1778*. Providence: The Preston & Rounds Co., 1898. E207.H7F4
Field, State of R.I.
  Field, Edward, ed., *State of Rhode Island and Providence Plantations at the End of the Century: A History*. Vol. 1. Boston: The Mason Publishing Company, 1902. F79.F45
Fish, Washington in Highlands
  Fish, Hamilton, Jr., *George Washington in the Highlands*. [Newburgh, N.Y.: The Newburgh News, 1932]. E312.25.F65
Fisher, Struggle for Am. Ind.
  Fisher, Sydney George, *The Struggle for American Independence*. 2v. Philadelphia: J.B. Lippincott Company, 1908. E208.F51
Fiske, Am. Rev.
  Fiske, John, *The American Revolution*. 2v. Cambridge, Mass.: The Riverside Press, 1896. E208.F55
Fitch, N.Y. Diary
  Fitch, Jabez, *The New York Diary of Lieutenant Jabez Fitch of the 17th (Connecticut) Regiment from August 22, 1776 to December 15, 1777*. New York: Colburn & Tegg, 1954. E281.F55 1954
Fitch, Some Neglected Hist. of N.C.
  Fitch, William Edwards, *Some Neglected History of South Carolina: Being an Account of the Revolution of the Regulators and of the Battle of the Alamance, the First Battle of the Revolution*. New York: The Neale Publishing Company, 1905. F257.F54
Fite, Book of Old Maps
  Fite, Emerson D., and Archibald Freeman, comps., *A Book of Old Maps Delineating American History from the Earliest Days to the Close of the Revolutionary War*. Cambridge: Harvard University Press, 1926. GA400.H65F5
Fitzmaurice, Life of Shelburne
  Fitzmaurice, Edmond George Petty-Fitzmaurice, 1st Baron, *Life of William, Earl of Shelburne*. 2nd and revised edition. Vol. 2. London: Macmillan and Col., 1912. DA512.L3F5 1912

Fleming, Autobiog. of Colony
  Fleming, Berry, comp., *Autobiography of a Colony: The First Half-
  Century of Augusta, Georgia*.   Athens, Ga.: University of Georgia
  Press, c1957.   F289.F55
Fleming, Battle of Yorktown
  Fleming, Thomas J., *The Battle of Yorktown*.   New York: American
  Heritage Publishing Co., Inc., c1968.   E241.Y6F54
Fleming, Beat the Last Drum
  Fleming, Thomas J., *Beat the Last Drum; The Siege of Yorktown, 1781*.
  New York: St. Martin's Press, 1963.   E241.Y6F55
Fleming, Hist. of Pittsburgh
  Fleming, George Thornton, *History of Pittsburgh and Evirons*. Vol. 1.
  New York: The American Historical Society Inc., 1922.   F159.P6F61
Fleming, Now We Are Enemies
  Fleming, Thomas J., *Now We Are Enemies; The Story of Bunker Hill*.
  New York: St. Martin's Press, c1960.   E241.B9F58   1960a
Fleming, Views
  Fleming, George Thornton, *Fleming's Views of Old Pittsburgh: A Port-
  folio of the Past*.   Pittsburgh: The Crescent Press, 1932.
  F159.P6F602
Flexner, Mohawk Baronet
  Flexner, James Thomas, *Mohawk Baronet: Sir William Johnson of New
  York*.   New York: Harper & Brothers, c1959.   E195.J659
Flexner, Washington in Am. Rev.
  Flexner, James Thomas, *George Washington in the American Revolution
  (1775-1783)*.   Boston: Little, Brown and Company, c1968.   E312.25.F69
Flick, Hist. of State of N.Y.
  Flick, Alexander C., ed., *History of the State of New York*.   Vol. 4.
  Port Washington, N.Y.: Ira J. Friedman, Inc., 1962.   F119.N65 1962
Fla. Hist. Quar.
  Florida Historical Quarterly.   Vol. 29.   Gainesville, Fla.:   Florida
  Historical Society.   F306.F65
Forbes, France and New Eng.
  Forbes, Allan, and Paul F. Cadman, *France and New England*.   Vol. 1.
  Boston: State Street Trust Company, 1925.   E265.F65
Forbes, Paul Revere
  Forbes, Esther, *Paul Revere and the World He Lived in*.   Boston:
  Houghton, Mifflin Company, 1942.   F69.R4175
Forbes, Second Battle
  Forbes, Charles Spooner, *The Second Battle of Bennington: A History
  of Vermont's Centennial, and the One Hundreth Anniversary of
  Bennington's Battle*.   St. Albans, Vt.: Advertiser Printing Co., 1877.
  E241.B4F6
Force, Am. Archives
  Force, Peter, comp., *American Archives*.   4th series.   Vol. 3.
  Washington, D.C., 1840.   E203.A51
Ford, Gen. Orders of Israel Putnam
  Ford, Worthington Chauncey, ed., *General Orders Issued by Major-
  General Israel Putnam, When in Command of the Highlands, in the
  Summer and Fall of 1777*.   Brooklyn, N.Y.: Historical Printing Club,
  1893.   E233.U56
Ford, Peculiar Service
  Ford, Corey, *A Peculiar Service*.   Boston: Little, Brown and Company,
  c1965.   E279.F6

Ft. Ticonderoga Museum, Bul.
  Fort Ticonderoga Museum, *Bulletin*.   Vol. 9. Ft. Ticonderoga, N.Y.
    E199.F75
Ft. Washington Account
  *Fort Washington: An Account of the Identification of the Site of Fort
  Washington, New York City, and the Erection and Dedication of a
  Monument thereon Nov. 16, 1901, by the Empire State Society of the
  Sons of the American Revolution, with the Cooperation of the Ameri-
  can Scenic and Historic Preservation Society*. New York, 1902.
    E241.W3S7
Ft. Washington Memorial
  *Fort Washington, November 16th, 1776: A Memorial from the Empire
  State Society of the Sons of the American Revolution to the Honor-
  able Mayor and Municipal Assembly of the City of New York, Praying
  for the Erection of a Suitable Monument to Mark the Site of Fort
  Washington*. [New York,] 1898. E241.W3S5
Fortescue, British Army
  Fortescue, J.W., *A History of the British Army*. Vol. 3.   London:
    Macmillan and Co., 1911. DA50.F73
Fraser, Stone House
  Fraser, Georgia, *The Stone House at Gowanus, Scene of the Battle of
  Long Island*. New York: Witter and Kintner, 1909. E241.L8F8
Freeman, Washington
  Freeman, Douglas Southall, *George Washington, A Biography*. Vols. 4,
    5. New York: Charles Scribner's Sons, 1951-1952. E312.F82
Freeman, Washington, abridgment
  Freeman, Douglas Southall, *Washington*. An abridgment in one volume
  by Richard Harwell of Freeman's seven volume *George Washington*.
  New York: Charles Scribner's Sons, c1968. E312.F83
French, Day of Con. and Lex.
  French, Allen, *The Day of Concord and Lexington, the Nineteenth of
  April, 1775*. Boston: Little, Brown, and Company, 1925. E241.L6F8
French, First Year
  French, Allen, *The First Year of the American Revolution*. Boston:
    Houghton Mifflin Company, 1934. E208.F73
French, Gage's Informers
  French, Allen, *General Gage's Informers*. Ann Arbor: The University
    of Michigan Press, 1932. E241.L6F85
French, Historic Concord
  French, Allen, *Historic Concord*. Concord, Mass.: The Riverside Press,
    c1942. F74.C8F865
Frontier Forts
  Pennsylvania, Indian Forts Commission, *Report of the Commission to
  Locate the Site of the Frontier Forts of Pennsylvania*. Vol. 1.
  Harrisburg: C.M. Bush, State Printer, 1896. F152.P36 (1916 edition
    F152.P363)
Frost, We Build a Navy
  Frost, Holloway H., *We Build a Navy*. Annapolis, Md.: U.S. Naval
    Institute, 1940. E182.F93
Frothingham, Bunker Hill
  Frothingham, Richard, *The Centennial: Battle of Bunker Hill*. Boston:
    Little, Brown, & Co., 1875. E241.B9F9
Frothingham, Charleston
  Frothingham, Richard, Jr., *The History of Charlestown, Massachusetts*.
    Charlestown: Charles P. Emmons, 1845. F74.C4F9

Frothingham, Siege
  Frothingham, Richard, *History of the Siege of Boston*.   4th edition.
    Boston: Little, Brown, and Comapny, 1873.   E231.F94
Frothingham, Washington
  Frothingham, Thomas G., *Washington, Commander in Chief*.   Boston:
    Houghton Mifflin Company, 1930.   E312.25.F94
Fuller, Battles
  Fuller, John Frederick Charles, *Decisive Battles of the U.S.A.*   New
    York: Thomas Yoseloff, Inc., c1942
Fuller, Decisive Battles of W. World
  Fuller, John Frederick Charles, *The Decisive Battles of the Western
    World, and Their Influence upon History*.   Vol. 2.   London: Eyre &
    Spottiswoode, 1955.   D25.F93
Futhey, Hist. of Chester Co.
  Futhey, J.Smith, and Gilbert Cope, *History of Chester County, Penn-
    sylvania*.   Philadelphia: Louis H. Everts, 1881.   F157.C4F9
Ganong, Origins
  Ganong, William F., *A Monograph of the Origins of the Settlements in
    New Brunswick*.   (Royal Society of Canada, Transactions, 2d series,
    Vol. 10, Section II).   Ottawa, 1904.   F1043.G24
Garner, Hist. of U.S.
  Garner, James Wilford, and Henry Cabot Lodge, *The History of the
    United States*.   Vols. 1, 2.   Philadelphia: John D. Morris and
    Company, 1906.   E178.G23
Garrett, Hist. of Tenn.
  Garrett, William Robertson, and Albert Virgil Goodpasture, *History of
    Tennessee, Its People and Its Institutions*.   Nashville: Brandon
    Printing Company, 1900.   F436.G23
Garvan, Arch. and Town Planning
  Garvan, Anthony N.B., *Architecture and Town Planning in Colonial
    Connecticut*.   New Haven: Yale University Press, 1951.   NA7235.C8G3
Gentleman's Mag.
  The Gentleman's Magazine.   Vol. 33.   London.   AP4.G3
Geog. Rev.
  The Geographical Review.   Vol. 30.   New York: The American Geographical
    Society.   G1.G35
Ga. Hist. Quar.
  Georgia Historical Quarterly.   Vol. 10.   Savannah: Georgia Historical
    Society.   F281.G2975
Ga. Hist. Soc., Coll.
  Georgia Historical Society, *Collections*.   Vol. 8.   Savannah, Ga.
    F281.G35
Gérard, Despatches
  Gérard, Conrad Alexandre, *Despatches and Instructions of Conrad
    Alexandre Gérard, 1778-1780: Correspondence of the First French
    Minister to the United States with the Comte de Vergennes*.   John
    J. Meng, ed.   Baltimore: The Johns Hopkins Press, 1939.   E249.F76
Gerlach, Schuyler
  Gerlach, Don R., *Philip Schuyler and the American Revolution in New
    York, 1733-1777*.   Lincoln: University of Nebraska Press, 1964.
    E207.S3G4
Germantown Hist. Soc., 150th Anniversary
  Germantown Historical Society, *Pictorial Souvenir . . . The 150th
    Anniversary of the Battle of Germantown, October 1 to 4, 1927*.
    Germantown, Pa.: The Society, 1928.   E241.G3G31

Germantowne Crier
  Germantowne Crier. Vol. 4. Germantown, Pa.: Germantown Historical
    Society. F159.G3G336
Gerson, Franklin
  Gerson, Noel Bertram, *Franklin, America's Lost State*. New York:
    Crowell-Collier Press, c1968. F436.G4 1968
Gerson, Nathan Hale
  Gerson, Noel Bertram, *Nathan Hale, Espionage Agent*. Garden City,
    N.Y.: Nelson, Doubleday, Inc., c1960. E280.H2G4
Gewehr, United States
  Gewehr, Wesley M., Donald C. Gordon, David S. Sparks, Roland N. Strom-
    berg, eds., *The United States: A History of Democracy*. 2nd edition.
    New York: McGraw-Hill Book Company, Inc., 1960. E178.1.G4 1960
Gilbert, Eastern Cherokees
  Gilbert, William Harlen, Jr., *The Eastern Cherokees*. (Smithsonian
    Institution, Bureau of American Ethnology, Anthropological Papers,
    No.23). Washington: U.S. Government Printing Office, 1943.
    E99.C5G35
Gilchrist, Ft. Ticonderoga
  Gilchrist, Helen Ives, *Fort Ticonderoga in History*. Fort Ticonderoga
    Museum, 1923? E199.G46
Gilman, Cambridge of 1776
  Gilman, Arthur, *The Cambridge of 1776*. 2nd edition. Cambridge, Mass.,
    1876. F74.C1G53
Gilman, Monmouth
  Gilman, Charles Malcolm Brookfield, *Monmouth Road to Glory, including
    the Court-Martial and Vindication of Major-General Charles Lee*.
    Red Bank, N.J.: Arlington Laboratory for Clinical and Historical
    Research, c1964. E241.M7G5
Gilman, Story of Boston
  Gilman, Arthur, *The Story of Boston: A Study of Independency*. New
    York: G.P. Putnam's Sons, 1889. F73.3.G48
Gilmore, N.H. Soldiers
  Gilmore, George Clinton, comp., *Roll of New Hampshire Soldiers at the
    Battle of Bennington, August 16, 1777*. Manchester, N.H.: Printed by
    John B. Clarke, 1891. E241.B4G4
Gilmore, Rear-Guard
  Gilmore, James Roberts, *The Rear-Guard of the Revolution*. By Edmund
    Kirke [pseud.] New York: D. Appleton & Company, 1886. E263.N8G4
Gipson, Br. Empire
  Gipson, Lawrence Henry, *The British Empire before the American Revolu-
    tion*. Vols. 2, 3, 4, 9, 10, 12. New York: Alfred A. Knopf, 1939-
    1965. DA500.G52
Gipson, Br. Empire, Caxton ed.
  Gipson, Lawrence Henry, *The British Empire before the American Revolu-
    tion*. Vols. 2, 3. Caldwell, Idaho: The Caxton Printers, 1936.
    DA500.G5
Gipson, Coming of Rev.
  Gipson, Lawrence Henry, *The Coming of the Revolution, 1763-1775*. New
    York: Harper & Row, 1962
Godcharles, Chronicles
  Godcharles, Frederic Antes, *Chronicles of Central Pennsylvania*. Vols.
    1, 2. New York: Lewis Historical Publishing Company, Inc., c1944.
    F149.G56

Godfrey, Washington's March
  Godfrey, Carlos E., *Washington's March to Trenton on Christmas Night
    in 1776.* Trenton: The Trenton Historical Society, 1924. E241.T7G5
Goodrich, First Michigan Frontier
  Goodrich, Calvin, *The First Michigan Frontier.* Ann Arbor: University
    of Michigan Press, 1940. F566.G66
Goold, Mitchell's Regt.
  Goold, Nathan, *History of Colonel Jonathan Mitchell's Cumberland
    County Regiment of the Bagaduce Expedition, 1779.* Portland, Me.:
    The Thurston Print, 1899. E263.M4G67
Gordon, Hist. of U.S.A.
  Gordon, William, *The History of the Rise, Progress, and Establishment,
    of the Independence of the United States of America.* Vols. 2, 4,
    London, 1788. E208.G66 Jefferson Coll.
Gore, Journal
  Gore, Obadiah, Jr., *The Revolutionary Journal of Lieut. Obadiah Gore,
    Jr.* R.W.G. Vail, ed. New York: The New York Public Library, 1929.
    E275.G68
Gottschalk, Lafayette
  Gottschalk, Louis, *Lafayette Joins the American Army.* Chicago: The
    University of Chicago Press, 1937. E207.L2G7
Gottschalk, Lafayette and Close of Am. Rev.
  Gottschalk, Louis, *Lafayette and the Close of the American Revolution.*
    Chicago: The University of Chicago Press, c1942. E207.L2G68
Gould, Storming the Heights
  Gould, Edward Kalloch, *Storming the Heights: Maine's Embattled Farmers
    at Castine in the Revolution.* Rockland, Me.: The Courier-Gazette
    Press, 1932. E263.M2G7
Gouvion, Washington's Map
  Gouvion, Jean-Baptiste, *Washington's Official Map of Yorktown.* (Na-
    tional Archives Facsimile 21). Washington: U.S. Government Printing
    Office, 1952. G3701.S331 1952.G6 Map Division
Graham, Br. Policy and Canada
  Graham, Gerald Sanford, *British Policy and Canada, 1774-1791: A Study
    in 18th Century Trade Policy.* London: Longmans, Green and Co.,
    1930. HF1533.G7
Graham, Gen. Joseph Graham
  Graham, William Alexander, *General Joseph Graham and His Papers on
    North Carolina Revolutionary History.* Raleigh, N.C.: Edwards and
    Broughton, 1904. E263.N867
Granite State Mag.
  Granite State Magazine. Vol. 6. Manchester, N.H. F31.G76
Grant, British Battles
  Grant, James, *British Battles on Land and Sea.* Vol. 2. London:
    Cassell & Company, Ltd., 188?. DA50.G761
Greene, Foundations
  Greene, Evarts Boutell, *The Foundations of American Nationality.* New
    York: American Book Company, c1922. E178.G75
Greene, Gen. Greene
  Greene, Francis Vinton, *General Greene.* New York: D. Appleton and
    Company, 1893. E207.G9G7
Greene, Mohawk Valley
  Greene, Nelson, ed., *History of the Mohawk Valley, Gateway to the West,
    1614-1925.* Vols. 1, 2. Chicago: The S.J. Clarke Publishing Com-
    pany, 1925. F127.M55H6

Hall-Quest, From Colony to Nation
  Hall-Quest, Olga (Wilbourne), *From Colony to Nation: With Washington
    and His Army in the War for Independence*. New York: E.P. Dutton &
    Co., Inc., c1966. E208.H22
Hall-Quest, Guardians of Liberty
  Hall-Quest, Olga (Wilbourne), *Guardians of Liberty: Sam Adams and
    John Hancock*. New York: E.P. Dutton & Company, Inc., c1963.
    E302.6.A2H16
Halsey, Old N.Y. Frontier
  Halsey, Francis Whiting, *The Old New York Frontier*. Port Washington,
    N.Y.: Ira J. Friedman, Inc., 1963. F119.H19 1963
Hamilton, Colonial Mobile
  Hamilton, Peter Joseph, *Colonial Mobile*. Revised and enlarged ed.
    Mobile, Ala.: The First National Bank of Mobile, 1952. F326.H22
    1952
Hamilton, Ft. Ticonderoga
  Hamilton, Edward Pierce, *Fort Ticonderoga, Key to a Continent*.
    Boston: Little, Brown and Comapny, c1964. E199.H25
Hamilton, Grenadier Guards
  Hamilton, Sir Frederick William, *The Origin and History of the First
    or Grenadier Guards*. Vol. 2. London: John Murray, 1874.
    UA652.G7H3
Hamilton, Hist. of Republic
  Hamilton, John C., *History of the Republic of the United States of
    America, as Traced in the Writings of Alexander Hamilton and of His
    Contemporaries*. Vols. 1, 2. New York: D. Appleton & Company, 1958.
    E302.1.H2
Hamilton, Johnson and Indians
  Hamilton, Milton Wheaton, *Sir William Johnson and the Indians of New
    York*. [Albany?]: University of the State of New York, State Educa-
    tion Dept., Office of State History, 1967. E195.J663
Hamilton, Papers
  Hamilton, Alexander, *The Papers of Alexander Hamilton*. Harold C.
    Syrett, ed. Vols. 1, 2. New York: Columbia University Press, 1961.
    E302.H247
Hanna, Florida
  Hanna, Kathryn Abbey, *Florida, Land of Change*. Chapel Hill: The
    University of North Carolina Press, 1948. F311.H3 1948
Hanna, Wilderness Trail
  Hanna, Charles A., *The Wilderness Trail, or the Ventures and Adven-
    tures of the Pennsylvania Traders on the Allegheny Path*. Vol. 2.
    New York: G.P. Putnam's Sons, 1911. F152.H24
Hardenbergh, Journal
  Hardenbergh, John Leonard, *The Journal of Lieut. John L. Hardenbergh
    of the Second New York Continental Regiment from May 1 to October 3,
    1779, in General Sullivan's Campaign against the Western Indians*.
    (Collections of Cayuga County Historical Society, No. 1). Auburn,
    N.Y.: Knapp and Peck, 1879. F127.C5C5 vol 1.
Hargreaves, The Bloodybacks
  Hargreaves, Reginald, *The Bloodybacks: The British Serviceman in
    North America and the Caribbean, 1655-1783*. London: Rupert Hart-
    Davis, 1968. E267.H35 1968b
Harlow, United States
  Harlow, Ralph Volney, *The United States: From Wilderness to World
    Power*. 3rd edition. New York: Henry Holt and Company, 1957.
    E178.1.H295 1957

Harper's Mag.
  Harper's New Monthly Magazine. Vols. 18, 21, 47, 50, 52, 53, 55, 63,
    67. New York: Harper & Brothers. AP2.H3
Harris, Groton Heights
  Harris, William W., *The Battle of Groton Heights.* New London: Charles
    Allyn, 1882. E241.G8H32
Hart, Am. Nation
  Hart, Albert Bushnell, ed., *The American Nation: A History.* Vols. 7-
    10, 26. New York: Harper & Brothers, 1905-1907. E178.A55
Hart, Commonwealth Hist. of Mass.
  Hart, Albert Bushnell, ed., *Commonwealth History of Massachusetts.*
    Vols. 2,3. New York: The States History Company, 1928. F64.H32
Hart, Sleeping Sentinel
  Hart, Edwin Kirman, *The Sleeping Sentinel of Valley Forge: A Romance
    of the Revolution.* Philadelphia, 1897. PZ3.H2495S
Hart, Valley of Va.
  Hart, Freeman H., *The Valley of Virginia in the American Revolution,
    1763-1789.* Chapel Hill: The University of North Carolina Press,
    1942. F232.S5H3 1942a
Harte, River Obstructions
  Harte, Charles Rufus, *The River Obstructions of the Revolutionary
    War.* New Haven, 1946. E271.H3
Hatch, Yorktown
  Hatch, Charles E., Jr., *Yorktown and the Siege of 1781.* (National
    Park Service Historical Handbook Series No. 14). Washington:
    Government Printing Office, 1957. E241.Y6H3 1957
Haven, 30 Days in N.J.
  Haven, Charles Chauncy, *Thirty Days in New Jersey Ninety Years Ago:
    An Essay Revealing New Facts in Connection with Washington and His
    Army in 1776 and 1777.* Trenton: The State Gazette Office, 1867.
    E232.H38
Havighurst, Geo. Rogers Clark
  Havighurst, Walter, *George Rogers Clark, Soldier in the West.* New
    York: McGraw-Hill Book Company, Inc., c1952. E207.C5H3
Havighurst, Proud Prisoner
  Havighurst, Walter, *Proud Prisoner.* Williamsburg, Va.: Colonial
    Williamsburg, c1964. E208.H38
Hawke, Colonial Experience
  Hawke, David, *The Colonial Experience.* Indianapolis: The Bobbs-
    Merrill Company, Inc., c1966. E188.H3
Haycox, Winds of Rebellion
  Haycox, Ernest, *Winds of Rebellion: Tales of the American Revolution.*
    New York: Criterion Books, c1954. PZ3.H3237Wj
Haywood, Tryon
  Haywood, Marshall DeLancey, *Governor William Tryon, and His Adminis-
    tration in the Province of North Carolina, 1765-1771.* Raleigh:
    E.M. Uzzell, Printer, 1903. F257.H43
Heathcote, Chester Co.
  Heathcote, Charles William, *History of Chester County, Pennsylvania.*
    West Chester, Pa.: Horace F. Temple, c1926. F157.C4H3
Heathcote, Washington
  Heathcote, Charles William, *Washington in Chester County.* [West
    Chester, Pa.?, 1932.] E312.27.H33

Henderson, Conquest of Old S.W.
  Henderson, Archibald, *The Conquest of the Old Southwest: The Romantic
    Story of the Early Pioneers into Virginia, the Carolinas, Tennessee,
    and Kentucky, 1740-1790*. New York: The Century Co., c1920.
    F396.H49
Henderson, N. Carolina
  Henderson, Archibald, *North Carolina: The Old North State and the New*.
    Vol. 1. Chicago: Lewis Publishing Company, 1941. F254.H45
Hersey, Heroes of Battle Rd.
  Hersey, Frank Wilson Cheney, *Heroes of the Battle Road*. Boston: Perry
    Walton, 1930. E241.L6H57
Heth, Diary
  Heth, William, *The Diary of William Heth while a Prisoner in Quebec*.
    B. Floyd Flickinger, ed. Winchester, Va.: Winchester, Virginia,
    Historical Society, 1931. E281.H56
Heusser, Forgotten Gen.
  Heusser, Albert H., *The Forgotten General, Robert Erskine, F.R.S.
    (1735-1780), Geographer and Surveyor General to the Army of the
    United States of America*. Paterson, N.J.: The Benjamin Franklin
    Press, 1928. E207.E7H6
Heusser, Washington's Map Maker
  Heusser, Albert Henry, *George Washington's Map Maker: A Biography of
    Robert Erskine*. Edited with an Introduction by Hubert G. Schmidt.
    New Brunswick, N.J.: Rutgers University Press, 1966. E207.E7H6 1966
Hicks, Federal Union
  Hicks, John Donald, George E. Mowry, Robert E. Burke, *The Federal
    Union*. 4th edition. Boston: Houghton Mifflin Company, 1964.
    E178.H59 1964
Higginbotham, Morgan
  Higginbotham, Don, *Daniel Morgan, Revolutionary Rifleman*. Chapel
    Hill: University of North Carolina Press, c1961. E207.M8H5
Hilliard d'Auberteuil, Essais
  Hilliard d'Auberteuil, Michel René, *Essais Historiques et Politiques
    sur les Anglo-Américains*. 2v. Bruxelles, 1782. E208.H64 Rare
    Book Coll.
Hinsdale, Old Northwest
  Hinsdale, Burke Aaron, *The Old Northwest*. New York: Townsend MacCown,
    1888. F479.H64
Historical Mag.
  The Historical Magazine. 2nd series. Vol. 3. Morrisania, N.Y.:
    Henry B. Dawson. E171.H64
Hist. and Philos. Soc. Ohio, Bul.
  Historical and Philosophical Society of Ohio, *Bulletin*. Vol. 10.
    Cincinnati. F486.H653
Hist. Soc. Montgomery Co., Bul.
  Historical Society of Montgomery County, Pennsylvania, *Bulletin*. Vols.
    2, 4. Norristown, Pa.: The Society. F157.M7H45
Hist. Soc. Montgomery Co., Historical Sketches
  Historical Society of Montgomery County, Pennsylvania, *Historical
    Sketches*. Vols. 2, 3, 4. Norristown, Pa.: Herald Printing and
    Binding Rooms, 1900-1910. F157.M7H5
Hist. Soc. Pa., Bul.
  Historical Society of Pennsylvania, *Bulletin*. Vol. 1. Philadelphia.
    F146.P33

Hulbert, Indian Thoroughfares
   Hulbert, Archer Butler, *Indian Thoroughfares*. (Historic Highways of
   America, Vol. 2). Cleveland: The Arthur H. Clark Company, 1902.
   E159.H92 vol. 2
Hulbert, Military Roads
   Hulbert, Archer Butler, *Military Roads of the Mississippi Basin: The
   Conquest of the Old Northwest*. (Historic Highways of America.
   Vol. 8). Cleveland: The Arthur H. Clark Company, 1904.
   E159.H92 vol.8
Hulbert, Ohio River
   Hulbert, Archer Butler, *The Ohio River: A Course of Empire*. New York:
   G.P. Putnam's Sons, 1906. F516.H91
Hulbert, Washington and West
   Hulbert, Archer Butler, ed., *Washington and the West: Being George
   Washington's Diary of September 1784, Kept during His Journey into
   the Ohio Basin in the Interest of a Commercial Union between the
   Great Lakes and the Potomac River*. New York: The Century Co.,
   1905. E312.8 1784
Hunnewell, Bibliography
   Hunnewell, James Frothingham, *Bibliography of Charlestown, Massachu-
   setts, and Bunker Hill*. Boston: James R. Osgood and Company, 1880.
   Z1296.C47H
Hunnewell, Century of Town Life
   Hunnewell, James Frothingham, *A Century of Town Life: A History of
   Charlestown, Massachusetts, 1775-1887*. Boston: Little, Brown, and
   Company, 1888. F74.C4H9
Hutchins, Courses of Ohio R.
   Hutchins, Thomas, *The Courses of the Ohio River Taken by Lt. Thomas
   Hutchins, Anno 1766, and Two Accompanying Maps*. Beverly W. Bond,
   ed. Cincinnati: Historical and Philosophical Society of Ohio, 1942.
   VK995.04H8
Hutchins, Topo. Description
   Hutchins, Thomas, *A Topographical Description of Virginia, Pennsylva-
   nia, Maryland, and North Carolina*. Frederick Charles Hicks, ed.
   Cleveland: The Burrows Brothers Company, 1904. E163.H985
Hutton, Col. Henry Bouquet
   Hutton, Lt. Gen. Sir Edward, *Colonel Henry Bouquet, 60th Royal Ameri-
   cans, 1756-1765*. Winchester, Eng.: Warren & Son, Ltd., 1911.
   E83.76.B76
Hutton, Washington Crossed Here
   Hutton, Ann Hawkes, *George Washington Crossed Here, Christmas Night,
   1776*. Philadelphia: Dorrance & Company, 1948. E232.H88
Ill. State Hist. Soc. Trans. for 1907
   *Transactions of the Illinois State Historical Society for the Year
   1907*. (Illinois State Historical Library Publication No. 12).
   Springfield, Ill.: Phillips Bros., 1908. F536.I34
Infantry Jl.
   Infantry Journal. Vols. 36, 44, 46. Washington, D.C.: The United
   States Infantry Association. UD1.I6
Ingles, Queen's Rangers
   Ingles, C.J., *The Queen's Rangers in the Revolutionary War*.
   [Montreal?,] 1956. E277.6Q6I5
Irving, Life of Washington
   Irving, Washington, *Life of George Washington*. Vols. 1-4. New York:
   G.P. Putnam & Co., 1855-1857. E312.I6

Jacobs, Tarnished Warrior
  Jacobs, James Ripley, *Tarnished Warrior, Major-General James Wilkinson*. New York: The Macmillan Company, 1938. E353.1.W6J3
James, Br. Navy in Adversity
  James, Capt. William Milbourne, *The British Navy in Adversity: A Study of the War of American Independence*. London: Longmans, Green and Co., Ltd., 1926. E271.J28
James, Life of Clark
  James, James Alton, *The Life of George Rogers Clark*. Chicago: The University of Chicago Press, 1928. E207.C5J3
James, Ohio Co.
  James, Alfred Procter, *The Ohio Company: Its Inner History*. Pittsburgh, Pa.: University of Pittsburgh Press, c1959. F517.J3
James, Oliver Pollock
  James, James Alton, *Oliver Pollock: The Life and Times of an Unknown Patriot*. New York: D. Appleton-Century Company, Inc., 1937. E302.6P84J3
Jefferson, Papers
  Jefferson, Thomas, *The Papers of Thomas Jefferson*. Julian P. Boyd, ed. Vols. 2, 4, 5. Princeton: Princeton University Press, 1950-1952. E302.J463
Jellison, Ethan Allen
  Jellison, Charles Albert, *Ethan Allen, Frontier Rebel*. Syracuse, N.Y. Syracuse University Press, c1969. E207.A4J4
Jenkins, Pa. Colonial & Federal
  Jenkins, Howard M., ed., *Pennsylvania Colonial and Federal: A History, 1608-1903*. Vol. 1. Philadelphia: Pennsylvania Historical Publishing Association, 1903. F149.J52
Jennings, Memorials
  Jennings, Isaac, *Memorials of a Century: Embracing a Record of Individuals and Events Chiefly in the Early History of Bennington, Vt., and Its First Church*. Boston: Gould and Lincoln, 1869. F59.B4J5
Jillson, Bibliog. of Clark
  Jillson, Willard Rouse, *A Bibliography of George Rogers Clark*. Frankfort, Ky.: Perry Publishing Co., 1958. Z8173.8.J5
Johnson, Orderly Book
  Johnson, Sir John, *Orderly Book of Sir John Johnson during the Oriskany Campaign, 1776-1777*. William L. Stone, ed. Albany: Joel Munsell's Sons, 1882. E233.J67 Microfilm 8525
Johnson, Papers
  Johnson, Sir William, *The Papers of Sir William Johnson*. Alexander C. Flick, ed. Vols. 4, 5, 6, 8, 10, 11, 12. Albany: The University of the State of New York, 1925. E195.J62
Johnson, Swedish Contrib.
  Johnson, Amandus, *Swedish Contributions to American Freedom, 1776-1783*. Vol. 1. Philadelphia: Swedish Colonial Foundation, 1953. E184.S23J62 pt. 7
Johnson, Traditions
  Johnson, Joseph, *Traditions and Reminiscences, Chiefly of the American Revolution in the South*. Charleston, S.C.: Walker & James, 1851. Microfilm 01291 reel 163 no.6E
Johnston, Campaign of 1776
  Johnston, Henry Phelps, *The Campaign of 1776 around New York and Brooklyn*. (Memoirs of The Long Island Historical Society, Vol. 3). Brooklyn, N.Y.: The Long Island Historical Society, 1878. F116.L87

Johnston, Harlem Heights
  Johnston, Henry Phelps, *The Battle of Harlem Heights, September 16,*
    1776, with a Review of the Events of the Campaign. New York: The
    Macmillan Company, 1897. E241.H2J7
Johnston, Minisink Battle
  Johnston, John W., and Albert Stage, *Centennial Celebration of the*
    Minisink Battle on the Actual Battle Field, July 22, 1879.
    Barryville, N.Y., 1879. E241.M6J7
Johnston, Nathan Hale
  Johnston, Henry Phelps, *Nathan Hale, Biography and Memorials.* New
    Haven: Yale University Press, 1914. E280.H2J74
Johnston, Storming of Stony Pt.
  Johnston, Henry Phelps, *The Storming of Stony Point on the Hudson,*
    Midnight July 15, 1779. New York: James T. White & Co., 1900.
    E241.S8J7
Johnston, Yorktown
  Johnston, Henry Phelps, *The Yorktown Campaign and the Surrender of*
    Cornwallis, 1781. New York: Harper & Brothers, 1881. E241.Y6J7
Jones, Hist. of N.Y.
  Jones, Thomas, *History of New York during the Revolutionary War, and*
    of the Leading Events in the Other Colonies at that Period. E. F.
    De Lancey, ed. 2v. New York: New York Historical Society, 1879.
    E263.N6J7
Jones, Savannah
  Jones, Charles Colcock, ed. and tr., *The Siege of Savannah in 1779,*
    as Described in Two Contemporaneous Journals of French Officers in
    the Fleet of Count D'Estaing. Albany, N.Y.: Joel Munsell, 1874.
    E241.S26J72
Journal of Am. Hist.
  Journal of American History. Vols. 10, 25. New York: The National
    Historical Society. E171.J86
Journal of Mod. Hist.
  The Journal of Modern History. Vol. 17. Chicago: The University of
    Chicago Press. D1.J6
Journal of South. Hist.
  The Journal of Southern History. Vol. 11. Lexington, Ky.: Southern
    Historical Association. F206.J68
Kain, Operations on Del.
  Kain, C. Henry, *The Military and Naval Operations on the Delaware in*
    1777. Philadelphia, 1910. F158.1.C58 no.8
Kaler, Old Falmouth
  Kaler, James Otis, *The Story of Old Falmouth.* By James Otis [pseud.].
    New York: Thomas Y. Crowell & Co., c1901. F29.P9K2
Kegley, Va. Frontier
  Kegley, Frederick Bittle, *Kegley's Virginia Frontier: The Beginning*
    of the Southwest. The Roanoke of Colonial Days, 1740-1783.
    Roanoke, Va.: The Southwest Virginia Historical Society, 1938.
    F229.K26
Keim, Rochambeau
  Keim, DeB. Randolph, *Rochambeau.* (59th Congress, 1st Session, Senate
    Document 537). Washington: Government Printing Office, 1907.
    E265.R68
Kelley, Historic Elizabeth
  Kelley, Frank Bergen, comp., *Historic Elizabeth, 1664-1914.* Eliza-
    beth, N.J., 1914. F144.E4K29

Larrabee, Decision
    Larrabee, Harold A., *Decision at the Chesapeake*. New York: Clarkson
    N.Potter, Inc., c1964. E271.L3
Lathrop, Black Rock
    Lathrop, Cornelia Penifield, *Black Rock, Seaport of Old Fairfield,
    Connecticut, 1644-1870*. New Haven: The Tuttle, Morehouse & Taylor
    Company, 1930. F104.B52L35
Lauvrière, Brève Histoire
    Lauvrière, Emile, *Brève Histoire Tragique du Peuple Acadien*. Paris:
    Librairie d'Amérique et d'Orient Adrien Maisonneuve, 1947.
    F1038.L35
Lawrence, Storm over Savannah
    Lawrence, Alexander A., *Storm over Savannah: The Story of Count
    d'Estaing and the Siege of the Town in 1779*. Athens, Ga.: The
    University of Georgia Press, c1951. E241.S26L3
Leake, John Lamb
    Leake, Isaac Q., *Memoir of the Life and Times of General John Lamb*.
    Albany: Joel Munsell, 1857. E207.L22L4
Leboucher, Histoire
    Leboucher, Odet Julien, *Histoire de la Derniere Guerre, entre la
    Grande-Bretagne, et les États-Unis de l'Amérique, la France,
    l'Espagne et la Hollande, depuis Son Commencement en 1775, jusqu'a
    Sa Fin en 1783*. Paris: Brocas, 1787. E208.L42 Jefferson Coll.
Leckie, Wars of America
    Leckie, Robert, *The Wars of America*. New York: Harper & Row, c1968
    E181.L45
Lee, Hist. of N.America
    Lee, Guy Carleton, ed., *The History of North America*. Vols. 4-6.
    Philadelphia: George Barrie & Sons, c1904. E178.H7
Lee, Memoirs of War
    Lee, Henry, *Memoirs of the War in the Southern Department of the
    United States*. Robert E. Lee, ed. New York: University Publish-
    ing Company, 1869. E230.5.S7L49 Office
Lefler, North Carolina
    Lefler, Hugh Talmage, *North Carolina: History, Geography, Government*.
    Revised edition. New York: Harcourt, Brace & World, Inc., c1966.
    F254.L365 1966
Leiby, Hackensack Valley
    Leiby, Adrian C., *The Revolutionary War in the Hackensack Valley:
    The Jersey Dutch and the Neutral Ground*. New Brunswick: Rutgers
    University Press, c1962. F142.B4L4
Lengyel, Arnold
    Lengyel, Cornel, *I, Benedict Arnold: The Anatomy of Treason*. Garden
    City, N.Y.: Doubleday & Company, Inc., c1960. E278.A7L42
Lewis, Adm. De Grasse
    Lewis, Charles Lee, *Admiral De Grasse and American Independence*.
    Annapolis: United States Naval Institute, c1945. E265.L45
Lewis, Hist. and Govt. of W. Va.
    Lewis, Virgil A., *History and Government of West Virginia*. New York
    American Book Company, c1922. F241.L673 1922
Lewis, Indiana Co.
    Lewis, George Elmer, *The Indiana Company, 1763-1798: A Study in
    Eighteenth Century Frontier Land Speculation and Business Venture*.
    Glendale, Calif.: The Arthur H. Clark Company, 1941. F517.I67

Lexington-Concord Battle Rd.
    U.S. Boston National Historic Sites Commission, *Interim Report of the
        Boston National Historic Sites Commission . . . Pertaining to the*
        Lexington-Concord Battle Road. (86th Congress, 1st Session, House
        Document 57). Washington: Government Printing Office, 1959.
        F72.M7U5
Lillie, Cambridge in 1775
    Lillie, Rupert Ballou, *Cambridge in 1775.* Salem, Mass.: Newcome &
        Gauss Co., 1949. F74.C1L55
Lodge, Story of Rev.
    Lodge, Henry Cabot, *The Story of the Revolution.* New York: Charles
        Scribner's Sons, 1903. E208.L83
Lonergan, Ticonderoga
    Lonergan, Carroll Vincent, *Ticonderoga, Historic Portage.* Ticon-
        deroga, N.Y.: Fort Mount Hope Society Press, c1959. F129.T5L65
Long Is. Hist. Soc. Quar.
    The Long Island Historical Society Quarterly. Vol. 1. Brooklyn,
        N.Y.: The Society. F116.L875
Lonsdale, Atlas of N.C.
    Lonsdale, Richard E., *Atlas of North Carolina.* Chapel Hill: The
        University of North Carolina Press, 1967. G1300.L6 1967 Map
        Division
Lord, Atlas
    Lord, Clifford L., and Elizabeth H. Lord, *Historical Atlas of the*
        United States. Revised edition. New York: Henry Holt and Company,
        c1953. G1201.S1L6 1953
Lossing, Field-Book of Rev.
    Lossing, Benson John, *The Pictorial Field-Book of the Revolution.* 2v.
        New York: Harper & Brothers, 1859-1860. E208.L882
Lossing, Life of Washington
    Lossing, Benson John, *Life of Washington: A Biography, Personal,*
        Military, and Political. Vols. 1, 2. New York: Virtue and
        Company, 1860. E312.L88
Lossing, Washington, A Biography
    Lossing, Benson John, *Washington, A Biography.* Vols. 1,2. Phila-
        delphia: George Barrie's Sons, c1914. E312.L885
Lossing, Washington and Am. Republic
    Lossing, Benson John, *Washington and the American Republic.* Vols.
        1, 2. New York: Virtue & Yorston, 1870. E312.L886
Lovell, Israel Angell
    Lovell, Louise Lewis, *Israel Angell, Colonel of the 2nd Rhode Island*
        Regiment. New York: G.P. Putnam's Sons, 1921. E263.R4A6
Lovell, Journal
    Lovell, Solomon, *The Original Journal of General Solomon Lovell, Kept*
        during the Penobscot Expedition, 1779. Boston: The Weymouth Histor-
        ical Society, 1881. F74.W77W7 no.1
Lowell, Hessians
    Lowell, Edward Jackson, *The Hessians and the Other German Auxiliaries*
        of Great Britain in the Revolutionary War. Port Washington, N.Y.:
        Kennikat Press, Inc., 1965. E268.L9 1965
Ludlow, War of Am. Independence
    Ludlow, John Malcolm, *The War of American Independence, 1775-1783*
        New York: Longmans, Green, and Co., 1899. E208.L96
Lundin, Cockpit
    Lundin, Leonard, *Cockpit of the Revolution: The War for Independence*
        in New Jersey. Princeton: Princeton University Press, 1940.
        E263.N5L8

Lunny, Early Maps of N. Am.
   Lunny, Robert M., *Early Maps of North America*.   Newark, N.J.: The
   New Jersey Historical Society, 1961.   GA401.L8
Lydekker, Faithful Mohawks
   Lydekker, John Wolfe, *The Faithful Mohawks*.   Cambridge, Eng.: The
   University Press, 1938.   E99.M8L93
Maclay, Hist. of U.S. Navy
   Maclay, Edgar Stanton, *A History of the United States Navy, from 1775
   to 1894*.   Vol. 1.   New York: D. Appleton and Company, 1895.
McClintock, Washington's Camp
   McClintock, Emory, *Topography of Washington's Camp of 1780 and Its
   Neighborhood*.   [Morristown?,] N.J., [1894?].   E236.M12
McCrady, S. Carolina 1775-80
   McCrady, Edward, *The History of South Carolina in the Revolution,
   1775-1780*.   New York: The Macmillan Company, 1901.   E263.S7M13
McCrady, S. Carolina 1780-83
   McCrady, Edward, *The History of South Carolina in the Revolution,
   1780-1783*.   New York: The Macmillan Company, 1902.   E263.S7M14
McDowell, Revolutionary War
   McDowell, Bart, *The Revolutionary War*.   Washington, D.C.: The
   National Geographic Society, c1967.   E208.M12
MacElree, Along W. Brandywine
   MacElree, Wilmer W., *Along the Western Brandywine*.   2nd edition.
   West Chester, Pa.: F.S. Hickman, 1912.   F157.C4M22
Macintyre, Admiral Rodney
   Macintyre, Capt. Donald, *Admiral Rodney*.   New York: W.W. Norton
   & Co., Inc., 1963.   DA87.1.R6M3 1963
McIver, Washington in French and Indian War
   McIver, Brig. Gen. George Wilcox, *Washington in the French and Indian
   War*.   Washington, D.C., 1932.   E312.23.M16
Mackenzie, Br. Fusilier
   Mackenzie, Frederick, *A British Fusilier in Revolutionary Boston*.
   Allen French, ed.   Cambridge: Harvard University Press, 1926
   E267.M15
Mackenzie, Diary
   Mackenzie, Frederick, *Diary of Frederick Mackenzie, Giving a Daily
   Narrative of His Military Service as an Officer of the Regiment of
   Royal Welch Fusiliers during the Years 1775-1781 in Massachusetts,
   Rhode Island, and New York*.   Vol. 1.   Cambridge, Mass.: Harvard
   University Press, 1930.   E267.M17
Mackenzie, Kings Mt.
   Mackenzie, George C., *Kings Mountain National Military Park, South
   Carolina*.   (National Park Service Historical Handbook Series, No.
   22).   Revised edition.   Washington, 1956.   E241.K5M3 1956
Mackesy, War for America
   Mackesy, Piers, *The War for America, 1775-1783*.   Cambridge: Harvard
   University Press, 1964.   E208.M14
McKown, Am. Revolution
   McKown, Robin, *The American Revolution: The French Allies*.   New York:
   McGraw-Hill Book Company, c1969.   E265.M27
McMaster, Hist. of People of U.S.
   McMaster, John Bach, *A History of the People of the United States,
   from the Revolution to the Civil War*.   Vol. 3.   New York: D.
   Appleton and Company, 1891.   E301.M16

MacMunn, Am. War
　　MacMunn, Lt. Gen. Sir George, *The American War of Independence in
　　　Perspective. London: G. Bell & Sons Ltd., 1939. E208.M15
MacNeill, Valley Forge Landmarks
　　MacNeill, Aimes Junker, *Valley Forge Landmarks, including Generals'
　　　Quarters during the Time of the Encampment, 1777-1778*. Whitford,
　　　Pa.: Stephen Moylan Press, 1958. E234.M3
MacWethy, Book of Names
　　MacWethy, Lou D., Comp., *The Book of Names, especially Relating to*
　　　the Early Palatines and the First Settlers in the Mohawk Valley.
　　　St. Johnsville, N.Y.: The Enterprise and News, 1933. F118.M19
Madison, Papers
　　Madison, James, *The Papers of James Madison*. William T. Hutchinson
　　　and William M.E. Rachal, eds. Vols. 1, 2. Chicago: The University
　　　of Chicago Press, 1962. JK11.M24
Mag. of Am. Hist.
　　Magazine of American History, with Notes and Queries. Vols. 1, 3-8,
　　　10. New York: A.S. Barnes & Co., 1877-1883. E171.M18
Maggs Bros. Berthier
　　Maggs Bros., Ltd., *The American War for Independence as Related in
　　　the Unpublished Manuscript Journals and Plans of Alexander Berthier*.
　　　. . . London, 1936. Z6616.B54M2
Mahan, Influence of Sea Power
　　Mahan, Alfred Thayer, *The Influence of Sea Power upon History, 1660-
　　　1783*. 25th edition. Boston: Little, Brown, and Company, 1919.
Mahan, Navies
　　Mahan, Alfred Thayer, *The Major Operations of the Navies in the War
　　　of American Independence*. Boston: Little, Brown, and Company, 1913.
　　　E271.M22
Mahan, Royal Navy
　　Mahan, Alfred Thayer, *Major Operations of the Royal Navy, 1762-1783*.
　　　Boston: Little, Brown, and Company, 1898. E271.M21
Malone, Am. Origins
　　Malone, Dumas, and Basil Rauch, *American Origins to 1789*. New York:
　　　Appleton-Century-Crofts, 1964. E178.M25
Malone, Cherokees
　　Malone, Henry Thompson, *Cherokees of the Old South: A People in
　　　Transition*. Athens: The University of Georgia Press, c1956.
　　　E99.C5M3
Marine Corps Gaz.
　　Marine Corps Gazette. Vol. 34. Quantico, Va.: The Marine Corps
　　　Association. VE7.M4
Marshall, Atlas
　　Marshall, John, *Atlas to Marshall's Life of Washington*. Philadelphia:
　　　J. Crissy, 1840. E312.M359 Atlas
Martelaer's Rock Assn., 3rd Annual Rept.
　　Martelaer's Rock Association, *Third Annual Report and Year Book, 1919-
　　　1920*. West Point, N.Y., 1920. F127.C2C6
Martyn, Artemas Ward
　　Martyn, Charles, *The Life of Artemas Ward, the First Commander-in-
　　　Chief of the American Revolution*. New York: Artemas Ward, 1921.
　　　E207.W2M38
Md. Hist. Mag.
　　Maryland Historical Magazine. Vols. 41,57. Baltimore: Maryland
　　　Historical Society. F176.M18

Mason, Ft. Lernoult
  Mason, Philip P., *Detroit, Fort Lernoult, and the American Revolution*.
    Detroit: Wayne State University Press, 1964.
Mason, James Harrod
  Mason, Kathryn Harrod, *James Harrod of Kentucky*. Baton Rouge:
    Louisiana State University Press, c1951. F454.H3M3
Mason, Stars on the Sea
  Mason, F. van Wyck, *Stars on the Sea*. Philadelphia: J.P. Lippincott
    Company, c1940. PZ3.M3855St
Mass. Hist. Soc., Battle of Bunker Hill
  Massachusetts Historical Society, *The Battle of Bunker Hill*. Boston:
    The Society, 1968. E241.B9M3
Mass. Hist. Soc., Proc.
  Massachusetts Historical Society, *Proceedings*. Vols. 17, 20, 67.
    Boston: The Society. F61.M38
Mather, Refugees of 1776
  Mather, Frederic Gregory, *The Refugees of 1776 from Long Island to
    Connecticut*. Albany, N.Y.: J.B. Lyon Company, 1913. E263.N6M4
Mathews, Mark of Honour
  Mathews, Hazel C., *The Mark of Honour*. Toronto: University Press,
    1965. E277.M43
Matloff, Am. Military History
  Matloff, Maurice, ed., *American Military History*. Washington, D.C.:
    Office of the Chief of Military History, United States Army 1969.
    E181.M33 1969
Matthews, Twenty-One Plans
  Matthews, John, *Twenty-One Plans, with Explanations, of Different
    Actions in the West Indies, during the Late War, by an Officer in
    the Royal Navy, Who Was Present*. Chester: J. Fletcher, 1784.
    E271.M43 Office
May, Brookline in Rev.
  May, Margaret Elizabeth, *Brookline in the Revolution*. (Brookline
    Historical Publication Society Publications No. 3). Brookline,
    Mass.: The Riverdale Press, 1897. F74.B9B8
Mays, Edmund Pendleton
  Mays, David John, *Edmund Pendleton, 1721-1803: A Biography*. Vol. 2.
    Cambridge: Harvard University Press, 1952. F230.P425
Meredith, Am. Wars
  Meredith, Roy, *The American Wars: A Pictorial History from Quebec to
    Korea, 1755-1953*. Cleveland: The World Publishing Company, 1955.
    E181.M5
Merrens, Colonial N.C.
  Merrens, Harry Roy, *Colonial North Carolina in the Eighteenth Century*.
    Chapel Hill: The University of North Carolina Press, c1964. F257.M4
Meyer, Highland Scots of N.C.
  Meyer, Duane Gilbert, *The Highland Scots of North Carolina, 1732-
    1776*. Chapel Hill: The University of North Carolina Press, c1961.
    F265.S3M4 1961
Mich. Hist. Mag.
  Michigan History Magazine. Vol. 14. Lansing: Michigan Historical
    Commission. F561.M57
Middlebrook, Maritime Conn.
  Middlebrook, Louis Frank, *History of Maritime Connecticut during the
    American Revolution, 1775-1783*. 2v. Salem, Mass.: The Essex
    Institute, 1925. F99.M63

Middlebrook, Salisbury Cannon
  Middlebrook, Louis Frank, *Salisbury Connecticut Cannon, Revolutionary War*. Salem, Mass.: Newcomb & Gauss Co., 1935. UF534.C8M5 Office
Miers, Blood of Freedom
  Miers, Earl Schenck, *Blood of Freedom: The Story of Jamestown, Williamsburg, and Yorktown*. Williamsburg, Va.: Colonial Williamsburg, 1958. F234.W7W7 vol.3
Miers, Yankee Doodle Dandy
  Miers, Earl Schenck, *Yankee Doodle Dandy*. Chicago: Rand McNally & Company, c1963. E208.M47
Mil. Affairs
  Military Affairs: Journal of the American Military Institute. Vols. 1, 15, 17, 19, 20. Washington, D.C.: American Military Institute. E181.M55
Mil. Engineer
  The Military Engineer. Vols. 23, 31, 40, 41, 45, 48, 55. Washington: Society of American Military Engineers. TA1.P85
Military Review
  Military Review. Vols. 30, 43. Fort Leavenworth, Kansas: U.S. Army Command and General Staff College. Z6723.U35
Mil. Ser. Institution, Jl.
  Military Service Institution of the United States, *Journal*. Vols. 50, 51. Governors' Island, N.Y. U1.M6
Miller, Triumph of Freedom
  Miller, John C., *Triumph of Freedom, 1775-1783*. Boston: Little, Brown, and Company, 1948. E208.M5 1948
Miller, W. Va. and Its People
  Miller, Thomas Condit, and Hu Maxwell, *West Virginia and Its People*. Vol. 1. New York: Lewis Historical Publishing Company, 1913. F241.M65
Mo. Hist. Rev.
  Missouri Historical Review. Vol. 55. Columbia: State Historical Society of Missouri. F461.M59
Mitchell, Battles Am. Rev.
  Mitchell, Joseph Brady, *Decisive Battles of the American Revolution*. New York: G.P. Putnam's Sons, c1962. E230.M5
Mitchell, Discipline and Bayonets
  Mitchell, Joseph Brady, *Discipline and Bayonets: The Armies and Leaders in the War of the American Revolution*. New York: G.P. Putnam's Sons, 1967. E255.M64
Mitchell, Twenty Battles
  Mitchell, Joseph Brady, and Sir Edward S. Creasy, *Twenty Decisive Battles of the World*. New York: The Macmillan Company, c1964. D25.M52
Mohr, Fed. Indian Relations
  Mohr, Walter H., *Federal Indian Relations, 1774-1788*. Philadelphia: University of Pennsylvania Press, 1933. E93.M74
Montmort, Vioménil
  Montmort, Roger, Comte de, *Antoine Charles du Houx, Baron de Vioménil, Lieutenant-General of the Armies of the King, Second in Command under Rochambeau*. Englished by John Francis Gough. Baltimore: The John Hopkins Press, 1935. E265.V56
Month at Goodspeed's
  The Month at Goodspeed's Book Shop. Vol. 29. Boston. Z999.G655

Montross, Rag, Tag and Bobtail
  Montross, Lynn, *Rag, Tag and Bobtail: The Story of the Continental
    Army, 1775-1783*. New York: Harper and Brothers, c1952. E255.M66
Montross, War through the Ages
  Montross, Lynn, *War through the Ages*. New York: Harper & Brothers,
    c1944. U27.M6
Moore, Diary of Am. Rev.
  Moore, Frank, *Diary of the American Revolution from Newspapers and
    Original Documents*. 2v. New York: Charles Scribner, 1859-1860.
    E208.M82
Moore, Gen. John Stark
  Moore, Howard Parker, *A Life of General John Stark of New Hampshire*.
    Boston: Spaulding-Moss Company, c1949.
Morales Padrón, Spanish Help
  Morales Padrón, Francisco, *Spanish Help in American Independence*.
    Madrid: Publicaciones Españolas, 1952. E249.M675
Morgan, Gentle Puritan
  Morgan, Edmund Sears, *The Gentle Puritan: A Life of Ezra Stiles,
    1727-1795*. New Haven: Yale University Press, 1962. LD6330 1778.M6
Morison, Growth of Am. Republic
  Morison, Samuel Eliot, and Henry Steele Commager, *The Growth of the
    American Republic*. 5th edition. Vol. 1. New York: Oxford Uni-
    versity Press, 1962. E178.M85 1962 (4th edition E178.M85 1950)
Morison, Hist. of Am. People
  Morison, Samuel Eliot, *The Oxford History of the American People*.
    New York: Oxford University Press, 1965. E178.M855
Morison, Jones
  Morison, Samuel Eliot, *John Paul Jones: A Sailor's Biography*.
    Boston: Little, Brown, and Company, c1959. E207.J7M6
Morris, Enc. of Am. Hist.
  Morris, Richard B., ed., *Encyclopedia of American History*. Updated
    and Revised. New York: Harper & Row, c1965. E174.5.M847 1965
Morris, Peacemakers
  Morris, Richard B., *The Peacemakers: The Great Powers and American
    Independence*. New York: Harper & Row, c1965. E249.M68
Morrison, Indiana
  Morrison, Olin Dee, *Indiana, "Hoosier State": New Historical Atlas
    of Indiana*. Athens, Ohio: E.M. Morrison, 1958. G1401.S1M6 1958
    Map Division
Morrison, Ohio in Maps
  Morrison, Olin Dee, *Ohio in Maps and Charts: A Historical Atlas*.
    Athens, Ohio, 1956. G1396.S1M6 1956 Map Division
Morton, Colonial Va.
  Morton, Richard Lee, *Colonial Virginia*. Vol. 2. Chapel Hill: The
    University of North Carolina Press, 1960. F229.M75
Mowat, East Fla.
  Mowat, Charles Loch, *East Florida as a British Province, 1763-1784*.
    Berkeley: University of California Press, 1943. E173.C15 vol.32
    and F314.M78
Munger, Hist. Atlas
  Munger, William P., ed., *Historical Atlas of New York State*. Phoe-
    nix, N.Y.: Frank E. Richards, 1941. G1250.M 1941 Map Division
Munsell, Annals of Albany
  Munsell, Joel, *The Annals of Albany*. Vol. 4. Albany, N.Y.: Joel
    Munsell, 1853. F129.A3M9

Murdock, Bunker Hill
  Murdock, Harold, *Bunker Hill: Notes and Queries on a Famous Battle*.
    Boston: Houghton Mifflin Company, 1927. E241.B9M9
Murdock, Earl Percy Dines Abroad
  Murdock, Harold, *Earl Percy Dines Abroad: A Boswellian Episode*.
    Boston: Houghton Mifflin Company, 1924. E267.M968
Murdock, 19th Apr. 1775
  Murdock, Harold, *The Nineteenth of April 1775*. Boston: Houghton   ✓
    Mifflin Company, 1923. E241.L6M7
Murray, Notes on Sullivan Exped.
  Murray, Louis Welles, ed., *Notes from Craft Collection in Tioga
    Point Museum on the Sullivan Expedition of 1779. . . .* Athens, Pa.,
    1929. E235.M97
Murray, Old Tioga Pt.
  Murray, Louise Welles, *A History of Old Tioga Point and Early Athens,
    Pennsylvania*. Athens, Pa., 1908. F159.A9M9
Murray, Order Book of Ft. Sullivan
  Murray, Louise Welles, comp., *Order Book of Fort Sullivan and
    Extracts from Journals of Soldiers in Gen. Sullivan's Army Relating
    to Fort Sullivan at Tioga Point, Pennsylvania, 1779*. Athens, Pa.,
    1903. E235.M98
Myers, Hist. of W. Va.
  Myers, Sylvester, *Myer's History of West Virginia*. Vol. 1. [New
    Martinsville, W. Va., 1915]. F241.M99
Myers, Story of N.J.
  Myers, William Starr, ed., *The Story of New Jersey*, Vol. 1. New York:
    Lewis Historical Publishing Co., Inc., c1945. F134.M97
National Geographic
  The National Geographic Magazine. Vol. 61. Washington, D.C.: The
    National Geographic Society. G1.N27
N.P.S., Guilford
  U.S. National Park Service, *Guilford Courthouse, National Military
    Park, Greensboro, North Carolina*. Washington, D.C., 1940.
    E241.G9U5 1940
Naval Docs. of Am. Rev.
  U.S. Naval History Division, *Naval Documents of the American Revolu-
    tion*. Vols. 1-4. Washington: Government Printing Office, 1964-66
    E271.U583
Neatby, Quebec
  Neatby, Hilda Marion, *Quebec: The Revolutionary Age, 1760-1791*.
    Toronto: McClelland and Stewart Limited, c1966. F1032.N34
Neilsen, Burgoyne's Campaign
  Neilsen, Charles, *An Original, Compiled and Corrected Account of
    Burgoyne's Campaign, and the Memorable Battles of Bemis's Heights,
    Sept. 19, and Oct. 7, 1777*. Albany: J. Munsell, 1844. E233.N41
Nettels, Roots of Am. Civ.
  Nettels, Curtis Putnam, *Roots of American Civilization: A History of
    American Colonial Life*. New York: F.S. Crofts & Co., 1938.
    E188.N48
Nettels, Washington
  Nettels, Curtis Putnam, *George Washington and American Independence*.
    Boston: Little, Brown and Company, 1951. E312.25.N4
New Brunswick Hist. Soc., Coll.
  New Brunswick Historical Society, *Collections*. Vol. 36. St. John,
    N.B. F1041.N53

N.H. State Papers
New Hampshire State Papers. Vol. 26. Concord, N.H.: Edward N.
Pearson, 1895. F31.N42
N.J. Hist. Soc., Proc.
New Jersey Historical Society, Proceedings. Vols. 69, 70. Newark,
N.J. F131.N58
New York, Am. Rev. in N.Y.
New York (State), Division of Archives and History, The American
Revolution in New York: Its Political, Social and Economic Signifi-
cance. Albany: The University of the State of New York, 1926.
F123.N565
N.Y., Bennington Program
New York (State) University, Executive Committee on the One Hundred
and Fiftieth Anniversary of the American Revolution, Souvenir Pro-
gram, One Hundred Fiftieth Anniversary of the Battle of Bennington.
Albany, 1927. E241.B4N5
N.Y., Calendar of Hist. MSS.
New York (State) Secretary of State, Calendar of Historical Manu-
scripts Relating to the War of the Revolution in the Office of the
Secretary of State, Albany, N.Y. 2v. Albany: Weed, Parsons and
Company, 1868. E263.N6N6
N.Y. City during Am. Rev.
New York Mercantile Library Association, New York City during the
American Revolution. New York, 1861. E263.N6N72 and F128.44.N5
N.Y. Common Council, Manual
New York (City) Common Council, Manual of the Corporation of the City
of New York. Vols. for 1854, 1857, 1858, 1859, 1861, 1864, 1866,
1868, 1869, 1870, 1871. New York. F128.1.N53
N.Y. Hist. Soc., Collections
New-York Historical Society, Collections. Publication Fund Series.
Vols. 13, 14. New York, 1881-1882. F116.N63
N.Y. Hist. Soc. Quar.
The New-York Historical Society Quarterly. Vols. 32, 36, 40, 41,
42, 45. New York: The Society. F116.N638
N.Y. Hist. Soc., Quar. Bul.
New-York Historical Society, Quarterly Bulletin. Vols. 2, 3, 7, 8.
New York: The Society. F116.N638
N.Y. Hist.
New York History. Vol. 19. Cooperstown: New York State Historical
Association. F116.N865
N.Y., New York in Rev.
New York (State) Comptroller's Office, New York in the Revolution as
Colony and State. 2nd edition. Albany: Brandow Printing Company,
1898. E263.N6N442
N.Y. Publ. Lib., Bul.
Bulletin of the New York Public Library. Vol. 37. New York.
Z881.N6B
N.Y., Saratoga and Burgoyne
New York (State) University, Executive Committee of the One Hundred
and Fiftieth Anniversary of the American Revolution, One Hundred
Fiftieth Anniversary of the Battle of Saratoga and the Surrender of
Burgoyne. Albany, 1927. E241.S2N6
N.Y. State Hist. Assn., Proc.
New York State Historical Association, Proceedings. Vol. 14. Albany.
F116.N86

N.Y. State Hist. Assn., Quar. Jl.
  New York State Historical Association, *Quarterly Journal*. Vols. 3,
    8-12. Albany. F116.N865
N.Y., Sullivan-Clinton Campaign
  New York (State), State Historian, *The Sullivan-Clinton Campaign in
    1779*. Albany: The University of the State of New York, 1929.
    E235.N55
N.Y., Sullivan Journals
  New York (State), Secretary of State, *Journals of the Military
    Expedition of Major General John Sullivan Against the Six Nations
    of Indians in 1779*. Auburn, N.Y.: Knapp, Peck & Thomson, 1887.
    E235.N53
Newport Hist. Soc., Bul.
  Newport Historical Society, *Bulletin*. Nos. 6, 51. Newport, R.I.
    F89.N5N615
Newsome, Growth of N.C.
  Newsome, Albert Ray, and Hugh Talmage Lefler, *The Growth of North
    Carolina*. Yonkers, N.Y.: World Book Company, c1940. F254.N48
Newton, Vermont Story
  Newton, Earle Williams, *The Vermont Story: A History of the People of
    the Green Mountain State, 1749-1949*. Montpelier: The Vermont
    Historical Society, 1949. F49.N49
Nickerson, Turning Point
  Nickerson, Hoffman, *The Turning Point of the Revolution; or, Burgoyne
    in America*. Boston: Houghton Mifflin Company, 1928. E233.N63
Nields, Washington's Army in Del.
  Nields, John P., *Washington's Army in Delaware in the Summer of 1777*.
    n.p., 1927. E233.N66
Niles, Chronicles
  Niles, Hezekiah, *Chronicles of the American Revolution*. Alden T.
    Vaughan, ed. New York: Grosset and Dunlap, 1965. E203.N69 1965
Niles, Hoosac Valley
  Niles, Grace Greylock, *The Hoosac Valley: Its Legends and Its History*.
    New York: G.P. Putnam's Sons, 1912. F127.H73N6
Noel Hume, 1775
  Noel Hume, Ivor, *1775, Another Part of the Field*. New York: Alfred
    A. Knopf, 1966. E263.V8N6
Nolan, S.E. Penna.
  Nolan, James Bennett, *Southeastern Pennsylvania*. Vol. 1. Philadel-
    phia: Lewis Publishing Company, Inc., c1943. F157.A18W6
N.C. Booklet
  The North Carolina Booklet. Vols. 3-6, 8. Raleigh: The North Caro-
    lina Society of the Daughters of the American Revolution.
    E241.M8N7 1904 and F251.N86
N.C. Hist. Rev.
  The North Carolina Historical Review. Vols. 30, 31. Raleigh: State
    Department of Archives and History. F251.N892
Northumberland Co. Hist. Soc., Proc.
  The Northumberland County Historical Society, *Proceedings and
    Addresses*. Vol. 6. Northumberland, Pa.: The Susquehanna Press.
    F157.N8N7
Norton, Orderly Book
  Norton, Ichabod, *Orderly Book of Capt. Ichabod Norton of Col. Mott's
    Regiment of Connecticut Troops Destined for the Northern Campaign
    in 1776, at Skeensborough (now Whitehall), Fort Ann and Ticonderoga,
    N.Y., and at Mount Independence, Vt.* Robert O. Bascom, ed. Fort
    Edward, N.Y.: Keating & Barnard, 1898. E263.C5C59

Norton, Sullivan's Campaign
  Norton, A. Tiffany, *History of Sullivan's Campaign against the Iroquois*. Lima, N.Y., 1879.   E235.N88
O'Callaghan, Doc. Hist. of N.Y.
  O'Callaghan, Edmund Burke, *The Documentary History of the State of New York*. Vols. 1, 3, 4.   Albany: Charles Van Benthuysen, 1850-1851.   F122.D64
O'Dea, Washington
  O'Dea, Arthur J., *Washington and His Army in Bergen County, November 13th-21st, 1776*. Hackensack, N.J.: Bergen County Bar Association, 1957.   E232.O4
Ohio Arch. and Hist. Soc., Pub.
  Ohio Archaeological and Historical Society, *Publications*.   Vols. 6, 10, 12.   Columbus, O.   F486.O51
O.P.S. Portfolio
  The Old Print Shop Portfolio.   Vol. 7.   New York: Harry Shaw Newman.   NE1.O63
Old York Rd. Hist. Soc. Bul.
  Old York Road Historical Society Bulletin.   Vol. 3.   Jenkintown, Pa.   F146.O58
O'Meara, Guns at the Forks
  O'Meara, Walter, *Guns at the Forks*.   Englewood Cliffs, N.J.: Prentice-Hall Inc., c1965.   F159.P604
Onderdonk, Rev. Incidents
  Onderdonk, Henry, Jr., *Revolutionary Incidents of Suffolk and Kings Counties; with an Account of the Battle of Long Island, and the British Prisons and Prison-Ships at New York*.   New York: Leavitt & Company, 1849.   E263.N605 and E263.N6056
Ontario History
  Ontario History.   Vol. 52.   Toronto: Ontario Historical Society   F1056.O58
Ostrander, Old Saratoga
  Ostrander, William S., *Old Saratoga and the Burgoyne Campaign*.   Schuylerville, N.Y., 1897.   E233.O86
Pag. Am.
  The Pageant of America: A Pictorial History of the United States.   Ralph Henry Gabriel, ed.   Vols. 2, 6.   New Haven: Yale University Press, 1927-1929.   E178.5.P195
Palmer, Atlas of World Hist.
  Palmer, Robert Roswell, ed., *Atlas of World History*.   Chicago: Rand McNally & Company, c1957.   G1030.R3 1957
Palmer, Clark of the Ohio
  Palmer, Frederick, *Clark of the Ohio: A Life of George Rogers Clark*.   New York: Dodd, Mead & Company, 1929.   E207.C5P18
Palmer, L. Champlain
  Palmer, Peter Sailly, *History of Lake Champlain, from Its First Exploration by the French in 1609, to the Close of the Year 1814*.   Albany: J. Munsell, 1866.   F127.C6P2
Palmer, River and Rock
  Palmer, Dave Richard, *The River and the Rock: The History of Fortress West Point, 1775-1781*.   New York: Greenwood Publishing Corporation, c1969.   F129.W7P17
Palmer, Steuben
  Palmer, John McAuley, *General Von Steuben*.   New Haven: Yale University Press, 1937.   E207.S8P3

Paoli Massacre Proc.
  *Proceedings on the Occasion of the Dedication of the Monument on the
  One Hundreth Anniversary of the Paoli Massacre, in Chester County,
  Pa., September 20, 1777.* West Chester, Pa.: F.S. Hickman, 1877.
  E241.P2P9
Parkman, Pontiac
  Parkman, Francis, *The Conspiracy of Pontiac.* 2v. London: J.M. Dent
  & Sons, Ltd., 1943-1944.
Pasley, Sea Journals
  Pasley, Sir Thomas, *Private Sea Journals, 1778-1782.* Rodney M.S.
  Pasley, ed. London: J.M. Dent & Sons, Ltd., 1931. DA87.1.P35A3
Passano, Hist. of Md.
  Passano, L. Magruder, *History of Maryland.* 5th edition. Baltimore:
  Wm. J.C. Dulany Company, c1901. F181.P28
Patterson, Knight Errant
  Patterson, Samuel White, *Knight Errant of Liberty: The Triumph and
  Tragedy of General Charles Lee.* New York: Lantern Press, c1958.
  E207.L47P35
Patterson, Peekskill
  Patterson, Emma Lillie, *Peekskill in the American Revolution.* Peeks-
  kill, N.Y.: The Friendly Town Association, Inc., 1944. F129.P37P3
Patton, Yorktown
  Patton, Jacob Harris, *Yorktown.* New York: Fords, Howard, and Hulbert,
  1882. E241.Y6P3
Paullin, Atlas
  Paullin, Charles Oscar, *Atlas of the Historical Geography of the
  United States.* John K. Wright, ed. (Carnegie Institution of
  Washington Publication No. 401). Washington, 1932. G1201.S1P3 1932
  Map Division
Pausch, Journal
  Pausch, Georg, *Journal of Captain Pausch, Chief of the Hanau Artillery
  during the Burgoyne Campaign.* William L. Stone, tr. Albany: Joel
  Munsell's Sons, 1886. E233.P33
Paxson, Am. Frontier
  Paxson, Frederick Logan, *History of the American Frontier, 1763-1893.*
  Students' edition. Boston: Houghton Mifflin Company, c1924.
  E179.5.P343
Payne, Concord Bridge
  Payne, Robert, *Concord Bridge.* By Howard Horne [pseud.]. Indiana-
  polis: The Bobbs-Merrill Company, Inc., c1952. PZ4.P347Co
Pearson, Schenectady Patent
  Pearson, Jonathan, and others, *A History of the Schenectady Patent in
  the Dutch and English Times; Being Contributions toward a History
  of the Lower Mohawk Valley.* J.W. MacMurray, ed. Albany: Joel
  Munsell's Sons, 1883. F129.S5P3
Peckham, Pontiac
  Peckham, Howard Henry, *Pontiac and the Indian Uprising.* Chicago: The
  University of Chicago Press, 1961.
Peckham, War for Independence
  Peckham, Howard Henry, *The War for Independence: A Military History.*
  Chicago: The University of Chicago Press, 1958. E230.P36
Pell, Ethan Allen
  Pell, John, *Ethan Allen.* Boston: Houghton Mifflin Company, 1929.
  E207.A4P38

Prentice, Hist. of N.Y. State
  Prentice, William Reed, *History of New York State*.   Syracuse: C.W.
    Bardeen, 1900.   F119.P92
Preston, Battle of R.I.
  Preston, Howard Willis, *The Battle of Rhode Island, August 29th, 1778*.
    Providence: State Bureau of Information, 1928.   E241.R4P9
Preston, Gentleman Rebel
  Preston, John Hyde, *A Gentleman Rebel: The Exploits of Anthony Wayne*.
    New York: Farrar & Rinehart, Incorporated, 1930.   E207.W35P93
Preston, R.I. Hist. Background
  Preston, Howard Willis, *Rhode Island's Historic Background*.   2nd
    edition.   Providence: State Bureau of Information, 1933.
    F76.R334 no.3^a
Preston, Rochambeau
  Preston, Howard Willis, *Rochambeau and the French Troops in Providence
    in 1780-81-82*.   Providence, R.I., 1924.   E265.P92
Princeton Battle Mon.
  *The Princeton Battle Monument: The History of the Monument, a Record
    of the Ceremonies Attending Its Unveiling, and an Account of the
    Battle of Princeton*.   Princeton, N.J.: Princeton University Press,
    1922.   E241.P9P9
Princeton Univ. Lib. Chron.
  The Princeton University Library Chronicle.   Vol. 13.   Princeton, N.J.:
    The Friends of the Princeton Library.   Z733.P93C5
Pugh, Cowpens Campaign
  Pugh, Robert Coplin, *The Cowpens Campaign and the American Revolution*.
    Ph.D. thesis on microfilm.   Ann Arbor: University Microfilms, 1951.
    Microfilm AC-1, no.2722
Pulsifer, Bunker Hill
  Pulsifer, David, *An Account of the Battle of Bunker Hill, Compiled
    from Authentic Sources*.   Boston: A. Williams and Co., 1872.
    E241.B9P9
Pusey, Wilderness Rd.
  Pusey, William Allen, *The Wilderness Road to Kentucky*.   New York:
    George H. Doran Company, c1921.   F452.P95
Putnam, Memoirs
  Putnam, Rufus, *The Memoirs of Rufus Putnam*.   Rowena Buell, comp.
    Boston: Houghton, Mifflin and Company, 1903.   F483.P94
Quaife, Capture
  Quaife, Milo M., ed., *The Capture of Old Vincennes: The Original
    Narratives of George Rogers Clark and of His Opponent Gov. Henry
    Hamilton*.   Indianapolis: The Bobbs-Merrill Company, 1927.   F534.V7C6
Quaker Hist.
  Quaker History.   Vol. 52.   Haverford, Pa.: Friends Historical Associa-
    tion.   BX7635.A1F6
Ramsay, Revolution of S.C.
  Ramsay, David, *The History of the Revolution of South Carolina, from
    a British Province to an Independent State*.   2v.   Trenton, N.J.:
    Isaac Collins, 1785.   E263.S7R17 Jefferson Coll.
Ramsey, Annals of Tenn.
  Ramsey, James Gattys McGregor, *The Annals of Tennessee to the End of
    the Eighteenth Century*.   Kingsport, Tenn.: Kingsport Press, 1926
    F436.R24
Randall, Dunmore War
  Randall, Emilius Oviatt, *The Dunmore War*.   Columbus, O.: Fred J.
    Greer, 1902.   E83.77.R26 1902

Randall, Hist. of Ohio
  Randall, Emilius Oviatt, and Daniel J. Ryan. *History of Ohio: The
  Rise and Progress of an American State*. Vols. 1, 2. New York:
  The Century History Co., 1912. F491.R18
Rankin, Am. Rev.
  Rankin, Hugh F., *The American Revolution*. New York: G.P. Putnam's
  Sons, c1964. E203.R3 1964
Rankin, N.C. in Rev.
  Rankin, Hugh F., *North Carolina in the American Revolution*. Raleigh:
  State Department of Archives and History, 1959. E263.N8R3
Raum, Trenton
  Raum, John D., *History of the City of Trenton, New Jersey*. Trenton:
  W.T. Nicholson & Co., 1871. F144.T7R2 Toner Coll.
Rayback, Richards Atlas
  Rayback, Robert J., ed., *Richards Atlas of New York State*. Phoenix,
  N.Y.: Frank E. Richards, 1959. G1250.R5 1959 Map Division
Reade, Dedication Exercises
  Reade, Philip Hildreth, *Dedication Exercises at the Massachusetts
  Military Monument, Valley Forge, Pa*. Boston: Wright & Potter
  Printing Company, 1912. E263.M4R3
Reed, Campaign to Valley Forge
  Reed, John Frederick, *Campaign to Valley Forge, July 1, 1777 -
  December 19, 1777*. Philadelphia: University of Pennsylvania Press,
  c1965. E233.R33
Reed, Valley Forge
  Reed, John F., *Valley Forge, Crucible of Victory*. Monmouth Beach,
  N.J.: Philip Freneau Press, 1969. E234.R36
Reeder, Story of Rev. War
  Reeder, Russell Potter, *The Story of the Revolutionary War*. New York:
  Duell, Sloan and Pearce, c1959. E208.R4
Reid, Guilford
  Reid, Courtland T., *Guilford Courthouse National Military Park, North
  Carolina*. (National Park Service Historical Handbook Series No. 30).
  Washington, 1959. E241.G9R4
Revel, Journal
  Revel, Gabriel Joachim du Perron, Comte de, *Journal Particulier d'une
  Campagne aux Indes Occidentales (1781-1782)*. Paris: Henri Charles-
  Lavauzelle, 1898? E265.R44
Revel, Map of Yorktown
  Revel, Gabriel Joachim du Perron, Comte de, *A Map of Yorktown*.
  Princeton, N.J.: The Princeton University Library, 1942. E241.Y6R47
  Rare Book Coll.
Revue Historique de l'Armée
  Revue Historique de l'Armée. Special Issue Dedicated to the Franco-
  American Comradeship in Arms. Paris: Ministere de la Guerre, 1957.
  E183.8.F8R4
Revue Maritime
  La Revue Maritime, new series, No.195. Paris: Societe d'Éditions
  Géographiques, Maritimes, et Coloniales. V2.R4
Reynolds, Albany Chronicles
  Reynolds, Cuyler, comp., *Albany Chronicles: A History of the City
  Arranged Chronologically*. Albany, N.Y.: J.B. Lyon Company, 1906
  F129.A3R4
Reynolds, Old St. Augustine
  Reynolds, Charles B., *Old Saint Augustine: A Story of Three Centuries*.
  St. Augustine, Fla.: E.H. Reynolds, 1888. F319.S2R36

R.I. Hist. Mag.
  The Rhode Island Historical Magazine. Vol. 5. Providence. F76.R35
R.I. History
  Rhode Island History. Vols. 7, 24. Providence: Rhode Island Histor-
    ical Society. F76.R472
R.I. Hist. Soc., Collections
  Rhode Island Historical Society, *Collections.* Vol. 6. Providence.
    F76.R47
Rice, Allegheny Frontier
  Rice, Otis K., *The Allegheny Frontier: West Virginia Beginnings.*
    Lexington: The University Press of Kentucky, 1970. F241.K5
Richards, Pa.-German in Rev. War
  Richards, Henry Melchior Muhlenberg, *The Pennsylvania-German in the
    Revolutionary War.* (The Pennsylvania-German Society, Proceedings
    and Addresses, Vol. 17). Lancaster, Pa., 1908. F146.P23 vol.17
Richardson, Washington
  Richardson, William H., *George Washington and Jersey City.* (Reprinted
    from N.J. Historical Society, Proceedings, Apr. 1933). Jersey City,
    N.J., c1933. E312.25.R49
Richardson, Washington and Powles Hook
  Richardson, William H., *Washington and "The Enterprise against Powles
    Hook," a New Study of the Surprise and Capture of the Fort, Thurs-
    day, August 19, 1777.* Jersey City, N.J.: The New Jersey Title
    Guarantee and Trust Comapny, 1929. E241.P24R52
Rider, Battle of R.I.
  Rider, Sidney S., *The Centennial Celebration of the Battle of Rhode
    Island, at Portsmouth, R.I., August 29, 1878.* Providence: Sidney
    S. Rider, 1878. F76.R52
Ridpath, New Complete Hist.
  Ridpath, John Clark, *The New Complete History of the United States
    of America.* Official Edition. Vols. 5, 6, 7. Washington: Ridpath
    History Company, 1905. E178.R633
Riker, Evacuation Day
  Riker, James, *"Evacuation Day," 1783: Its Many Stirring Events. . . .*
    New York: Printed for the Author, 1883. E239.R57
Ristow, Services
  Ristow, Walter W., *The Services and Collections of the Map Division.
    The Library of Congress.* Washington: Government Printing Office,
    1951. Z733.U63M28 1951
Roberts, Arundel
  Roberts, Kenneth, *Arundel: A Chronicle of the Province of Maine and
    of the Secret Expedition against Quebec.* Garden City, N.Y.:
    Doubleday, Doran & Company, Inc., 1938. PZ3.R54263 Ar 9
Roberts, Cowpens
  Roberts, Kenneth, *The Battle of Cowpens: The Great Morale-Builder.*
    Garden City, N.Y.: Doubleday & Company, Inc., 1958. E241.C9R6 1958
Roberts, March to Quebec
  Roberts, Kenneth, comp., *March to Quebec: Journals of the Members of
    Arnold's Expedition.* New York: Doubleday, Doran & Company, Inc.,
    1940. E231.563 1940
Roberts, Rabble in Arms
  Roberts, Kenneth, *Rabble in Arms.* Garden City, N.Y.: Doubleday &
    Company, Inc., 1946. PZ3.R54263Rab6

Robertson, Diaries
  Robertson, Archibald, *Archibald Robertson, Lieutenant-General Royal Engineers, His Diaries and Sketches in America, 1762-1780.* Henry Miller Lydenberg, ed. New York: The New York Public Library, 1930. E275.R66 Office
Robertson, Spanish Town Papers
  Robertson, Eileen Arnot, *The Spanish Town Papers: Some Sidelights on the American War of Independence.* New York: The Macmillan Company 1959. E271.R73 1959a
Rochester Hist. Soc. Pub.
  Rochester Historical Society Publication Fund Series. Vol. 3. Rochester, N.Y.: The Society, 1924. F129.R7R58
Rogers, Conn. Naval Office
  Rogers, Ernest Elias, *Connecticut's Naval Office at New London during the War of the American Revolution.* (The New London County Historical Society, Collections, Vol. 2). New London, 1933. F102.N7N8 vol.2
Rogers, Groton Heights
  Rogers, Ernest Elias, comp., *Sesquicentennial of the Battle of Groton Heights and the Battle of New London, Connecticut.* New London: Fort Griswold & Groton Monument Association, 1931. E241.G8C6
Rogers, Journal
  Rogers, William, *The Journal of a Brigade Chaplain in the Campaign of 1779 against the Six Nations under Command of Major-General John Sullivan.* Providence: Sidney S. Rider, 1879. F76.R52
Rogers, New Doane Book
  Rogers, John Pugh, *The New Doane Book: Bucks County's Bandittories of the Revolution.* 2nd edition. Doylestown, Pa.: Bucks County Historical Society, 1952. E280.D6R6 1952
Roosevelt, Winning of West
  Roosevelt, Theodore, *The Winning of the West.* 3v. New York: G.P. Putnam's Sons, 1894-1895.
Roscoe, Picture Hist.
  Roscoe, Theodore, and Fred Freedman, *Picture History of the U.S. Navy.* New York: Charles Scribner's Sons, 1956. E182.R84
Rose, Journal
  Rose, John, *Journal of a Volunteer Expedition to Sandusky from May 24 to June 13, 1782.* (Reprinted from The Pennsylvania Magazine of History and Biography, July and October 1894). Philadelphia, 1894. E238.R81
Roseboom, Hist. of Ohio
  Roseboom, Eugene Holloway, and Francis P. Weisenburger, *A History of Ohio.* Columbus: The Ohio State Archaeological and Historical Society, 1954. F491.R76
Rosengarten, Am. Hist. from Ger. Archives
  Rosengarten, J.G., *American History from German Archives.* Lancaster, Pa., 1904. E268.R83
Rouse, Virginia
  Rouse, Parke, Jr., *Virginia: The English Heritage in America.* New York: Hastings House, c1966. F226.R6
Royal Soc. Canada, Proc.
  Royal Society of Canada, *Proceedings and Transactions.* 2nd series. Vols. 5, 10. Ottawa. AS42.R6
Royal United Service Instn., Journal
  Royal United Service Institution, *Journal.* Vol. 57. London. U1.R8

Royaumont, La Fayette et Rochambeau
  Royaumont, Louis de, *La Fayette et Rochambeau au Pays de Washington.*
    Grenoble: J. Rey, 1919. E265.R66
Russell, Lexington
  Russell, Francis, *Lexington, Concord, and Bunker Hill.* New York:
    American Heritage Publishing Co., 1963. E263.M4R8
Ruttenber, Obstructions of Hudson
  Ruttenber, Edward Manning, *Obstructions to the Navigation of Hudson's
    River.* . . . Albany: J. Munsell, 1860. E263.N6R9
Ruttenber, New Windsor
  Ruttenber, Edward Manning, *History of the Town of New Windsor, Orange
    County, N.Y.* Newburgh, N.Y.: The Historical Society of Newburgh
    Bay and the Highlands, 1911. F129.N6R9
Sanderlin, 1776: Journals
  Sanderlin, George William, comp., *1776: Journals of American Indepen-*
    dence. New York: Harper & Row, 1968 E210.S2
Sanderson, Lynn in Rev.
  Sanderson, Howard Kendall, *Lynn in the Revolution.* Vol. 1. Boston:
    W.B. Clarke Co., 1909. F74.L98S2
Sargent, Life of André
  Sargent, Winthrop, *The Life and Career of Major John André, Adjutant-
    General of the British Army in America.* William Abbatt, ed. New
    York: William Abbatt, 1902. E280.A5S33
Savelle, Foundations
  Savelle, Max, *The Foundations of American Civilization: A History of
    Colonial America.* New York: Henry Holt and Company, 1942. E188.S29
Scenic and Historic Am.
  Scenic and Historic America. Vols. 1-4. New York: The American
    Scenic and Historic Preservation Society. E151.A55
Scharf, Hist. of Md.
  Scharf, John Thomas, *History of Maryland, from the Earliest Period
    to the Present Day.* Vol. 2. Baltimore: John B. Piet, 1879.
    F181.S31
Scharf, Hist. of Phila.
  Scharf, J. Thomas, and Thompson Westcott, *History of Philadelphia,
    1609-1884.* Vol. 1. Philadelphia: L.H. Everts & Co., 1884.
    F158.3.S4
Scharf, Westchester Co.
  Scharf, John Thomas, *History of Westchester County, New York.* Vol. 1.
    Philadelphia: L.E. Preston & Co., 1886. F127.W5S3
Scheer, Rebels and Redcoats
  Scheer, George F., and Hugh F. Rankin, *Rebels and Redcoats.* Cleve-
    land: The World Publishing Company, c1957. E275.S3
Schenck, N. Carolina
  Schenck, David, *North Carolina, 1780-'81: Being a History of the
    Invasion of the Carolinas by the British Army under Lord Cornwallis
    in 1780-'81.* Raleigh: Edwards & Broughton, 1889. E263.N8S3
Schlarman, From Quebec to New Orleans
  Schlarman, Joseph H., *From Quebec to New Orleans: The Story of the
    French in America.* Belleville, Ill.: Buechler Publishing Company,
    1929. F1030.S33
Schwab, Fort No. Eight
  Schwab, John Christopher, *The Revolutionary History of Fort Number
    Eight on Morris Heights, New York City.* New Haven, 1897.
    E230.5.S39

Sigsby, Timothy Murphy
  Sigsby, _____, _Life and Adventures of Timothy Murphy, the Bene-
    factor of Schoharie._ Middleburgh, N.Y.: The Middleburgh Gazette,
    1912. E275.M975
Simcoe, Military Jl.
  Simcoe, John Graves, _Simcoe's Military Journal. A History of the
    Operations of a Partisan Corps, Called the Queen's Rangers, Com-
    manded by Lieut. Col. J.G. Simcoe, during the War of the American
    Revolution._ New York: Bartlett & Welford, 1844. E277.6.Q6S5
    Rare Book Coll.
Simms, Frontiersmen of N.Y.
  Simms, Jeptha R., _The Frontiersmen of New York._ Vol. 2. Albany,
    N.Y.: George C. Riggs, 1883. E263.N6S5
Simonds, South Boston
  Simonds, Thomas C., _History of South Boston; formerly Dorchester
    Neck, now Ward XII. of the City of Boston._ Boston: David Clapp,
    1857. F73.68.S7
Sinclair, Westward the Tide
  Sinclair, Harold, _Westward the Tide._ New York: Doubleday, Doran &
    Co., Inc., 1940. PZ3.S6154We
Singer, S.C. in Confederation
  Singer, Charles Gregg, _South Carolina in the Confederation._ Phila-
    delphia, 1941. E263.S7S53 1941
Sipe, Fort Ligonier
  Sipe, Chester Hale, _Fort Ligonier and Its Times._ Harrisburg, Pa.:
    The Telegraph Press, 1932. F152.S57
Sipe, Indian Wars of Pa.
  Sipe, Chester Hale, _The Indian Wars of Pennsylvania._ Harrisburg,
    Pa.: The Telegraph Press, 1929. E78.P4S54
Sklarsky, Boldest Venture
  Sklarsky, I.W., _The Revolution's Boldest Venture: The Story of General
    "Mad Anthony" Wayne's Assault on Stony Point._ Port Washington,
    N.Y.: Kennikat Press, 1965. E241.S8S55
Sloane, French War and Rev.
  Sloane, William Milligan, _The French War and the Revolution._ New
    York: Charles Scribner's Sons, 1893. E178.A51 and E208.S63
Smith, Arnold's March
  Smith, Justin Harvey, _Arnold's March from Cambridge to Quebec._
    New York: G.P. Putnam's Sons, 1903. E231.S65
Smith, Delaware Co.
  Smith, George, _History of Delaware County, Pennsylvania._ Phila-
    delphia: Henry B. Ashmead, 1862. F157.D3S6 1907
Smith, French at Boston
  Smith, Fitz-Henry, Jr., _The French at Boston during the Revolution._
    Boston: Privately Printed, 1913. E265.S66
Smith, Monmouth
  Smith, Samuel Stelle, _The Battle of Monmouth._ Monmouth Beach, N.J.:
    Philip Freneau Press, 1964. E241.M7S5
Smith, Princeton
  Smith, Samuel Stelle, _The Battle of Princeton._ Monmouth Beach, N.J.:
    Philip Freneau Press, 1967. E241.P9S6
Smith, St. Clair Papers
  Smith, William Henry, ed., _The St. Clair Papers: The Life and Public
    Services of Arthur St. Clair._ . . . Vol. 1. Cincinnati: Robert
    Clarke & Co., 1882. F483.S15

Smith, Sandy Hook
    Smith, Samuel Stelle, *Sandy Hook and the Land of the Navesink*.   Mon-
    mouth Beach, N.J.: Philip Freneau Press, 1963. F142.M7S6
Smith, School Hist. of Ga.
    Smith, Charles H., *A School History of Georgia*. Boston: Ginn &
    Company, 1893. F286.S64
Smith, Struggle for 14th Colony
    Smith, Justin Harvey, *Our Struggle for the Fourteenth Colony*. 2v.
    New York: G.P. Putnam's Sons, 1907. E231.S654
Smith, Tour of Four Great Rivers
    Smith, Richard, *A Tour of Four Great Rivers, the Hudson, Mohawk,
    Susquehanna, and Delaware, in 1769*. Francis W. Halsey, ed. New
    York: Charles Scribner's Sons, 1906. F122.S63
Smith, Trenton
    Smith, Samuel Stelle, *The Battle of Trenton*. Monmouth Beach, N.J.:
    Philip Freneau Press, 1965. E241.T7S6
Snell, Saratoga
    Snell, Charles W., *Saratoga National Historical Park, New York*.
    (National Park Service Historical Handbook Series No. 4). Wash-
    ington, D.C., 1950. E241.S2S68
Sobel, Am. Revolution
    Sobel, Robert, *The American Revolution: A Concise History and Inter-
    pretation*. New York: Ardmore Press, c1967. E208.S7
Soc. for Army Hist. Res., Jl.
    The Society for Army Historical Research, *Journal*. Vols. 6, 8, 13, 15,
    17. London. DA49.S6
Somerset Co. Hist. Quar.
    Somerset County Historical Quarterly. Vol. 5. Somerville, N.J.:
    Somerset County Historical Society. F142.S6S6
Sons of Am. Rev., Maine at Valley Forge
    Sons of the American Revolution, Maine Society, *Maine at Valley Forge*.
    Augusta: Burleigh & Flint, 1910. E234.S695
Sons of Am. Rev., Rev. Characters
    Sons of the American Revolution, Connecticut Society, General David
    Humphreys Branch, No. 1, *Revolutionary Characters of New Haven*.
    New Haven, Conn., c1911. E263.C5S64
Sons of Am. Rev., Old Suffolk Reg.
    Sons of the American Revolution, Massachusetts Society, *Register of
    Old Suffolk Chapter, 1900*. Boston, c1901. E202.3.M38C52
Sons of Am. Rev., Washington's Journey
    The National Society of the Sons of the American Revolution, *Cele-
    bration of the One Hundred and Thirty-Ninth Anniversary of the
    Journey of General Washington from Philadelphia to Cambridge to
    Take Command of the American Army, June 23 - July 3, 1775*. Wash-
    ington, 1914. E312.27.S79
Sons of Rev., N.Y., Year Book (1896)
    Society of Sons of the Revolution in the State of New York, *Year
    Book, 1896*. New York: Exchange Printing Company, 1896. E202.4.N67
Sons of Rev. in Va. Mag.
    Sons of the Revolution in the State of Virginia, *Quarterly (or Semi-
    Annual) Magazine*. Title varies. Vols. 3, 9. Richmond, Va.
    E202.4.V4
Sosin, Revolutionary Frontier
    Sosin, Jack M., *The Revolutionary Frontier, 1763-1783*. New York:
    Holt, Rinehart and Winston, c1967. E179.5.S68

Sosin, Whitehall and Wilderness
  Sosin, Jack M., *Whitehall and the Wilderness: The Middle West in
    British Colonial Policy, 1760-1775.*   Lincoln, Neb.: University of
    Nebraska Press, 1961.   F483.S6
Soulés, Histoire des Troubles
  Soulés, Francois, *Histoire des Troubles de l'Amérique Anglaise.* Vol.
    4.   Paris, 1787.   E208.S72 Jefferson Coll.
S.C. Hist. Mag.
  The South Carolina Historical Magazine.   Vol. 66.   Charleston: The
    South Carolina Historical Society.   F266.S55
Sparks, Washington's Writings
  Sparks, Jared, ed., *The Writings of George Washington.*   Vols. 3, 4,
    5, 6, 7, 8.   New York: Harper & Brothers, 1847.   E312.7 1847
Spaulding, Geo. Clinton
  Spaulding, Ernest Wilder, *His Excellency George Clinton, Critic of
    the Constitution.*   New York: The Macmillan Company, 1938.
    E302.6.C6S7
Spears, Anthony Wayne
  Spears, John Randolph, *Anthony Wayne, Sometimes Called "Mad Anthony".*
    New York: D. Appleton and Company, 1903.   E207.W35S7
Spears, Hist. of Our Navy
  Spears, John Randolph, *The History of Our Navy, from Its Origin to
    the End of the War with Spain, 1775-1898.*   Vol. 1. New York:
    Charles Scribner's Sons, 1899.   E182.S74
Speed, Wilderness Rd.
  Speed, Thomas, *The Wilderness Road: A Description of the Routes of
    Travel by which the Pioneers and Early Settlers First Came to
    Kentucky.*   (Filson Club Publications No.2).   Louisville: John P.
    Morton & Co., 1886.   F466.F48 no.2 Office
Stanley, For Want of a Horse
  Stanley, Lt. Col. George F.G., ed., *For Want of a Horse, Being a
    Journal of the Campaigns against the Americans in 1776 and 1777
    Conducted from Canada, by an Officer Who Served with Lt. Gen.
    Burgoyne.*   Sackville, N.B.: The Tribune Press Limited, 1961.
    E267.F66
Stark, Antique Views
  Stark, James H., *Stark's Antique Views of ye Towne of Boston.*   Boston:
    Morse-Purce Co., c1907.   F73.37.S73
Stark, Loyalists of Mass.
  Stark, James H., *The Loyalists of Massachusetts and the Other Side of
    the American Revolution.*   Boston: James H. Stark, 1910.   E277.S79
Staten Is. Historian
  The Staten Island Historian.   Vols. 4, 7.   Richmond, N.Y.: Staten
    Island Historical Society.   F127.S7S68
Staten Is. Inst. Arts Sci., Proc.
  Staten Island Institute of Arts and Sciences, *Proceedings.*   Vol. 7.
    Staten Island, N.Y.   Q11.S9
Stedman, Am. War
  Stedman, Charles, *The History of the Origin, Progress, and Termination
    of the American War.*   2v.   London, 1794.   E208.S81 Office
Steel, Am. Campaigns
  Steele, Matthew Fortney, *American Campaigns.*   Vol. 2.   Washington:
    United States Infantry Association, 1939.   E181.S856
Stephenson, Washington
  Stephenson, Nathaniel Wright, and Waldo Hilary Dunn, *George Washington.*
    2v.   New York: Oxford University Press, 1940.   E312.S82

Stevens, Exploring Penna.
  Stevens, Sylvester Kirby, Ralph W. Cordier, and Florence O. Benjamin,
  Exploring Pennsylvania: Its Geography, History, and Government.
  New York: Harcourt, Brace and Company, c1957. F149.S76 1957
Stevens, Wilderness Chronicles
  Stevens, Sylvester Kirby, and Donald H. Kent, eds., *Wilderness
  Chronicles of Northwestern Pennsylvania.* Harrisburg: Pennsylvania
  Historical Commission, 1941. F152.F87
Stevens, Yorktown Handbook
  Stevens, John Austin, *Yorktown Centennial Handbook.* New York: C.A.
  Coffin & Rogers, 1881. E241.Y6S8
Steward, St. Domingo Legion
  Steward, Theophilus Gould, *How the Black St. Domingo Legion Saved the
  Patriot Army in the Siege of Savannah, 1779.* (The American Negro
  Academy Occasional Papers No.5). Washington: The American Negro
  Academy, 1899. E241.S26S8 and E185.5.A51 no.5
Stewart, Battle of Red Bank
  Stewart, Frank H., *History of the Battle of Red Bank.* Woodbury,
  N.J., 1927. E241.R3S8
Stewart, Foraging
  Stewart, Frank H., *Foraging for Valley Forge by General Anthony Wayne
  in Salem and Gloucester Counties, New Jersey, with Associated Hap-
  penings, and Foraging in Salem County for the British Army in Phila-
  delphia by Colonel Mawhood and Major Simcoe, 1778.* Woodbury, N.J.:
  Gloucester County Historical Society, 1929. E234.S87
Stiles, Brooklyn
  Stiles, Henry R., *A History of the City of Brooklyn.* Vol. 1. Albany,
  N.Y.: J. Munsell, 1869. F129.B7S8
Stiles, Diary
  Stiles, Ezra, *The Literary Diary of Ezra Stiles, D.D., LL.D., Presi-
  dent of Yale College.* Franklin Bowditch Dexter, ed. 3v. New York:
  Charles Scribner's Sons, 1901. BX7260.S8A3
Stiles, Itineraries
  Stiles, Ezra, *Extracts from the Itineraries and Other Miscellanies of
  Ezra Stiles, D.D., LL.D., with a Selection from His Correspondence.*
  Franklin Bowditch Dexter, ed. New Haven: Yale University Press, 1916.
  F7.S85
Stiles, Letters and Papers
  Stiles, Ezra, *Letters and Papers of Ezra Stiles, President of Yale
  College, 1778-1795.* Isabel M. Calder, ed. New Haven: Yale Univer-
  sity Library, 1933. LD6330 1778 .A3
Stimson, My Story
  Stimson, Frederic Jesup, *My Story: Being the Memoirs of Benedict
  Arnold.* New York: Charles Scribner's Sons, 1917. PZ3.S86My
Stone, Brandywine
  Stone, Frederick D., *The Battle of Brandywine. . . .* Philadelphia,
  1895. E241.B8S8
Stone, Burgoyne
  Stone, William Leete, *The Campaign of Lieut. Gen. John Burgoyne and
  the Expedition of Lieut. Col. Barry St. Leger.* Albany, N.Y.: Joel
  Munsell, 1877. E233.S88
Stone, Hist. of N.Y. City
  Stone, William Leete, *History of New York City, from the Discovery to
  the Present Day.* New York: Virtue & Yorston, 1872. F128.3.S89

Utica Pub. Lib., Bibliography
  Utica Public Library, *Bibliography of Sullivan's Expedition against
    the Six Nations in 1779.* Utica, N.Y., 1929. Z1238.U88
Valley Forge Park Comm., Report
  Valley Forge Park Commission, *Report,* for 1906 and for 1908. Phila-
    delphia: James Hogan, 1910. E234.P393
Van Alstyne, Empire and Independence
  Van Alstyne, Richard Warner, *Empire and Independence: The Inter-
    national History of the American Revolution.* New York: John Wiley
    & Sons, Inc., 1965. E208.V28
Vanderpoel, Hist. of Chatham, N.J.
  Vanderpoel, Ambrose Ely, *History of Chatham, New Jersey, from Its
    Earliest Settlement through the Revolutionary War.* Chatham, N.J.:
    The Chatham Historical Society, 1959. F144.C49V2 1959
Van de Water, Lake Champlain and Lake George
  Van de Water, Frederick Franklyn, *Lake Champlain and Lake George.*
    Indianapolis: The Bobbs-Merrill Company, c1946. F127.C6V3
Van Doren, Mutiny in Jan.
  Van Doren, Carl, *Mutiny in January: The Story of a Crisis in the
    Continental Army. . . .* New York: The Viking Press, 1943. E255.V26
Van Doren, Secret History
  Van Doren, Carl, *Secret History of the American Revolution.* New York:
    The Viking Press, 1941. E277.V23 1941a
Van Dusen, Connecticut
  Van Dusen, Albert Edward, *Connecticut.* New York: Random House, c1961.
    F94.V3
Van Dusen, Middletown and Am. Rev.
  Van Dusen, Albert Edward, *Middletown and the American Revolution.*
    Middletown, Conn.: James D. Young Company, 1950. F104.M6V3
Van Every, Ark of Empire
  Van Every, Dale, *Ark of Empire: The American Frontier, 1784-1803.*
    New York: William Morrow and Company, 1963. E310.V3
Van Every, Co. of Heroes
  Van Every, Dale, *A Company of Heroes: The American Frontier, 1775-
    1783.* New York: William Morrow and Company, 1962. E263.N84V3
Varney, Patriots' Day
  Varney, George Jones, *The Story of Patriots' Day, Lexington and
    Concord, April 19, 1775.* Boston: Lee and Shepard, c1895.
    E241.L6V32
Vt. Hist.
  Vermont History, new series. Vols. 24, 27. Montpelier: Vermont
    Historical Society. F46.V55
Vt. Hist. Soc., Proc.
  Vermont Historical Society, *Proceedings.* Vol. 11. Montpelier.
    F46.V55
Vt. Life
  Vermont Life. Vol. 9. Montpelier: Vermont Development Commission.
    F46.V54
Vestal, Washington
  Vestal, Samuel Curtis, *Washington the Military Man.* (Honor to George
    Washington pamphlet series, Albert Bushnell Hart, ed., Pamphlet
    No. 10). Washington: United States George Washington Bicentennial
    Commission, 1931. E312.H77 no. 10
Va. Cavalcade
  Virginia Cavalcade: History in Picture and Story. Vols. 1, 2, 4, 7,
    13. Richmond: Virginia State Library. F221.V74

Va. Mag. Hist. and Biog.
  The Virginia Magazine of History and Biography.   Vol. 53.   Richmond:
    Virginia Historical Society.   F221.V91
Vose, Journal
  Vose, Joseph, *Journal of Lieutenant-Colonel Joseph Vose, April-July
    1776.*   Henry Winchester Cunningham, ed.   Cambridge: John Wilson
    and Son, 1905.   E232.V96
Vrooman, Clarissa Putman
  Vrooman, John J., *Clarissa Putman of Tribes Hill: A Romantic History
    of Sir William Johnson, His Family, and Mohawk Valley Neighbors
    Through the Flaming Years, 1767-1780.*   Johnstown, N.Y.: The Baronet
    Litho Company, Inc., 1950.   PZ3.V958Cl
Vrooman, Forts and Firesides
  Vrooman, John J., *Forts and Firesides of the Mohawk Country, New York.*
    Philadelphia: Elijah Ellsworth Brownell, 1943.   F127.M55V7
Wall, Convention Army
  Wall, Alexander James, *The Story of the Convention Army.*   New York,
    1927.   E233.W16
Wallace, Appeal to Arms
  Wallace, Willard Mosher, *Appeal to Arms: A Military History of the
    American Revolution.*   New York: Harper & Brothers, c1951.   E230.W3
Wallace, Col. Wm. Bradford
  Wallace, John William, *An Old Philadelphian, Colonel William Bradford,
    the Patriot Printer of 1776.*   Philadelphia: Sherman & Co., 1884.
    E263.P4B7 Office
Wallace, Hist. of S.C.
  Wallace, David Duncan, *The History of South Carolina.*   Vol. 2.   New
    York: The American Historical Society, Inc., 1934.   F269.W25
Wallace, Traitorous Hero
  Wallace, Willard Mosher, *Traitorous Hero: The Life and Fortunes of
    Benedict Arnold.*   New York: Harper & Brothers, c1954.   E278.A7W26
Wallace, United Empire Loyalists
  Wallace, W. Stewart, *The United Empire Loyalists: A Chronicle of the
    Great Migration.*   Toronto: Glasgow, Brook & Company, 1914.
    E277.W19
Walworth, Saratoga
  Walworth, Ellen Hardin, *Saratoga - The Battle - Battleground - Visi-
    tor's Guide.*   New York: The American News Company, c1877.
    E241.S24W24
Ward, Battle of L.I.
  Ward, Samuel, *The Battle of Long Island: A Lecture, Delivered before
    the New-York Historical Society, February 7, 1839.*   New York:
    William Osborn, 1839.   E241.L8W2
  Note: Reprinted, with different type and pagination, from Knicker-
    bocker Magazine, Apr. 1839.
Ward, Del. Continentals
  Ward, Christopher L., *The Delaware Continentals, 1776-1783.*   Wilming-
    ton: The Historical Society of Delaware, 1941.   E263.D3W3
Ward, Revolution
  Ward, Christopher L., *The War of the American Revolution.*   John
    Richard Alden, ed.   2v.   New York: The Macmillan Company, 1952.
    E230.W34
Warden, Boston
  Warden, Gerard B., *Boston, 1689-1776.*   Boston: Little, Brown and
    Company, c1970.   F73.4.W37

World Book
  The World Book Encyclopedia. Vol. 16. Chicago: Field Enterprises
    Educational Corporation, c1967. AE5.W55 1967
Wright, Fabric of Freedom
  Wright, Esmond, *Fabric of Freedom, 1763-1800*. New York: Hill and
    Wang, c1961. E208.W9
Wroth, Abel Buell
  Wroth, Lawrence Counselman, *Abel Buell of Connecticut, Silversmith,
    Type Founder & Engraver*. Middletown: Wesleyan University Press,
    1958. NK7198.B9W7 1958
Wynne, Gen. History
  Wynne, John Huddleston, *A General History of the British Empire in
    America*. Vol. 1. London: W. Richardson and L. Urquhart, 1770.
    E188.W98
Yale Library Gaz.
  Yale University Library Gazette. Vol. 21. New Haven, Conn.
    Z733.Y17G
Zobel, Boston Massacre
  Zobel, Hiller B., *The Boston Massacre*. New York: W.W. Norton &
    Company, Inc., c1970. E215.4.Z6 1970

ABOUT THE AUTHOR

David Sanders Clark, a graduate of Yale with an M.A. in American History from Harvard, since retirement from government service has been devoting his time to research and writing in American history. His earlier publications include *The Moravian Mission of Pilgerruh, American Travelers and Observers in the British Isles, 1850-1875 and 1875-1900; A Bibliography, Directory of Planning Agencies of the National Capital Region, A Guide to Sources of Information Pertinent to Planning a Transportation System for the Washington Metropolitan Area,* and genealogies of the Sanders, Otis, Terry, Clark, Hubbard, and Livingstone families. Mr. Clark also edited *Letters from Europe, 1865-1866,* by Amy Grinnell Smith and Mary Ermina Smith, *Postmaster Clark and the Burglars,* and *Two Anti-Slavery Sermons,* by William Davis Sanders.